Rethinking Indian Political Institutions

Anthem South Asian Studies
Series Editor: Crispin Bates

Other titles in the series:

Brosius, Christiane *Empowering Visions* (2005)

Mills, Jim (ed) *Sport in South Asia* (2005)

Joshi, Chitra *Lost Worlds: Indian Labour and its Forgotten Histories* (2005)

Dasgupta, Biplab, *European Trade and Colonial Conquest* (2005)

Kaur, Raminder *Performative Politics and the Cultures of Hinduism* (2005)

Rosenstein, Lucy *New Poetry in Hindi* (2004)

Shah, Ghanshyam, *Caste and Democratic Politics in India* (2004)

Van Schendel, Willem *The Bengal Borderland: Beyond State and Nation in South Asia* (2004)

Rethinking Indian Political Institutions

Edited by

CRISPIN BATES AND SUBHO BASU

Anthem Press

Anthem Press
An imprint of Wimbledon Publishing Company
75-76 Blackfriars Road, London SE1 8HA
or
PO Box 9779, London SW19 7QA
www.anthempress.com

This edition first published by Anthem Press 2005
This selection © Wimbledon Publishing Company 2005

Editorial matter © Crispin Bates & Subho Basu 2005
Individual articles © individual contributors

British Library Cataloguing in Publication Data
A catalogue record for this book is available from the British Library.

Library of Congress Cataloguing in Publication Data
A catalog record for this book has been requested.

Cover illustration: Empics

1 3 5 7 9 10 8 6 4 2

ISBN 1 84331 079 1 (Hbk)
ISBN 1 84331 080 5 (Pbk)

Printed in India

CONTENTS

Rural Politics

CONTRIBUTORS

Crispin Bates is a senior lecturer in modern South Asian history in the School of History & Classics at the University of Edinburgh. He completed his Ph.D. at Cambridge University, UK, and has published on various aspects of Indian social and economic history, but mostly concerning rural Indian (and tribal) labour in central India and labour migration. He is a former Research Fellow of Churchill College Cambridge, visiting Professor at the Ecoles des Hautes Etudes in Paris, and Fellow of the Institute of Oriental Culture, University of Tokyo; he has recently completed a history of India entitled *Subalterns and the Raj* (London: Routledge, forthcoming) and edited *Community, Empire and Migration* (Palgrave Macmillan, 2001; Orient Longman, 2003). Work in progress includes a monograph on adivasis in Madhya Pradesh and a political history of India since independence (with Subho Basu).

Dr. Subho Basu completed his Ph.D. at Cambridge University. He is presently an Assistant Professor at Syracuse University where he teaches Indian History in general and nationalist politics in the late nineteenth and early twentieth century in particular. A former fellow of the Centre of South Asian Studies and Wolfson College Cambridge, visiting fellow at the Maison des Sciences de l, Homme, Paris, and teaching fellow at the School of Oriental and African Studies, University of London, he has published widely on the politics of industrial workers in Bengal. He has recently published with Oxford University Press a book entitled *Does Class Matter? Colonial Capitalism and Workers, Resistance in Bengal 1890–1940* and has edited with Prof. Suranjan Das of Calcutta University a book on *Electoral Politics in South Asia* published in March 2000 by K.P. Bagchi Press, Calcutta.

Bharat Dahiya has a multi-disciplinary background in urban and regional development planning, geography and political science, which has strongly influenced his research. He completed his Ph.D. thesis, *Whither urban governance? Self-help civil society, political conflicts and environmental services in Chennai, India*, at the University of Cambridge, UK, and is currently working in the Urban Development Unit of the World Bank. Bharat actively participates in the policy initiatives of several international institutions as well as advising civil society organisations working towards the goal of sustainable urban development. He has written extensively on the issues of governance and civil society, and initiated numerous projects on local environmental services in South Asia.

Evelin Hust studied political science, economics and classical indology at the universities of Freiburg, Sussex and Heidelberg. Presently she is the representative of the South Asia Institute of the University of Heidelberg in Delhi. She completed her Ph.D. in 2001 in Heidelberg, entitled *A Million Indiras Now? Political Presence and Women's Empowerment in Rural Local Government in India* (Delhi: Manohar 2004). Other publications include (co-edited with M. Mann), *Urbanisation and Governance in India* (Delhi: Manohar 2005); (co-edited with C. Weiß, T. Weichert & H. Fischer-Tiné), *Religion-Macht-Gewalt. Religiöser Fundamentalismus, und Hindu-Moslem-Konflikte in Südasien* (Frankfurt: IKO Verlag 1996); 'Political Representation and Empowerment' in *Heidelberg Papers in South Asian & Comparative Politics*, No. 6, September 2002; 'A Million Indiras Now?' in *Women's Link* (2002), 8 (2), pp. 2–6; and 'Political "Empowerment" of Women through Legislation? Case study Orissa', in Pinto, A. & Reifeld, H. (eds.), *Women in PRI*, (New Delhi: ISI 2001), pp. 166–194.

Sumi Madhok is Mellon Research Fellow, Department of Politics, School of Oriental and African Studies, University of London, where she completed her Ph.D. on *Autonomy, Subordination and the Social Woman: Examining rights narratives of rural Rajasthani women.* She is now preparing this for publication. Her other publications include: A Limited Women's Empowerment: Politics, The state, and Development in North West India', *Women's Studies Quarterly*, nos. 3&4, Spring/Summer (2003) and Heteronomous Women? Hidden Assumptions in the Demography of Women' in Maya Unnithan-Kumar (ed.), *Reproductive Agency, Medicine and the state: Cultural Transformations in Childbearing* (Oxford: Berghahn Press, 2004).

Jos Mooji is a Senior Lecturer in Public Policy and Development Management at the Institute of Social Studies, the Hague, Netherlands, and was formerly a visiting fellow at the Centre for Economic and Social Studies, Hyderabad, India. Since early 2001, she has been working on a project, entitled 'Comparative Studies of Public Policy Processes in India', as well as several short term research projects all related to governance and the social sector in India. She is the author of *Food Policy and the Indian state. The Public Food Distribution System in South India*, published by Oxford University Press, New Delhi in 1999, and several articles in international and Indian journals.

Veena Naregal is a lecturer in the Departments of Asian Studies and Radio-TV-Film at the University of Texas, Austin. Her most recent publication is *Language Politics, Elites, and the Public Sphere: Western India Under Colonialism* (London: Anthem Press, 2001). Her multi-disciplinary interests include postcolonial theory, alternative modernities and contemporary cultural politics.

Bhavana Padiyath is a journalist and researcher, who has served as a correspondent for two of India's leading English dailies – *The Times of India* and *The Indian Express*. She is particularly interested in questions related to urban political processes and policy. In 1997 Bhavana completed her masters from Cambridge University in Social and Political Science Department. Currently she is working towards her Ph.D. at Cambridge on the political institutional arrangements in Bombay city. She also continues her freelance writing from her new home in California.

Pamela Price took her B.A. at Wellesley College and her Ph.D. at the University of Wisconsin-Madison. She is Professor of South Asian History at the University of Oslo, Norway. Her publications include *Kingship And Political Practice In Colonial India* (Cambridge, 1996) and "Revolution and Rank in Tamil Nationalism" (*Journal of Asian Studies*, 1996). She is soon to publish "Kin, Clan and Power in Colonial South India" in a volume edited by Indrani Chatterjee and is currently involved in fieldwork in village Andhra Pradesh on issues of honour and self-respect in village politics and inter-personal relations.

Sanjay Ruparelia studied for a Ph.D. at Cambridge University and is now a member of the Political Science department at the New School University, New York. He is presently rewriting his dissertation on the United Front Government in India between 1996–1998 with a view to publication.

INTRODUCTION

I

On 28 February 2002, in Godhara, a little known railway station of Gujarat, in an unprecedented case of arson nearly fifty-eight passengers on the Sabarmati express lost their lives. Many of those who perished in this dreadful fire were volunteers of a militant Hindu nationalist organisation namely Vishwa Hindu Parishad (translated as World Hindu Council and popularly called VHP). These volunteers were returning home from a rally in Ayodhya where the VHP was trying to construct a Ram temple on the site of a sixteenth century mosque named after India's first Mughal emperor Babar.

The temple agitation, periodically orchestrated by Hindu nationalist organisations from 1989 onwards, has unfailingly provoked communal eruptions in the country resulting in large casualties[1]. The February 2002 agitation was no exception to this trend: only this time the stakes were higher. As soon as news of the murderous arson spread, the VHP cashed in on the tragedy by calling for a total strike in Gujarat. The strike escalated into widespread well-orchestrated attacks on Muslim minorities, worsening – in the process – the relationship between India and Pakistan, already tense in the wake of the Kargil war, nuclear tests, and terrorist assaults in New Delhi and Kashmir. The Indian media, and politicians opposed to Hindu nationalist organisations, and human rights activists alleged that the Bharatiya Janata Party, the ruling political party in Gujarat and a sister Hindu nationalist organisation of the VHP, had used state power to assist the attacks on Gujarati Muslims. The police played a crucial role by their conspicuous failure to suppress the riots. Many alleged that the police provided assistance to Hindu rioters and refused backing to the army when it was called in to restore normality. Even according to the conservative estimates of the Hindu nationalist state government of Gujarat, nearly 2000 people lost their lives and over a hundred thousand were rendered homeless. Gujarat became again a crucial example of the state's failure to maintain law and order in India.

The Gujarat incident brought to the fore the crucial significance of the state-society relationship in India where state institutions have staged a strategic retreat in the face of organised violence against minorities and women. This poses a crucial paradox. The Indian state remains an over-developed state with an ever-increasing number of paramilitary forces[2], bureaucrats and sophisticated technocrats[3]. Yet the state has been completely unable to control violence against the most vulnerable segments of the population. How do we explain the inability of the Indian state to stem the tide of growing violence, ethnic conflicts and increasing sense of insecurity among its less affluent citizens or ethnic and religious minorities? Apparently the state in India enjoys an unusual degree of political power to suspend civil liberties of the population in order to meet these threats and to provide security to its citizens[4]. Yet it is powerless to do so. This conundrum has placed the Indian state at the centre of political analysis.

II

Historians have devoted considerable attention to the nature of state formation in pre-colonial[5] and colonial India[6]. The state in post-colonial India has also been analysed in close detail. Pioneering scholars, such as Gunnar Myrdal, formulated the theory of the soft state to explain the inability of underdeveloped countries to eradicate poverty, arguing that the soft state is soft on powerful elites but hard on the powerless segments of the population[7]. Hamza Alavi put forward the thesis of the over-developed state in South Asia, based upon his reading of the role played by the bureaucracy and army in Pakistan. Alavi argued that the colonial state effected a bourgeois revolution in South Asia and created a vast repository of bureaucrats, along with a disproportionately large security apparatus, intended to subordinate rather than maintain any sort of democratic order. Subsequently, the state has been the focus of considerable sociological scrutiny. Marxist scholars and political activists have often sought to explain the class character of the Indian state in terms of the dominant coalitions of social classes that underpin the political practice of state policies. The most sophisticated analysis of the Indian state along these lines can be found in the work of Pranab Bardhan[8]. Bardhan explains the policies of the Indian state in terms of a dominant coalition of proprietary classes comprising large industrialists, small industrialists, rich peasants and public sector bureaucrats.

Many American-trained political scientists have applied the method of interest group analysis to explain the functioning of the Indian state and political economy. Most prominently among them, Rudolph and Rudolph, in their path breaking work on the Indian political economy, have shown how the tensions between the alternate imperatives of command and demand polities impact upon political life[9]. Recently, following Huntingdon's work on the overheated polity arising from competitive political mobilisation, Atul Kohli has sought to explain how fraction-ridden Indian elites at different levels of the Indian polity have been engaged in destabilising competitions, which has resulted in the deinstitutionalisation of the political system, incapacitating the state's ability to maintain public order[10].

These works have expanded our understanding of the functioning of the Indian state. However, a problem lies in the treatment of the Indian state as a single political entity. The varied operations of diverse forms of institutions that characterise the Indian state cannot be comprehended in such mono-tonal terms. The state encompasses complex layers of political institutions that operate in a variety of ways in different contexts. Social contexts in local-ity, state and nation[11], to evoke an older historical work on the subject, need to be identified in order to understand the functioning of the state. Indeed, instead of talking about the Indian state as a monolithic entity, it is preferable to talk about the state as the sum total of myriad forms of political institutions in order to develop a more comprehensive understanding of the sub-conti-nental kaleidoscope of political institutions and their immediate social envi-ronments. At every stage political institutions are implicated in diverse social nexuses that inform and influence their functioning. Any investigation of the Indian state thus needs to be located in terms of its multi-layered structure and its relationship to the wider society within each layer.

This volume aims to explore various aspects of the twentieth century Indian state ranging from the central government level down to local level in the states, cities and villages. It considers both political economic frameworks and the ideological and discursive processes that inform and influence them. It con-tends that the functioning of the Indian state cannot be comprehended simply by looking at the changes at the political centre, but are fundamentally influ-enced by developments in the wider civil society. Thus it aims to bring together a number of insightful essays on multiple aspects of the Indian state as a means to understand the interactive processes that constitute it.

The approach adopted in this volume is particularly crucial in the light of recent changes in the wake of globalisation and liberalisation. The twin processes of globalisation and liberalisation have supposedly undermined the economic autonomy of the Indian state, certainly the centralisation of fiscal powers, and have thus strengthened the regionalisation of the polity[12]. At the same time, these processes have strengthened state control over the population through innovations in information technology and have enabled the security apparatus at different levels to become more powerful. These significant changes in the nature of the functioning of the Indian state can be better understood if we situate the individual institutions of the state within a long term historical context and submit them to serious sociological scrutiny. The institutions considered in this volume include primarily those that attempt to foster social consent through rudimentary forms of democratic accountability, such as the national parliament, state assemblies, urban municipal governments, and rural government institutions such as panchayats. Whilst individual chapters throw light on the nature of the operation of different institutions of the state at different levels of hierarchy, the volume collectively intends to analyse and illuminate the changes taking place in the nature and functioning of the Indian state as a whole. By analysing institutions of the Indian state in the context of their interactions with societal relationships at different levels, our approach will address the wider question of state-society relationships rather than simply narrating stories (however entertaining) of high politics.

III

The chapters in this volume range over the political institutions of India from the central to the grass roots level. It begins with institutions that operate at the central level. The first chapter by Jos Mooji addresses the nature, process and institutional contexts of the liberalisation of the Indian economy. Comparing two attempts at the liberalisation of the Indian economy under Rajiv Gandhi and Narasimha Rao, Mooji asks: What have been the political factors that made a transition from planning to the market possible in the 1990s but not in the 1980s? The chapter critically reviews some of the political science literature that deals with the political processes and institutions in the 1980s and the 1990s that made reform difficult or feasible. It analyses the various contributions to this debate and discusses the work of authors such as Kohli, Varshney, Bardhan, P. Patnaik and others. Through the lens of economic policy changes, the chapter thereby contributes to our rethinking of Indian political processes and institutions. A particular emphasis is placed on the variety of pressures impinging upon the government and the contrast between state-centred, contingent, societal, and external pressures. It is suggested that it was perhaps the relative decline of the Congress party and the threat from political extremists that may have directed attention elsewhere and helped to make reform possible. Societal, fiscal and external pressures also played an important role in undermining the centralised Indian state. This weakness of the federal state has somewhat contrarily permitted both populist and elite pressures to bear heavily upon policy-making: hence the continuation of liberalising reform since the BJP came to power, despite the party's overt commitment to a policy of *swadeshi* and the re-imposition of restrictions on foreign access to the Indian market. Continuing economic reform has been made further practicable by changes within the governing coalition, which has become more diverse, fluid and fragmented, as compared with the 1980s. A final influence has been changing ideas about the role of the state. The growth of the black economy and the broken promises and failures of the 'Congress era' up until 1996 caused many people to realise that the state simply cannot any longer (if it ever could) fully control and direct the progress of the Indian economy. It is for this reason that questions of wealth redistribution are increasingly by-passed in favour of policies intending to increase access to education and the participation of the low castes and under-privileged in the business of government itself. Meanwhile, the elites look increasingly to private enterprise and opportunities overseas rather than the manipulation of government patronage as a means to profit. Curiously however, most explanations of the reform process – according to Mooji – remain state-centred, despite the evidence that many of its motivations lie elsewhere. One might suggest that this could be perhaps be because many economists and academics have themselves a vested interest in the state-centred approach.

In the second chapter Sanjay Ruparelia focuses on the institutional parameters of regime formation as defined in the constitution and its impact on the political strategies of governing parties. Ruparelia particularly explores the prospects and limits of the practice of secularism in contemporary India through an analysis of the impact of, and recent arguments over, the institutional design of its democratic regime. One of the most striking developments of Indian politics in the last decade was the emergence of the Bharatiya Janata Party (BJP) as the single largest party in the *Lok Sabha* (lower house of parliament). The BJP espouses a politics of *Hindutva* (Hindu cultural nationalism), which many critics argue threatens to undermine the secular, plural fabric of the nation through efforts to create a politics of religious majoritarianism. However, despite its relative electoral success, the BJP was able to form a coalition Union government only after striking political bargains with other regional parties. These coalition partners forced the BJP to abandon the pursuit of its more controversial programs, in exchange for their varying degrees of support, in the formal political arena. Thus to some extent the latter was forced to dilute its agenda of *Hindutva*. Despite the BJP's relegation to the position of second largest party again in the *Lok Sabha* in the general election of 2004, their *Hindutva* agenda nonetheless remains a potent threat, given the tensions between pragmatists and ideologues within the party and its associated organisations. Proponents of *Hindutva* have sought to fulfil their aims using a variety of extreme measures either 'on the streets' in order to change the texture of everyday life, or through unilateral interventions in the realm of elite politics which altered the terms of political debate in their favour. Indeed, their desire to transform the official secular doctrine of the Indian state within the formal political arena presently inspires their demands for a review of the basic features of the Constitution. The chapter argues that to grasp the ways in which this scenario evolves requires one to examine the larger institutional design of the Indian polity. Three features matter in particular: a plurality-rule (first-past-the-post) electoral regime, a strong cabinet government in a parliamentary regime and a federal party system with several constitutional safeguards. Such features comprise necessary, though not sufficient, conditions for Indian secularism to survive. Ultimately, though, the prospects and quality of a secular politics requires its reiterative practice within a wider and deeper form of democratic politics.

From the central level institutions, we move on to a consideration of the institutions that operate at state level and explore the crucial societal relationships that underpin them. The third chapter thus focuses on the dynamics of personal rivalry in the Janata Dal Party in Karnataka state in the last fifteen years. Building on field research undertaken in recent years, Pamela Price discusses the conflict between Ramakrishna Hegde and Deve Gowda and the way this conflict resulted in a split in the party, leading to the formation of Ramakrishna Hegde's Lok Shakti Party. The Lok Shakti is cited as an example of a trend in Indian politics for political parties at provincial level to be formed around the charisma of single persons. Further personality and political conflict in the Janata Dal led last year to the formation of the Janata Dal (U) and the Janata Dal (S). Overall, the chapter aims to describe the politics of charisma, and the manner in which it has assumed an increasingly important role in the struggle for political power. A tentative explanation of the phenomenon is offered, suggesting the politics of personality to be a consequence of globalisation, and the undermining of traditional loyalties to class, caste, faction and community.

In the fourth chapter in this volume, Veena Naregal looks at the institutions of the media and their connections with the politics of marketability of the media primarily at a regional level. The past few years have seen issues of representation and ideology being displaced as central aspects of media debates. Instead, the right to control distribution territories has emerged as an increasingly important question, first, in the film and popular music industries, and now, in far more serious ways, in the cable and satellite television industries. These shifts towards the depoliticisation of media correspond with the penetration of the media markets by indigenous and western transnational corporate organisations. With networks of political patronage and control increasingly tied up with large potential revenues in the media distribution networks, these developments highlight the desire to assert direct control over the public sphere. Nevertheless, despite its rhetoric of withdrawal, these changes have come about through manipulation of media law by the state. This has led to a situation where the increasing ideological volatility in the public sphere – signified by attacks on cultural difference – have gone hand in hand with the expansion of the media sector and its privatisation since the early 1990s. This chapter examines these emerging trends with respect to Mumbai, focusing on the consolidation in the cable and satellite television industries which demonstrates the growing integration between corporate interests, local political and media networks. The resulting data is used to interrogate recent shifts and contestations over media policy.

The fifth chapter, by Bhavana Padiyath, moves from provincial politics to the study of urban political institutions, focusing on the largest metropolis of India, namely Mumbai. It examines the institutional impact and political outcomes of the post-independence planning enterprise and concludes that Mumbai is a city that is basically frozen because of its land laws, development control rules and zoning regulations. 1991 census figures reveal that while the population of Greater Mumbai (a 428 square kilometre area) grew by 8 per cent over the previous decade to touch 9.9 million, the count for the Mumbai Metropolitan Region as a whole rose to 12.5 million, indicating the pressures on land and scarcity of housing that have put real estate prices in the city beyond the reach of most citizens. The socio-economic and political compulsions that have led to the inelasticity of Mumbai's land market are examined in this chapter, alongside the various projects that benchmark the urban planning process in the city. A primary endeavour of this chapter is to demonstrate the powerlessness of the purported beneficiaries of urban planning schemes and to explain how the governing elite and other political actors influenced the various agendas at work and profited from this asymmetrical structuring of social space in the city. The uneven institutional impacts of these projects on various classes and communities, and their political responses are outlined, along with the manner in which they influence and actuate each other. Included in the study is a review of the formal political, legal and administrative entities in operation within the democratic regime, like the body of legislation, parties, and the bureaucratic mechanisms that set the parameters of policy and ensure its implementation. The chapter argues that closer attention needs also to be paid to other regularised channels of interaction and exchange which, although not formally codified, attempt to bridge the expanse between the official channels of 'state' and the dense network of systems within 'civil society' that seek to negotiate their mutual terms of interaction with the powers that be. The chapter reviews the role of these formal and informal institutional settings in engendering and accentuating the segmentation pervading several sectors of the city's socio-economic landscape – land, housing, transportation, environment, spheres of production, information and social stratification. An attempt is finally made to examine how popular initiatives have sought to counter this sealing of democratic options and spaces through the erection of new institutional platforms from a variety of vantage points.

In chapter six, in a detailed discussion of the urban politics and environmental infrastructure, Bharat Dahiya deals with the nature of urban politics of waste disposal in the city of Chennai. Combining historical investigation with an urban policy framework, Dahiya demonstrates the crucial need for the democratic accountability of civic administration to ordinary citizens. Based on empirical research in the Chennai city, he carefully explains the emergence of autonomous civil society in Chennai city through the activities of grass roots organisations which work towards improving urban living conditions. These civil society activities have tended to reenergise ordinary citizens into action. The very success of such activities has threatened the political turf of politicians who have often refused co-operation with civil society organisations. As a result, opportunities to improve governance and living conditions in urban areas are lost. Yet such activities often could not over come the social fault lines between rich and poor, citizens' initiatives being more often concentrated in the prosperous municipal districts than in the poorer areas of the city, causing environmental social divisions based on wealth. Dahiya's paper highlights the salience of maintaining the urban environmental infrastructure in Indian cities and the problems associated with the political institutions of the state and emerging civil society in general when it comes to addressing such issues. He concludes by arguing for a greater autonomy of civil society action combined with accountable state administration at local level.

From the larger urban settings of Mumbai and Chennai the volume moves on to consider the small rural market town of Bolpur. This chapter investigates the evolution of town polity in terms of the establishment of the political institutions related to the developmental state from the opening years of the twentieth century. With the rise of the developmental state these small towns witnessed the emergence of a grid of state-controlled public institutions, ranging from electric power generating houses and nationally owned banks through to schools and hospitals. These institutions define the parameters of a small town polity. The chapter argues that the social structure of such rural town polities evolves in relation to a variety of political institutions. Political, social and economic access to such institutions affects the life chances of the rural-town population and informs the social stratification process. Thus class structure in these rural towns is determined not by production processes, but by the consumption of educational and health services as well as the ability to garner resources from state-run institutions. The advent of democracy and the emergence of elected social institutions, such as municipal government, has created a class of political entrepreneurs who negotiate between and seek to access these institutions in order to utilise their resources. Yet the formalised centralised bureaucratic structure of such institutions play little meaningful role in economic redistribution. As a consequence, political alignments remain fluid and often depend upon a populist anti-institutional overtone. This explains the success of populist politicians such as Mamata Banerjee's appeal to the urban masses over the more highly institutionalised corporatist structure of the Communist Parties.

Chapters in the final section of this volume analyse the rural political institutions in India and how these institutions create a political framework of participation, language of mobilisation, and a wider discourse of political rights. The eighth chapter, by Sumi Madhok, seeks to problematize the right of political office and political participation in the lives of rural, poor and illiterate women. It examines in particular the conflict between public individualism which informs the functioning of 'public institutions' and the social doctrines sanctioning private freedoms which make political participation possible. The chapter begins by examining the tension between the public and private view of the person as seen in the encounter of rural women with political rights in India. These engagements with political rights take on two different forms. These forms correspond with the two different understandings of the self that come into being as a result of these engagements. The first understanding of the self is primarily in terms of a right bearing agent, the second assumes the form of an embedded relational self. More often than not these forms intersect. The engagements with political rights and the reformulation of meanings that accompanies these are, it is argued, indicative of their particular capacities, and more specifically, of their moral autonomy. Finally it is argued that the articulation of and commitment to political rights, which is not always evident in their action, compels us to look for ways in which we can capture conceptually their capacities and the effects ensuing from the particular skills of individuals – skills referred to as 'political literacy'. In order to illustrate the argument, the chapter examines the moral encounter with the idea and language of 'rights' of a group of rural women known as the *sathins* involved in a state sponsored development program for women in the North Western Indian State of Rajasthan. The *sathins* are largely illiterate or semi literate and belong principally to the lowest castes. The fieldwork was conducted in the districts of Jaipur and Ajmer over a period of eight months, between September 1998 and April 1999.

Madhok concludes that the negotiations of the *sathins* with political rights take the form of an interpretative exercise that results in new meanings both moral and linguistic. Some of these meanings are born out of a desire by women to weave some of their existing moral values together with new values with which they have come into contact and have acquired. It is argued that these linguistic meanings are therefore essentially efforts, both practical and intellectual, to increase the comprehensibility of rights-based ideas within an existing moral framework, articulating thereby the encounter between 'modernity' and 'tradition'.

From these discussions of the political rights of women in rural India the ninth chapter moves to the historical and political processes of the construction of panchayati raj and the wider processes involved in the construction of the notion of the Indian village as the quintessential representative of Indian civilisation. The discourse on panchayati reform thus dwells on the nature of rural empowerment and the discourse of rural social reconstruction. The chapter begins with the premise that the Indian village community is firmly embedded in the orientalist imagining of India. The composition of these village committees and the powers they are believed to have exercised has varied enormously over time and from province to province. Gandhi was a firm believer but hardly an unequivocal champion of village self-government. Village communities must not exist as disconnected units, he argued, but be held together by a system of co-operation and integration. Gandhi recommended a massive decentralisation of government after independence, the higher centres of governmental power being reduced and the organ of administration becoming the *panchayat*, organised into village, town, district, provincial and all-India units of government. However, Gandhi, C.R. Das and others in the I.N.C. were not the only advocates of panchayats. As the nationalist struggle progressed, Gandhi became more ambitious for the idea of village self-government, but so too did the British, who made panchayats and village co-operatives the foundation of their reformed constitution.

Post independence, the Gandhian ideal was abandoned, but a limited programme of panchayati raj was instituted in several states. The problem with these panchayats is that they were set up largely for developmental reasons, and although panchayats were constituted at village level (including always a certain number of women and members of the scheduled or '*backward*' castes and tribes), most often the executive powers lay at block level, where a block *Samiti* (committee) was constituted by delegates from a number of villages. There was thus very little continuity with the primarily judicial panchayats of the 1920's, let alone Charles Metcalfe's or even Gandhi's idea of little village republics. Panchayats were constituted in many villages, but they had few responsibilities beyond village drainage, street lighting, sanitation and the arbitration of petty disputes. The dispersal of development thus remained largely in the hands of officials.

During Rajiv Gandhi's government of the mid 1980s, a committee – chaired by H.M. Singhvi – proposed the re-organisation of panchayati raj institutions and the setting up of effective village level committees. Soon after, the first of several Constitutional Amendments was proposed making it legally binding upon all states to establish a three-tier system of panchayats at the village, intermediate and district level, each of them to be appointed by direct election. Following the passage of this bill into law as the 73rd Constitutional Amendment Act of 1993, the states introduced in some cases radical measures which delegated significant powers and responsibilities onto panchayats. In 1996 the *Lok Sabha* then passed a bill extending the proposed panchayati system into Scheduled (i.e. adivasi or tribal) areas. This bill went so far as to oblige state governments to devolve all responsibility for planning and development onto the panchayats – a radical restructuring of the juridical position of the panchayats, which state level administrations are only now beginning to come to terms with. The question remains to be answered whether this new enthusiasm for panchayati rule is likely to fare any better than those that have gone before, and whether it is a long cherished dream finally come true, or merely the latest twist in a struggle for power and control over government expenditure between central and state governments and village elites. This chapter surveys the origins of the idea of panchayati raj, the present-day issues, and points tentatively towards a conclusion and prediction of future developments.

The final chapter in the volume focuses more precisely, by means of a case study, on one aspect of the 73rd Constitutional Amendment. This amendment, apart from making elections to the panchayati raj institutions (PRI) mandatory, introduced a reservation of no less than 33 per cent of seats and positions for women. Evelin Hust begins by tracing the background of this revolutionary step, from which it becomes clear that many advocates expected that the reservation for women would lead to women's empowerment. The paper then sets out to explore whether this is really taking place, and begins by questioning the very meaning of empowerment itself. Thus, the reservation for women might ensure that a substantive number of women manage to get into formal positions of power. Whether these women can really exercise power and become empowered in a more general sense, however, needs to be empirically tested. By presenting results from fieldwork conducted in the eastern state of Orissa, Evelin Hust attempts to do this. The field research (a quantitative survey in 1998/99 and a qualitative one in 1999/2000) was conducted in two blocks that differ in their socio-political history and in the present economic position and women's status. Female and male incumbents of the PRI are the focus of analysis, so the results are analysed by gender as well as by region.

Generally speaking women were found to be younger, less educated and poorer than their male colleagues and to participate less in the decision-making process. They also spent less time on their work for the *panchayat* than the male politicians, although those in the 'developed' block spent rather more time than those in the less developed block. Women hardly took any part in public meetings, and work to be done outside the confines of the *panchayat* office was often taken care of by male family members. Very few women decided themselves to participate in elections, but there is a perceptible gap between the regions: those in the 'developed' block being more autonomous. Around 60 per cent of the women did not face a contest, but more than 35 per cent of the men also faced no rival. It appears therefore that unanimous decisions are cherished by traditional village communities, and are not necessarily linked to gender.

Perhaps depressingly, the reasons given by village communities for the (s)election of a specific woman were simply her education and willingness, or that of her husband. Interestingly though, quite a number of *gaanjhias* (women married in the village of origin) were elected, for they are less confined in their social intercourse with men. Generally speaking, male villagers were not very happy with the reservation system. As to empowerment: most elected women perceived a gain in knowledge, interest in politics, and an enhanced status in the family and village community. And more women than men, especially in the 'developed' block, spoke about doing something specifically for women and children. This offers some hope that a more gender-balanced rural development might take place in the future. 70 per cent of elected women wished to remain in the institutions, or even aspired for higher positions, especially those in the more forward block. This is a possible indicator of their confidence and belief in their abilities.

Generally speaking, it appears that some empowerment has taken place for the elected women. The impact on the women remaining outside the institutions appears to be feebler. In the *backward* block it seems that the elected women became removed from the female constituency. However, most women were still happy that other women were elected and perceived that they now had access to their elected representatives, which was not the case before. These results indicate that undeniably a process of empowerment has been started by the reforms in local self government in rural India, at least in the case of Orissa, but that progress has been rather more successful in the better-placed regions. This points to the all-pervasive effects of inequality in Indian society and the need for additional measures. This in turn depends on a continuing political will to put these reforms into practice. However, positive changes do seem to have occurred in both of the regions of Orissa studied, and the sheer quantitative impact of one third of female representatives being created should not be underrated. In this respect gains from reservation are already perceptible, but it will be a long lasting process, and additional strategies have to be adopted if there is to be a greater impact on women's life in general. Furthermore, whether other states have been, or will be, as efficacious as Orissa in extending democracy at a local level, remains an open question.

IV

The examples and studies in this volume interpret the term political institution in an eclectic fashion. This invariably results from looking at diverse forms of institutions associated with the developmental state in India and locating their functioning in relation to society. We hope thereby to suggest some of the ways in which the institutional designs of the Indian state inform and influence social texture and in turn are shaped by the social texture that surrounds them. The volume deliberately refrains from looking at institutions simply in terms of high politics, but attempts to explain the dynamism of the Indian state as a whole by examining it at different levels and in different contexts. In recent years, a regular refrain in both scholarly circles and popular journalistic media has been to highlight the supposed 'de-institutionalisation' of the Indian polity. This volume indicates that this term is perhaps less valid than might be supposed. Within a thriving democracy, with a rapidly growing economy, Indian political institutions are undergoing a process of reactivation. It is indeed true that the institutional design of the state at its apex demands serious reform. The first-past-the-post electoral system and over-centralisation has enabled a small number of political elites to exercise enormous power over a country of one billion people with diverse language, religion and cultural traditions. In many ways these institutional designs, based upon the Indian constitution, have possibly restrained extreme political formations – such as the RSS (Rashtriya Svayamsevak Sangh) and their political representatives – from exercising control over the Indian political system. But on the other hand, the first-past-the-post system has enabled parties to exercise much wider power than their regionally concentrated, rather thin layer of mass support might otherwise permit.

Another visible political de-institutionalisation that has mesmerised observers of contemporary India has been the decline of the Congress party organisation. The obvious displacement of the Congress from the centre of Indian politics – notwithstanding their electoral success in 2004 – and the Congress' internal organisational entropy is undoubtedly a reflection of political realignment in Indian society. However, it needs to be remembered that politics in India in recent years has become a truly mass affair. The participation of the less affluent citizens in Indian politics no doubt challenged both the Congress and BJP primarily due to their failure to reinvent themselves in accordance with changing social configurations and their articulation in electoral and agitational politics. The BJP has lost support by retreating into its old alliance with the RSS whilst relying excessively on unrealistic propagandist electioneering. The Congress, however, has learnt its lesson in coalition politics in recent years. It has gained few more votes than before, but has entered instead into diverse forms of coalition in order to regain access to political power and preserve its dwindling mass base. It is ironical that Sonia Gandhi's relative inexperience in politics proved to be her greatest asset. Abandoning the highly authoritarian practice of Indira Gandhi, she has relied more upon the collective leadership of seasoned Congress politicians. The Congress party is thus now far more disciplined and cohesive. Sonia Gandhi also readily renounced the formal trappings of power and projected a more neutral and technocratic image of the party by enabling Manmohan Singh to become the new Prime Minister following the 2004 election. The suave, technocratic and supposedly non-political image of Manmohan has enabled him to concentrate more on governance. Sonia meanwhile has been able to concentrate on the management of the party and coalition and has taken upon herself the burden of electoral campaigning. Pragmatic strategising has thus facilitated the emergence of a novel institutional process of coalition building within the ruling party, whilst a more flexible political approach has gained the Congress new acceptance and stemmed the rapid corrosion in its mass base.

A further form of political deinstitutionalisation has been linked, by some observers, with economic liberalisation, privatisation, the absolute decline in state enterprise, and the relative decline in development expenditure. This has resulted in state institutions enjoying a far less prominent place in daily economic life than they did in the first twenty or thirty years after independence. Yet as the same time as political deinstitutionalisation has become apparent in certain areas of the body politic, this volume draws attention to the rise or revitalisation of new forms of political institution. The increasing activism of rural panchayats suggests the growing salience of a novel form of politics at the grass roots level. The much used and frequently abused term (*panchayat*) has thus gained a fresh lease of life as a political institution since their successful use by the Left Front in West Bengal and the erstwhile Janata Party in Karnataka. The 74th constitutional amendment concerning local self-government institutions has transformed panchayats into an institution of the new mass era in Indian politics, providing both a source of self-empowerment for hitherto marginalised groups and a focal point for rural economic and developmental transactions. Indeed, in areas where such reforms were not implemented, de-institutionalisation has become far more apparent and the political system has been thrown into crisis. In recent years in a long corridor extending from the Nepal border in Bihar, down through the adivasi regions of Jharkhand, the thickly forested hilly areas of Orissa and Chattisgarh to the dalit and advasi areas of Andhra, revolutionary Maoist movements have raised their head again. In recent state assembly elections in February 2005 voter apathy combined with Maoist violence and police counter-terrorist measures contributed to a very low turnout in certain districts of Jharkhand. By contrast, in insurgency-devastated Kashmir, people voted in large numbers in *panchayat* elections in January 2005, notwithstanding the reluctance of Kashmir Huryat (an alliance of dissident political parties) to endorse these elections. Institutions at local level can thus provide new means for the mobilisation of popular energies in the transactional politics of development, despite the reluctance of more formal political leadership to become involved.

Urban political institutions cannot be explained in such clear terms, as in both rural market towns and large urban centres the political institutions are more complex. Here we find that the electoral and democratic dynamism of politics is enmeshed with diverse state institutions that tend more often than not to restrict the power of marginalised social groups and force them to confront the far better-entrenched institutional power of elites. This is especially true in cities such as Mumbai where the complex arrangement of institutions lies far beyond the reach of the city's slum dwellers or even the middle class working population. The land question in Mumbai is crucially indicative of this powerlessness and the opaqueness of institutions that often enables corruption to thrive and penetrate even the highest echelons of city government.

Political institutions cannot, however, be simply explained in terms of the juxtaposition between popular democratic institutions and bureaucratic entanglements. Bureaucracy has its own institutional dynamism and autonomy that can reshape and influence such crucial areas as popular media. Bureaucratic control can seriously impinge upon popular media which are thereby enmeshed in networks of corporate power, elected political patronage, and commercial and revenue transactions. This is evident in the arena of state level politics as the state often functions as the crucial intermediary layer between an increasingly dysfunctional centre and a dynamic grass roots level of politics. A final crucial political institution in popular state politics is the ill-defined Weberian concept of charisma and its role in garnering popular following. Through an investigation of these various institutions, the present volume presents a montage of the complex arrangements within a variety of Indian political institutions. It is the intention thereby to provide a framework for understanding the changing nature of democracy, governance and civil society in South Asia at a time when the subcontinent is facing both dramatic opportunities and unprecedented threats to its security. The interconnectedness of poverty, alienation, communal and ethnic violence and international conflict are widely apparent. So too are the connections between governance, human, economic and strategic security. We hope that the examples we have addressed might allow a more optimistic perspective on future developments by illuminating key issues and by demonstrating the innovation and resourcefulness of ordinary Indians in recent years. As democracy has widened, and old structures of authority have diminished, the Indian citizen has clearly a far larger part to play in the shaping of political institutions than ever before. With improvements in communications and the increasing transparency of public life, the ordinary citizen is also now better equipped to exercise that power. It is to be hoped that future political trends will nurture this new found agency and that growing popular participation and governmental accountability within India, will enable Indians to face the challenges of globalisation and to play a more effective and responsible role within the wider world.

1

STAGES IN THE SUCCESS AND FAILURE OF ECONOMIC REFORM IN INDIA: A REVIEW OF THE LITERATURE

Jos Mooji[1]

1. Introduction

In the past 15 years, several political scientists have tried to understand and explore 'liberalisation' reforms in India: first, the efforts in the 1980s and why they failed, and later, the apparent success of the reforms in the 1990s. This chapter reviews the literature that focuses on the latter – and still ongoing – reform process. It does not discuss the impact of economic reform as such, instead concentrating on political explanations for the reforms: the success or failure of both stages of reforms and the relative absence of opposition to them. The terms 'reform' or 'reforms' are used here rather loosely. I do not refer to specific monetary or financial measures, but rather to the whole process of change from a more state-regulated economy to a more market-oriented economy.

The real beginning of the economic reform process in India is widely viewed as having been in 1991. There had been earlier episodes of economic liberalisation: first, during the post-Emergency rule of Indira Gandhi (1980–4) and later during Rajiv Gandhi's regime (1984–9), but the pursuit of liberalisation policies during the 1990s was much more significant. In 1991, a new government, headed by PV Narasimha Rao and with Manmohan Singh as Finance Minister, announced its first reform measures almost immediately after taking office in June 1991, and continued to introduce new reform measures in various key economic sectors during its term. The first measures aimed at stabilisation and included a substantial currency devaluation and deflationary measures. They were followed by structural adjustment reforms, including the removal of controls on private industrial investment, a reduction of price controls, reforms of the banking system and the opening-up of the economy to foreign trade and investment.[2] In some other economic areas (such as labour laws, agriculture and public enterprises), however, reforms have so far been either less radical or entirely absent.

The desire to reform did not end in 1996 when the Congress (I) government was replaced by a coalition headed by the Janata Dal, or in 1998, when a coalition led by the Bharatiya Janata Party (BJP) took over. These governments, as well as the subsequent BJP-led governments, continued to direct the Indian economy away from regulation and central planning, and towards a more open market economy. The reforms seem to be fairly well consolidated, and although a policy reversal back to a more planned economy cannot be ruled out altogether, there is no indication that this is likely to happen in the near future.

The immediate trigger for reform in 1991 was an acute balance of payments crisis. When the new government took charge, it was faced with an immediate liquidity crisis: foreign exchange reserves barely sufficed to cover two weeks of imports.[3] The rupee was devalued almost immediately, and various loans from the International Monetary Fund helped to resolve the immediate problems. Other measures related to industrial policy and trade were introduced shortly afterwards.[4]

The acute crisis and the feeling of urgency that accompanied the reform process may explain its some drastic steps were taken immediately, but they cannot explain its continuation and consolidation. Other factors have to be taken into account to understand the success of these reforms: how they survived and indeed increased, and why there was so little opposition towards them. As with all policy changes, some groups stood to win while others faced losses – and some of the latter are well organised and capable of mounting considerable resistance to unpopular legislation.

Three principal characteristics of the consolidation of the 1990s reforms makes them particularly intriguing. First is their success compared to the reforms introduced earlier in the 1980s, especially by Rajiv Gandhi. Early in 1986 Rajiv Gandhi announced a 'judicious combination of deregulation, import liberalisation and easier access to foreign technology'.[5] Soon, however, this liberalisation ran into problems, the pace of change slowed and eventually almost stopped.[6] So why should something that failed in the 1980s succeed in the 1990s, especially since, at first sight, the conditions in the 1980s were so much more favourable? Rajiv Gandhi had come to power on an enormous wave of sympathy after the assassination of his mother, Indira Gandhi. He headed a large majority (415 out of 545 seats) in the Indian lower house, the *Lok Sabha*,[7] while the reforming Congress (I) party of Narasimha Rao had just over 40 per cent of the *Lok Sabha* seats.

A second characteristic of the reforms of the 1990s is the apparent lack of organised opposition. India is a democratic country in which interest groups are allowed to participate. As a result, opposition to the reforms could easily have become influential and could have resulted in a policy reversal. As Jenkins states:

> Governments in democratic political systems have generally been thought to face greater obstacles in bringing about economic reform, mainly because their hold on power relies on electoral consent. In genuinely liberal democracies, anti-reform interests have more political space and resources to influence electorates motivated largely by narrowly defined short-term economic considerations.[8]

Yet this principle seems not to have applied in the Indian case. Thirdly, some of the chief politicians in the old regime had a number of relevant interests. Narasimha Rao was a senior member of the Congress (I) party and had been in the ministries of both Indira Gandhi and her son.[9] Manmohan Singh had held various posts in the Indian bureaucracy before he joined the government in 1991, and was known, again according to Shastri, 'to be part of the earlier mode of India's economy bureaucracy. His associates describe him as a regulator'.[10] The Narasimha Rao government was a Congress (I) government, which meant that it had no one to blame but its own predecessors for the rigidity and economic stagnation that the reformers aimed to change. Historically, the Congress (I) party itself bore the brunt of blame for this situation. Moreover, there was no 'honeymoon' period,[11] during which new governments are given the benefit of the doubt and have opportunities to introduce radical new policies. Despite these obstacles, the new government pursued its reforms with some consistency, although perhaps not as quickly as some of the reformers would have preferred, and certainly not to the same extent in each sector and every region of the country. But on the whole, there is no disagreement about the fact that the economic orientation of India in the early 21st century is distinctly different from that of 10–15 years earlier.

I now turn briefly to the abortive reform programme of the 1980s, and then examine in detail the various interpretations of the later reforms, highlighting four different kinds of explanation for the successful consolidation of these reforms. Finally, I make some general observations with regard to the relation between the reform process on the one hand and some of India's political institutions on the other.

2. The Failed Reform Process in the 1980s

The heyday of the Nehruvian paradigm was already over in the mid-1980s when Rajiv Gandhi announced the initiation of a reform programme.[12] Faith in the socialist path of development had gradually eroded: industrial growth had slowed down after the 1960s and almost everyone agreed that the main redistributive measures, such as land reform, had failed. Anti-poverty policies had been unsuccessful, and there was a growing consensus as to the inefficiences of the public sector. The international context, too, had undergone major changes. With the emergence of the newly industrialising countries (NICs), India was left behind. Moreover, from the end of the 1970s onwards China was turning into a market economy; it was followed, to a limited extent, by the Soviet Union in the 1980s. An increasing number of Indian economists and bureaucrats were educated in American universities and became influenced both by neoclassical economics and the American way of life.[13] Generally, the force of anti-colonial and nationalist sentiments had declined. As a result of all this, many of India's leaders in the 1980s were, according to Kohli, 'more willing to open the economy to and learn from the West than the leaders of the post-independence generation'.[14]

In this seemingly fertile ground, Rajiv Gandhi's early reforms nonetheless failed. There are a number of different interpretations that explain both the reforms and their failure. Patnaik emphasises the interests of metropolitan capital in the economic reform process. The devaluation of the local currency, which often accompanies liberalisation 'helps to keep raw material export prices from the third world low'. Moreover such "liberalisation" 'opens up avenues of profitable investment for metropolitan capital in a period of crisis'.[15] Aside from external pressures, Patnaik emphasised the role of internal pressure as 'perhaps even more decisive'.[16] He analysed the push for liberalisation as the response of big business to the stagnation in public investment, which itself should be seen as a result of the fiscal crisis. Investment opportunities for private enterprise were limited, certainly in comparison to the expansion of the command over capital. Businesses were in search of growth opportunities, and therefore supported domestic decontrol, delicensing and deregulation.[17]

Another class-based explanation with a slightly different emphasis was developed by Harriss and Rubin.[18] These authors argued that the reforms could be seen as an attempt to change the relationship between the Indian state and the main economic classes, and aimed thereby to remove some of the obstacles to growth.[19] The reforms were an attempt to move the state away from patronage politics and towards a more developmental role, albeit an openly elitist one.[20] The reforms, according to Harriss, failed as a result of the compromised nature of class power and the weakness of the state as an organisation.

Kohli has emphasised the role of interest groups more than classes. He argued that when Rajiv Gandhi came to power, there was an 'illusion of autonomy' after a massive electoral victory. This victory freed Rajiv Gandhi – if only momentarily and artificially – from coalitional entanglements and interest-group pressures.[21] This freedom was curtailed when mass support for Rajiv Gandhi's government faltered. Congress was defeated in several states and Rajiv himself was increasingly perceived as 'pro-rich'. Opposition developed from almost all sides, in particular from the Congress rank and file, from the left-wing opposition and from rural interest groups.

Another argument which has been made for the failure of the reforms highlights their poor management, and the lack of political skills of those implementing them. Manor refers to Rajiv Gandhi's lack of political expertise and his lack of awareness over the 'need to build support for this major change in policy. He shared his mother's central misconception that India could be governed by mere assertion from the apex of the political system'.[22] Other observers have argued that the reforms were too piecemeal and left too much of the system intact, and that the phasing of the reforms was ill thought through.[23]

Most contemporary contributors to the debate about the failed reform of the 1980s were pessimistic about the possibility of subsequent major policy shifts. Harriss suggested that 'a real attempt to liberalise the economy probably would require the establishment of a more authoritarian regime, able to ride over the powerful interests represented in the dominant coalition'.[24] Kohli, too, concluded with a note of scepticism regarding the possibility of introducing reforms in a democratic setting:

> It would...be absurd to deny that powerful leaders like Indira Gandhi or Rajiv Gandhi can initiate some policy changes that they and their advisors deem necessary. There are, however, fairly sharp limits on how far and how fast a liberalisation program can be implemented in a democracy... The need to build broad coalitions pulls these fragile democratic governments in policy directions other than those that may best promote an efficient and competitive economy.[25]

This widespread scepticism proved to be misplaced. In the early 1990s a new drive towards economic liberalisation was introduced, and this time with more success.

3. Economic Reform After 1991

Compared to the 1980s, the reforms in the 1990s have attracted more attention and debate. Most of the contributions to the debate have tried to explain the success of the present reform process and the relative absence of opposition,[26] and in particular have attempted to trace the political factors that made a transition from a planned to a market economy possible. A few contributions stress the fact that this transition is not yet complete and that there have been reforms in some sectors, but not in others. The variation between the various states and the role of state governments has also been debated.

Four different kinds of approaches can be discerned in the explanations of the reforms. The first is a state-centred approach, focusing on the political process, the management of the reforms and the importance and the strength of the ideas behind them. The second approach emphasises contingent factors, in particular the importance of identity politics, which have diverted public attention from economic policies. The third is a society-centred approach, focusing on the changing class composition in the dominant coalition, which may have facilitated economic reforms. The fourth stresses external influences, in particular those exercised by the World Bank and the International Monetary Fund (see table 1 for an overview of these four approaches and the principle authors associated with them).

Table 1 Explanations of Economic Reforms in the 1990s

Type of Explanation		Authors
State-centred	– political management and skills	Chhibber 1995
	– institutions and mechanisms	Jenkins 1995a, 1995b, 1999
	– emphasis on personality of the reformers and their background	Manor 1995
		Panini 1995
	– political parties and electoral processes	Root 1998
	– ideas as a source of change	Shastri 1997
Contingencies	Identity politics is a mass politics issue, and diverts the attention from economic policies	Varshney 1999
Society-centred	changes with regard to diversity, fluidity and fragmentation in the coalition of dominant interest groups	Bardhan 1998
External pressure	Influence of Bretton Woods institutions	Bhadhuri and Nayyar 1996 Patnaik 2000 Patnaik and Chandrashekar (1995)

Note: Most authors refer to several factors in their analysis of the economic reforms, although there is usually a main emphasis in their explanation.

State-centred Explanations

Most authors writing about the economic reforms of the 1990s utilise 'state-centred' explanations. One of the fullest accounts is Jenkins' detailed investigation of the political mechanisms that have made the reform process possible.[27] Jenkins describes these mechanisms under three different headings: incentives, institutions and skills. With regard to incentives, he argues that the political elite is willing to take risks (i.e. introduce reforms), because it is confident that the reforms will not fundamentally alter the political arena or its privileged position. Most Indian politicians are 'survivors': they have been able to adjust to different circumstances and have even changed party loyalty if necessary. They know the rules of the game and expect that even amidst or after reforms they will be able to continue to collect illegal income and strengthen their networks of patronage. This, in Jenkins' account, is the first incentive. The second is that the political elite, fully aware of both the flexibility and malleability of interest groups, is confident that these groups will adjust to altered circumstances and find new ways for coalition-building, when forced to do so.[28] The reforms may even provide new opportunities for earning illegal incomes, strengthening support bases, and carrying on 'Politics as usual'.[29]

In the second category, 'institutions', Jenkins describes the formal (mainly federal) and informal (mainly party networks) institutions. The way these institutions work helps the political elite to implement the reforms with surprising efficiency. The influence of the federal system means that nationwide opposition to reforms is less likely to emerge. The impact of reforms varies from state to state. There are winners and losers; some will resist but others won't. The result is competition among states rather than a joined effort to reverse national policies. Second, the federal structure fragments interest groups which otherwise might organise at a national level. Lastly, the fact that state governments, headed by parties that are in opposition at the central level, sometimes cooperate with central government policies lessens the likelihood of opposition parties mounting an effective opposition to these policies at the national level. Moreover, the federalist structure provides for multiple reform experiments and learning processes, which may help to absorb the shocks of reform.[30]

The political parties are described by Jenkins mainly in terms of the networks of relationships that they help to sustain. An important characteristic of Indian political parties is their porousness: the boundaries between party- and non-party networks are fuzzy, and enterprising individuals/politicians may control various networks of influence. These networks can be exploited when negotiating policies and accommodating interests, but also for the purpose of intelligence-gathering. The porousness lengthens the time horisons of the politicians – a crucial factor in the sustainability of the reforms.[31]

Jenkins' third heading, 'skills', refers to the tactics used by politicians and party elites, which enabled them to introduce the reforms by stealth without being noticed by the political 'radar screen'. The reformers tried – successfully – to cloak change in the disguise of continuity. By claiming one thing but doing another, and by introducing *de facto* reforms when official policy statements stress continuity, reforms could be introduced without much opposition.

One of the most interesting aspects of Jenkins' interpretations is his description of 'real democracy'. In contrast to the idealist image of democracy underlying much of the 'good governance' agenda, Jenkins shows that the capacity of the Indian state to introduce reform policies is due to the underhanded and often opaque tactics that are made possible by democratic institutions. The Indian state manages to combine being capable with a lack of transparency, despite the association of these two concepts in the 'good governance' ideologies of various international agencies. At the same time, Jenkins criticises the cynical view of the Indian democracy as being entirely in the clutches of powerful interest groups capable of preventing any reform that would negatively affect their interests.

One of the limitations of Jenkins' account is that it does not address the substance of the reforms. He explains why a reform process can succeed in India and analyses the political mechanisms that made the reform possible. The same mechanisms could, however, facilitate a reform process of an entirely different nature.

Other authors, Manor, Panini and Shastri,[32] with or without reference to Jenkins, have stressed the stealth characteristic of the reforms, although they put their main emphasis elsewhere. Panini starts by saying that the reforms in India 'are regarded as another instance of the imperialist design of the International Monetary Fund (IMF) and the World Bank'.[33] India, according to Panini, was too weak to withstand this pressure. Initially there was resistance from various sides, but this has weakened as a result of, on the one hand, the compromising attitude of the government, which was willing to make special adjustments to accommodate particular interests, and on the other hand, the impacts of the reforms themselves, as various interest groups, initially opposed to the reforms, began to realise the potential advantages of the reform process.

Manor describes the reform process as cautious and limited. The reformers were very careful not to threaten any vested interest, attempting both to satisfy all interest groups and appeal to the whole electorate. According to Manor, the sequencing of the reforms has thus been very effective:

Changes in policy have been announced in modest steps, but steadily, with something new every week or two. In most cases, each innovation has affected only a limited sector of the economy and a small number of interests. After one announcement which is liable to displease a particular set of interests, the government carefully postpones further steps which they might dislike for a while, to let resentment dissipate. Political opponents of the reforms are thus picked off one at the time, in turns, to prevent them from uniting.[34]

Compared to Jenkins' analysis, Manor places greater emphasis on the personality, experience and insights of the main actor in the process: PV Narasimha Rao. According to Manor, the reforms were managed and controlled by a small group of people around the Prime Minister. These reformers were determined and consistent in pursuing their objectives. The decision not to advertise the reforms broadly is ascribed to Narasimha Rao. He was realistic enough to realise he would not succeed in selling the reforms to large crowds at large meetings. Instead, he opted for a low-key approach to the reforms and generally has worked towards a de-dramatisation of politics.[35]

This 'who' question is also raised by Shastri, but where Manor stresses the determination of Narasimha Rao (contrasted with the impatience, confusion and inconstancy of Rajiv Gandhi), Shastri investigates the public image of both leaders. Rajiv Gandhi was seen as modern, young, dynamic and an outsider to politics. Initially this was an advantage, but very soon his emphasis on science and modernisation was identified as pro-urban and pro-rich. Narasimha Rao, on the other hand, had a history in the old Congress party and was known for his intellect and caution. His credibility assisted the reform programme, especially since he had so far never been a rabid supporter of economic liberalisation.[36]

Although Shastri, like Jenkins, mentions the political skills and careful management of the reforms, her main argument is a different one. What she stresses is the importance of ideas as a source of policy change. In her interpretation, the reform process started in the late 1970s and early 1980s, when various committees, headed by senior administrators who were more market-friendly than their predecessors, wrote their policy reports. These ideas were further developed during the Rajiv Gandhi regime. Although many of the policy ideas could not be implemented, the strength of the new discourse increased. The ideological orientation of the key decision-makers and economic advisors changed further, a process which was helped by the entry of the so-called 'laterals' within the bureaucracy. These laterals were usually relatively young and had trained outside India, notably in the USA. They sometimes had prior professional experience in the World Bank or in the academic world and were not used to the hierarchy and rigidity of the

Indian bureaucracy. They may not have been real ideologues but, according to Shastri, once they were faced with the excessive centralisation and bureaucratisation of the Indian government, they wanted to correct these inefficiencies. These corrections were then identified with reform. Moreover, compared to normal members of the Indian Administrative Service, these laterals were freer to develop new ideas and to explore new avenues in their work because they had more alternative career options than the normal bureaucrats.[37]

So, although Rajiv Gandhi had to backtrack on his reform policies, the ideas and convictions regarding the necessity of reform created during his own and the previous government, continued to gather strength within the bureaucracy, and when Narasimha Rao came into office the plans were all ready to be implemented. The bureaucratic policymakers had only to wait for the gradual opening of the 'windows of opportunity' to introduce the reforms in a carefully sequenced way.

According to Shastri the shift from the Nehruvian 1950s discourse to the new market-oriented ideology is now complete.[38] In this respect, Shastri's analysis is diametrically opposed to several others, which have emphasised that the reformers downplayed (as they had to) the importance of the changes and obscured their real intentions, and that there has been *no* ideological revolution in government thinking.[39] Panini, for instance, makes the point that the 'socialist values stressing equality continue to dominate the political discourse in India'.[40] The ambivalence vis-à-vis traders and business, partly based on Gandhian ideals, is far from extinct in India. There is 'a pragmatic consensus in favour of liberalisation', according to Panini, but 'the programme is yet to gain legitimacy in terms of ideologies and values'.[41]

To sum up the discussion so far, there are various interpretations of the Indian reform process which prioritise the role of the state. These interpretations posit different emphases: ideas, determination of the main politicians, management and skills, institutions and incentives within the Indian bureaucracy. Existing analyses allow us to look into the kitchen of Indian policymaking, as it were, and show us the conditions in which the policy elite designs its policies and what kind of accommodation, compromising and negotiation, partly behind closed doors, takes place during the implementation phase.

The limitation of some of these studies (particularly Jenkins, but also Manor and Shastri) is the neglect of the wider political economy in which these processes are located. The emphasis is on political processes and mechanisms *per se*, but little effort is made to explain the substance of these processes, the content, the direction in which the political processes are leading the economy and society, and ultimately what is at stake. In short these studies offer political science without political economy.

Emphasising Contingencies – Identity Politics

An interesting interpretation of the reforms and the broad support they generated is developed by Varshney.[42] His account falls within the category of 'state-centred' approaches, stressing the role of key players within the Indian state who have pushed the reforms. His main emphasis, however, is on the more general political circumstances which enabled these reformers to go ahead without attracting much attention. According to Varshney, there existed contingent circumstances which had nothing to do with the reforms but which made them possible.

According to Varshney, scholars generally assume that reforms, once they are there, become a central issue in political debates and therefore become dependent upon the political support they can muster.[43] Varshney claims that this centrality of reforms need not be the case. In a situation in which other issues dominate what he calls 'mass politics',[44] reformers can proceed quietly as long as they refrain from policies which could turn into mass political issues.

Mass politics in India centres around identity issues, especially since the 1990s, during which Hindu nationalism was a rising force. After the 1991 elections, the Hindu nationalist Bharatiya Janata Party (BJP) was the second largest party in the country after Congress (I). It had played a key role in the movement for the demolition of the Babri mosque in Ayodhya in north India, and in the Hindu–Muslim riots that emerged in several parts of the country. This, plus the issue of reservations for the lower castes, led to mass politics centring around identity and communalism, and a realignment of the main political parties. In Varshney's words, '[c]oalitions were increasingly formed against Hindu nationalists, not against the Congress. To begin with, the left – the Communists and the lower caste Janata Dal and its allies – disliked the reforms, but *they disliked Hindu nationalism even more.*'[45] Subsequent budget proposals could pass the Indian parliament, not because the opposition parties were in favour, but because Hindu–Muslim relations and caste animosities had become the prime determinants of political coalitions.[46]

Varshney uses the same concepts, mass and elite politics, to explain why reforms have been successfully executed in some areas and not in others. 'Reforms that touch, directly or primarily, elite politics have gone farthest: a large devaluation of the currency, a restructuring of capital markets, a liberalisation of the trade regime, and a simplification of investment rules.' Reforms that have positive political consequences in mass politics have been implemented, but reforms that have potentially negative or highly uncertain consequences in mass politics have either been completely ignored, or pursued half-heartedly.[47]

This interpretation of the Indian reforms is overlooked in the general literature about economic reforms, but may well be relevant to some other reforming countries, especially in eastern Europe and the former Soviet Union, where identity politics and ethnic conflicts likewise dominate mass politics. At the same time, several questions remain.

First, the distinction between mass and elite politics is not altogether satisfactory. Varshney rightly states that questions of identity have come to dominate the political arenas, not only on the streets but also in the parliament and the bureaucracy. He acknowledges that mass political issues can enter and profoundly influence elite politics. 'In democracies, especially poor democracies, mass politics can redefine elite politics, for an accumulated expression of popular sentiments and opinions inevitably exercises a great deal of pressure on elected politicians.'[48] But what is also true is that this mass political sentiment is partly orchestrated by elite politicians. Just as elites attempt to make use of the masses in order to pursue their concerns and interests, mass mobilisation both responds to and influences the actions of elite politicians. In other words, the distinction between elite and mass politics is often not so clear-cut. Elite concerns and interests may be pursued by mass mobilisation.

Moreover, the opposition between elite and mass suggests that the groups are in some way homogeneous. However, within both mass and elite there are important divisions, both in relation to how people position themselves with regard to political issues (i.e. whether or not they sympathise with the Hindu nationalists) and with regard to other factors and issues. The industrial elite, for instance, differs from the rural elite, and may pursue different interests in different ways (they may even be internally divided). The 'mass–elite' opposition discourages an examination of more complex relationships and contradictions that may influence political affiliations.

Second, there is an unexplored contradiction in Varshney's interpretation. On the one hand, he makes the argument that the reformers could introduce changes relatively easily while people were more interested in issues other than the reforms. This is the contingency argument. On the other hand, the reformers can only push ahead in those sectors in which changes primarily affect – and are beneficial to – the elite. The reformers avoided pushing reforms with potentially negative or uncertain effects for large numbers of people, which would foreground the reforms in mass politics. This is the 'selective implementation' argument. These two arguments do not sit easily together; in fact, the second argument makes the first redundant. The only evidence that would prove the contingency argument would be if reforms with adverse effects for large numbers of people had been implemented without much resistance. The fact that Varshney complements his contingency argument with the 'selective implementation' argument therefore weakens his claim that it was communalist politics which helped in the introduction of the reforms. The question remains: what was the role of the contingencies, and how important was the selective implementation?

A third issue that is not addressed by Varshney concerns the origins and support base of the reforms. If we accept his interpretation, we understand the *context* in which the reforms could be pushed, but why there was a group of reformers who made use of the opportunity is not explained. In this respect, Varshney's theory needs to be complemented with another one which explains not only the political context which shaped the opportunity, for reforms but also the reason for of the reforms themselves.

4. Society-centred Explanations

Society-centred approaches are relatively rare in explanations of economic reforms in India, but one that falls into this category is Bardhan's analysis. In a recent epilogue to his influential book 'The Political Economy of Development in India', he attempted to explain the socio-political background of the reforms of the 1990s.[49]

Like other observers, Bardhan notes that the reforms have generated little serious opposition. This does not mean, he argues, that there have been no substantive reforms, but rather that they were introduced by stealth, as Jenkins has also argued. Bardhan, however, does not completely agree with Jenkins,[50] and goes on to argue that much has remained the same as when he wrote his interpretation of stagnation 15 years ago. There is still a 'staggering burden of government subsidies, placating various powerful interest groups'.[51] According to Bardhan, '[o]n the whole one should not exaggerate the extent of shift in the basic political equilibrium in spite of all the impressive changes that have taken place in economic policy'.[52]

But Bardhan also acknowledges that there are important changes and realignments in the composition and attitudes of the dominant coalition that have made the reforms more acceptable.[53] On the one hand, the dominant coalition itself has become more diverse, fluid and fragmented. On the other hand, ideas about the preferred role of the state have changed. 'There is a slow, and at times grudging, acceptance within the bureaucracy that the Indian state has overextended itself in the economy, far beyond the limits of its administrative capacity' (ibid: 131). So, Bardhan stresses continuity – the fact that the old system of subsidies and patronage networks continues to exist – but he also acknowledges that the changed attitudes and new realignments within the dominant coalition were important backdrops against which the reforms could take place.

Another such context is the specific process of democratisation in India: the shift of political power from the traditional elites to the lower castes. To quote Bardhan at length, there is a

> major disjuncture between politics and economics in India so far as market reform is concerned. On the one hand, we are told that in recent years the era of market reform has arrived in India, and that there is a measure of political consensus that it is inexorable and irreversible. On the other hand, some of the major political events in the last decade or so that have captured public imagination constitute a phenomenon that is essentially anti-market: the propagation of group equity and caste rights, the carving of markets for new jobs in the public sector in pro- tected niches, special dispensations and patronage for newly emergent groups, rampant caste-based violations of the institutional insulation of economic governance – all amounting to a drowning of considerations of efficiency in the name of intergroup equity.

> Cynics may even argue that the retreat of the state implied by economic reform is now more acceptable to the upper classes and castes, not only because the regulatory and interventionist state has become too burden- some for the Indian economy, but also because these classes and castes are now losing their control over state power in the face of the emerging hordes of lower castes, and thus opting for greener pastures in the private sector (and abroad)[54]

This valuable contextualisation of the Indian reform process provides part of the explanation of why reforms have become popular. A new economic envi- ronment, in which setting up a business is regarded with less suspicion and to which entry is less constrained, may provide a way out for the many educated but unemployed upper-caste young people whose access to jobs within the government is limited.

Bardhan concludes his epilogue with a note of caution about the prospects of the reform process. Gandhi's anti-market, anti-big capital, small-is-beautiful populism has become part of India's collective identity, and there are other reasons too which result in a 'none-too-hospitable climate for market reforms'.[55]

The epilogue contains several interesting ideas, and complements some of the other interpretations discussed above in the sense that Bardhan's approach is a political-economic one addressing the content of the reforms, not only the circumstances under which reforms can be implemented. But the paper is also somewhat contradictory, since it aims to explain two things at the same time: 1) reforms and the fact that they proceeded, and 2) the fact that their progress is slow. The fact that they exist is related to the realignments and changing attitudes within the dominant coalition and to the changing political cal landscape in which high castes lose access to the state. Political and cultural factors constrain the reforms and cause, if not overt, certainly some less open forms of opposition. It is not clear how the two arguments relate together. Bardhan's interpretation is a valuable contribution to the debate about the politics of the reforms, but the overall argument is still in need of some more elaboration.

Emphasis on External Pressure: The Role of the Bretton Woods Institutions

Surprisingly, most of the authors discussed so far (e.g. Jenkins, Varshney, Bardhan) have not mentioned the role of international institutions in the reform process. An exception is Panini, who mentioned the pressure of the International Monetary Fund (IMF) and the World Bank. Another exception is Shastri, who highlighted the educational and professional background of the bureaucrats and 'laterals', who often have prior professional experience in one of the international financial institutions.

For Patnaik, Bhaduri and Nayyar these international institutions are crucial to their explanation of domestic economic reforms.[56] Bhaduri and Nayyar discuss the 'hidden script' of liberalisation. They analyse the Washington Consensus and point out that questioning this consensus has become difficult for people who want to pursue a career in the normal establishment. Their analysis of this 'hidden script' is very similar to the interpretation of Patnaik, who in addition also discusses the political effects of the reforms in much more detail.

According to Patnaik, the fiscal crisis which triggered the reforms in 1991 was not so much the result of populist and costly policies undertaken by the *dirigiste* government, as many people assume, but of liberalisation policies undertaken before 1991. The standard response to a fiscal crisis is to liberalise further, which from this perspective is, of course, the wrong treatment. The Bretton Woods institutions played a major role in diagnosing the crisis and prescribing further liberalisation. Hence, a crucial question is, which interests do these institutions represent? These certainly include, according to Patnaik, those of the multinational corporations (MNCs): 'Trade liberalisation no doubt enables MNCs to capture third world markets at the expense of local producers by providing or arranging for loans or export credit. Likewise the wooing of MNCs to undertake investment in third world economies opens up very profitable investment opportunities for them; and the sale of public sector assets as well as the removal of restrictions on taking over local companies enables them to buy their way cheaply into business empires in third world economies.'[57] Furthermore, it is consumers in the metropolitan region of the world who benefit from cheap exports of tropical products and imports of staple food products. Most important, however, are the interests of international financial capital, a point also made by Bhaduri and Nayyar. Patnaik observes that:

> The point is that the Bretton Woods programme, with its emphasis not just on trade liberalisation but on the removal of restrictions on capital flows, on 'financial liberalisation' and on currency unification and convertibility, serves above all the interests of international finance capital by prising open third world economies to its unhindered access, exit, and operation. True, the programme represents a convergence of interests between the MNCs; international finance capital; sections of the domestic third world bourgeoisie anxious to break out of the straitjacket of the national economy; kulak and landlord elements lured by the promise of export agriculture (a promise that is not necessarily realised subsequently as prices crash); and sections of the third world elite that benefit from 'globalisation' in terms of access to opportunities and commodities. But it bears the unmistakable stamp of international finance capital.[58]

The economic effect of liberalisation, according to Patnaik, is not so much export-led growth, but rather the import of crisis and stagnation. In India, industrial growth in the periods 1990–1 and 1997–8 was lower than in the preceding five years (i.e. 5.9 per cent as compared to 8.4 per cent).[59] There is also evidence of a slowdown of agricultural growth and an increase in rural poverty. An important question then is how these reforms could sustain themselves, and why there is not more opposition. This, suggests Patnaik, is because an abridgement of democracy has taken place, and it has happened in three different ways.

The first is the strategic shaping of policy and public opinion. There is a small group of people involved in economic policymaking, many of whom have previously been employees of the IMF or World Bank. Individual members of the media or academic researchers are influenced by grants of well-paid assignments. Independent, critical academic work becomes more difficult to undertake in an era in which universities and research have become increasingly market-driven. A second factor explaining lack of opposition is that at a certain point there is no way back. '[I]f people suffer under neo-liberal economic policies, they could suffer even more from attempts to break out of these policies, i.e. in the aftermath of the speculative outflow which would accompany any effort to change neo-liberal policies.'[60] Lastly, liberalisation policies effect changes on the political arena. According to Patnaik, globalisation in India has intensified communalism, fundamentalism and secessionism. These movements have become more important in Indian politics and have led to a shift in political discourse away from economic policies towards issues raised by these movements. Under these circumstances, implementation of the reforms has become easier, and is even justified by some on the grounds that reforms will stimulate modernisation and would help to overcome traditionalism and backwardness.[61]

Patnaik's emphasis on the international context is a valuable addition to the other theories and models discussed above (and makes one wonder, in fact, how it is possible that this element has been neglected by so many others). However, it is important to qualify Patnaik's argument. Patnaik's interpretation of the role of finance capital tends towards a conspiracy theory, because there is so little empirical description and analysis of how the interests of the MNCs and of international finance capital have become dominant within the Bretton Woods institutions. One may observe and conclude that the policy *outcome* serves finance capital well, but for a full explanation it is also necessary to analyse the *process*. What are the procedures and mechanisms through which the MNCs and international finance capital have become so influential? In other words, Patnaik's (but also Bhaduri and Nayyar's) analysis on this point is deductive, where one would have welcomed some more empirical detail about the processes of policymaking within the international financial institutions and the Indian state. It is an analysis of structure without process.

5. By Way of Conclusion – Reforms and India's Political Institutions

In the preceding sections I have reviewed various interpretations of the economic reforms in India of the 1980s and 1990s. It has become clear that there are different kinds of explanations, some focusing more on the state, others more on contextual or social factors. I will conclude by mentioning a few issues that have not yet been discussed in much detail, but that are relevant in the context of this book, and that could be taken up in further research.

A first issue relates to the *role of the federal structure in the reform process*. There are two opposite views in the literature on this issue: one negative and one more positive. Guhan and Weiner both argue that 'the states' response so far to economic reforms has been grudging at best and non-cooperative at worst'.[62] Three reasons are presented to explain this. First, endemic political instability in the states. State governments have a time duration of 2 to 3 years, making a real commitment to long-term development unlikely. Second,

interest groups opposed to aspects of economic reform (trade unions, agricul-
turalists, etc.) are well-organised at the state level. And lastly, the reluctance of
state functionaries to 'give up the patronage and the rents that are acquired
through the regulatory system'.[63] By contrast, Jenkins describes the federalist
structure as an institution that has facilitated the reform process considerably.
He gives a number of reasons, summarised in the previous section.

Although the interpretations of Guhan and Weiner on the one hand and
Jenkins on the other are opposed to each other, I tend to think that both contain some truth. The federal structure can help (and has) but can also obstruct –
and has obstructed – the reform process. Together these two interpretations
point not only to the diversity within India (states differ very much from each
other) but also to the internal contradictions that exist within many of India's
institutions. Institutions or people within institutions may sometimes cooperate with each other (or work in the same direction) and sometimes they do not.
The Indian state and its institutions are not homogeneous units, but fragmented and sometimes internally contradictory. It is important to understand
why and under which conditions (federal) institutions play one role and why
in other contexts they play another.

A second issue is the relation between the reforms and good governance.
Currie analyses the impact of the economic reforms on governance, and the
way in which the World Bank has dealt with this issue in the case of India. He
concludes that the impact of the reforms on democracy is mixed. Delicencing
has reduced the scope for corruption while social welfare has been compromised by the removal of subsidies.[64] Neither the World Bank nor other international lenders have ever tried systematically to pressure India to improve its
governance. This pressure was selective for a number of reasons: probably
because India was an active reformer; because the leverage of the World Bank
was not sufficient; and because the good governance agenda is applied in a
partial and *ad hoc* manner in any case.[65]

Jenkins makes another observation. His work is a critique of the feasibility
and internal consistence of the good governance agenda itself, and he shows
that there is both competence and capacity, in that the Indian state has been
able to introduce and subsequently pursue a structural adjustment programme. But the way in which the state has done so is, however, not a classic
example of 'good governance'. It involved a 'decided lack of transparency,
and even corruption' or, in other words, 'the "competent" management of
policy reform necessitates the use of decidedly un-"transparent" tactics'.[66]

What both analyses suggest is that 'good governance' was never an important
concern, neither for the international agencies that supported India's reform,
nor for the Indian politicians who managed to introduce the reforms. Economic
concerns came first; concerns with governance were secondary at best.

Nevertheless, in the long run the reforms may have a positive impact on governance. Along with economic reforms, some of the reforming states have implemented or are in the process of implementing various types of administrative reforms, using computers to improve service delivery, to monitor policy implementation, and to shorten the distance between stake-holders and government. In principle, these measures could enhance a wider participation of stakeholders in policy processes and improve government accountability.

A third issue is the relationship between the reforms and the increased importance of caste politics and lower caste representation in India's bureau-cracy and political institutions. This increased representation (job reservation, etc.) has been viewed by Bardhan as essentially anti-market, qualities such as efficiency and merit being valued less than issues of group equity and caste rights. The inevitable result of this 'drift towards the *backward* and lower castes'[67] is that the traditionally privileged access of the upper castes to the state is constrained; as Bardhan suggests, this could be one of the reasons why the upper castes tend to support pro-market policies – they seek for greener pastures outside the state now that their traditional state pastures are becoming dryer and less accessible.[68]

Indeed, the effect of the reforms could be that these greener pastures are found. The result may be that while the lower castes are winning on one side, they are losing on another. Due to their disadvantaged position in terms of social capital, it will be difficult for them to make use of the new opportunities to the same extent as the higher caste groups.[69]

I will make one final observation. Most interpretations of the reform process in the 1990s emphasise the positive capacity of the Indian state to introduce and pursue radical policies, emphasising the strength, rather than the weakness, of the state. This emphasis reflects the fact that the Indian state was – and is – competent, and that the policy elite was – and is – skilled and able to manage the reform process well. But it also reflects a reluctance on the part of most scholars whose work is reviewed in this paper to look beyond state-centred explanations, and to contextualise the reform process within the wider political economy of India, and the changes therein. To combine the study of the processes within the state with the study of the political-economic context remains one of the major challenges for future research on the politics of economic reform.

2

THE TEMPTATIONS OF PRESIDENTIALISM: AN EXPLANATION OF THE EVOLVING POLITICAL STRATEGY OF THE BJP

Sanjay Ruparelia

On 26 January 2000, India marked the fiftieth anniversary of its Constitution. The National Democratic Alliance (NDA), a coalition of 22 political parties that formed the Union (federal) government in September 1999, chose to mark the milestone in an unusual way. On February 22nd, it established a National Commission of recognised experts of various political persuasions whose explicit purpose was to review the workings of the Constitution. The body was set up to consider ways in which the Constitution might be reformed in order to serve the interests of the country in light of its present imperatives. One particular issue was vigorously debated in public discourse: the instability of the Centre. The reason for this was quite simple. Since 1989, India had conducted five general elections, none of which produced a single-party majority Union government. None of the eight multiparty coalition governments which emerged – with the exception of the minority Congress administration under Narasimha Rao (1991–6) which engaged in horse-trading and vote-buying to gain a parliamentary majority in 1993 – survived for the mandated five-year term in office. Simply put, they either broke into rival factions during their tenure in power or succumbed to political blackmail exerted by parties providing external parliamentary support. Given this, the issue of governmental instability and its presumed negative effect upon the formulation, execution and implementation of public policy (which is contested by certain studies of economic liberalisation), assumed great importance in the minds of many observers and citizens.

The terms of reference of the review commission were notably limited. The commission was to conduct its inquiry within the bounds of India's present regime and was not to interfere with the 'basic structure' of the Constitution. Generally speaking, the basic structure encompasses provisions which ensure the separation of powers between the executive, legislature and judiciary; commitment to the principles of secularism and fundamental rights; and, more debatably, a parliamentary form of cabinet government. Other important features of the Indian democratic regime included its 'first-past-the-post' electoral system and federal party system with strong consociational features. These structures, which together framed the rules of democratic government in India, were considered to be beyond the scrutiny of the commission. Yet despite this, caution and scepticism were urged in many quarters. KR Narayanan, the country's President, declared that 'we have to decide whether it is the Constitution which has failed us, or whether it is we who have failed the Constitution'.[1] Opposition parties, many of which were avowedly secular in their politics, expressed more vociferous dissent. They reacted strongly to the Government's decision and alluded to a 'hidden agenda' within the review process. This allusion concerned the potential motives harbored by elements within the Sangh Parivar – a family of militantly Hindu, cadre-based religious organisations – which espoused a doctrine of *Hindutva* (Sanskritic-based cultural nationalism). These groups, as well as senior figures in the NDA government, argued for the adoption of a presidential form of government. Such a change, the opposition asserted, would violate the basic parliamentary structure of the polity. The Sangh Parivar's political party wing, the Bharatiya Janata Party (BJP), which was the political fulcrum of the NDA, was quick to assure the opposition, as well as the wider public, that such a reform was indeed beyond the ambit of the constitutional review. Yet many critics of the BJP, and the Sangh Parivar more generally, were sceptical of this pledge, given the lack of coherence in the Government's position. The debate prompted two obvious questions: why did non-party elements within the Sangh Parivar openly advocate a presidential form of government? And why does the BJP, as the party wing of the Parivar, equivocate about such a proposal?

To answer these questions, we have to explore the extent to which we can make sense of the recent politics of Hindu nationalist forces through an analysis of the functioning of political institutions at the Centre under its tenure.[2] Observers of post-1947 Indian politics have generally eschewed a formal institutionalist approach for the often-touted reason that explaining the politics of India – given its geographical size and cultural diversity on the one hand, combined with the particularity of its multifarious indigenous social practices on the other – through use of general analytical categories would distort our understanding.[3] In contrast, recent analyses of Indian politics by comparativist scholars – such as Alfred Stepan, Arend Lijphart and Eswaran Sridharan – have drawn attention to the ways in which certain institutional features of the Indian democratic regime have shaped its political trajectory in significant ways.[4] In so doing, such studies have exposed the hazard of subscribing to a doctrine of Indian exceptionalism.

Yet one of the main limitations of these explicitly institutionalist analyses is that they obscure, or even fail to examine, the ways in which political agents seek to overcome, subordinate and indeed interpret the constraints imposed by political institutions in their pursuit of power. Given this, I want to assess the impact of India's democratic regime on the recent politics of the BJP by distinguishing three levels of political institutions: first, the design of the electoral system, party system and form of government; second, intermediary political institutions, such as the Council of Ministers, parliamentary committees and other administrative bodies of governance; and third, political parties, which exhibit a dual identity since they constitute both formal organisations that are governed by the incentives of larger institutional structures, as well as informal networks of influence that are capable of extending their activities beyond the boundaries of the formal political arena. My general argument is that while these political institutions structured the options and shaped the expectations of political actors in the Sangh Parivar, the extent to which they guided political action depended on their political judgement. To put it differently, political actors may, if skilful enough, deploy strategies and tactics which subordinate formally established procedures and roles of decision-making. Institutions do not determine outcomes; rather they structure choices and signal incentives which political actors must appraise strategically.[5] Political actors have the capacity to reflexively engage with the institutions within which they pursue various political aims.

This essay examines these issues in the following manner. Section one traces the origins of some of the basic institutional features in the Indian democratic regime during the 1950s and 1960s. Section two charts ways in which the original practice of secular politics was undermined by both cynical and programmatic political entrepreneurs, who sought to mobilise forces of religious intolerance in their quest for power, from the 1970s to the late 1980s. And sections three and four analyse the reasons for the changing political strategy of the BJP in its search for power in the mid to late 1990s.

1. The Origins of Secular Politics in Post-colonial India: The Early Decades

Historically, post-colonial India's secular career originated in two ways. The first was through its active practice.[6] This owed much to a single person: Jawaharlal Nehru. Nehru was one of the most dominant political figures of the Congress party, which famously secured the country's self-rule. In his eyes, secularism required a committed refusal to recognise religious identities in the public arena. It was not a coherent ideological doctrine (it was not a term or article included in the Constitution), rather, it was an active maxim of political practice. Given the vagaries of fortune and contingency, to live up to this principle involved the exercise of prudence and political judgement.

In the violent aftermath of India's tragic partition at Independence in 1947, the country's nationalist elites were divided about the future political identity of the post-colonial state. The creation of Pakistan as an explicitly Muslim political community encouraged voices of Hindu nationalism, some of which even existed within the Congress, to argue for a state committed to the interests of the Hindu majority. Nehru, however, firmly resisted such claims. Instead, he argued for an improvised, open conception of 'Indianness'. This conception was a layered, plural and modern act of self-invention. Its triumph during this crucial juncture of history was partly assisted by contingency. The legitimacy of the Hindu card was effectively destroyed with the assassination of Mahatma Gandhi by a member of the forces of Hindu nationalism (as a result, it would take nearly four decades before its legitimacy revived politically). But what also proved decisive was Nehru's decision to assuage the fears of Muslims in India by using the coercive powers of the state to restore public order during this tumultuous period. Secular India was an imagined modern political identity, and as with all political identities and interests, it could only come into being through actual political activity.

Other constitutive aspects of this imagined identity also emerged during this formative period. They arose in the course of the country's Constituent Assembly debates (1946–9).[7] Through their deliberations, they produced a Constitution, promulgated on January 26th 1950, which declared India a sovereign political community. The state that emerged was a federal, democratic republic. One of its guiding purposes was to modernise some of the *backward* ways and customs of its peoples according to the presumed universal logic of world history (in Nehru's eyes).[8] In this particular respect, the constitutional process, and the beliefs which underlay it, matched to a great extent the picture of the motives and myths of modern constitutionalism.[9]

However, a very striking feature marked the vision which inspired the modern Indian state: its advocacy of intense pluralism. Put simply, it did not seek to create a uniform narrative which subdued multiple, overlapping, plural identities. Rather, Nehru's vision of 'Indianness' was an intensely manifold conception. To be Indian required one, in a sense, to mediate this larger, distant identity through more intimate, local sources of the self.

Therefore, certain features of the Indian Constitution strove to *protect* the country's irreducible cultural plurality – its own very 'strange multiplicities'.[10] This account of national identity manifested itself in three different ways.[11] First, a sense of region and nation emerged together: their self-definitions were parallel. Regional sources of identity (such as a Marathi, Bengali or Tamilian) acquired institutional reality in the federal structure of the democratic polity. Initially, these geographical units were multilingual, but by the mid-1950s were reorganised within the democratic process to fashion linguistic regional identities. Second, the defence of group identities on grounds of religion involved a two-way process. On the one hand, customary religious laws, codes and practices of minority communities – which included Muslims, Sikhs, Christians, Jains and Buddhists – were recognised. On the other hand, social reform of customary Hindu practices, many of which undermined human dignity among the lower strata of the highly unjust caste order, were pursued. The purpose of these reforms was to assuage minority religious communities' anxiety over potential Hindu supremacy and, more directly, to dismantle unjust social conventions which governed within the highly unequal caste hierarchy. Third, to further the opportunities of lower caste orders within society, the Constitution guaranteed reservations (quotas of affirmative action or compensatory discrimination) in public institutions for these stigmatised social groups.

In doing so, it transformed these social identities, which varied immensely given the deeply context-specific nature of actual caste orders, into distinct, legally prescribed (e.g. Dalits as Scheduled Castes, Adivasis as Scheduled Tribes) political identities in the public domain. Taken together, these three sets of consociational measures, handled differently according to the general criteria of democratic equality, served to encompass a range of diverse claims. The improvised, layered and plural conception of Indianness which emerged was the modern idea of India itself.

There were two other features of the polity, resulting from the Constituent Assembly debates, which deserve notice: a first-past-the-post electoral regime and a parliamentary form of responsible cabinet government. These democratic procedures also proved significant in forging a centrist political system. Notably, the decision to adopt them was not informed by sustained deliberation over their presumed impact on actual political outcomes with respect to secularism. In fact, there was little debate over the classic fears of democracy – the ways in which this system of rule would coexist with large sections of the poor, dispossessed and illiterate – that marked democracy's original career in Europe.[12] Rather, these procedures were part and parcel of the attempt to devise effective mechanisms of power-sharing in a deeply plural society.

2. The Decline of Secular Politics in the 1980s: Political Folly and Ideological Conflict

In retrospect, the 1950s and 1960s proved to be the apogee of secular politics in post-colonial India. Much of this owed a great deal to the active prudence of India's governing Nehruvian elites. This in large part inspired the various measures of the Constitution which gave India's plentiful minorities a sense of inclusion. However, by the 1980s, most observers realised that the practice of secular politics was in serious decline. Indeed, the severity of this problem was seen in the revival of a political voice arguing for an explicitly religious national identity.

A direct threat came in the form of a resurgent Sangh Parivar, which championed the doctrine of *Hindutva* as essential to any proper self-understanding of India. This counter-ideology, and the arguments which inspired it, was a complex phenomenon. On the one hand, it accused the Indian state of duplicity; that is to say, it argued that alleged secularists intervened on the pretext of social reform in the religious affairs of the Hindu community, yet refused to enact similar measures against regressive customs in other minority religious communities.[13] In so doing, claimed proponents of *Hindutva*, so-called secularists capitulated to unjustified demands for the autonomy of such groups; violated the principles of liberty, equality and neutrality with respect to matters of religion in the public domain; and as a result, unfairly stigmatised the Hindu majority as an inherently dangerous entity. In short, Nehruvians, despite their rhetorical claims to the contrary, practiced a form of 'pseudo-secularism'. On the other hand, however, the doctrine of *Hindutva* didn't advocate a form of politics which abstained from appeals made in the name of religion in public affairs. In fact, the BJP espoused the maxim of 'one nation, one people, one culture'. This greatly obscured the syncretic, plural character of India, and promoted a distorted, unitary image of Hinduism. The BJP argued that *Hindutva* defined the genuine foundation of the Indian nation; a nation previously 'subjugated' by 'foreign' – Mughal and British – conquerors. Thus the BJP traded politically on this sense of deep cultural injury in order to change both the structure and dense texture of actual social relations.

The criticism of Nehruvian secular politics was accurate on several counts. Many important initiatives were taken by the modernising state to reform Hindu customs that were deemed *backward* in the late 1940s and through the 1950s. (This is not to say that such efforts of reform were absent in minority religious communities; yet they weren't pursued under the sovereign auspices of the legislative majority.[14]) Moreover, in terms of actual electoral politics, the Congress party's relative success in the 1950s and 1960s owed much to electoral appeals courting various group identities, which were mobilised locally by dominant Brahminical elites. It must be noted that while Nehru's actions failed to observe strictly the idea of secularism according to a liberal Western paradigm, he was careful not to wield the language of religion in political rhetoric explicitly. However, Indira Gandhi recklessly abandoned Nehru's prudence during her time in power in the 1970s and early 1980s. Under her aegis, the notion of secularism was radically diverted from its original intention (despite the ironic fact that Mrs Gandhi formally introduced the term into the Constitution). If Nehruvian secularism was about refusing to court ethno-religious identities in the public domain, Mrs Gandhi's understanding meant giving explicit, equal recognition to such identities. In this manner, Mrs Gandhi cynically exploited the fears of various minority groups situated in different regions – most notably Assam, Kashmir and Punjab – for short-term electoral purposes. In doing so, she roused and assisted extremist forces that gradually escaped her control. She gave legitimate political space to other parties – such as the BJP – with more singular, sectarian agendas.

For a variety of reasons, the end of the 1980s saw the Congress party in a state of rapid political decline. In contrast, the electoral fortunes of the BJP were rising. To mobilise public support for its agenda, the latter campaigned for the construction of a Ram *mandir* (temple) upon an occupied religious site in the pilgrimage city of Ayodhya. It was in Ayodhya that *Hindutva*'s deadly potential was realised. In the name of restoring lost Hindu honour, religious zealots belonging to the Sangh Parivar demolished the Babri *Masjid* on the disputed ground on December 6th 1992. In so doing, they unleashed India's worst communal riots since Partition. The practice of secular politics had reached its nadir.

The trauma of Ayodhya convinced many observers that allowing the BJP to capture Union power, despite its partial attempt to dissociate with extremists in the Sangh Parivar, would simply produce further mayhem and tear the social fabric of the country apart. The party had suffered electorally in the state assembly elections between 1993–5 following the destruction of the Babri *Masjid*. However, many observers accurately believed that the country's first general election after 'Ayodhya' would provide a more reliable test of the BJP's political fortunes.

3. A Temporary Reprieve from *Hindutva*: The Compulsions of Coalition Politics

In the spring of 1996, India went to the polls for its eleventh general election. Strikingly, the BJP emerged as the single largest party in the *Lok Sabha*. The party's decision to enter a limited number of seat-sharing alliances with regional parties, such as the Akali Dal and the Haryana Vikas Party (HVP), paid significant dividends in Punjab and Haryana, where its victories were sweeping, as well as with the Samata Party, a faction of the Janata Dal, in Bihar, where its success was more limited. However, as in 1989 and 1991, the popular verdict was inconclusive. Given that the BJP was the largest party, President Shankar Dayal Sharma asked its leader, Atal Bihari Vajpayee, to form the government and prove its majority on the floor of the house within two weeks. Vajpayee was a relative moderate within the BJP's ranks, and publicly opposed the events in Ayodhya. Indeed his wing of the party refrained from making the strident attacks conducted by the Rashtriya Svayamsevak Sangh (RSS), Vishwa Hindu Parishad (VHP) and Bajrang Dal against minority groups. Instead Vajpayee appealed to the public about the importance of probity in public life, given the array of scandals implicating the Congress, and unity in national affairs, in light of the sense of social instability produced during VP Singh's government between 1989–91. Vajpayee also downplayed the most controversial measures in their party manifesto: the abrogation of Article 370 in the Muslim-majority state of Jammu and Kashmir (which gave special asymmetric rights to the region), the imposition of a Uniform Civil Code (which threatened minority customary codes) and the construction of a Ram Temple at Ayodhya. However, in a stormy motion of confidence, not a single opposition party crossed the floor of the *Lok Sabha*; a surprise, given the disconcerting ease with which parties in India's parliament routinely break political ranks. Vajpayee's Ministry was forced to resign, and make way for a coalition of avowedly secular parties belonging to the third force, dubbed the United Front, which went on to form the Union government. The BJP's first taste of Union power – a period of miserable political isolation – lasted a mere thirteen days.

The United Front, fearing the threat of *Hindutva*, resisted the BJP's attempt to seize control of the central government. One bloc comprised regional parties (such as the TDP, DMK, TMC and AGP) – many of which represented non-Hindi speaking region-states in the south and east – which opposed the culturally uniform agenda of the BJP. Another bloc was composed of 'socialist' parties, which explicitly promoted the interests of middle and lower caste groups against the Sankritised Hinduism of the BJP.[15] Both groups' political identities were forged in important ways by concerted political mobilisation. However, they were also a long-term function of the semi-consociational design of India's democratic regime. Reservations (quotas of compensatory discrimination) on grounds of caste politicised social groups that benefited from such policies. Initially, these geopolitical units were multilingual, but by the 1960s, despite Nehru's initial reluctance, had been reorganised to fashion linguistic regional identities that informed the development of distinct party systems in these states. Indeed, given the impact of federalism, these political identities manifested themselves in various intersecting ways. The identity of specific parties' main political rivals in their respective regional domains, the issues which animated their political contests, the social groups over whom they competed for votes and partisan loyalty, and the discursive idioms within which these various political struggles were conducted: all of these differed substantially. In contrast, BJP votaries, more than any other party or bloc, consisted of social groups which inhabited zones of privilege with respect to status, wealth and authority: the party's social base was disproportionately urban, upper caste, upper class and male. Yet the constitutional design of specific political institutions helped forge diverse political identities, which resisted the monolithic, intolerant political designs of the BJP.

In the eyes of many secularists, the formation of the United Front Government was a critical victory against the forces of *Hindutva*. However, more astute observers, such as Sudipta Kaviraj, realised that its formation was only a reprieve.[16] The presence of thirteen parties (which in some cases comprised mere political cabals) within the UF, a coalition which contained divergent political agendas, threatened to escalate into unmanageable conflicts of interest. Moreover, the coalition's minority status as a Union government exposed it to the whims of its parliamentary supporters. Although the first pessimistic scenario failed to materialise, the second did: in November 1997, a politically desperate Congress party withdrew its support from the UF on the fig-leaf pretence of the Jain Commission Report, whose interim findings indicted the DMK in Rajiv Gandhi's assassination, causing the Government to collapse. As a result, the parties entered the competitive fray once again to contest the ensuing twelfth general election in March 1998.

During the tenure of the United Front, the BJP underwent a serious appraisal of its electoral prospects, and revised its political strategy. Aware of the fact that an intolerant image drove away both potential voters and political allies, the party's ruling elites strategically agreed to truncate the agenda of *Hindutva* in the formal political arena. The abrogation of Article 370 in Jammu and Kashmir, the imposition of a Uniform Civil Code and the construction of a Ram Temple at Ayodhya: the BJP put all of these controversial measures on the political back-burner. Doing so allowed it to strike a deal with a number of region-based parties, most of which entered electoral pacts with the BJP on the purely tactical grounds of defeating their various political opponents in their respective regional arenas.[17]

Why did the BJP take these decisions? I would argue that they derived their force from the centrist logic of the Indian electoral regime, federal party system and parliamentary system of cabinet government. A first-past-the-post electoral system disproportionately rewards and punishes parties' vote shares in terms of the number of parliamentary seats they win. In order to win a majority of seats, parties are forced to extend their appeal across the party system. Thus in a deeply diverse, plural polity such as India, a first-past-the-post regime creates strong incentives for parties to occupy the middle ground of a country's politics: to deploy a relatively consensual political rhetoric and advance a moderately centrist programme of public action. By doing so, parties have a greater chance of success in appealing to a wide cross-section of voters amidst a divided political opposition. Of course, the rules of the electoral game do not *determine* the political actions of parties. Rather, they *inform* the political calculi of respective party elites by outlining the consequences of not following strategies capable of forging 'manufactured' electoral majorities.[18] Party elites ought to consider these implications seriously in their respective political strategies if they seek to win office. The BJP failed sufficiently to appreciate such concerns prior to the eleventh general election in 1996. In espousing the rhetoric and programme of *Hindutva* during the campaign, they antagonised the majority of the electorate. The party's political calculus changed during its tenure in opposition during the UF (in contrast, the Congress was stubbornly blind to the new logic of the electoral game).

Second, a parliamentary form of cabinet government encouraged the BJP to express less extreme political postures as well. In single-party cabinet governments, the cabinet may exercise its concentration of formal powers to a great extent. However, in multi-party cabinet governments, no single party can easily impose its political will upon its coalition partners. Successful courses of action often require the party elites of such governing coalitions to manufacture consensus amongst disparate political interests through negotiation, accommodation and compromise. The BJP, though the single largest party in the *Lok Sabha*, knew it could not secure a mandate to govern alone. Moreover it realised its inability to extend its electoral appeal in those regions of the east and south which proved unresponsive, if not directly confrontational, towards its politics. Hence it decided to shelve its controversial proposals to attract support from existing political rivals in order to form a majority-winning coalition.

This changed course of action reaped great dividends in the twelfth general election and proved decisive after the electoral verdict was declared. The BJP, which crafted a larger coalition of parties during the short-lived tenure of the United Front, emerged once again as the single largest party in the country. Its governing coalition secured the greatest bloc of seats – just short of a majority – in the *Lok Sabha*. Again, it was invited to form the Union government. Having convinced enough parties that extreme aspects of the *Hindutva* agenda would not be pursued in office, the BJP managed to secure a majority vote in the *Lok Sabha*. The party of Hindu nationalism, having temporarily renounced its most controversial ideological programmes, finally captured the power of Union rule.

4. Alternative Strategies of Political Rule: Inherent Tensions within the Sangh Parivar

Control of the central government through its espousal of a more moderate political agenda partly confirms the arguments put forward by institutionalists. The constitutional design of India's democratic regime – its plurality-rule electoral regime, federal party system and parliamentary form of cabinet government – promoted a relatively centrist form of politics. The BJP, given its intense desire to capture the power of Union rule, was forced to abide by the logic of the country's democratic structure. In doing so, it was compelled to forsake the complete realisation of *Hindutva* in the formal political arena.

Having seized the power of Union rule, the BJP continued its concerted effort to project a moderate political image. It authored with its coalition partners a National Agenda for Governance, which advocated a consensual programme of action. It was bereft of any mention of abrogating Article 370, formulating a Uniform Civil Code or constructing a temple in Ayodhya. Moreover none of these items were on the party's National Council meeting agenda in Gandhinagar in early May, which saw the leadership of the organisation change hands from LK Advani to Kashubhai Thakre, neither of whom would publicly discuss these issues. With the exceptions of Vajpayee, Advani and Murli Manohar Joshi, politicians with known links to the RSS were relegated to junior posts within the cabinet. The BJP conceded grudgingly several ministerial posts.[19] Indeed these various measures, which appeared to restrict the BJP's political manoeuverability, drove one frustrated senior party functionary in Uttar Pradesh to lament that

> although we are the largest party in the ruling coalition at the Centre, we also seem to be the weakest. Consider, after all, the pressure that has been put on us by smaller parties and the compromises we made on one issue after another.[20]

A noted political journalist echoed, in praise, these laments:

> The politics of social exclusion that the BJP has carried forward to new extremes is self-limiting in the domain of representative democracy.[21]

The exigencies of coalition politics, which acquired salience due to the structure of India's centrist democratic regime, served to delimit the politics of *Hindutva*.

However, the actual record of events during the BJP coalition's first tenure in power at the Centre reduced the confidence of such expectations. Instances where the BJP sought to implement its *Hindutva* agenda in the formal political arena quickly drew effective opposition from secular parties. But political struggle does not simply consist of following the rules of the game within the formal institutions of the state. More often than not, it also involves attempts by political agents to realise their political aims by subverting or circumventing such conventions of rule through tactics of stealth and obfuscation.[22] These tactics include the manipulation of the terms of existing political debate, and the wider discourse that informs and partly constitutes such debates, to their own partisan advantage; and the promotion or effective condoning of acts of aggression 'on the street', which seek to mobilise committed followers while introducing fear into the dense social texture of everyday life. Indeed it can also entail attempts to change the rules of rule themselves.

This is particularly true regarding the actions of political parties. On the one hand, parties are formal organisations in the public arena, which contest for governmental power according to political and legal conventions. On the other hand, parties are also informal networks of influence which pursue partisan goals through various political strategies outside the realm of the state.[23] In this regard, the Sangh Parivar was forced to contend with two 'overriding strategic problems'.[24] First, in order to escape its political isolation the party needed to expand its relatively narrow social and regional bases of support through skilful strategies of coalition-making. Undoubtedly a crucial aspect of such a strategy enjoined it to assuage the fears expressed by potential allies by striking compromises, which removed the most controversial aspects of militant *Hindutva* from the Government agenda. In other words, the political cost of ideological purity was certain electoral defeat. Adopting a pragmatic posture allowed the party a more realistic opportunity to capture the power of Union rule. This first strategic problem defied simple resolution, however, since it was interwoven with a second. The BJP was not in a position simply to ignore extremists within the Sangh Parivar's ranks. The party was to distance itself radically from the very organisations which distinguished its politics and mobilised its key ideological support on the streets. Moreover these cadre-based ranks, given their doctrinal austerity, were unlikely to accept compromises of their ideological programme without a fight. Indeed there were good reasons to expect them to apply political pressure upon the Government to stand by its original programme of action. Consequently there was an inherent tension within the political strategy of the Sangh Parivar in the context of multiparty coalitions,[25] which yielded two distinct outcomes. In the first scenario, the BJP acted at cross purposes with other organisations of the Sangh Parivar in their mutual struggle to dominate the political agenda on their own terms. In the second, which recurred more frequently, the various elements of the Sangh Parivar spoke with more than one political voice, 'offering a weighted, and ambiguous, mix of appeals'.[26]

Several examples illustrate the ways in which the BJP sought to contend with these tensions. The most vivid example of the BJP's evasion of conventional procedures was obviously its unilateral decision to exercise India's nuclear option at Pokhran in May 1998. In doing so, it marked a decisive shift in the country's foreign policy. Observers were well aware of the BJP's desire to acquire the status of a nuclear weapon state;[27] the party's election manifestos openly avowed such intentions. Key sections of the atomic energy and defence establishments also supported exercising the nuclear option (as did earlier political dispensations, including Narasimha Rao's Congress administration in 1995). Nonetheless the timing of the tests, as well as the process of consultation which informed its decision-making, betrayed a strategy of stealth and obfuscation which the BJP pursued in order to escape its particular dilemma: the pressures of domestic coalition politics. Upon coming to power at the Centre, the Defence Minister George Fernandes asserted the Government's intention of establishing a National Security Council to undertake a strategic defence review in order to formulate a new foreign policy. This was important given that parties, both of the opposition as well as those – such as the TDP – supporting the Government, were reportedly against, or at least ambivalent towards, changing the country's existing nuclear doctrine. The opposition asserted that any decision regarding the nuclear option would have to earn the confidence of Parliament.

Yet the BJP simply evaded these institutional constraints. No attempt was made to set up a National Security Council or a Defence Review Committee prior to the tests. The Cabinet was certainly not informed of the decision to proceed with them. Indeed even the Defence Minister was reportedly not privy to the timing of the decision until the last minute; he remained outside the inner circle of decision-makers, which included top RSS leaders, and was informed only hours before the tests actually occurred. The decision to test the nuclear devices, given the minimum one-month prerequisite required to prepare for the explosions, was taken in mid-April, only a month after the BJP came to power. It betrayed the overwhelming influence of the Sangh Parivar, whose frustration with the exigencies of coalition negotiations encouraged radical political action.

Having conducted the tests, the BJP proceeded to manipulate the terms of political debate in an overtly partisan manner. The national euphoria which initially accompanied the tests effectively silenced the opposition. The Congress party was reduced to protesting against the BJP for attempting to exploit the success of the tests for itself; the former merely claimed that Pokhran II reflected a collective effort, which originated in the country's nuclear policy initiated by the Nehru–Congress dynasty decades earlier. Other members of the opposition such as IK Gujral, the former Prime Minister of the United Front, claimed that they also would have exercised the nuclear option if they had remained in power. In other words, the BJP's handling of Pokhran provoked the opposition into a defensive position and eliminated any middle political ground: the question of whether the decision to test was desirable on either strategic or ethical grounds was simply not raised.[28] To raise such a question amidst popular euphoria was to risk being labelled as 'anti-national', a risk that proved too daring for any party to take. Moreover the BJP's political management of the tests showed how it tried to manipulate the event towards its own partisan objectives. The hawkish Home Minister LK Advani, a central figure in the movement to destroy the Babri *Masjid* in Ayodhya in the early 1990s, effectively dared Pakistan to escalate conflict in Jammu and Kashmir by recklessly declaring that Indian forces would pursue a policy of 'hot pursuit' into Pakistani-occupied territory. By doing so, he refocused world attention[29] upon the violently disputed Himalayan state. Ironically the militancy towards Pakistan, in the context of two avowed nuclear weapon states, backfired upon Advani's refusal (in line with India's enduring policy) to admit third-party intervention in the conflict. The severity of the stakes involved commanded international scrutiny. The escalation of tensions with Pakistan reached an alarmingly dangerous degree, resulting in a renewed wave of insurgency in the region. The BJP, unable to abrogate Article 370 of the Constitution in government given the exigencies of coalition politics, exploited the decision to test the nuclear devices both to legitimate further military presence on the ground in the state of Jammu and Kashmir (already at 500,000 troops), and to construe the exercise of the country's nuclear option as central to the national interest. Rather than deter the possibility of military conflict, the acquisition of nuclear weapons para-doxically furnished a tenuous cover for conventional military engagements. In doing so, it exposed the dubious pretext which drives theories of nuclear deterrence; namely that the devastating implications of using nuclear weapons would breed rational, political restraint. The condition on the ground of the strife-torn region of Jammu and Kashmir simply grew worse, and resulted in the first ever ground war between two declared nuclear powers in Kargil in the summer of 1999.

Attempts by the BJP to introduce any policy measure that betrayed a Hindu nationalist agenda, attracted fierce criticism and political contestation. Where these initiatives were advanced in the formal political arena, and when they required political negotiations with other parties, they were effectively stymied. This was evident during the Conference of state Education Ministers and Secretaries in late October 1998, which gathered in New Delhi to discuss ways to improve various aspects of primary and secondary school curricula. Many of the details of the conference were scripted by the Human Resource Development Minister, Murli Manohar Joshi, a stalwart member of the RSS and an outspoken proponent of *Hindutva*, to embody a Hindu nationalist approach. The schedule of events included a presentation by PD Chitlangia, who apart from being an industrialist from Calcutta, occupied an important post within the Vidhya Bharati, the educational arm of the RSS. The itinerary also proposed opening the conference with the singing of a hymn to Saraswati Vandana, the Hindu goddess of learning, instead of the national anthem. If these items of the agenda served symbolic purposes, Joshi also surreptitiously attempted to introduce more substantive changes to the ways in which schooling was conducted. An appendix attached to the working papers that circulated amongst the delegates prior to the conference contained a report of a 'group of experts' relating to pedagogical matters. Notably, the report was drafted at the All-India Conference of the Vidhya Bharati, the educational arm of the RSS, in August 1998. It recommended changing the content of primary and higher educational curricula to reflect an 'Indianised, nationalised and spiritualised' leitmotif: for example, incorporating the *Vedas* and Upanishads into basic teaching and making Sanskrit a compulsory subject. The report also proposed amendments to Article 30 of the Constitution, which confers to minority groups special dispensation over the conduct and design of their educational institutions. Joshi plainly wanted to extend his *Hindutva* educational designs further.

However the attempt to receive official political sanction from state representatives for such reforms was thwarted. The Minorities Commission objected that amending Article 30 would deprive minority groups of their statutory rights to special educational autonomy, and violate the 1958 Supreme Court ruling which defended these entitlements as absolute. Additionally, senior leaders of many regional parties, including coalition partners of the BJP in Government, protested vehemently against the communalised agenda of the Human Resource Development Minister. Over half of the quorum of assembled delegates threatened to boycott the opening forum. Their fulminations worked: Joshi was forced to retreat swiftly, remove the appendix report from the working papers, cancel the Chitlangia speech and revert to the customary singing of the national anthem. The episode demonstrated that in joint decisions in the formal political arena, where threats of political vetoes could be credibly exercised, endeavors to promote *Hindutva* were by and large effectively rebuffed.

Yet in other areas Joshi's *Hindutva* designs achieved greater success. In June 1998 the Human Resources Development Minister reconstituted the Indian Council of Historical Research (ICHR). Customarily, the ICHR's composition was expected to accommodate a range of different viewpoints, and to represent several members of the previous board to ensure continuity. However Joshi's appointments included several well-known figures[30] who played a direct role in the VHP campaign to destroy the Babri *Masjid* in Ayodhya. Moreover, several of these figures, given their views regarding the *Masjid* controversy, were accused of lacking professional integrity by the World Archaeological Congress Conference held in 1994. Protests by prominent Left historians (such as Professor Irfan Habib) failed to alter the decision, which was justified by claiming that earlier versions of the Council reflected a domination by the Left. In a similar fashion, Joshi revamped the entire apex membership of the Indian Council of Social Science Research (ICSSR). These incidents attested to the importance which the Sangh Parivar attached to securing both the senior and junior posts of key cultural portfolios.

Another strategy adopted by the BJP was simply to vacillate over key decisions. This was illustrated by its failure to serve justice in the case of the Srikrishna Commission Report into the causes of the Mumbai riots in December 1992–January 1993. The Maharashtra state government, which originally received the report on 16 February 1998, repeatedly delayed its public release until August 1998, when it was compelled to meet a statutory six-month deadline in early August. However, upon its release the *Shiv Sena*–BJP state government tabled their Action Taken Report (ATR) in the Maharashtra state legislative assembly, which rejected the validity of the report for its 'pro-Muslim, anti-Hindu' bias. The reason was obvious: the report accused the leadership of the *Shiv Sena* and its *sainaks* of deliberately instigating a frenzy of violence against Muslims. Given this, opposition parties organised demonstrations against the *Shiv Sena*–BJP coalition. The Congress attacked the latter and demanded the resignation of Joshi as Chief Minister. The Left parties concurred with the demands made by the Congress, and also requested the Government to arrest and prosecute those figures accused of criminal acts in the report. Rumours circulated that the Maharashtran state-unit of the BJP was eager to table the report, given its indictment against the *Shiv Sena*, in order to appear politically responsible and to gain leverage over its unruly coalition partner. This distancing was politically expedient, as the increasingly violent tactics of the *Shiv Sena* had alienated big business interests, which otherwise supported these parties. Ultimately, however, the Union Home Minister Advani declared that the report failed to provide sufficient grounds for dismissal of the state government, and argued that the latter was not bound legally to accept the report in any case. The political culprits of India's worst communal riots since Partition, having captured the reins of power at the Centre through coalition strategies, eluded the judicial arm of the state.

Having escaped from a potential political quagmire unscathed, the *Shiv Sena* and other *Hindutva* elements continued to mobilise politically on anti-Muslim slogans, which inspired a number of deplorable acts. These began shortly after the BJP-led coalition came to power. In early May 1998, Bajrang Dal activists besieged the home of MF Husain, a well-known Muslim visual artist, for his allegedly blasphemous paintings. Further attempts to arouse anti-Muslim sentiment saw the *Shiv Sena* disrupting a concert given by Ghulam Ali, a *ghazal* singer from Pakistan, and declaring that Pakistani sportsmen would be barred from playing in Mumbai. Perhaps the fiercest protests against cultural expressions that offended an allegedly 'proper' Hindu sensibility, were vividly displayed towards the end of 1998 in violent demonstrations against the screening of *Fire*, a film produced by Deepa Mehta, which explored the theme of lesbianism within the context of an extended family household in urban India. Mehta's film passed the scrutiny of the censor board unscathed: both the sequence and content of the scenes remained untouched. Nevertheless, elements of the Sangh Parivar, unwilling to recognise the censorship board's authority, pursued coercive tactics on the streets with the complicity of the state apparatus.

On November 25th a fringe religious organisation, the Jain Samata Valini, petitioned the Minister of state for Cultural Affairs of the *Shiv Sena* Maharashtra state government to prohibit screenings of *Fire*, on the grounds that its content denigrated the Ramayana. The initial failure of the *Shiv Sena* to respond publicly to the appeal camouflaged its actual designs. By the end of the week lower-level officials of its party machine, which received de facto sanction from Chief Minister Joshi, orchestrated cadre-led protests against screenings of the movie in Mumbai. Such agitations occurred in New Delhi as well. Disturbingly, police forces in both cities reportedly watched such displays of violence without intervening. The outcome of these efforts fulfilled their original intent. The disruption of performances and vandalism of cinemas forced authorities in both cities to suspend showings of *Fire* indefinitely. Moreover the deplorable actions of such politicised mobs resulted in the film being sent back to the censor board for a second review, on the dubious pretext that if its showing evoked such genuine outrage from disapproving sections of urban society, then surely it must contain vulgar, objectionable elements mistakenly overlooked in its initial review. A vigilante politics of the street undermined the authority of the law that permitted the free expression of divergent views.

Yet the most ominous example of ways in which elements within the Sangh Parivar sought to realise their agenda of *Hindutva* was through acts of terror on the ground. In September 1998 a series of vicious attacks against Christian missionaries and their organisations occurred in Jhabua district of

Madhya Pradesh. While the identity of those who perpetrated the crimes was not completely verified, many suspected the involvement of *Hindutva* organisations. This suspicion increased when the Central Secretary of the VHP, Mr. Prem Sharma, defended the atrocities by saying they represented 'expressions of the anger of patriotic Hindu youth against anti-national forces', which was a 'direct result of the conversion efforts' of Christian missionaries in the region. In an effort to contain the damage of these remarks, the organisation's General Secretary, Acharya Giriraj Kishore, condemned the attacks and asserted that Sharma's statement was not a defence. At the centre, the BJP sought to distance itself from the events, yet conspicuously failed to condemn Sharma's conduct.

Similar incidents occurred elsewhere in the country as well. Other acts of violence against Christian minority groups over the summer included the desecration of a statue at the college of Jesus and Mary in New Delhi, the murder of priests and nuns in Bihar, and incidents of corpse exhumation and bible-burning in Gujarat. The series of atrocities against religious minorities reached their nadir in January 1999. Acts of desecration against Christian places of worship in the Dangs district of Gujarat compelled the Prime Minister to criticise the VHP but without pursuing the matter further. The Home Minister adopted an even less critical posture in the aftermath of the murder of a Christian missionary, Graham Stewart Staines, and his two sons in Orissa. Again, as in previous instances, the Union Home Minister denied knowledge of the Bajrang Dal's involvement in the killing. From the vantage point of the Sangh Parivar, the purpose of committing these acts was clear: to introduce intense fear into the everyday lives of ordinary citizens. Unable to institutionalise their virulent ideology within the formal political arena of the state, *Hindutva* organisations have increasingly resorted to realising their aims on the ground, unilaterally, in connivance with, or even opposed to, the BJP at the centre.

In sum, pressures within the Sangh Parivar raised the issue introduced at the start of this paper: the current review of the Constitution which took place under the auspices of the present BJP coalition Government. Hindu extremists were dissatisfied with their current political situation. They wished to adopt a presidential form of government in order to evade the bounds imposed by the exigencies of coalition politics, a form of politics which emerged through trends set in motion by a plurality-rule electoral regime, a parliamentary form of cabinet government and a federal party system with strong consociational features. These institutional structures could not by themselves secure a secular politics, which can only flourish through its active, daily political practice. However, without them, the prospects for secularism would be arguably much worse.

3

IDEOLOGICAL INTEGRATION IN POST-COLONIAL (SOUTH) INDIA: ASPECTS OF A POLITICAL LANGUAGE

Pamela Price

1. Introduction

This essay discusses aspects of political integration in south India, focusing on the last quarter of the 20th century.[1] In it I attempt to link issues of personal and group identity to discourses on a moral community which are implicit in the language of politicians.

The observation that ideology does not play a major role in political dynamics has often been found in both scholarly writing and journalistic commentary on Indian politics. In the early 1980s, Narain and Mathur noted that factional conflicts and party desertions, among other phenomena, had led to the widespread belief that ideological elements were negligible in political practice.[2] James Manor, for example, went so far as to argue that political *anomie*, or 'normlessness', was evident from the years 1973–4 onward. He defined *anomie* as:

> insufficiency or absence of norms, rules, standards for conduct and belief…an inadequacy of forces…to regulate appetites, behaviour and social life, so that a person experienced disorientation and unease.[3]

Atul Kohli characterised political developments in the 1980s in terms of the widespread focus on the personalities of political leaders in the midst of processes of deinstitutionalisation.[4] In their article from 1984, however, Narain and Mathur took exception to the reigning opinion, arguing that ideology was a significant force in Indian politics. Even before the striking emergence of the Hindu nationalist Bharatiya Janata Party on the national stage, they found that nationalism, of various sorts, was a common theme throughout the country. Armed with these and other insights from more recent research, I describe below another course in this discussion.

Sudipta Kaviraj, Partha Chatterjee, TN Madan and Satish Saberwal made major contributions to debates about Indian politics and society in the 1990s. As John Harriss has pointed out, while differences in theory and approach exist among them, these writers share a point of view in that they perceive major cultural gaps in state–society relations in India, between elites and sub-alterns on the one hand, and modernity and tradition on the other.[5] Harriss finds that Kaviraj and Chatterjee represent a point of view which focuses on differences between westernised elites and vernacular-speaking masses, differences in political language and assumptions about the role and functioning of the state.[6] Harriss points out that Madan and Saberwal have been more preoccupied with distinctions between the 'modern' notions of elite[7] and the norms of traditional, segmented society.[8] This essay suggests that one can disaggregate the issue of the role of ideology to find that substantial groups in the population have differing notions of authority, political responsibility and the relationship of the person to the state.

The work of Pradeep K Chhibber posits the suggestion of a method for examining the relationship between values and ideas on the one hand, and institutions and groups in political society on the other. He has argued for the unusually important role of political parties in state and society relations in India, compared to most long-term democracies.[9] Because of the relative lack of associations in 'civil society', he argues that political parties play the decisive role in structuring state–society relations. It is not voluntary associations, but *jatis* (subcastes) with which politicians must deal as they build the coalitions they need to capture political office. Combining Chhibber's observation with insights from the considerable literature on caste and politics, we can suggest that electoral competition and the politics thereof shape the orientation of fellow caste members to governance, while political parties reflect, in the nature of their transactions, values which are found in caste society and institutions important to its organisation and reproduction, including temples, *maths* (monasteries) and patron–client relationships.

One problem facing governance in India is that there exists a tension between the desire of the state for integration on the one hand and, on the other, processes of electoral competition that play on division – for example, in the selection of candidates to stand for election according to caste background. David Gilmartin recently described this tension as existing between the state's 'appeal to a larger moral unity' and the operation of a 'wide range of particularistic identities'.[10] He was discussing the emergence of Muslim nationalism and demand for a separate state of Pakistan in the context of the development

of new types of particularistic identities and processes of political competition
in the twentieth century. He analyses Mohammad Ali Jinnah's claims for
Pakistan as a symbol of moral unity against the politician's awareness of the
divided nature of Muslim society, with divisions based in major part on caste,
tribe, *biradari* and family connections.[11] Gilmartin's comments allow us to
expand on Narain and Mathur's assertion that ideological elements in Indian
politics revolve in the main around nationalist goals:

> Whether 'imagined' (à la Benedict Anderson) or a product of the
> transformations of modernity (à la Ernest Gellner), nationalism, as a form
> of moral community, gained meaning only in relationship to the ongoing
> production and operation of the more particular identities that structured
> politics and everyday life. Though configured morally as transcending
> local status divisions and distinctions, nationalism cannot be portrayed as
> something standing apart from them. As historians of communalism have
> shown, arenas of local cultural competition produced *simultaneously* deep
> status divisions and a vision of moral community. This pattern marked the
> emergence of nationalism in the public realm as well.[12]

In recent decades there has appeared scholarship focusing to varying degrees
on issues of religious identity and nationalism. Writers on the colonial period
have explored social and political processes leading up to the creation of
Pakistan,[13] while post-colonial developments in Sikh and Hindu nationalism
have fuelled interest in religious nationalism in general.[14] Other types of
nationalism have been the subject of research, including the Dravidian movement, the Maratha nationalism of *Shiv Sena* and indigenous peoples' movements. I have argued elsewhere that appeals to group and personal honour are
a common theme in these nationalist movements, having pursued this issue
with work on the Dravidian movement in Tamil Nadu.[15] Using Karnataka as
my main case below, I will take a related approach in discussing issues of
personal evaluation and political integration as they relate to party politics.

2. Honour and Caste

By the end of the twentieth century, in many parts of India political parties
had emerged which claimed explicitly to represent the interests of specific
castes or groups of castes. Examples which have received much attention in
the press include the Janata Dal (speaking for *backward* castes in general), the
Bahujan Samaj Party (for Dalits) and the Yadava-dominated Samajwadi
Party. The appeals of these parties fall under the category of nationalism in
the sense that Paul Brass used in his groundbreaking study of nationalism in

north India: a group's decision that it has a shared (culture/social) identity and seeks to support its interests politically.[16]

It has long been observed that caste calculations in Indian democracy, for example in the selection of candidates and in electoral campaigning, has contributed to the consolidation of political identity based on caste membership and the politicisation of caste relations.[17] At issue is not only the desire of many people in an electoral constituency to be represented by a person of their own caste, but the politics of appointment in the Legislative Assemblies and Councils. In Karnataka, MLAs (Members of the Karnataka Legislative Assembly) from a specific caste are commonly perceived as representing that caste and it is a question of showing appropriate respect to the caste that one of their MLAs be selected as a Minister. It is an issue of caste honour that representatives are appointed to other less prominent, but nevertheless, influential positions. Without always emerging explicitly as a phenomenon of community formation, issues of group honour are significant in Karnataka, as in other parts of India.

However, the link between political parties and state-society relations has implications beyond merely the sharpening of caste and religious differences. In most electoral contests in India, in order to acquire power and influence in a state, and/or to be elected to the *Lok Sabha*, politicians have to make factional alliances and develop electoral support beyond their particular caste base. They have to move beyond their specific emerging or consolidated cultural/social nationalisms and present, explicity or implicitly, visions of – or references to – moral community which speak to the common understanding of the mass of voters. In short, politicians need a political language which can be widely comprehended.

It is my contention here that references to honour and respect – and self-respect – in spheres of party politics go beyond nationalist or casteist appeals. I argue that, without making explicit, formalised references to a moral community (such as Gilmartin does in his article on the Pakistan movement), politicians in Karnataka and elsewhere in India refer in their political language to common norms of appropriate behavior. They create visions of social relationships which can resonate with basic values and understandings among ordinary people. In the spring of 1998 this vision was perhaps best summed up in the words written in large letters in English across the back of the driver's seat of an auto-rickshaw in Mysore City: 'Give Respect & Take Respect'.

Recent scholarship provides evidence that public shows of honour and respect were an integral part of political culture in south Indian institutions of worship and rule in the late precolonial and colonial period.[18] When we examine material relating to everyday social exchanges in the twentieth century, it becomes clear that respect behavior and concern with 'face' (*moka*) have been major preoccupations. MN Srinivas' research on values in rural life in

Karnataka discussed the importance of face, while the novels of the famous Kannadiga novelist, Anantha Murthy, vividly illustrated that daily interactions in villages in mid-twentieth century Karnataka were characterised by reciprocal shows of respect.[19] We can attribute the practice of respect behaviour to the mild tenor of social exchange in Malgudi, the fictitous Kannadiga town which is the site of action in the many English-language novels of RK Narayan.[20] References to respect can be linked with notions of morality in social intercourse, which are a fundamental element of life for the rural population, as well as for people living in towns and identifiable neighborhoods in cities. References to respect and honour also resonate with popular acceptance of social segmentation in caste as the natural order of things. Politically, references to honour and respect suggest acceptance of domination and subordination as being appropriate in social and political relations, while notions of self-respect, on the other hand, fuel low-status peoples' desire for dignity and recognition.

I will elaborate on these points below. At this point, I aim to show that references to personal and group honour are an integral part of political language and the presentation of self among politicians in Karnataka.[21]

3. Respect in the Discourse of Politicians

A close reading of politicians' comments in the English-language Karnatakan press[22] leads to the conviction that issues of respect, maintaining self-respect and being treated with respect by others – in particular, by other politicians – is a major preoccupation in Karnatakan politics. In a speech given in April 1998 at a district-level convention of BJP and *Lok Sabha* party workers in Karnataka, Ramakrishna Hegde, former Union Commerce Minister and a major political figure in Karnataka, linked the display of respect to a general need to reform values:

> The tendency among the people to respect a person when he was in power and ignore him when he was out of power should go. People should change their attitude.[23]

Linked with the receiving of respect for one's person is the honour of one's *jati* or caste cluster. Issues of caste self-respect come into being, for example, in the selection of ministers to the Chief Minister's cabinet, since a minister represents his caste group and is presumed to work to support its projects, such as colleges, hospitals, and so on. Calls for Kannadiga self-respect do not by any means reach the frequency or level of emotional intensity that one finds with appeals to Telugu self-respect in Andhra. However, such appeals can also be made, as evidenced by former Prime Minister Deve Gowda, when he asked for votes for his party in the general election held early in 1998:

> [I]n the name of the self-respect of the people of Karnataka. "Please vote for Dal, if you are true progenies of Goddess Bhuvaneshwari or if Kannada blood flows in you…"[24]

Sitaram Kesri's statement upon resigning as Congress president, after a national campaign in which he was continuously overshadowed by Sonia Gandhi, received front page attention in Bangalore:

> "Have you not seen how things took shape during the last two months. No man with self-respect could tolerate this", he said without elaborating.[25]

Like BJP supporters elsewhere in India, Kannadiga enthusiasts for *Hindutva* will write about the demolition of the Babri *Masjid* as 'an act of self respect on the part of Hindus'.[26] The controversial Dr A Ravindra, Commissioner of the Bangalore City Corporation, tried to mobilise citizens to solve serious problems with the city's infrastructure by initiating a self-respect movement, the Swabhimana Movement.[27]

What is perhaps more common than references to one's own self-respect or that of one's group, are claims that an opponent has acted in such a way as to lose his self-respect. For example, a Congress spokesman asserted that it was 'unfortunate' that Janata Dal ministers had joined an organisation started by Ramakrishna Hegde to compete with the Dal because they, knowing well that their party government would not survive for more than two months, went to the extent of giving up their self-respect'.[28]

Several months later the General Secretary of Hegde's organisation called on Transport Minister and senior Janata Dal leader PGR Sindhia to leave the Dal after the latter had complained to the Governor that 'it was suffocating to be in the party', presumably because of one or two major party bosses. Ugrappa, the General Secretary, said:

> Mr. Sindhia has to exhibit political will by revolting against the leaders who have been responsible for stifling internal democracy within the Janata Dal. Pointing out that Mr. Sindhia had declared that there was a suffocating atmosphere within the Janata Dal, Mr. Ugrappa said no leaders with self-respect could remain in that party.[29]

One example of the preoccupation with respect or personal honour is the frequency with which politicians will claim in a news interview that they have been humiliated by another person or group of people. Claims of humiliation appear prominently in reasons given by politicians for leaving a party or threatening to leave, representing themselves as having been intolerably insulted, and seeking sympathy from members of the public. One story from the *Hindu* told of a case in a district town where a Mr. Lakshminarasimiah and other Janata Dal members were reported to be 'deserting the party to join the Lok Shakti' because of the 'humiliation heaped on them' and because of 'not being consulted on organisational matters at the district level'.[30]

In another case, a Dal man joined Hegde's organisation, purportedly to save the honour of others, because 'his supporters, who had been with the party for a long time' had been humiliated.[31]

Probably the most prominent use of humiliation in political discourse in the spring of 1998 was the penultimate sentence in the letter which Chandrababu Naidu, Chief Minister of Andhra Pradesh, wrote to Deve Gowda about his decision to adopt a neutral stance toward the new BJP government. Naidu began his letter, published in the Bangalore edition of the *Hindu*, with a reference to the 'immense pain' he had suffered when he learned through the media that the United Front, of which he was the convenor, had decided to overlook his candidacy for the post of Speaker of the *Lok Sabha*, instead preferring to support a Congress candidate. He refered directly to his 'pain' twice more, in addition to other similar references to the lack of respect shown him, and finally ended: 'I consider this an act of insult and humiliation to my state, my party and me. In such [a] painful situation I have no choice but to disassociate myself from the United Front'.[32]

Claims of humiliating treatment are complemented in discourse with claims of betrayal and attempts to take revenge. I will illustrate this point with reference again to the incident mentioned earlier, of Janata Dal ministers supporting Ramakrishna Hegde's organisations. Hegde, forced out of the Dal earlier by his rival Deve Gowda, had started his own political party, Lok Shakti, and allied himself with the BJP during the *Lok Sabha* election. It was widely assumed in Karnataka that part of Hegde's motivation was to take revenge against Deve Gowda by ruining the Dal. He had succeeded in enticing Ajaykumar Sarnayak, a Janata Dal Minister, to join Lok Shakti and to stand for election to the *Lok Sabha*, representing Bagalkot District. Sarnayak won the election, necessitating a by-election in June. The Bagalkot correspondent for the *Deccan Herald* wrote:

Betrayal by Mr. Ajaykumar Sarnayak was the main campaign issue for the Janata Dal leaders though they touched other issues like [the] Upper Krishna Project...and [the] nuclear tests by the BJP-led Central government.

state leaders including Chief Minister J.H. Patel…who toured the consistuency during the election campaign urged the people to teach a lesson to the Lok Shakti-BJP alliance for the betrayal by Mr. Sarnayak.[33]

Pursuing the topic of respect in interviews with politicians, as well as journalists, university scholars and observers of the political scene, I found my informants to be, for the most part, keen to discuss respect and self-respect in politics in Karnataka. E Raghavan, a Bangalore-based political commentator with the *Economic Times of India*, argued implicitly that concerns with acquiring and maintaining respect were an aspect of the so-called 'feudal' nature of contemporary politics in Karnataka and elsewhere in India. He was concerned in the main with the relative lack of emphasis on policy in contemporary politics: 'The feudal mindset is the focus on personal loyalty and the personal relationships in politics.'[34] He remarked that a 'feudal system is built into politics' and argued that the feudal element came not only from the precolonial polity, but from what he called 'the British feudalism', which he found in the strict hierarchy of the apparatus of the current Indian Administrative Service: 'Ordinary people were subservient to the Indian Civil Service and there was widespread respect for the officers'. Toward the end of the interview when I asked him about the importance of symbolic displays of respect in public shows, he asserted, somewhat disconnected:

> What is more important is whether someone gets something accomplished before another and earns respect. Having a huge bungalow and 10 dogs gives respectability… Respectability is what politicians want. Respectability comes from wealth, achievement and power. A politician often will have both wealth and power [if not achievement].'[35]

Preoccupation with public image is a major concern for politicians generally, but it is of particular significance in an electoral system. In large democracies like the United States and India such a preoccupation can appear to take on obsessive dimensions. According to a sometime journalist and former MLA, image was everything for politicians. And he added, 'A politician lives on paper'.[36] A sociologist in Bangalore suggested that, since so many people in Karnataka had access to television, appearances on television had surpassed the political significance of print in creating and maintaining image:

> TV is important as a medium to convey status. So actions of protocol – getting what kind of garland, who is introduced first, what kind of chair one sits on – these visible signs of honour are exceedingly important.[37]

He elaborated on the kind of public exposure some politicians and/or their supporters sought:

> [Tamil Chief Minister] Jayalalitha allowed her MLAs to prostrate them-
> selves before her in public. For ordinary people her honour would thus
> go up. One's honour goes up "in inverse proportion to the subservience
> of others".

> The cut-out culture is new to Karnataka. Here, too, the bigger the cut-out,
> the higher the honour of the politican. You try to make the cut-out of
> your leader the highest – 20 feet, 30 feet... Or one will deface public
> walls – the competition here is to show the honour of one's leader. The
> competition will be over who can cover the most walls with posters or
> slogans of one's ruler – to increase his honour.[38]

In India the public image of a politician takes on a special dimension because of the particular representational nature of politicians in relation to their core constituencies, however these may be defined. For rural communities in particular, the very person of the leader is representative. A constituency tends to feel that its political leader's rank and status reflects on that of the group. The caste cluster that Deve Gowda comes from, the Vokkaligas, 'were greatly honoured' when he became Prime Minister of India and during the time that he was in office in Delhi he made frequent trips to his home district to take part in occasions of public honouring.[39] According to another political scientist, an important reason for the Lingayat community's shift from the Congress Party to the Janata Dal was the treatment meted out to a Lingayat Chief Minister of the state, a Congressman, by Rajiv Gandhi. Veerendra Patil had suffered a stroke and, in a less than gracious manner, Rajiv dismissed him from his post: 'The Lingayat community was insulted and withdrew support from Congress in the next election'.[40]

Among politicians and those close to the political scene, *stannamana* is the status which one receives as a result of political engagement, either by being elected to office or by important service to the party. By itself, *mana* is the intrinsic honour and respect one has because of inner qualities, as opposed to *gaurava*, the respect one has earned through one's actions. Self-respect, as mentioned earlier, is translated often as *swabimana*; however, while a politician may feel increased self-respect when he wins an election, *stannamana* is recognition from others.[41]

Whether or not one has received recognition appropriate to one's *stannamana* is frequently an issue which lies at the base of conflicts. When the Chief Minister makes ministerial or other appointments, the issue of balancing the representation of important castes, along with the issue of recognising persons, is deemed by the Chief Minister to be, for various reasons, worthy of a post. With the deinstitutionalisation of parties over the last 20 years implying the lack of formal organisation and meaningful positions in party hierarchies, the issue of recognition for services rendered has become increasingly volatile. Party members may feel that they have earned status through their party work that has not been recognised by appointment, and that they have not been treated with the respect they feel they deserve. My notes from an interview with KH Srinivasa, Janata Dal politician and then Political Secretary to the Chief Minister, clarified this point:

> There is no definition of a party worker or a party cadre. So how can party workers get respect? [As things stand now] they are power-oriented and think that without an [appointed] position they cannot do anything. So they say that they have no *stannamana*. In this loose party structure it is hard to get respect; they feel that they are nobody.[42]

During an interview with a Vokkaliga, Janata Dal MLA, Putte Gowda, in which he and some of his associates elaborated on respect and *stannamana*,[43] we discussed displays of respect and having self-respect in politics. He stated that politics takes place in communities, and that a community member and his group want 'due respect' shown to them. Gowda argued that a leader cannot satisfy all of the groups and this so-called lack of respect results in conflict. I asked him if it would therefore be correct to say that conflicts [over appointments, nominations, patronage, and so on] are expressed in terms of respect relations. He answered that this was the case. Conflict, he felt, was expressed as an issue of respect shown or withheld and the undermining of self-respect. I also brought up the term *stannamana* and Mr. Gowda explained (to the accompaniment of laughter from the dozen or so others in the room) that *stannamana* is 'a pure Kannada word'. 'Every politician wants *stannamana*', he elaborated. 'If you have *stannamana*, you have status'. It seemed that all those present agreed that the overall translation of *stannamana* was 'status'. 'If you have *stannamana*, people will be with you', Mr Gowda concluded: 'Where there is status, there is people.'[44]

After some discussion among themselves, the group indicated that it was important that I understood that, even if the word *mana*, which Putte Gowda translated as 'respect shown', was part of the construction of the word *stannamana*, this did not mean the a person with *stannamana* was a good person. Putte Gowda explained: 'If you have a good son, if you have a good wife, if you are a good MLA, you will receive respect.' But, he added, a corrupt politician will not have the respect which is due to a man with *mana*, but he will have *stannamana*.

What does the political language of honour and respect tell us about political integration in south India in general and Karnataka in particular? For those familiar with post-colonial history in south India, self-respect movements in Tamil Nadu and Andhra Pradesh come to mind. In Tamil Nadu the movement for non-Brahmin caste assertion, the Self-Respect Movement initiated by EV Ramaswami Naicker, became strongly linked to Tamil cultural nationalism and support for the Tamil language. So-called Dravidian nationalism generated the two political parties, DMK and ADMK, which have dominated Tamil Nadu since 1967. In Andhra Pradesh, the ruling Telugu Desam Party, which became galvanised under the leadership of a popular movie star, commonly articulates as its goal the support of Telugu self-respect.

Powerful self-respect movements have not yet appeared in Karnataka; however, the language of self-respect is widely associated with lower caste uplift. The journalist Raghavendra Rao argued that notions of self-respect are more important to low status groups, in terms of caste or class, than they are to 'the bourgoisie':[45]

[Notes from interview] Politicians appeal to the weakest notion of *swabimana* [self-respect]. *Swabimana* is a strong concept, referring to one's identity. But castes [in Karnataka] don't get much out of these mobilisations.

Mana does not mean honour – which is a European word that is hard to find Kannada meanings for – it is better to translate it as respect or dignity. Honour is not so good to use with *mana*. Status is a better word to use to translate *mana*. Notables have authority – here, *mana* is an elite concept.

Self-respect is something different... Servants in the house used to wear shabby clothes, now they will dress nicely and want to be treated with respect. They have self-respect. So *swabimana* can/does tie in with the democratic ideal. This translates as self-respect in politics – my vote gives me respect. I am somebody when I vote.

The comments of Raghavendra Rao suggest that references to respect in political discourse are multivalent, referring both to the status of elites and a desire for social emancipation. References to respect and the vocabulary of honour (including 'humiliation' and 'betrayal') also bring the distant spheres of district and particularly state and national politics closer to the everyday experiences of the mass of people, resonating with common concerns and notions of appropriate relations in a community. Below I will outline conventional values of honour and respect as they appear in selected scholarship and literature. While personal identity and civil social exchange are included in the range of meanings expressed in the language of respect, it would seem that in a political context, notions of hierarchy and dominance are the salient ideological elements.

Aspects of Honour and Respect

We saw above that there are several words in Kannada which refer to honour and respect; these words reflect the fact that there exist different types of respect. Furthermore, a word, like the commonly used *mana*, can have different meanings in different contexts. Here I explore some of the issues for consideration referring to respect and self-respect in political discourse.

One of the few discussions of honour and respect in English scholarship on Karnataka is that of MN Srinivas. In his field research in the 1940s and 1950s Srinivas found that there was much preoccupation with *moka* or 'face' among villagers.[46] People struggled to maintain face in public and were sensitive to insults in public. Self-respect was associated with face, with the word *mana*, meaning self-respect in this context. A man with a keen sense of self-respect was referred to as a *manishta*, which had two near synonyms in *gauruvasta* and *maryadasta*. Srinivas discussed the characteristics of a man with *mana*:

> A *manishta* kept his word, and he also discharged his obligations scrupu-
> lously. He paid creditors on time, and he gave the gifts he was required
> to. He did not easily brook an insult. If he was not strong or aggressive
> enough to react instantly to an insult, he showed his resentment by silent
> non-cooperation.[47]

Robert J Zydenbos discussed *mana* and the related *mariyade* in his study of post-colonial Kannada fiction. He found *mana* and *mariyade* in the fiction he examined to be an issue of obedience to the strictures of caste and maintaining the honour of one's caste and, thus, one's family standing:

> [C]aste is linked to *maryade*, which is usually variously translated as
> 'honour', 'dignity' or 'decency...[After discussing a novel in which the
> heroine loves a man of another caste], [f]rom all this it follows that
> *maryade* or *mana*, 'honour', is *not* a quality showing a personal desire for
> general, impersonal justice, with reliability, strength of individual char-
> acter and personal integrity, as is the general Western view. Rather,
> it...means subjection in deference to the rules of the caste, into which
> one is born not through one's own will.[48]

Rather than competing interpretations, the views of Srinivas and Zydenbos can be seen as different aspects which one needs to explore in the complex evaluation of the self and others in Karnatakan social life. Another aspect of respect relations is to be found in two novels dealing with village life by the widely known Kannada writer UR Anantha Murthy. Anantha Murthy, born a Brahmin in 1932, grew up in Malenad, a hilly area of rural Karnataka. Our main interest here is his novel *Bharathipura*, which shows a wide range of social interaction among caste groups in the village of the novel's title.[49] The novel was written in Kannada in the 1970s while the author was staying in a village in Malenad. A socialist of the Lohiaite movement, Anantha Murthy travelled extensively in that area during electoral campaigns and campaigns for the abolition of landlordism.[50]

In *Bharathipura* the young Brahmin landlord in the village comes back from university in the UK, and decides that the ex-untouchables in the village will not act to escape their low status until the village god is demystified for them. He endeavours to mobilise them to enter the temple of the god and touch the icon. As DR Nagaraj summarises in his introduction to the recent English translation of the novel:

> [T]his chapter [fourteen]…gives us the philosophical vision that informs the novel. A certain kind of super revolutionary, whatever be his or her ideological moorings, treats the world and its people as meaningless things. S/he has to invest them with meaning. The will to create such meaning may also destroy both the self-respect and self-image of the objects of change.[51]

Amidst the action of the novel, as the protagonist struggles against the prejudices of both caste society and ex-untouchables, one can observe continuous and common shows of courtesy in everyday encounters, the gestures of respect, graded according to caste, that characterise conventional interactions in the village. In his novel, *Samskara: A Rite for a Dead Man*, first published in Kannada in 1965, Anantha Murthy referred explicitly to such gestures as those of courtesy, respect and fear.[52]

Samskara was made into a movie in 1970; it aroused controversy in India and was shown on university campuses in the United States. The noted scholar and poet, AK Ramanujan, published an English translation of the novel in 1976. It tells of a village Brahmin of great learning, respect and integrity who loses his self-respect and becomes tortured by self-questioning after having intercourse with the low-caste concubine of a deceased decadent Brahmin neighbour. The novel traces his painful attempts to construct a new self-image for himself, a new identity. Ramanujan wrote in the afterward to his translation:

> All the battles of tradition and defiance, asceticism and sensuality, the meaning and meaninglessness of ritual, dharma as nature and law,

desire (*kama*) and salvation (*moksha*) have now become internal to Praneshacharya [the protagonist]. The arena shifts from a Hindu village community to the body and spirit of the protagonist...

...[T]he story moves very much like a *rite de passage*. It is well known that many types of ritual, especially rites of initiation, have three states: 'separation', 'transition' ('margin or limen') and 're-incorporation'. In and through such rituals, individuals and groups change their state or status. Such a change of state is often symbolised (as in this book) by a change of place – a going-away, a seclusion and a coming back...

So a *samskara* is not only the subject of the work but the form as well.

[Praneshacharya] moves through the three stages – though we see him not entirely into the third state, but only on its threshold. Will he, can he, ever integrate it with his old ways, his past *samskara*? We do not know. We only see him mutating, changing from a fully evolved socialised brahmin at one with his tradition towards a new kind of person; choosing himself, individuating himself and 'alienating' himself. We are left, 'anxious, expectant', like [Praneshacharya] at the end of the novel.[53]

With the insights of Ramanujan we learn something of the existential realm of respect and self-respect. When I met Anantha Murthy in May 1998, my concern was with the portrayal of civil intercourse in *Bharathipuram* and *Samskara*. I was struck by the ever-presence in the books of respect relations in village life. Amidst the dramatic action, the breaking of taboos and the challenging of superior caste status, there was an undertone of common civility in conventional gestures of courtesy and respect.

In response to my saying that his novels portray relations of respect in the communities he writes about, Anantha Murthy responded that people are unconscious of self-respect in social relations. His grandfather, he told me, treated lower caste people with the respect which they held by virtue of their own social place. Mr. Murthy recalled that he once asked a Kuruba gardener how he related to Vokkaligas [a dominant caste cluster in Karnataka]. The Kuruba answered with a list of ways in which Vokkaligas are superior in customs (having higher status customs) and other ways in which Kurubas have the status advantage. In the gardener's view, both communities had high and low aspects, and these balanced each other in a way that made for some ambiguity as to which had the higher overall status. Each could have pride in their own group, and there was mutual awareness. Murthy believed that a higher caste man had an innate respect for a lower caste man and that this unconscious awareness was a part of everyday life.

It would seem then that the language of honour and respect in political discourse in Karnataka can overlap with conceptions of civil intercourse that touched on notions of community belonging. However, a notable pattern is revealed in these social exchanges. The respect relations in *Bharathipura* function to maintain the local dominance of the protagonist's plantation-owning Brahmin family. Examining major sources for the generation of values and practices of honour and respect, one finds that these values and practices maintain a structure of relationships which institutionalises inequality. However, the inequalities can be and often are challenged.

4. Learning Respect in Everyday Practice

Surely notions of honour and respect among ordinary people, along with many ideas of authority and power, are informed by participation in activities of worship in religious institutions. As C Fuller recently reminded us, *puja* (worship) in Hinduism consists of acts of honouring the gods.[54] It appears likely, however, that the most important generation of these norms is found in the behavioural disciplines which maintain the conventional family as the basic unit in a segmented social order. We find these norms in the political values which support the solidarity of the kin groups of clan and *jati* segments, and which still in many parts of rural and urban India allows them to reproduce political values themselves.

We need to think in terms of the administration of the affairs of the families which make up these social segments. We need to examine the administration of interpersonal interactions within familial groups as they work to sustain themselves and celebrate the live of their members. Administration is carried out in face-to-face relationships in which age and gender are important determinants of the formal hierarchy – the face which the unit shows the world.

I asked NP Shankarnaraya Rao how a child in Karnataka learns about honour and respect. Shankarnaraya Rao, around retirement age at the time of the interview, holds an MA in anthropology and is an acute observer of life in Karnataka. He was adamant that there was 'no conscious training in honour and respect'. For one thing, he pointed out, there is no compulsory need to attend school, so poor children are not socialised through the school system. They learn about honour and respect, he felt, in the relations of 'love and affection in the family'. Children were taught by example, for the most part. Shankarnaraya Rao did however suggest that there is one occasion when the child will be consciously instructed in correct behaviour – the marriage festivity and its attendant rituals:

Children will learn by practice, looking (in the case of boys) at their fathers... Let's say that grandparents come to visit their children and grandchildren. As they leave the children will touch their feet and they may be instructed, "You must behave like this".[55]

Rao also argued that there are linguistic registers indicating respect, and that Kannada appears to be no different than Tamil generally in this. He emphasised that the use of these registers is not conscious, but internalised. In an earlier interview, when asked about *stannamana*, he commented: '[S]*tannamana* exists because in our mind are joint family lineages… *Stannamana* emanates from the joint family system where, (for example) according to age one has position'.[56]

What follows is based on my experience of conventional kin relations as I have learned them from anthropological and historical accounts, fiction, movies and observation. The head of the unit of kin is usually the oldest male and he is supposed to rule; he is not simply a manager. His rule is personal and he commands personal respect. This respect is to be shown through a range of behaviour of subordination appropriate to the age and gender of the kin subjects within the tiny domain of the head of kin, or segment head. His position is supported by ideologies of honour and high status responsibility that are found in the worship and ritual of his subclan or *jati*. Generally worship consists of acts of honouring the deities, who in turn rule the cosmos. Within the conventional husband–wife relationship, many women consider their husbands analogous to god and honour them in a manner akin to worship of their deities.

Everyone in the kin domain has honour, with the oldest male head of the unit taking, formally, the royal function – assuming the function of a kingly ruler. As the highest-ranking member of the segment, the head represents and protects it. A slight to any member of the segment is perceived to dishonour all, but the head takes the formal lead in regaining lost honour and status. He also protects the honour of the group by enforcing adherence to its code for conduct, punishing misbehaviour. Restrictions on the movements of women, and the responsibility of men in the group to protect them, is well-known. A man whose family members act inappropriately suffers humiliation and shame in part because of his presumed failure to rule effectively.

It is in the respect behaviour of his group subordinates that the authority of the head is recognised and protected. An insult from a member of the group signifies rebellion against the head's rule. Despite outward shows of order, group relations – particularly among brothers and cousins – can be highly conflicted. The conflicts can involve disagreement over control of unit assets, but will often be expressed in terms of respect. There will be quarrels over appropriate shows of respect or the lack of respectful behaviour. In some contexts and situations, therefore, there will be competition for honour and authority in the group, depending on its size and constitution, and on the personalities of members.

Satish Saberwal has argued for the importance of social learning in segmented structures as a major influence in forming notions of the nature of public responsibility in India:

Indian society has been notable both for the strength of its intra-familial and intra-caste bonds and for its difficulties with public authority on a durable basis. Under these conditions, *impersonal* normative orders cannot reasonably be expected to rise – nor easily sustained.[57]

Saberwal also observes that 'the directions for one's conduct, and interpretations of fresh experience – even in the megasocietal institutions – are often framed by small-scale moralities…'[58] Following Saberwal I suggest that, as the socio-technical frame of interaction has expanded in south India, far beyond the relatively small range of interaction for most people in the eighteenth and nineteenth centuries, the ideology of personal administration through respect behaviour has been applied to new types of domains. Formal and informal institutions of personal rule – including factions in political parties – are anchored ideologically in notions of personal authority and rule which find their support in social and political relations in the social, cultural and political domains. The practice of appropriate interaction is anchored in notions of respect shown appropriately.

5. Domain Building and Politicians

From the discussion above we can see that respect relations occur with reference to domains, for example, of kin, caste and village. Here I will discuss a different type of domain, where politicians carry out transactions where notions of honour and respect play important roles.

Several scholars have written about the intensive networking which Indians carry out as a means to achieve various ends in their lives. Adrian Mayer and Mark Holmström developed models for the construction of 'action-sets, a kind of networking among politicians in, respectively, Madhya Pradesh and Karnataka. Both anthropologists did their research in connection with elections as they investigated the ways local politicians went about attaining office. Mayer in particular relied on transaction theory to argue that a politician constructs networks of persons who are obliged to him in one way or another, and that these networks are activated at election time for the purpose of getting him elected. As Holmström explained:

Picture an action-set as a number of chains radiating out from the central individual, the originator, the person with a special reason for organising it.

Some of the chains are also connected to each other by extra links, away from the centre. I persuade A, who persuades B, who persuades C and D; but A is also putting pressure on D, by virtue of some quite different relation to him. The action-set consists of all the people who can be persuaded to act and to persuade others because they are linked to me directly or through intermediaries; and between each pair of individuals the relation, the basis for persuasion, may be different.[59]

Mayer's work can be seen as an analysis of how Indian politicians used 'vote banks' to get elected in the 1950s and 1960s. A politician established a relationship of mutual obligation with a powerful patron – a leader in a community or locality – by doing him a favour, for example for the disposal of the local leader when he was in office. At election time the community leader would instruct his clients to vote for the politician; he thus constituted a vote bank for the politician. In the 1970s, however, as increasing numbers of low-status groups became mobilised, vote banks became less common, as the authority of local 'Big Men' began to be questioned. Other strategies for election had to be employed.

Holmström's work was influenced by Mayer's formulations, but he argued that relationships in action-sets were based on premises other than simple self-interest. Not only can support for the politician in action-sets be based on agreement with his ideological stands, but Holmström found in his research in Karnataka in the 1960s that respect for the person of the politician played an important role.[60] This respect could have its basis in several different kinds of relationships: 'including family relationship, economic obligation, indebtedness for past favours, the prestige of wealth or birth, and respect for honourable conduct (*manam, mana-mariyatai*)'.[61] Holmström noted that he also includes the category of respect toward a friend, even though that is not governed under the term *mariyatai*, which, he argued, pertains to unequal relationships.[62] He commented on action sets and corrupt actions:

The campaign was full of accusations of bribery, which is considered disgraceful; yet it is unlikely that those who may have accepted bribes, to line up support for a candidate or to get him the ticket [to stand for election], regarded the transaction quite cynically as an economic one. Any present puts one under an obligation, particularly when it is given some time before the counter-demand is presented; and in such cases it is possible to save one's self-respect by seeing the transaction as one involving tokens of mutual respect.[63]

Holmström seemed to believe that preoccupations with self-respect were so important in people's calculations of the morality of their actions, that a person making a bribe or accepting one would not see himself as purely self-interested:

> Everyone agrees that politics is a dirty business and is cynical about the motives of others, but the common value system, on which the 'big men' base their conception of the respect owed to them, makes it difficult to regard one's own motives in the same way. Relative cynicism is almost universal, because political behaviour falls so far short of an ideal most people would like to believe in.[64]

Action-sets still exist as a technique in reaching specific political goals; however, if we take Mayer's and Holmström's work as a guide, action-sets have altered in their nature. With the deinstitutionalisation of party organisations which began in the 1970s, it perhaps gives a more complete picture of politicians' concerns to speak of them as constructing fluid domains of influence as they struggle to expand the range of their personal power. As personal followings have become more important in the structure of political action, politicians increasingly rely on their personal capacity to put key figures in the state bureaucracy, business and wider society under obligation to them, not just to be exploited or activated at election time, but continuously. This is partly because an MLA in India, first and foremost, is a 'fixer', someone who can solve problems for others, particularly members of his constituency and his community.[65] Solutions to problems probably more often than not require a departure from formal procedures of decision-making on the part of state and national bureaucrats.

The political landscape in Karnataka, then, contains politicians' informal, overlapping domains of personal networks, domains which make no distinction between the procedural boundaries of state administration and the administration of non-state-originated enterprises of one sort or another. For a major politician, it is partly as the master of fluid network domains that he seeks to avoid loss of face: to manage his public image as a person who is protective of his self-respect. The irony here is that in the view of the solid middle classes in Karnataka, as elsewhere in India, a politician is a person with no self-respect. I was told repeatedly that no person with self-respect could think of going into politics, because of the depth of the moral compromises involved in deal-making and in financing party activities.

6. The King Conundrum in Post-Colonial Politics

As I mentioned above, Raghavendra Rao's comments on the connection between voting and assertions of self-respect for some groups of low-status people indicate elements of emancipation in ideologies of respect. Respect and honour for many politicians, on the other hand, are notions anchored in values of political hierarchy, belonging to a complex of values which commentators in India find reflect 'feudal' elements in Indian polity. Discourses among politicians hold direct references to (south) Indian 'feudalism' and ideas of monarchical rule.

In January 1998, when six Dal partymen had joined the Rastriya Nava Nirmana Vedike, the non-party organisation started by Ramakrishna Hegde, there had been cries of betrayal. A news conference was held, at which the six men offered explanations for their action. One of their supporters claimed in the course of the proceedings that 'only some *pallegars* (chieftains) were ruling the Janata Dal. A situation had developed where honest workers would be forced to go out'.[66]

Palegars were the chiefs and little kings of south India, found in Andhra and Tamil Nadu as well as Karnataka, who alternatively served or rebelled against larger kings in the seventeenth century and contributed to the disintegration of the larger kingdoms in the eighteenth century. Political commentators occasionally wrote about political life in Karnataka as '*Palegar* politics', and the term was reasonably well known in the state. I do not think that a direct historical link can be made between political bosses like Deve Gowda – against whom the charge of *palegar* was occasionally made – and seventeenth- and eighteenth-century chieftains. However, in that such petty rulers are portrayed in nineteenth-century writing, at least, as highly protective of their honour, it is useful to consider the term in the context of this discussion.

While references to royal symbols and feudal images in political commentary appeared in the 1990s with greater frequency than earlier, it is unlikely that most writers use historical references according to a theory of political culture. Often the references appear to be rhetorical flourishes. In 1992, for example, Mahendra Prasad Singh outlined a scenario which would seem to have its base in the Gangetic Plain. He found Indian politics becoming:

some sort of a medieval fort-holding operation between warring *caudillos*; extraparliamentary mass movements and parliamentary disorders by the opposition swarm over governmental forces almost instantly after an electoral mandate (Singh 1992:308).

An editorial in the *Deccan Herald* intoned the same motif in writing about the murder of Y.S. Raja Reddy, father of the Andhra Pradesh Congress President. Referring to factional conflict in rural Andhra, the writer stated:

To many it is like a throwback to the clash of chieftains and warlords of the feudal era because the violence is mostly sparked off by feuds between the rich and powerful sections of the region (*Deccan Herald*, 26/5/98).

The most developed use of these metaphors comes not from a journalist or news commentator, but from a politician with long experience in the Congress Party, P.V. Narasimha Rao, Prime Minister of India from 1991 to 1996. His thoughts on Indian political culture appear in his autobiographical novel, *The Insider*, which was published early in 1998. Most of the action is based in the fictional state of Afrozabad, which bears a close resemblence to Rao's own state, Andhra Pradesh (Narasimha Rao, 1998). The book was treated in the press as an exposé. For example, one writer noted that Chief Ministers in the novel appear more like medieval 'chieftains' than 20th century parliamentarians, and added that Rao 'tells us more about the inner workings of the Congress, and hence India's rulers, than any other book in the last fifty years' (Mishra, 1998:57).

The period of action in the novel is mainly the 1950s and 1960s; Rao explains in 'A Note from the Author' that he had begun the novel more that twenty years before its publication. The political language employed by Narasimha Rao belongs equally to commentary of the 1990s. It would appear that, if the novel can be used as a source for political values during the Nehru period, there are continuities, at least at the level of state politics, from the post-Independence decades to the 1990s. These continuities would seem to be in politicians' conceptions of the nature of the status of office and their strategies for the establishment of informal domains of influence.

Narasimha Rao has the second Chief Minister of Afrozabad, Chaudhuri, give voice to a perception of the politicians' creed which is common in the English language press today. As he runs through a list of Members of the Legislative Assembly, he thinks, 'The common motivation: power. The common point of unity: self. That was the game, by whatever name you chose to call it' (Narasimha Rao, 1998:206). Chaudhuri exclaims to Rao's idealistic protagonist, 'Political power is my ideology, if you can call it that, which ideologues like you don't!' and he later ruminates about politicians:

'who had come into the political field with an entirely self-centered approach... They had spent all their lives chasing transient glory, worshipping the false god of political power for its own sake' (Narasimha Rao:324).

The 'political field' was a favorite motif for Chaudhuri to whom Rao gives a common refrain, emphasised in italics:

In the political field, frailty was the banner held aloft over each person's chariot, glaring and prominent, announcing only vulnerable points to the wide world. Which proceeded to see nothing, hear nothing – but evil (Narasimha Rao 1998:207).

Narasimha Rao often characterises relations among the MLAs in *The Insider* as 'feudal' in quality: 'The activity was political, but the minds behind it were feudalistic and implacable all the way' (Narasimha Rao, 1998:549). For Rao the political culture of India at all levels during the period of the novel was monarchical: all men of public authority 'reigned' and 'Democracy in action at best consisted of the question "Who should reign?"'. He introduces the first Chief Minister of Afrozabad thus:

> He had all the attributes of a medieval king-iron-handed administration, cruelty, sadism, egocentrism, intolerance, arbitrariness, aggressiveness, ruthlessness, sexual licence as of right. He was also like a medieval chieftain...whose attitude towards the Central authority was never really cooperative or cordial... He appeared on the verge of revolt all the time; yet he never actually revolted, since there was nothing to revolt against, really (Narasimha Rao, 1998:130).

Narasimha Rao carries the royal imagery further when, twenty years later in his novel, Indira Gandhi becomes Prime Minister. His protagonist, Anand thought to himself:

> In his opinion...[he] was attempting to save her from the queenly and dynastic image that was being fostered by her sycophants. The attempt to appoint Indira Gandhi as the new regent was understandable in a country where kingship had been the main building block of the socio-political structure for centuries (Narasimha Rao, 1998: 586).

Narasimha Rao articulates a point of view which seems to reflect at the least some opinions on contemporary political style and practice. Relevant to the discussion here is that Narasimha Rao's main characters are periodically preoccuped with their personal honour, with self-respect, revenge or the humiliation of rivals. References in political discourse to *palegars*, chieftains, or kings do not necessarily indicate a direct inheritance of south India's precolonial monarchical heritage. The political cultures of kinship and worship reproduce hierarchical conceptions of honour in which the person with highest status in a domain reigns. Elsewhere, in a study of precolonial and colonial monarchical culture in the Tamil country, I argued that all actors in monarchical systems had honour and that they were in competition to enhance their honour, an enhancement which was consolidated by public recognition of the new honour status. In such flexible and fluid hierarchies of rank honour, all with honour ruled the domains under their control, large or small. The person who in the course of competition received the greatest recognition of honour was the highest-ranking ruler, with royal status.

This notion of being the highest of the high, the ruler of rulers, appears to be reproduced in contemporary political culture and is reflected in symbolic actions in political performances in public. Tamil Nadu is well-known in south India for the utilisation of monarchical symbols, particularly in the ADMK, the political party of former Chief Minister, Jayalalitha. Kannadigans tend to be proud that their politics generally avoid the displays of glorified status and, sometimes, abject subordination that have occurred in Tamil Nadu. People commonly point to the lack of interest of their great film actor, Rajkumar, in entering into politics in the state. An old man close to the political scene in Mysore City related that Rajkumar had said to his public, 'I am not a deity for you to pray to' (Ramana, 7 January 1998). This is stark contrast to Jayalalitha, who presented herself as the queen of the Tamils.

This not to say that royal symbolism in practice or rumor was absent in Karnataka in 1997–8. At a campaign rally of Lok Shakti, Ramakrishna Hegde's party, in April 1998, among the chairs on the main platform were three throne-like models for the chief guests among the politicians. Hegde and a chief guest distributed Mysore turbans and red and gold cloths to men on the platform in the course of the proceedings. Public honouring of politicians in Karnataka commonly includes the presentation of turbans, one type modelled from the period of the erstwhile Kingdom of Mysore in the southern part of the state, and one style coming from northern Karnataka (G.S. Hegde Ajjibal, 26 December 1997). The Mysore turban is called the *peta* and is named with reference to a Wodeya king of Mysore who wore the *peta*.

A local Janata Dal politician, former president of a mandal (block) *panchayat* in western Karnataka, related a story to the effect that former Chief Minister Bangarappa, a low status caste (Idaga) leader, had given money to be honoured by a gold crown by members of his caste community:

Outsiders, who will not know the whole story, will believe that he must be a great man to have been so honoured. It is fairly common to pay to be honoured in public. This is a way of turning black money into white money... Recieving a gold crown shows that you are equal to god – you have divinity (Ramnath, 25 December 1997).

A Karnataka Administrative Service officer who had served as private secretary for the leader of the Opposition in the Karnataka Legislative Council remarked that giving a crown to a leader was 'adoring your leader' (V.N. Torgal, 29 April 1998) Along the same lines the Resident Editor of *The Times of India* in Bangalore argued that the politician who is 'in the limelight is worshipped' throughout India: 'People will forget about his nefarious

actions. He is a great man. Nobody goes into his background. He is a hero...'
(H.S. Balram, 10 June 1998).

The expression '*palegar* politics' and references to Indian politics as 'feudal' are used as negative criticism of political behaviour, suggesting departures from norms of civility and decency. However, as the evidence above indicates, monarchical references are also used by politicians and their followers to make statements about the kind of status a leader has or, at least, strives for.

7. Conclusion

The language (and symbolism) of honour and respect in political discourse is a different order of ideology than, say, calls for a Muslim nation, a Pakistan. This political language is, however, one which ordinary men and women can understand. It is a language which resonates with a wide range of important values in both ordinary and extraordinary experience. As such this language assists the functioning of political parties as hinges between the person and the state, between state and society. However, the process of amalgamating the particularisms of local society in electoral politics ties intimately with competitive processes of identity formation, of status definition. When I write about ideological integration, I am discussing a *kind* of integration, not postulating a smooth or even necessarily a fully successful process. Along with honour there is humiliation, with respect one finds also betrayal. Politicians represent such defeats in a manner which most people comprehend.

4

THE FIGHT FOR TURF AND THE CRISIS OF IDEOLOGY: BROADCASTING REFORM AND CONTEMPORARY MEDIA DISTRIBUTION IN INDIA

Veena Naregal

Until the 1990s, dissemination of news through print and the commercial cinema represented the most significant media presences in the Indian context. The factors that shaped the historical and political context of discussion in the public domain include: the limited nature of participation and access to print media for large segments of the population; the predominance of upper-caste agents, especially in the print media; the internal divisions, on the one hand, between English and regional language audiences, and between the regional language reading publics on the other. Within this larger scenario, the links between big business houses and Indian news media, especially the press, in the post-Independence period, have been fairly well documented.[1] As Robin Jeffrey's work has well shown, the expansion in the market for political news and the consumer base from the 1980s onwards has resulted in a phenomenal rise in the circulation of regional-language newspapers.[2] Significant as these trends have been, it is debatable if they have brought about any fundamental shifts in reversing the relations of power underlying the structure of the public sphere, especially those pertaining to the nature of ownership, participation and access.

Parallel to these connections, but less analysed in terms of their implications for the nature of the Indian public sphere, have been the relations between the entertainment media and speculative capital and the informal sectors of the money markets. Students of popular Indian cinema have long known that, with its nationwide markets and growing international audiences, the commercial film industry is an attractive area for the investment of unaccounted profits. In fact, with banks unwilling to finance film production until recently, the 'parallel' economy has been the main source of funds for the entertainment business, estimated currently to have an annual turnover of approximately Rs 3750 crores.[3] Although not known for their intellectual content, the output of these media industries remains an important aspect of the Indian public sphere in so far as varieties of commercial cinema in Hindi and South Indian languages and popular music have helped define a cultural mainstream more than any other cultural form. In reaching out to larger audiences than the printed media, cinema represented one of the most important sites in which the experience of a general public was created and contested until the growth in television in the 1990s. What is particularly interesting, is that, compared to the patronage available to print media from national and provincial business elites, and for broadcasting through state funds, commercial cinema – whose products, above all, helped extend the public sphere beyond that defined by upper-caste cultural elites – has survived mainly through exploiting surplus merchant capital available through parallel money markets.[4] There is a growing literature that demonstrates how the interdependence of legitimate big business and the illegitimate activities of the 'parallel' sector, such as labour racketeering, bootlegging and manipulation of unions, sustain the efficiency of capitalist economies in different parts of the world, including those of advanced industrial, western democracies.[5] More specifically, links between organised crime and the entertainment industry in the US and elsewhere have also been documented.[6] In the US, there has been longstanding evidence of the infiltration of Hollywood labour unions, including some major ones, by the underworld. Similarly, the Music Company of America, starting off in the 1920s as a talent agency and band-booking company with alleged links with the Chicago mafia, has gone on to become one of Hollywood's most powerful TV, film and recording conglomerates.[7] However, given the scale and importance of Hollywood's output, its relation vis-a-vis leading banks has been the exact reverse of the situation of the Indian film industry: the financial health of several banks remains intrinsically tied up with fortunes of Hollywood companies. Thus, perhaps uniquely within the scenario of Indian capitalistic modernity, the links between mainstream and informal sectors do not only have a significance in the economic context; rather, they have been integral to patronage structures of popular culture and the dissemination of a 'low-brow' cultural mainstream, thereby impacting in important ways upon the public sphere.[8] Most notably, Jan Breman's work has emphasised the almost complete paucity of work on the informal sector;[9] this is particularly true in the context of large Indian cities such as Mumbai.[10] One may additionally emphasise the need to pose questions about the diverse ways in which intersections between formal and informal economies are increasingly implicated in shaping circuits of ideological and cultural production, distribution and consumption, especially in the Indian context.

1. Informal Networks and Popular Culture

In this section I will sketch the contours of the role of under-capitalised informal networks in shaping circuits of patronage, production and distribution of popular cultural products in post-colonial India. The Indian film industry makes about 900 films per year. Big budgets and inflated star fees are considered essential by most mainstream Bollywood directors for a chance of box-office success. And yet, as Madhav Prasad's work has shown, Indian film production has been dominated by surplus merchant capital and a large number of independent producers who, at best, are small scale entrepreneurs hoping to capitalise on the availability of low-wage casual labour, the enormous wage differences between stars, 'character actors' and 'extras', and relying on renting all requisite technical resources, demonstrating that the industry remains characterised by under-capitalisation and fragmentation.[11] Recent developments notwithstanding, a current industry report tells us that film-financiers comprise mainly of diamond merchants, brokers, builders and other such people with large amounts of liquid cash to spare, which they lend out at rates as high as 36–48 per cent per annum.[12] In addition, in a situation characterised by an acute scarcity of exhibition outlets,[13] and where distribution and exhibition are seen as the most profitable aspects of the film business, the industry has long been seen as a distributors' market.[14] Distributors, and more recently, music companies – the main parties to profit by a film's success – have been the other source of commercial film finance.[15] Up until the early 1980s, these links between 'black' money and commercial film production were still contained within relatively unthreatening proportions, with only occasional rumours about a well-known underworld figure putting up money for a film involving some minor actress whom he admired.

However, with the expanding market for film-based and other media products such as audio cassettes and videos in the 1980s, and now cable and satellite TV, the underworld has become seriously interested in the lucrative returns available through the entertainment and media industry.[16] Peter Manuel's study on the audio cassette and video boom shows the extent to which this expansion in the 1980s relied on piracy and use of other illegal means.[17] Clearly, the growing markets for media products tapped the potential of the informal sector in augmenting distribution networks, even as the increasing rivalry between segments of the entertainment industry such as music and film production seemed to present underworld elements with a ripe opportunity to emerge as important mediators over copyright, distribution and profit claims. This, of course, was not the first time that the help of underworld goons had been sought to resolve feuds over big money or other types of economic and industrial disputes: since the 1970s especially, *Shiv Sena*, the right-wing party set up by Bal Thackeray with a nativist agenda for Bombay, was able to acquire a great deal of influence largely by presenting itself as a useful intermediary for all kinds of dealings between the 'clean' capitalistic core of the economy and its parallel sectors, especially by providing quick solutions through the use of intimidation and violence.

The extension of this role into cultural 'patronage' was novel. If evidence were needed of the growing involvement of the underworld in the entertainment business, it was provided in the gunning down of Gulshan Kumar, the ambitious and self-made 'audio-cassette king' in Bombay on August 12 1997.[18] More than anyone else, Gulshan Kumar rewrote the rules of the music business in India through the 1980s and 1990s. Starting off as small-time fresh-juice vendor in Delhi, he got into the audio-cassette business in 1978, first with a petty service and repair shop. Realising that the market was ripe for expansion, he is said to have made huge profits through bootlegging and cheap, pirated versions of expensive HMV cassettes, HMV being the monopolist market leader at the time. Soon after he set up his own legitimate but controversial recording company, T-series, which introduced what were called 'cover versions'. Initially, these 'cover versions' were rerecordings of old film hits, but he soon began to issue such 'duplicates' of current movie releases. At the time of his death, besides his flagship company, Super Cassettes, Gulshan Kumar presided over a Rs 500 *crore* business empire that had diversified into soap and detergents, electronics manufacture, CDs and video production, and even film production.[19] Gulshan Kumar was one of the biggest names in the film and entertainment business when he was shot dead, allegedly because he failed to acquiesce to extortionist demands. Subsequently, the difficulties in obtaining finance for film-making have presented the mafia with easy openings to step into film production. Industry sources claim that at a conservative estimate, approximately 30–35 per cent of the films are financed by underworld money.[20] Besides, the presence of mafia money has been useful in securing dates from top stars to keep production on schedule.[21] More recently, with the growing international attention towards Indian commercial cinema, the mafia has been mainly interested in securing overseas rights, as a way of money laundering.[22]

Until recently, the realms of commercial cinema and popular music have routinely received analytical disdain from the English-language press and sections of the liberal-nationalist and left-oriented intelligentsia. This stems partly from bourgeois anxiety over the possible contamination of middle class culture from contact with the 'low-brow', even while it reflects the difficulties of posing the question of what constitutes the 'popular' in an intensely stratified and linguistically divided post-colonial society. However, the last few years have seen the growth of an interesting body of work that aims to conceptualise the cultural terrain occupied by Indian commercial cinema, and understand its modes of address, narration, and reception.[23] Mindful of the unique way in which relations between institutions of cinema and politics have evolved in India, recent work has also tried to probe the connections between large collectivities such as cinema audiences and political behaviour[24] or, for example, the historicity of regional cinema audiences and their links with class and debates about cultural values.[25] It has been suggested that the emerging economic and ideological context of the post-reforms period has seen some important shifts in cinematic form and its mode of production, arising from a new capital base, the emergence of a nexus between cultural corporations and reputable directors, the adoption of management techniques, and new aesthetic strategies.[26] However, despite these attempts to confer a belated partial official acknowledgement of film production as an industry, and attempts to regularise financial flows into film-making, other media trends in recent times have only accentuated linkages between the extension of audiences, the expansion of capitalism, informal sectors of the economy and underworld elements. For, as much as the lure of growing profits in the media industries, it was clearly the mafia attack on film producer Raakesh Roshan in connection with its demands for the international rights of his recent hit that apparently impelled the government to make available partial bank loans to fund film-production.[27]

It is in this context that the rest of this essay attempts to elaborate on media reform and distribution in India in the post-liberalisation period. The recent expansion in media audiences has occurred primarily through the deregulation of the broadcasting sector that dismantled the government monopoly over TV and radio transmission, and the consequent growth of privately owned cable and satellite TV networks in the 1990s. The next two parts of this essay will examine the direction of media reform and the environment it has created, followed by an account of the ways in which television audiences have been expanding through increasing integration between corporate interests and local media networks. The discussion in the last section will focus mainly on developments in Mumbai.[28] Given the city's position as India's financial capital and home to the Hindi film industry, and as an important centre for media and advertising industries, these contemporary links between media distribution, big enterprise, local networks and the underworld are unsurprisingly most visible there.

2. Media Reforms in the 1990s

Crucial to the liberalisation of economies across the world, and leading to the privatisation of state enterprises, deregulation of business sectors and cutbacks in state subsidies and welfare expenditure since the 1980s, has been the emergence of a global media system, which has actively facilitated the expansion of markets for corporate wares, and its cultural valorisation, mainly through advertising but also through other programming and commercial practices. Not surprisingly, the deregulation and privatisation of previously state-run national broadcasting systems has been an important adjunct of these processes of economic liberalisation. The media reforms that coincided with economic liberalisation in India since 1991 ought to be viewed against these wider changes. The debate about permitting foreign media firms to set up operations in India applied to both the print and the electronic media. But for a range of reasons, including the low credibility enjoyed by the official broadcasting agency, Doordarshan, it has proved easier to push through measures that first facilitated these changes in the case of the electronic media.

Drafted in 1997, more than five years after private satellite channels, including several in regional languages, had been beaming to Indian audiences, the Indian Broadcast Bill and its antecedent documents were quite candid in reviewing the contradictions under which broadcasting currently operated in India.[29] Whereas a large number of foreign broadcasting entities, uplinked from outside the country, successfully beamed their programmes to Indian audiences with hardly any restrictions under Indian laws, at this point Indian entrepreneurs and companies were not permitted to own radio or TV stations except for All India Radio (AIR) and Doordarshan (DD).[30] Ironically, as things stood, all the private satellite channels, including the popular regional channels such as Zee, Sun, and so on, were registered in some foreign country, so that they were technically 'foreign' channels beaming into India. And yet, the official stance insisted on emphasising the need to put a regulatory framework in place *in order to* counter the impact of this 'invasion of Indian skies by foreign satellite channels'.[31]

Briefly, broadcasting services comprise two main categories of companies: broadcasting entities, either as terrestrial or satellite channels, and entities that provide delivery services like cable distribution or DTH (direct to home). The Broadcast Bill proposed to restrict cross-holding of licences across these two categories, ostensibly to prevent concentration of control. The Bill was silent about how existing instances of the same group of companies holding sizeable simultaneous interests in distribution and broadcasting services would be treated. The Broadcast Bill went through subsequent drafts, but never actually made it to Parliament. Even by the time of its first draft, instances of cross holdings were glaringly obvious: the case of Subhas Chandra-owned Zee TV and Siticable (a joint venture between Rupert Murdoch's News Corp and Chandra's Zee Telefilms), and again AsiaNet in Kerala controlled entities engaged in broadcasting and distribution.

Ever since the Emergency, key issues in discussions on media reform have been those of autonomy and the need for government to forsake control of AIR and DD. However, the arrival of privatised commercial broadcasting has seen the focus of debate shift away from principles of free expression to questions of economic control and the permissible levels of consolidation within the industry. When the constitutional guarantee of free speech was invoked, it was with an altogether new accent. In what has been hailed as a landmark judgement in the context of Indian media regulation, in February 1995 the Supreme Court upheld the rights of the cricket association to give telecast rights to an agency of its choice, in a case between the Ministry of Information and Broadcasting and the Bengal Cricket Association.[32] Dismissing the exclusive claims of Doordarshan for these rights, the bench rejected the state's attempt to monopolise control over broadcasting, declaring that airwaves were public property. In doing so, the ruling opened the door to commercial bidding and the market for telecast rights.

With legislation on the issue of cross-holdings perpetually at the proposal stage, the situation on the ground does little to inspire confidence that deterrence of cross-holdings is a priority for current media policy in India. Political instability may be the immediate reason for the apparent inability of successive governments since 1992 to proceed with policy initiatives. But the present impasse in media regulation in India can, perhaps, be quite justifiably viewed as a smokescreen under which the necessary structural changes, that might otherwise have met with greater resistance, have been covertly carried out. For, despite their failure to seek parliamentary endorsement for the proposed laws, successive governments have throughout this period been characteristically open to representations and recommendations from foreign, 'indigenous' and NRI media corporations. This clearly corresponds with the pattern that Rob Jenkins has noted.[33]

3. Corporate Lobbies and Media Reform

The most concrete instance of the state's malleability has been its willingness to entertain advisory notes commissioned by a number of foreign satellite broadcasters. A significant example was the report submitted on behalf of the Working Group of the Broadcasting Industry of the American Business Council to the Parliamentary Committee on the Broadcasting Bill, ostensibly as a response to the document put out by the Indian Ministry of Information and Broadcasting in 1996. Entitled the 'Survey of National Broadcasting, Cable and DTH Satellite Laws' (henceforth called the Paul Weiss Survey), this document claimed to be 'a useful tool in determining how media laws elsewhere should be interpreted and what their relevance was to the debates over the shape of the (Indian) Broadcasting Bill'.[34] The Survey presented data about the existing laws with respect to foreign, cross-media ownership and uplinking restrictions, and the efficacy of auctioning licences for DTH and cable service providers in certain selected countries. It maintains a studiously factual approach.[35] However, it was clearly intended as an advocacy document meant to influence the course of Indian media law reform, leaving little doubt on this count about its implied inferences and preferences. This was borne out by the apparently close concurrence between key assumptions of the Paul Weiss Survey and the argument in the I&B Ministry's 1996 document.[36] Noting the wisdom of using a 'suitably adapted' comparative approach, the Ministry document had proceeded through a process of elimination to surmise that the basic framework of the proposed Broadcasting Bill ought to be modelled on British law. Corroborating this, the survey implies that since none of the countries chosen for comparison had the combination of provisions envisaged in the Indian draft bill, it would be undesirable for the Indian law to bring in restrictions on foreign ownership and cross-holdings, or insist on mandatory requirements on uplinking, including the use of Indian-held satellite capacity to reach Indian audiences.

Having thus disposed of the issues of ownership and control, and their implications for the vitality of the public sphere, the only remaining gesture within official thinking on media policy has been to speak of countering the 'invasions from the sky' with avowals to preserve 'our national identity'. And yet, the I&B document seemed only too eager to concede the failure of state-sponsored public broadcasting. It was abjectly stated that territorial delimitation and the issue of permitting foreign equity had 'lost their relevance' due to the advances of satellite technology. The document goes on to state baldly that as DD and AIR were unlikely to meet the aspirations of the people in terms of the variety and plurality of programmes required in India, the only available alternative was to 'develop our own indigenous private broadcasters who can provide to our people an alternative to the foreign satellite broadcasters'.[37] Relinquishing its previously self-proclaimed eminence as chief propagandist, current Indian media policy strikes one as a largely vacillating response to the crisis in the state's legitimacy, compounded by an opportunistic unwillingness to give up the advantages of being the regulatory authority. Therefore, the 1996 I&B document recognised with most exemplary pragmatism that the development of quality cable networks required substantial investment, and given this, that entrepreneurs would have to be assured of a certain security through licensing terms and 'a near exclusivity in a reasonably large area of operation', making it 'imperative that the number of cable operators in the country ... be as minimal as possible'.[38]

Now it seems that the Broadcasting Bill has been superseded by the Nariman Report on Convergence, which recommends the setting up of a new authority called the Communications Commission 'to facilitate and regulate (by means of regulations, orders and directions), all aspects of telecommunication and broadcasting, and other communications including all aspects of convergence in these services'. The newly envisaged Convergence Bill, which subsumes all issues pertaining to broadcasting and convergence, was placed before Parliament in August 2001 but has not yet been passed. Meanwhile, consolidation within the industry has proceeded apace, barely checked by piecemeal guidelines. One such set has been the guidelines on uplinking, announced in June 1998, which allowed satellite channels with resident Indian equity of not less than 80 per cent to uplink through VSNL or to set up their own uplinking earth station.[39] This was followed by admitting all satellite channels, irrespective of equity cap, to uplink from India, though it was not mandatory for all channels broadcasting to Indian audiences to uplink from Indian territory.[40] The much-awaited announcement allowing Direct-to-Home broadcasts, aimed at a small rich segment of the viewership, came in late 2000.[41] However, it has apparently generated little enthusiasm among existing media companies, possible reasons for the lack of interest being the stipulated restrictions on foreign equity and cross-holdings, along with the heavy licence fees being proposed.

Given the generally ad hoc approach that has guided media reform until now, cable networks have been allowed to achieve their phenomenal growth in connectivity in a short timespan. This has effectively meant the claiming of areas in Mumbai and elsewhere as 'belonging' to one or the other of the MSOs or the few large independent operators who now survive in the business. With subscription revenues and the potential to sell advertising time at rates being determined by the number of households reached by each network, the right to control 'distribution territories' rather than ideological contestation has emerged as the paramount consideration in media debates and the corporate strategies of media firms. Evidently, the stakes are indeed high.

4. The Emerging Distribution Scenario: Audiences, Informal Networks and Consolidation

Considering that the 1991 Gulf War marked the beginning of foreign satellite broadcasting in India, the fact that cable television now reaches more than 25 million Indian homes is an index of the fast pace of growth within the new television distribution industry.[42] Cable TV has made deep inroads into the political economy of urban and semi-urban lives. Closely-built apartment blocks with a high concentration of resident populations presented an ideal breeding ground initially for film-based cable TV services, especially in cities like Mumbai. With the video boom and the falling cost of video-cassette rentals, the business potential for localised cable networks grew. However, the scope of such operations changed with the coming of satellite channels and the privatisation of the media sector. With cable emerging as the medium for disseminating satellite broadcasts, cable distribution and satellite transmissions came together to form the core of the exhibition sector of the television industry.

Today, most cable homes are located in the major cities, yet given that the appeal of the audiovisual electronic media transcends the literacy barrier, and the lack of other information and entertainment facilities in smaller cities and non-urban areas, the potential for further expansion seems huge. Indian subscribers mostly receive the broadcast signal for a monthly fee, either directly from the major cable distribution companies or their franchisees. The appearance of cable TV saw several small local operators set up shop in each locality, using the relatively cheaper co-axial overground cables to transmit the signal from their control rooms to individual homes. Subsequently, the entry of major business houses like Hindujas, Zee TV's delivery-services arm, Siticable, RPG and Rahejas as leading players in the media distribution sector have seen attempts to upgrade to the more efficient but expensive fibre-optic technology. Bearing out the lucrative possibilities in the cable industry, the entry of the big business houses into the distribution sector has impacted upon the pace of developments, enabling increased connectivity, consolidation of existing networks and major changes in the relationships between broadcasting companies and viewers. But with the prospect of providing telecommunication, commercial and banking services through cable networks, it is evident that the scale of changes is not limited to the business landscape within a single industry. The major players in the Indian industry evidently realise this and, having staked out their claims in the larger cities, they are now making concerted attempts to establish control over the markets for cable TV audiences in the provincial urban centres. The recent cable wars in the Western region show that the intense competition among these large cable companies (MSOs or Multi-System Operators) for control over larger and larger territories is now spilling over into the smaller cities.[43]

The battle to control the new electronic media exemplifies one of the key sites through which the changing nature of state-society relations in the post-economic reforms period in India can be analysed, but few such systematic attempts have been made. The ongoing consolidation within the industry has been accompanied by high levels of volatility, seen equally in the all-too-common allegations of the use of force between rival companies and operators, as well as in the high rate of mergers and acquisitions observed at different levels within the cable business. Generally speaking, this volatility stems from the fast pace at which cable networks have expanded and the fact that the entry of foreign satellite TV and the growth of the cable industry have occurred in an almost completely unregulated fashion. Similar arguments about the absence of norms and the need for regulation are frequently used by the MSOs, while placing all blame for alleged unruliness squarely on the smaller operators, their local franchisees. However, it remains equally true that because of the size of their operations, especially in the unstable political conditions of the post-liberalisation period, the large cable distribution entities have been in a position to enjoy significant clout, by means of which they are able to lobby for congenial legislation at the national level. Moreover, in their quest to maximize their reach and control of the market, they are also wont to strike local deals with all manner of political bosses and power brokers. In other words, the extensive instability within the cable industry is related to the ways in which the new media technologies have been able to integrate communicative networks, local politics and power equations with the interests of big corporate houses.

The consolidation of cable networks through the entry of *desi* (indigenous/ NRI [Non-Resident Indian]) corporate houses like Essel's Siticable, Hinduja-owned IN Cablenet and the equally pugnacious Rahejas-promoted Hathway Datacom Ltd, have significantly altered ground-level equations between political bosses, local business persons and big enterprise, both in Mumbai and elsewhere. For, in addition to being scarcely regulated and allowing direct access to resident populations, the cash-rich nature of the cable business has been an obvious attraction to political bosses hoping to enhance their local influence. The high returns and intense rivalry between the large MSOs has often meant that they have been willing to take the help of underworld strongmen to establish their 'territorial rights'. Many such individuals have been appointed distributors for specific territories, resulting in the emergence of a new breed of entrepreneurs that include the relatively small number of local cable operators who now control cable transmission in each suburb. Such alliances between the world of big business, the underworld and local politics is not entirely new to Mumbai, but the very nature of cable distribution has enhanced the significance of the connection between large commercial stakes and territorial control. This scenario has led either to enhanced control for existing political leaders or, in other instances, to shifts in the distribution and bases of local power networks. For instance, in one Mumbai suburb, I was told that the small group of eight cable operators who now survive in the locality were all friends at a local school where they knew the son of a popular local *Shiv Sena* leader who had recently made it big in city circles. All this has obvious implications for the changing nature of today's public sphere and the shifts in emphases within contemporary political discourse.

5. The Changing Face of Cable TV in Bombay

Around the time CNNI first came to India in 1992, cable operations mush-roomed as a cottage industry within urban neighbourhoods. Given its cultural ethos, Mumbai could hardly have been an exception. It almost seemed that anyone who owned a VCR and had some spare time and funds in hand was willing to start single channel networks for a handful of subscribers, who were usually residents within the same housing complex or the adjoining slum. Belonging as they did to quite poor neighbourhoods, often their only claim to entrepreneurship was their driving compulsion to earn a little income from the few extra resources they may have had in comparison to nearby residents. However, cable TV was clearly lucrative because it was capable of attracting a potential audience from households across the socio-economic spectrum.

Since its arrival, the cable TV scenario in Mumbai has changed dramati-cally within the space of just a few years. To begin with, those who had been in the video rental business were easily attracted to the business opportunities presented by cable TV. As one operator who has survived in the business put it, the idea came to him when he started renting out his VCR to recover the cost of the hired cassettes his family watched at home – the first cable chan-nel was a way of seeing films and also showing them to a few others in the zopadpatti (slum) where they lived.[44] The idea evidently caught on among mid-dle class youth too: as another operator admitted, he first thought of it in col-lege because it would be frequently talked about in the group he hung out with at the tuition classes he attended.[45] When CNNI and the other foreign channels started beaming into India on a free-to-air basis, the prospects seemed attractive enough for many of them to invest in a dish antenna and other cable equipment to track and distribute signals. At that point, the costs involved were between Rs 70,000–100,000, which had to be raised from pri-vate sources, as no banks were willing to advance loans to aspiring cable busi-nesses. Almost all the cable operators who started out around 1992 were men in their late twenties or so, with little previous technical training or skills. But many of those who have lasted as independent operators today are the smaller number who came from families that owned other local businesses or retail outlets or, at least, had the wherewithal to capitalise on their close per-sonal ties with 'leading' local families and persons with political connections. The growth of cable services after 1992 produced a new crop of neighbour-hood operators who quickly grew in confidence on account of the incentive of quick returns through their minute knowledge of the locality, its layout and informational networks, in which they worked. At this stage, most operators charged an average of between Rs 40–60 per month per connection. Collections may have been somewhat irregular, yet operations evidently generated attractive monthly returns, mostly in cash payments, with enough scope for servicing undeclared points that brought in untaxed income. The industry grapevine abounds with stories about the flashy ways of this set of young, newly moneyed operators who made good, despite little or no formal education or training of any kind.

But as the number of channels increased, larger distribution companies with the funds to invest in more centralised operations that could cover wider areas began to move in. They were helped by their ability to negotiate deals with broadcasting entities that had bigger audience-reach than that which the average neighbourhood operator could service. These changes occurred from around 1995 onwards. Alongside the entry of the big corporate houses into the cable market, the Cable Regulation Act was also passed in 1995. This made it obligatory for cable operators to register themselves at the local post office and pay a fixed tax of Rs15 per subscription point per month. Aiming to move operations to an altogether different scale, the MSOs began by taking over small 'patches', with the aim of eventually controlling operations over large territories. This set in motion a whole raft of changes that for the first time unravelled for Indian audiences the organisational logics and principles implied and assumed by commercial private broadcasting. Since 1995, the cost of monthly subscriptions has gone up. In mid 1998, most local operators in Mumbai showed between 40 and 46 channels, out of which between 10 and 13 were pay channels. Their monthly charges were around Rs 125–150 for middle class localities and about Rs 70–80 in the poorer neighbourhoods. Out of this, most operators pay about Rs 30 to the MSO and Rs 15 as entertainment tax per (declared) point on a monthly basis.

In many Mumbai suburbs, as elsewhere, local operations are often dominated by relatives or cohorts of political bosses or MLAs in the area, or state or central ministers. With some of these businesses extending to several thousand points, the impunity with which important local operators adopt strong-arm tactics is often directly proportionate to the 'strength' of their respective political connections. As one of my informants candidly admitted, the son of a prominent Sena leader in the Dahisar area was in the cable business to nurse his political ambitions.[46] Besides, he went on, a second son was a well-established builder (once again pointing to the affinity between control over the real-estate and cable-distribution markets) and the family owned several other businesses. Therefore, my informant rationalised, money could not have been the main reason. Rather, cable operations was a good way to get popular and establish a good reputation among the local people, which was why the aspiring leader combined the cable business with his *samaj seva* (social service) – like securing school admissions, finding jobs or intervening to remove bureaucratic delays. Such claims of 'public-spiritedness' notwithstanding, given the scale of income generation enabled by dominance over densely populated resident colonies, it is not just idle speculation to say that many operators, if not directly related to local political leaders, are simply 'front men' managing these areas as 'collection fiefdoms'.

Many such operators have benefited enormously from the bargain, earning enough to invest some of their own earnings into smaller cable businesses or in other enterprises elsewhere. With operations of this size, local operators with some political clout may also subcontract parts of 'their' territory to former colleagues servicing the area, who now survive as subordinates taking their signals from the local 'cable boss' for a fixed fee per point. Needless to say, an important attraction in this arrangement is that these points that are thus leased out remain undeclared for the purposes of tax or other payments. Covering large territories, it is not surprising that the major operators also develop a good understanding with the local police. Many of them talk quite willingly about their regular contact and cordial relations with the local police station, often disclosing with some pride that their signals are received in the local DSP's office and also that as a measure of their 'goodwill', they run public service announcements about law and order or essential services at the request of the police, free of cost.[47]

With broadcasting companies, delivery systems (MSOs) and local distributors/operators emerging as the three tiers in the transmission link, the stage was set for a power struggle between each of these groups as they sought to manoeuvre themselves into the most favourable position to maximize potential control over operations and collections. This scenario has only been aggravated by the fact that operations have been allowed to proceed largely with few formal rules and codes. Developments since then have mostly cohered around tensions between these three groups over the all-important factors of reach and revenue share. Broadly, these can be divided into conflicts between broadcasters and MSOs on the one hand, and MSOs and their local distributors and franchisees on the other. Within this general framework, the design of MSOs has been to manoeuvre towards a monopolistic control over 'their' territories wherever possible. Industry bosses are agreed that the future of the broadcasting and large distribution companies lies in advancing this commercial logic; in turn, increasing profits would be largely dependent on bringing in a pay-per-view structure. Keeping a tab on the precise number of connections is a key issue and, not surprisingly, the main bone of contention has been the need to introduce technical and legislative means that would force local operators to fully declare their subscriber base.

6. MSO Strategies and Cable Operators

It is estimated that cable and satellite TV reaches about 3 million households in Bombay. The competition between the three large cable companies in

Mumbai has been intense. Both Siticable and the Hinduja-owned IN Cablenet entered the cable market in the city in late 1995. The Rahejas-controlled Hathway Cable and Datacom was the third major entrant. Starting off as builders, the Rahejas now have a serious investment interest in current media technologies and aim to become national players in these fields. Besides these, three partners of IN Cablenet's founders who broke away in late June 1999 have recently floated a fourth cable distribution entity in Mumbai, Win Cable and Datacom.[48] Despite evident signs of consolidation and ruthless competition, local cable operators continue to work on an informal basis. Undoubtedly, urban congestion and the difficulties of technical monitoring are contributory factors. Reliable estimates of reach and market share are therefore hard to come by in the cable distribution business. For all practical purposes, both companies and local operators seem to work with two parallel sets of claimed figures: subscriber bases are inflated for publicity purposes and for the benefit of advertisers, but as far as concerns bargaining over dues either with government agencies or broadcasting entities, declared connectivity tends to be grossly underplayed.

Even so, by conservative estimates, Mumbai was thought to have about 1500 cable operators in May 1999, out of which 75–80 per cent were affili-ated with IN Cablenet, 16–18 per cent with Hathway and 4–7 per cent with Siticable. ISiti's influence is mainly restricted to the suburbs of Kurla, Ghatkopar and Thane areas among the suburbs along the Central local rail-way line, and Borivili in the Western suburbs. On the other hand, Hathway boast of their sole dominance in the important South Mumbai segments of Churchgate, Nariman Point and Colaba. Besides this, they have carved a size-able presence in the central suburbs through the merger with a major operator, Sri Bhavani of Chembur. In the Western suburbs, Hathway claim to control an important chunk of the market in Mahim and Matunga and now with their recent strategic alliance with Kohli's Win Cable, Hathway is seeking to increase its hold in the adjoining Western suburbs of Bandra, Khar and Santacruz. Capitalising on the major involvement of the parent company, Raheja Builders, in real estate development in Mumbai, and using their detailed knowledge of local networks to pursue a policy of strategic alliances, Hathway have emerged as a powerful rival to the Hinduja cable company in Mumbai.

Starting operations from their main headquarters in Charni Road in South Mumbai, IN Cablenet had rapidly built up a powerful presence mainly in the Western suburbs all the way to Andheri East – the location of their present headquarters – through an aggressive policy that combined buying out oper-ators to establish direct control over strategic patches, with pressurising or persuading them to become affiliates and franchisees who then took signals from the IN Cablenet control rooms. As company officials admit, in other cities IN Network has gone in for joint ventures, but in Mumbai the preferred strategy was to work out a franchisee system. A common feed went out through the IN Cablenet trunk lines running through the 16 relay stations or company control rooms established in the city, along which they have arrangements with franchisee operators. In an attempt to get a head start over their rivals, the Hindujas are said to have delved deep into their pockets to pay sums varying from Rs 500 to Rs 5000 per point, depending on the profile of the locality, building up a total network of more than 1½ million homes in Mumbai. This aggressive takeover strategy was dictated by the aspiration to get ahead in the race to upgrade the entire network to fibre-optic cables, a technical necessity for the launch of DTH (Direct-to-Home) and Internet telephony, and other related commercial services like tele-shopping via the cable networks. On the other hand, Siticable and Hathway have not attempted to buy out local operators, preferring to work out partnership arrangements with local operators to receive signals from their respective control rooms in exchange for fixed monthly payments.

7. MSO-Franchisee Tensions: Upheavals Over Pay-TV

In retrospect, company spokespersons admit that the strategy of buying out operators through outright cash payments in a bid to establish direct control may not have been very prudent.[49] It was particularly unwise given that local operators frequently signed contracts to make over a certain number of points, but in the absence of any means for the company to verify the claimed subscription base or the actual number of points sold, the former retained control over all or a good portion of the network. Allegations that large revenues collected by ground-level operators do not reach the MSO are only too common in the cable business. The recent FIR filed by IN Cablenet against its erstwhile Presidents, Kohli and Radhakrishnan, who have now formed independent operations through Win Cable, testifies to the widespread nature of such practices in the industry. Such manoeuvres by the big cable companies to capture the market obviously affected the interests of the numerous local operators who had been around since the early 1990s. Unsurprisingly, there have been counter-moves to resist the advances towards consolidation and control. As rising levels of investment and competition from the big companies have pushed many operators out of the business, local operators in many parts of the country organised themselves to form pressure groups and even cooperatives at the local and regional level.[50] Today, local operations in many of the city suburbs are divided between an average of 8–10 operators, showing that an intermediate level of consolidation has been reached. Now the fight is really about control over profits between the MSOs and these reasonably well-established local players.

In order to establish themselves in the Indian market, all the channels initially beamed on a free-to-air basis. But by mid 1998, that had begun to change. Claiming that the present 30:70 ratio of the revenues from subscription to advertisements available to broadcasting companies operating in India (apparently the exact reverse of these figures is true for most Western countries) was economically unviable, many foreign channels, starting with STAR Sports in March 1998, followed by Discovery, ESPN National Geographic, Sony's AXN and others, decided to 'go pay'. This meant that the channel signals would now be encrypted and need to be decoded separately by the cable operator before they could be transmitted, in principle only to those homes that paid a monthly fee per pay channel, collectible through the cable operator. This was a clear signal, if any were needed, that media companies were gearing up to exploit the full potential of privatised commercial television in India. The two ways currently available to regulate the reception of satellite broadcasts are direct-to-home (DTH) transmission through an expensive individualised domestic dish antenna and decoder, or the introduction of set-top boxes in each cable home. In the industry jargon, these changes towards a more transparent subscriber base fall under the term of 'addressibility', for which all the big media firms and large distribution entities have been arduously advocating and lobbying. Such mechanisms would allow the exact number of home connections for each channel to be centrally monitored, so that access can be regulated strictly according to payment. However, the scheme to bring in the pay TV regime has so far enjoyed only a limited success. Since June 2000, many of these channels have gone pay; the full Zee bouquet of 11 channels was priced at Rs 35 a month ; the full STAR package was available for a monthly charge of Rs 30; ESPN and Star Sports cost Rs16 a month, and SONY had announced their package of four channels, and that AXN and CNBC would cost Rs 22 per month. And yet, these moves had not brought in the desired increases in collections. In early December 2001, STAR was reportedly in talks with MSOs to cut subscription rates in a move to optimise revenues.[51] Given that these firms have been primarily busy in rapidly expanding their connectivity in congested urban neighbourhoods, it has been difficult to establish a system of access against payment for each channel. Most customers may pay the increased subscription costs as more and more channels go pay. But in the case of already-existing connections, the local operator has as yet no means of stopping transmission to those who may prefer to continue watching while refusing to pay the increased charges.

This state of affairs has led to tensions and frequent confrontations between pay channel broadcasters and MSOs on the one hand, and a hostile campaign by MSOs against 'cunning' and 'unscrupulous' cable operators on the other. For instance, describing the 'sinister design' of the foreign channels to charge for transmissions that were initially offered free of cost, an IN Cablenet press release in May 1999 bewailed the 'plight' of the 'harried MSOs caught between the irate viewer and Shylock-like grip of the pay channels' as 'close to bankruptcy'.[52] Whatever the veracity of the above claims, what the statement makes clear – and as other industry sources corroborate – at stake in the fight between the MSOs and pay channels are issues of revenue and profit-sharing and the pressure to secure exclusive broadcasting contracts.

8. New Media Networks and the Limits of Civility

The turbulent turn of events at IN Cablenet which saw the murder of one of their directors, Mr Punjabi, in September 1998[53] and the acrimonious exit of the erstwhile president, Jagjit Singh Kohli, and two other partners Yogesh Shah and Yogesh Radhakrishnan in June 1999[54] are but two instances of the unruly scenario that prevails in the media distribution industry. In the latter instance, the trouble apparently started around the time IN Cablenet had to renew its contract with the ESPN distributor for India, Modi Entertainment Network (MEN) in March–April 1999. It seems that, despite merging their previous company with the Hinduja media company in 1994, Kohli and the other partners had continued to hold stakes in parallel enterprises alongside their positions within IN Cablenet. The Hindujas had entered the market with the claim that they intended to give cable operations a truly corporate identity. But in the bid to establish themselves, they found that they had to rely on the men who had been inducted – presumably on account of their reputedly formidable ground-level contacts. In a bid to gain an advantage over rival MSOs, the Hinduja management was apparently exerting pressure on MEN to sign an exclusive contract with IN Cablenet for distribution rights over Mumbai. As it turned out, MEN did not renew its contract with IN Cablenet at that point but chose to do a deal with Encore Electronics Ltd, the company jointly promoted by Kohli, Shah and Radhakrishnan, who then chose to sign a deal between IN Cablenet and Encore for the ESPN signals. Angry with these moves, the Hinduja management apparently asked the trio to leave; the three then lost no time in using their contacts to form a rival distribution entity, Win Cable and Datacom. It seems that IN Cablenet subsequently wrote to MEN on May 1 1999 unilaterally signing an agreement for ESPN. This has not been the only instance of such quarrels between pay channels and MSOs where, after initial resistance, the latter have agreed to increased charges by the pay channels.

Clearly, conditions in industry dealings border on the rapacious. It is not entirely coincidental that attempts to hasten the Indian TV scene closer to addressibility and the pay regime by expanding the fibre-optic network and paring operational costs have led to major upheavals in the newly privatised television industry, including the abovementioned murder of one of the IN Cablenet directors, Ram Punjabi. Mr Ram Punjabi was shot dead on the afternoon of 11 September 1998 as he was leaving his home in the Andheri area of Mumbai. As insiders will corroborate, this incident was hardly a unique case of violence in the cable industry, yet the seniority of the victim's position in this instance shows the serious conflicts caused by company policy and/or prevailing business practices. Immediate reports suggested that the crime was a *supari* killing (the slang term for underworld deals with hired assassins) related to the problem of extortion in the cable business and that the hired gunmen belonged to the Arun Gawli gang.[55] Police statements in subsequent reports suggested that the attack was related to Punjabi's efforts to rapidly expand the Hinduja network and simultaneously to upgrade it to fibre-optic cables, a project that evidently affected the interests of many smaller distributors who would suffer huge losses on account of the consolidation. With large cable networks emerging as the turf for a power struggle over revenue shares between political bosses, MSO officials, broadcasting entities, distributors, police, underworld operators (or *bhai log*, as they are known in local parlance) and government officials, it is unlikely that the exact combination of powerful interests behind the Punjabi murder will ever be clearly established. But this much remains incontestable: that the quest for consolidating revenues to be earned from broadcasting and distribution rights over larger and larger territories has intensified rivalries between contending parties. It is quite tenable to conclude that the arrival of new media technologies in India and their instant commercialisation has abetted an increase in the use of criminal means for economic control over the public sphere.

At another level, it was comparable pressure to consolidate business interests through creating larger and larger media networks that brought STAR and Zee to the negotiating table.[56] This occurred at a time when the government seemed poised to reconsider its ban on the launching of DTH services in India. Without suggesting any direct links between the two sets of events described above, it is at least significant that their timing overlapped closely, and that the underlying train of these developments stemmed from related industry conditions and the pressure to introduce addressibility and maximise profits. STAR TV was keen to be the first broadcasting entity to launch DTH services, but its attempt to do so in March 1997 failed. STAR TV had been looking for ways to reduce operational costs, reputedly on account of the pressure on Murdoch's investments in China and India. STAR and Zee already had a complicated web of alliances through their joint holdings in Siticable and Asia Television Ltd (ATL). But from late July 1998, reports began to appear that the two entities were moving closer to discussion of a possible merger of their interests and assets.[57]

By mid-September, firm plans were reported for the two sets of companies to merge, in order to create a new media conglomerate which would own at least seven channels in India, in addition to software production capabilities, advertising and marketing arms, as well as a cable distribution network in the major Indian cities through Siticable, a presence in the UK, USA and Africa through the Zee channels and in Europe through Zee Multimedia. If it had taken place, such a merger would have undoubtedly reduced competition, consolidated advertising revenues, rationalised operational costs and through these savings, as Vijay Zindal, the then CEO of Zee Telefilms observed, 'would have laid the foundation of pay TV in India'.[58]

At first glance, such corporate mergers between transnational entities may appear separated by a huge distance from the murky underside of ground-level interfaces that the cable TV networks are seen to depend upon. And yet, as the cable distribution industry has shown, what is common to current developments at both these levels is the operative belief that the protection of business interests and the 'rights' to distribute services has everything to do with the elimination of competition. It is arguable that the volatility within the industry, both on the ground and in its corporate organisation, simply mirrors this staunch belief in the efficacy of capitalist integration. Indeed, industry executives are aware that the problems in the industry are a result of the attempts to integrate local and big business interests through the new media networks. They admit there has been resistance from the 'unorganised' sectors, which has caused problems in appointing and formalising arrangements with distributors. For instance, acknowledging that there existed what he termed a 'social unrest' problem that people in the industry had to contend with, a top MSO executive attributed this problem to the 'huge gap' between corporate culture and the cultural backgrounds of franchisees and 'their style of operation'. He felt this would need to be resolved, and his company was looking into ways through which the 'tie culture could be made to gel with the style of local politics'.

9. Conclusion

This essay has tried to describe the conditions under which media audiences in India have expanded. Developments since the 1980s have accentuated the way in which increased audience sizes have been a function of a capitalist-democratic expansion, and of the growing complexities of the intersections between the formal and parallel sectors of the economy. The circumstances sketched out here serve as an important perspective towards understanding the increasing ideological volatility of the Indian public sphere in recent times, marked as it has been by a growing intolerance towards minority and dissenting or marginal points of view.

5

THE POLITICAL ECONOMY OF URBAN PLANNING THE CASE STUDY OF BOMBAY

Bhavana Padiyath

This essay examines the dynamics of development and growth in post-Independence Bombay.[1] It examines the manner and extent to which the Indian planning enterprise has been implicated in the wider domain of societal 'structures'[2] within which the state apparatus operates, and outlines the analytical grid within which Indian development planning ought to be located. It situates the dynamics at work within an active geographical arena, pertinent to a particular set of people in a particular place – in this case, the country's largest urban enclave.

1. Urban Development Planning : The Indian Context

Planning, here, is contextualised as the Indian state's attempt to lay the groundwork for capitalist growth and enhancement. The Bombay Plan of 1944, promulgated by eight prominent captains of industry, unequivocally viewed the strategic control of the key sectors of the economy by the public sector as an essential means to the primary accumulation of capital.[3] Cooperating with the state in this project has been the 'modern' sector, comprising the industrial and commercial bourgeoisie, the landholding classes, and the whole panoply of professional, service and small-scale sectors within the domain of industrial production and the reach of its markets.

Functionalist readings of the Indian state regard it, variously, as a neutral entity providing a socialist, 'developmentalist' impetus in its role as central allocator, or (in Miliband's sense of the term)[4] as a willing 'instrument' of class rule. The Rudolphs' Weberian notion posits the view of a technocratic 'self-determining' state, as does the neoliberal 'dogmatic *dirigisme*' model.[5] The latter was intended to invoke a simple contrast between the growth experiences of South Korea and India in a hard sell of the East Asian 'miracle' – a distinction perhaps too informed by a liberal economist's view of the relative success of each.

A contending – perhaps, more influential – formulation has been Pranab Bardhan's view of the Indian state as a handmaiden of dominant interest groups.[6] Such an approach too easily assumes a monolithic conceptualisation of the 'proprietory classes', ignoring the complexity of class structure in the countryside and the fractious nature of the urban bourgeoisie.[7] In the urban context, this approach is dismissive of the role of small industry and unionised labour in shaping the trajectory of India's capitalist development. Recent political economy literature provides a more nuanced perspective on the relationship between private interests and public policy in the context of Indian planning. It draws attention to the contradictions of state and class as they relate to accumulation and its sources.[8]

2. The Indian State and the Role of Planning

The crises of legitimacy and credibility faced by the Indian state – and by most post-colonial regimes – derive, as Hawthorn identifies,[9] from its incapacity to reconcile imaginatively 'in unpropitious conditions' the seemingly incompatible objectives of the developing world's political project: first, to establish a claim to political authority, and secondly, to achieve economic development. Planning must be regarded not only in terms of the latter, i.e. economic growth, but also in terms of the modalities of the claims to legitimacy established by the nascent nation state.

If we recognise that the administrative, judicial and law-enforcing apparatuses in the post-colonial Indian state were an almost undisturbed colonial legacy; if we recognise, that is to say, that the Congress regime's 'developmental' agenda 'on behalf of' the nation was, arguably, as vital as electoral sanction to its attempts to demarcate its representative status from that of its predecessor, it is only then that we are able to apprehend the planning process in terms of the problematic precepts of the Indian democratic idea. These precepts were confounded in actual practice by the system of single-party dominance. The Nehruvian tightrope act had sought to balance a Fabian agenda of redistributive growth with a charter of liberal fundamental rights that included property rights. The precariousness of the industry-agriculture compromise within the 'modern' sector, and the doctrinal struggles within Congress, led Nehru to invest faith in the Planning Commission, a technocracy formally situated outside the ruthless, restless terrain of procedural politics. Development planning, as an outcome of power struggles within the governing coalition, was, to invoke Poulantzas's phrase, part of the effort to 'prevent the social formation from bursting apart'.[10] It was also an instrument of power, serviceable in versatile ways.

As the Hegelian embodiment of a universal rationality overriding particular interests, the planning project has been invoked to legitimise the Indian state's 'socialist' ideology; and indeed its practices have increasingly tended towards the officious and the coercive. It has also proven expedient, in Chatterjee's Gramscian reading,[11] to interests in the 'modern' sector in transferring to the state the costs of constructing capital's 'hegemony' and maintaining its cohesion. As the state has attempted to appease entrenched feudal structures hostile to the capitalist agenda through 'demand' and 'vote bank' politics entailing the ad hoc division of political and economic spoils, it has had to come to terms with the dilution of its own autonomy.

The exigencies of synthesising the objectives of accumulation and legitimation have seen the Indian state in diverse contexts. To varying degrees it has served socialist interests in marshalling the economy's 'commanding heights', both conceding to the insistent demands of private capital, and gratifying its own need, as Byres recognises, 'to be reproduced as a system of political domination'.[12] It is within such a matrix that sites the state, in its institutional aggregate, within the scaffold of a social formation whose logic, contradictions and idiosyncrasies it can ill afford to ignore, that I seek to look at the unique pattern of concentrated growth in Bombay – the world's third most populous city. I take as my point of departure the built environment, and the manner in which it has both emerged from, and mediates between, the constitutive relations among social groups.

3. Bombay: Land, Population and Housing

India's industrial and commercial capital,[13] with a population of nearly 15 million, Bombay is also the country's largest urban enclave and capital of Maharashtra, its most industrialised and urbanised state. With its strong entrepreneurial ethos and a heavily migrant community,[14] post-Independence Bombay has been an island of corporatist *douceur de vivre* in what was, until not long ago, a sea of planned state intervention. The city has also been the scene of the most vocal articulations of working class resistance over the 150-year history of industrial capitalism in India.[15]

Over the past five decades, the rapid expansion in Bombay's scale and density, and the negligible investment in its built environment, have engendered new and fierce antagonisms related to control over the city's resources. The acute pressures on land – both as a means of production and a prime consumer good in short supply – and the scarcity in housing, have put real estate prices in the city beyond the reach of most citizens. A speculative and volatile property market has escalated residential and commercial property prices, in absolute terms, to levels surpassed only in Tokyo and central London.[16]

Over 60 per cent of Bombay's population – around six and a half million people – live in shanties on public and private land. Surveys indicate that approximately 50 per cent of these slum and pavement dwellers live below the official 'poverty line',[17] while a sizeable portion of the rest comprise blue-collar workers and a disaffected petit bourgeoisie – Breman's 'penny capitalists'[18] – who find the costs of regular housing too prohibitive, despite easily qualifying as middle class in other Indian towns. Until 1995, most of these people were designated 'encroachers', and continue to be denied title to their plots and forbidden access to municipal conservancy services.

The endemic collision between the dynamic capitalist core and the large concentrations of 'others' at the periphery has enhanced the search for the social cogency provided by cultural identity by and for Bombay's constituent communities. This has sharpened the competitive edges of the socio-economic framework in communal terms. Collective action, as a result, has been most effective when most particular and parochial in its concerns, and when the cosmopolitan spaces in politics have been drastically circumscribed. The rise and consolidation of the *Shiv Sena*, with its provocative and exclusionary rhetoric, attests to this potential in the politics of urban India.

The restricted supply of real estate in Bombay relates both to the city's peculiar geography, and its history of segmentation dating back to the colonial era.[19] Hemmed in by the Arabian Sea on the west and the Thane creek on the east, Greater Bombay, comprising the old island-city and its suburbs, is a peninsular strip of land measuring 438 square kilometres. Since the eighteenth century, after the city was built as a fort, the colonial state appropriated land from the indigenous population and enforced distinct settlement patterns, with British and Indian merchants occupying its south and north sections, relegating the 'natives' to outside its ramparts. Two subsequent surveys in the nineteenth century were designed to demarcate clear titles to the land for the collection of rent meant to accrue to the East India Company. The subsequent design of the city's expansion was oriented by this stratification based on race, class and caste determinants.[20]

Most planning interventions in the twentieth century, including the Town Planning Act of 1915 and the construction of the 'central' business district of Nariman Point, have concentrated population and services in the southernmost part of the island-city. This is a 30-degree peninsular wedge where the spatial concentration of population and services is particularly acute. The commercial and residential real estate markets are patterned in a geographical sense, becoming progressively less expensive in the northward direction. The city is served by two arterial roads and the Western and Central rail corridors,

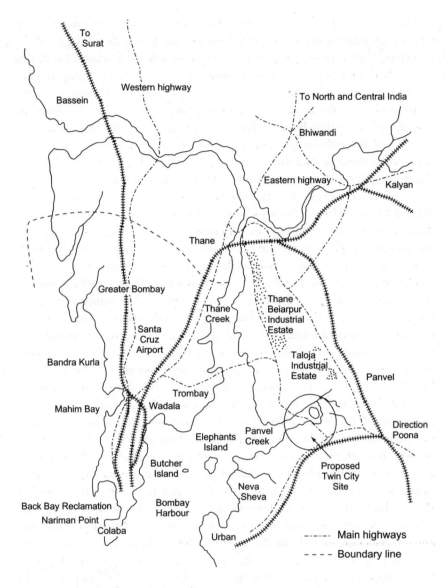

in addition to a third across the Thane Creek, that links the city to its vast geographical hinterland. Development has stretched linearly to dormitory townships on the mainland, so that commuting times are increasingly extended. The built environment, or what David Harvey calls 'created space',[21] incorporates both the neutral, unbounded physical space in which the engineer and planner typically work, and highly personalised, contested social space, where individuals, groups and organisations jostle and bargain to attain a reasonable degree of purchase upon the prevailing social order.

The 'creation' of space is a multidimensional process. In part, it is an outcome of institutional stances inscribed with the prevalent ideologies of the governing elite. In part, it is patterned by the dynamics of market forces that can easily produce results that are unanticipated and/or undesirable. In part, it reflects the extent to which popular pressures mandate and revise the terms and agendas of official discourse and structure attention in that direction. The spatial form that Bombay has assumed 'contains' all these social processes: and the policies and administrative strategies that have yielded the city's problematic development trajectory have been embedded in a mesh of dense and pervasive power relations. This is generally true of any planning exercise in any milieu. Institutional partisanship, alone, therefore, cannot explain the singularity of Bombay's socio-economic landscape in terms of the distributional disparity in land use, housing, transportation, spheres of production, information access and social stratification;[22] nor can it adequately account for the acrimonious politics that the process has engendered.

The answers lie in Bombay's role as a national metropolitan enclave encapsulated in a regional political system. On the one hand, with a vast economic hinterland that has traditionally surpassed much of Maharashtra's – even India's – geographical area, Bombay played a pivotal role in enabling the integration and consolidation of the domestic market as a national project, assigning national roles to its commercial and industrial bourgeoisie. On the other, the constellation of Bombay's political structures failed to articulate with the 'Congress system' at regional and national levels. In Maharashtra, the 'rural-urban' divide had been introduced fairly early into the political lexicon by the non-Maharashtrian capitalist class. The rift between the rich and medium peasantry of the intermediary Maratha caste and the non-Marathi capitalists (who had close commercial links with local capital in rural Maharashtra) threatened to split the party during the late 1950s, which saw vociferous demands for a separate Marathi-speaking state. The real trophy was Bombay, which the national Congress leadership was initially reluctant to cede to the proposed linguistic province. The central leadership finally buckled, expending great efforts to convince the Bombay-based financial and commercial interests that their stakes would not be undermined by the Maratha kulak leadership, who possessed very tenuous links to the capital city.

The two factions within the Congress were separately institutionalised as a compromise formula after Maharashtra was carved out of the erstwhile Bombay province in 1960. The Congress central leadership has to this day struggled to maintain the delicate rapprochement between the Maratha landed aristocracy in the Maharashtra Pradesh Congress Committee and the Gujarati-Marwari axis in the Bombay Pradesh Congress Committee, which continues to be a crucial source of party funding. Maharashtra, in 1960, accounted for 16.58 per cent of India's industrial output.[23] Half these industries and two-thirds of the state's industrial labour force were located in the Bombay Metropolitan Region (BMR)[24] – a 4,355 sq. km. area which, in addition to Greater Bombay, comprises 3 medium towns, 16 small towns, 7 urban centres and 995 villages. Since the 1870s, the wealthy Bombay Municipal Corporation had been the only civic body in the country with autonomous administrative powers. After the formation of Maharashtra state, these were severely circumscribed, and since then there have been rival axes of power for the city's control and management at the local and regional levels. While Bombay was meant to enable Maharashtra to actualise its growth potential, the city's local Congress structure, which derived its power and resources through its intimate connections with big business, had little clout in state politics.

To what extent, and in what manner, has Bombay's role as a national metropolitan enclave, orbited by a regional political system, influenced the urban planning enterprise? How has the territorial overlap of actors and institutions in the local, regional and national domains influenced the various agendas at work and profited from the asymmetrical structuring of social space in the city? This study attempts to untangle the multifarious strands of operation in each of these tiers through a focus on the city's land use policy in general, and the housing question in particular. A consciously contextual approach, it is hoped, will afford a basis upon which to challenge broad structural and game-theoretical explanations that consider local power structures and processes to be isomorphic with those at regional or national level, and attempts to impute overlapping agendas to a spectrum of political, bureaucratic, and social actors.

Politics and the People of Bombay

The strategy of alleviating poverty through growth was the primary thrust of the national development effort.[25] As India's economic hub, Bombay attracted a disproportionate share of industrial capital during the rapid growth phase between 1951 and 1965 when the annual national growth rate averaged 7.7 per cent per annum. The 1966 recession tightened a highly competitive white-collar job market, leaving unrealised the heightened expectations which arose with the creation of a separate state. Migration to Bombay in the 1950s was around 600,000, rising substantially during the 1960s to 850,000. The city's infrastructure was already creaking under the assault by waves of rural migrants escaping their surplus-extracting overlords who were still untaxed by the state. In the absence of institutional interventions, problems pertaining to their shelter needs were being addressed in an ad hoc manner.

The freesing of rents at 1940 levels and the granting of hereditary tenancy rights served as disincentives to private landlords who had traditionally provided tenement housing for the city's industrial labour force. By the mid-1960s, over a million of the city's residents were clustered in slum or pavement dwellings. These were mainly situated in the northern suburbs, in areas unsuitable for habitation – marshlands, garbage dumps, hillsides, under high-tension electric cables – and had practically no access to even rudimentary water, drainage and transport infrastructure. New migrations were rapidly reshaping community politics. As the permanence of the settlement grew, what was once neutral, undemarcated space became the 'turf' where the inhabitants sought to assert ownership claims, landlords and the state entrenched their control through the allocation of services, and political intermediaries sought to garner capital by siphoning money and votes.

The Role of Ethnicity

By the mid-1960s, the Congress was in the throes of a painful realignment, occasioned by the leadership vacuum after Nehru's death and the growing unreliability of its customary consensus-maintaining mechanisms. The Communist Party of India's split in 1964, state repression through its paramilitary and legal arsenal (evident during the unsuccessful public sector strike in 1960) and the inadequacy of the traditional means of seeking redress were extremely disquieting, even for entrenched or established workers. A large segment of Marathi-speaking youth, seeking non-manual or clerical employment, found themselves unequipped with the technical or professional expertise to avail themselves of the opportunities in the expanding chemical, fertiliser, banking and insurance sectors. So one balmy evening in June 1966, when a political cartoonist called Bal Thackeray, at a speech in Shivaji Park, announced the creation of the *Shiv Sena* (Shivaji's Army),[26] to restore Maharashtra to the 'sons of the soil', the city's marginalised youth were immediately presented with a sense of mission.

The structural constraints imposed upon labour by economic and ethnic segmentation have been formidable. One of the earliest studies of the Bombay labour market established how important kinship, caste and village networks were as axes of solidarity and organisation in the urban system.[27] They alert people to employment opportunities, sustain them initially in their new urban milieus, and fashion distinctive neighbourhoods along caste, ethnic or religious lines. In addition, the dynamics of industrialisation itself, beginning in the colonial era, exacerbated competition within the workforce through the division of labour and the divergence of workers' interests.[28] The intersection of land and labour markets forged strong ethnic subcultures within the *chawls* (tenements) and *khanwals* (eating houses), and the neighbourhood, particularly of the textile workers, was often the arena where both solidarities of class action were articulated and rivalries of the workplace were exposed.[29] Politicians, employers and the state have often exploited and occasionally exacerbated these sectional differences.[30] The labour market was less stratified among the Marathi-speaking white collar segment and it was to this constituency that the Sena's claim was addressed. In the absence of a vanguard party, Bombay's political space has always been up for grabs, and the Sena has often stepped in with its parochial message.

The Rise of the 'Planning Authority'

Feeding into the ghetto-avoidance behaviour of the middle class and the prescriptive territoriality found among the city's rival communities, were various municipal policies, designed to establish a regulatory framework for the ordering and organisation of the city's geography. In the Third Five-Year Plan, the state enunciated its intention to regulate and rationalise land use in individual cities through town and country planning. The end of the Plan period saw a crisis in capital accumulation, and state action began to proceed in intrusive and extractive directions.

Political expediency cautioned against taxing agricultural incomes or implementing rural land reform. The regional state governments were therefore urged, as part of a 'radical policy' in urban management, to set up planning authorities to create and manage regions encompassing expanding metropolitan areas. Bombay's first statutory development plan, published in 1964, recorded existing land use in the city, earmarked areas to be reserved for public amenities like recreation areas, hospitals, schools and markets, and designated the acquisition procedures and financial resources to be employed for the purpose. The regional planning board, set up three years later, emerged with a broader, more structured initiative.

The state's intention to intensify surplus extraction from the urban areas was made explicit in the Fourth Plan. It urged 'self-financing' mechanisms for urban development and a review of legislation 'which may be indirectly, but unduly hindering the re-development of private land and property for more intensive and economic use'.[31] This was to be achieved by widening the tax base through the optimal social use of urban land. Accompanying this initiative was the rhetoric of urban decentralisation – a concession to various demand groups that held the state culpable for their unfulfilled agendas.[32] National and regional leaderships were increasingly engaged in animosities with local populations over metropolitan development, accentuating the already formidable problems of governance. On the one hand, the increasingly vocal and expanding agrarian bourgeoisie sought regional development through industrial relocation. On the other, the expanding base of middle class taxpayers was becoming restive about its unheeded concerns over degraded living environments, housing scarcity, transport congestion and crime, not to mention anxieties about an overly bureaucratised state and the increasing influence of capital.

The 'institutionalised self-interest' of the state in sustaining the process of accumulation sits uneasily with the need to gain mass electoral support.[33] The use of the state's own capabilities to secure compliance through its bureaucratic, administrative and coercive apparatuses are a function of this structural contradiction, compounded, in the Indian case, by the array of what Weber called 'status groups' inscribed into the state.[34] The strengthening of demand politics was a reflection of the weakening authority of the state vis-à-vis these groups, and its need to preserve the 'unity' of the modern sector.[35]

The BMR and Dispersal Policies

The Bombay Metropolitan Regional Development Authority's regional plan in 1973 set in motion a major initiative to disperse population and economic activities to new areas in the BMR. An industrial location policy, and the creation of the twin city of New Bombay on the mainland, were part of this project. The failure of decentralisation initiatives was largely a result of the schizophrenic practices adopted during the decade.

The proposal to develop the satellite township of New Bombay was meant to divert two million people who would have otherwise lived and worked in Bombay to the mainland through housing and employment infrastructure along carefully planned rail corridors. The City and Industrial Development Corporation – a public limited company – was assigned the task of developing the total plan area of 343 sq. km., of which nearly 60 per cent was to be amassed from private holdings. The developed plots were to be granted on a leasehold rather than ownership basis, a reflection of the government's interest in marshalling the entire process of urban growth from the actual takeover of land, to its sale and development, and its subsequent use. It also ensured a key role for the state as a player and speculator in the property markets, putting the available housing in New Bombay outside the reach of the lower and middle classes.

Three decades later, New Bombay has emerged as another dormitory suburb of the metropolis, having failed to attract a critical mass of employment centres.[36] The project to rehabilitate the agricultural communities displaced by the land acquisition process was abandoned in 1981. Keen to cling on to prime real estate in the island-city, the state demonstrated little inclination to disperse the concentration of public and semi-public land use to the new township. Private developers have now taken over to cater to the upper-class and NRI (non-resident Indian) segments. The Bombay Municipal Corporation's 1964 development plan had earlier suggested that an investment of Rs.70 million to reorganise the existing infrastructure and exploit the vast vacant areas in Greater Bombay[37] would have generated more effective results. The city's entrepreneurial classes, seeking greater room for expansion, and opposed to the idea of a development tax, vetoed the proposal.

While the New Bombay project extended the urban sprawl, the Backbay Reclamation Project accentuated the intensity of land use in the island-city. Responding to the demands for more space for commercial use and upper-class accommodation in the vicinity of the central business district, the state government sanctioned the dredging of earth from the seabed at the city's southernmost end.[38] Developed over two phases, the project resulted in extremely concentrated urban expansion, straining the existing transport and civic infrastructure, and increasing commuting costs. By 1978, 73 per cent of the Backbay Area was under commercial use; this proportion had risen to 80 per cent by 1992.[39]

On the one hand, the New Bombay project extended the scale of urban dispersal. On the other, the premium on proximity to the commercial and residential infrastructure in south Bombay increased the inelasticity of the land 'market', which was far from transparent and did not witness a confrontation of demand and supply in the classical sense. The city's uncontrolled real-estate speculation began in the 1970s, fusing the builder-politician combination of interests. By the early 1970s, the city's industrial expansion had also nearly ground to a halt through physical saturation, and consequently state restrictions on the expansion of existing operations were introduced. The 1973 Industrial Location Policy sought to relocate the manufacturing sector to other areas of the Bombay Metropolitan Region.[40] This dispersed the industrial labour force to the eastern and extended suburbs and beyond, with a commensurate effect on the spatial pattern of property values.

Muslim weavers – the first to be hit by the downsising in the textile industry – relocated to the powerloom sector in the urban hinterland. Their traditional working class neighbourhoods, like Nagpada, Mominpura, Pydhonie and Madanpura, had already begun to be transformed into localities of small entrepreneurs and traders, with families seeking to augment income through the opportunities in the growing West Asian labour market. Between 1957 and 1977, the share of the island city in Bombay's total industrial employment declined from 84.3 per cent to 74 per cent, and then to a further 47 per cent in 1984.[41]

Indian industrial expansion, predicated as it was upon rapid turnover in the face of volatile and shifting demand, depended inordinately on cheap labour for its competitive edge.[42] The search for new labour markets outside Greater Bombay's geographical limits was an important attempt by capital to reshape conditions in the existing market.[43] Militant trade union radicalism had forcefully reared its head in Bombay in the 1970s, spurred no doubt by the Communist victory in West Bengal.

The Progress of the Shiv Sena

The city's industrial elite sought in the *Shiv Sena*'s tutelage an instrument against mobilisations more Left-leaning than they would have liked. Since its inception, the party had set about building a cadre drawn along paramilitary lines from the ranks of the underworld, from which it derived its ability to unleash mob terror. Its attempts to establish a foothold in the city's trade union scene by dislodging the Communist unions involved tactics that were notoriously blunt.[44] The city Congress boss, SK Patil, was simply echoing the business community's sentiment when he suggested, 'Let Thackeray use his manpower and someone else's money for some appropriate cause.'[45]

The *Shiv Sena* had also essayed, since its very inception, consciously to insert itself into the social life of the community through its network of *shakhas* (branches), job bureaux and *mitra mandals* (friendship forums). These emphasise an anti-individualistic, masculine Marathi idiom, and are venues where sporting events and public festivals are organised, newspapers are read and discussed, 'justice' is summarily dispensed by petty gangsters, and genuine welfare services are administered. The *shakhas* generated a young and committed leadership cadre and served to mediate the interests of class, gender, occupation and ideology through the lens of ethnicity.

Shanties and Cartels

By 1976, 41 per cent of the city's residents lived in shanties, most with no land tenure and outside the purview of any legal entitlement.[46] This led to a concentration of degraded neighbourhoods with few civic amenities, where the parallel administration and services run by the *shakhas* lent agency to local politicians, bureaucrats, and *dadas* (big brothers), with their proclaimed links with underworld syndicates.

Bombay is a city that is basically frozen because of its land laws, development control rules and zoning regulations. The arresting of rents at 1940 rates created serious problems of under-investment in housing stock. The state had amassed wide and peremptory powers to acquire and redistribute land through the Land Acquisition Act, 1894, The Maharashtra Slum Areas

(Improvement, Clearance and Redevelopment Act) 1971, The Maharashtra Housing and Area Development Act, 1976, and the Urban Land (Ceiling and Regulation) Act (ULCRA), 1976. While the implementation of these enactments was decidedly half-hearted, they put in place a Kafkaesque maze of controls that dampened supply in the real estate market.

The ULCRA, in particular, was a powerful instrument used to pursue a variety of political ends. Brought into effect during the Emergency, it was supposed to ensure the socialisation of urban land to pre-empt its monopolisation by powerful interests. It was meant to co-opt the armies of dishoused urban poor affected by widespread slum demolition operations, as well as the agricultural lobby antagonised by the move to impose limits on the size of transactable plots in rural areas.[47] Bombay's landowners' and developers' cartels were not particularly perturbed by the statute as it was, in the words of Maharashtra's most senior bureaucrat at the time, 'one of Mrs. Gandhi's showpiece legislations, punctured with as many loopholes as were deemed necessary to be rendered ineffective.'[48]

As Przeworski observes in his analysis of institutional reform, 'When the relation of forces is known and uneven, the institutions are custom-made for a particular party, person or alliance.'[49] The outcomes, in this case, were controlled *ex post* and results determined *ex ante*. There were vaguely defined exemptions from acquisitions under sections 20 and 21 of the ULCRA: in the 'public interest', if it caused 'undue hardship to the owner', or if housing was developed for the 'weaker sections'. With its flexibility, the ULCRA appeared less draconian than the Central Land Acquisition Act of 1894, under which around 600 acres had been acquired by the state for housing the middle and lower-income sections.[50] Moreover, agricultural land within urban areas was given a blanket exemption, as was industry, whose requirements were deemed to serve the 'common good'. The ULCRA and its implementation fused the builder-politician nexus, spawning an industry in the provision of different forms of franchises to pre-empt, by different means, the attachment of assets by the state.

While the regulatory regime did not restrict the availability of land per se – 200 exemptions under the ULCRA were cleared by chief minister Sharad Pawar during 1979 and 1980 alone – it centralised power in the hands of the political and bureaucratic bosses. By the 1970s, the housing policy of the BMR required the construction of 60,000 units annually. The supply of formal housing by the public and private sectors was a meagre 20,600 units, leading to a shortfall of nearly 40,000 units per year.[51] This demand-supply disjunction has been attributed to the concentration of ownership among a tight cabal that ploughed a controlled trickle of land annually for 'redevelopment' for higher middle class housing or commercial use. In 1984, 27 trusts and individuals were believed to possess 70 per cent of all exploitable vacant lands in Greater Bombay.[52] 4.2 million people – 51 per cent of the city's population – thus found themselves priced out of the city's formal housing sector in 1981.

As the city grew increasingly unmanageable, both institutional strategies and the structures of local political participation were transformed. There also emerged new legitimacy concerns that frequently pushed the governing élites to craft new urban policy compromises. After the end of the 18-month textile strike of 1982–84, which cost 80,000 workers their jobs, the powers that be in the bureaucracy and the cabinet were talking of their 'serviceable' assets (land) totalling nearly 600 acres in the heart of the city that could be employed to ease the 'pressure' on the mills.[53]

Where desirable locations were not freed by the market, the state sought to secure them by directly evicting the poor to the unserviced periphery. In 1981, as the World Bank negotiated with the Maharashtra government to incorporate slum improvement projects as part of its loan agreement, chief minister Babasaheb Bhosale announced his intention to relocate pavement dwellers outside the city limits.[54] 10,000 people were sent 30 km away from the city centre, before the Bombay High Court intervened to prevent further evictions.[55]

The urban planning exercise, through its very function of generating situational advantages, is subservient to the market principle.[56] Both the state housing board's scheme for the 'economically weaker sections' and the World Bank-sponsored 'sites and services' project, have been shaped by the exigencies of the property market.[57] Poor communities were relocated from the island-city to outlying areas, away from nerve centres and arterial routes, and from one another. Thus isolated in discrete clusters, they become more amenable to political control.

Poverty is an outcome of a series of entitlement failures in terms of endowment, exchange, production and consumption that prevent people from securing their rights.[58] The failure of employment and residential opportunities to maintain an equilibrium, and the severe scarcities of critical services, have imposed greater accessibility costs on some groups in the population relative to others.[59] The effects of this polarisation have typically gone hand in hand with class, caste, religious and gender determinants, and have accentuated as the size of the urban system has increased. Members of the Scheduled Castes, for instance, who comprise 4.8 per cent of Bombay's population, account for 31.7 per cent of the city's slum dwellers and 20.4 per cent of its homeless people.[60]

These multiple exclusions are compounded by the additional investment required of low-income households to secure access to services, infrastructure and information. A survey of pavement dwellers in Bombay revealed that the effective price they paid for water was twenty times the municipal fee.[61]

The spatial concentration of upper-class residential areas and commercial areas has compressed the transport networks along selected corridors. Moreover, private sector involvement in the housing sector rose from 50 per cent in the 1960s to 90 per cent in the 1980s.[62] This was achieved through substantial subsidies, diverting institutional funds to private profiteering.[63] Much of the political activity in the city can be interpreted as the struggle for the control over the hidden mechanisms of redistribution of urban resources. The city's slum communities have been effectively excluded from the negotiating and bargaining game by institutional barriers and the manoeuvres of other, better organised groups. The only participative structures at their disposal have been political parties – each chasing its respective limits of caste, communal and regional support.

The Sena's adoption, in the mid-1980s, of the Bharatiya Janata Party's ideological stance, was a calculated response to the possibilities presented by militant Hinduism in extending its influence from regional to national politics.[64] The party's long reign in the country's wealthiest civic body – *kamadhenu* (cash cow) in bureaucratic parlance – provided it easy access to a barrage of contracts, rents and taxes when real estate rates were soaring. In a well-oiled collaboration with Congress bosses in the state government, the Sena party made a windfall, easing ceilings on various categories of lands under the ULCRA.

The ascendance of the trading and commercial classes, the power of construction cartels and a growing underworld, had transformed the texture of civil society in the city, always noted for the predatory nature of its business ethic. By the mid-1980s, senior Sena and Congress bosses like Manohar Joshi and Sharad Pawar (known as 'the builder's chief minister'[65]) had acquired heavy stakes in the real estate, hotel and film sectors, with links extending deep into criminality.

Land Policies and Political Manipulations

In its own interests, and in the interests of regional 'hegemonies' commanding local processes of social and economic production, the state has employed regulatory tools such as development plans and shelter programmes to support a discourse that legitimises the oblique operations of Bombay's property 'markets'. Development plans – defining urban physical and social infrastructure, and outlining its present and future use – have, in practice, emerged as promotional rather than technical documents subordinate to the interests of influential 'stakeholders'.

Bombay's first development plan had, in an elitist fervour, prescribed area ratios and density limits that took housing in the city out of the reach of the lower middle class and the poor.[66] The plan effectively froze 3,067 hectares of land in the city and suburbs (an area almost half the size of the island city) for public amenities till such time as the municipal corporation could find the resources to acquire it. These 'reservations' were arbitrarily drawn and selectively enforced.[67] The Congress government in the state, and the Sena-controlled BMC, set up procedures for a spoils-sharing system and a price for releasing some of these areas from the irksome reservations.[68]

The second Development Plan in the 1980s saw the public claims to services being completely subordinated to the ownership claims of a few. 1,000,000 sq. metres, or 1 per cent of the city's lands, were lost to public use when they were surreptitiously 'dereserved' on a piecemeal basis without public notification.[69] The spate of dereservations, by bending government norms, kept the bureaucratic machinery well-oiled. Sharad Pawar dexterously used his 'ten per cent' quota (available to the chief minister for distributing public land on a discretionary basis) to fix potential troublemakers – journalists, key bureaucrats, judges, political colleagues, opposition members.[70]

Also at play are the state's own resource and patronage interests. Citing the lack of resources, the municipal corporation has implemented a mere 15 per cent of the proposals drawn up so far.[71] The D'Souza Committee set up to review the Development Plan document had deemed the plan to be within the corporation's means.[72] While ignoring the city's vital needs, the civic body has increased the wages of its 149,000 strong workforce more than twice as quickly as the consumer price index over the last three decades. Establishment costs, which accounted for 44 per cent of the BMC's costs in 1971, now consume 70 per cent of its revenue.[73] At the macro level, the thesis of 'urban bias'[74] in spatial policies related to infrastructure, import substitution and so on is not borne out by data on the allocative priority given to urban development in the Indian planning context. The combined investment in housing and urban development was less than 2 per cent of the total Plan outlay until 1974, and never crossed 3 per cent until the Eighth Plan (1992–7).[75]

Geographies of Restructuring

During the 1980s, the new geographies of restructuring in Bombay saw the space vacated by traditional industries like textiles quickly appropriated by informal production centres like the city's slums, or high-tech service centres catering to the exigencies of post-Fordian capital. Capital market reforms hastened the transformation, and the share of manufacturing employment in the city fell from 36 per cent in 1980 to 28.5 per cent in 1990. The share of the trade finance and service sectors rose from 52.1 per cent to 64.3 per cent of total employment.

In the Bombay Metropolitan Region (BMR), factory employment declined from 740,000 to 590,000 in the same period.[76] The overall decline in manufacturing and the trend to specialisation has coincided with an increase in informalisation. The city, which has traditionally served as a transport and distribution hub, has witnessed a mushrooming of technopoles, where literacy and low wages draw software production activity, clerical processes like international airline ticketing, and a panoply of services in finance, retailing, tourism and entertainment.

Spatially, this process has greatly extended the city's effective economic frontiers. The dispersed manufacturing is located in specialised areas – the extended suburbs, satellite centres in the BMR, and in nearby cities such as Pune and Nashik. Worst hit was the Thane-Belapur industrial heartland, which, throughout the 1980s, witnessed a 16 per cent loss in the industrial workforce.[77] The area, unsurprisingly, is a Sena bastion. Employment in the central business district (ironically, at the city's southernmost tip) dropped from 54.7 per cent to 47.5 per cent between 1970 and 1991[78] and there has been a sustained dispersal of the population to the north-eastern and north-western suburbs and beyond.

1991 census figures indicate the pressures on land and scarcity of housing that have put real estate prices in Bombay beyond the reach of most citizens. While the population of Greater Bombay grew by 8 per cent over the previous decade to touch 9.9 million, the count for the Bombay Metropolitan Region as a whole rose to 12.5 million. Most of the growth in the BMR during the decade of the 1980s was channelled to nodes on the northern fringe of Mira-Bhayander, Thane and Kalyan, where population growth rates averaged 21.1 per cent, 10.5 per cent and 7.1 per cent per annum respectively. This predominantly agricultural area witnessed a rash of illegal constructions in the late 1970s by private developers in violation of town planning regulations.[79] Most had political connections, and some like Hitendra Thakur and Pappu Kalani, who went on to become elected members of the Maharashtra legislature, had formidable criminal records. Public housing was able to meet only 8 per cent of the incremental demands of the formal housing sector,[80] and properties in Greater Bombay were largely out of the economic reach of the burgeoning professional and white-collar populations. They found themselves grappling to wrest amenities from fly-by-night developers and a lethargic officialdom, while having to commute long distances to the city using an outdated transport system.

By the end of the 1980s, speculative buying by an elite seeking capital enhancement in a lucrative land and property market had made real estate in Bombay among the most expensive in the world. The state was an active agent in the process, through income-tax auctions of prime properties. The effect of

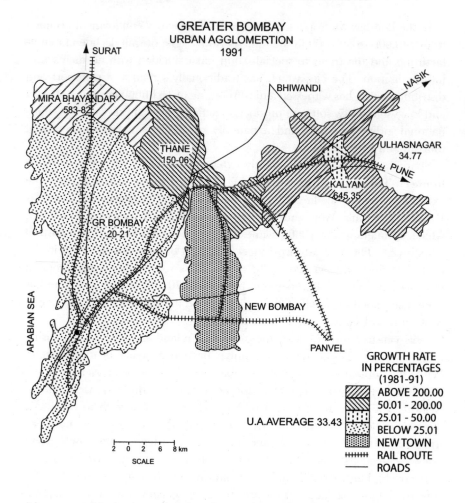

GREATER BOMBAY
URBAN AGGLOMERTION
1991

this geographical structuring has been most pronounced on the 'E' ward, housing the mill district. While Bombay's population grew by 38.1 per cent in the 1970s and 52.5 per cent in the next decade, population in the densely inhabited south-central pocket housing the mills and their workforce fell by 7.3 per cent between 1961 and 1991.[81]

The end of the textile strike and the subsequent riots led to the dispersal of Muslim workers and their retrenched Hindu colleagues to the extended suburbs, creating segregated ethnic enclaves. Girangoan – the mill hamlet – began its evolution into an estate of commercial complexes, with shops and tenements being rapidly converted into rudimentary export-processing zones for garments and jewellery. Thackeray's 'boys' – usually progeny of retrenched mill workers – found lucrative openings as labour contractors for these firms, and also in garnering protection money from local shopkeepers and traders. Often their services would be solicited by millowners, who were also landlords, to 'persuade' obdurate tenants to leave. With the 1984 bloodletting still fresh in memory, the Muslim traders in Lalbagh were more easily inveigled, for a lower compensation.

This decline in the city core effectively dissipated the *chawl*-level networks for mobilisation earlier controlled by the Girni Kamgar Union and the Communist trade unions. With over half the city's population huddled in slums by the late 1980s, most outside the purview of any legal entitlement, the concerned communities were often seen expending their energies on ensuring the security of their tenures and gaining access to land, finance and civic amenities. With the Congress having no ground-level organisation worth the name, and the Communists relegated to the factory floor, the *shakha* became the forum to meet these specific concerns through a parallel administration drawing heavily upon criminalised grassroots power structures. These neighbourhood grids of exchange served to programmatically link the secular and non-secular networks of social life.

Developments in the 1990s

With a shrill campaign against religious minorities, the *Shiv Sena*-BJP alliance garnered a rich harvest of 52 seats in the 1990 regional elections. The growing electoral support of the Sena since the late 1980s, as a leading daily observed, was 'out of desperation', rather than as an endorsement of its provocative posturing about a 'Hindu state'. 'Voters...found that other parties had failed to solve their basic problems like the provision of drinking water and shelter.'[82] The worst communal carnage in India's post-Partition history occurred in Bombay between December 1992 and January 1993, in response to the rasing of the Babri mosque in distant Ayodhya by the protagonists of the *Hindutva* alliance. Sparked by religious frenzy, the violence was sustained over a fortnight by a consortium of vested interests. Masselos[83] describes the wide array of agendas at work:

> While the *Shiv Sena* drive provided a core to the ongoing direction of the riots, there were other elements involved in what became an especially diffuse and dispersed series of events. In the slum areas whole sections of hutments were set alight in a manner that did not distinguish between Muslim and Hindu. Either slum landlords were setting off the fires in order to regain the land and to rent it out again for higher key money, or the original owners of the land were making use of the state of anarchy to clear the land so they could build on it, something they could not do while the shanties were on it. In some cases, perhaps, branches of various political parties in the slums were paying off party rivals and in others there was probably a clear involvement of rival gangs

to settle scores with opponents to gain control of the slums and the various activities that went on in them.

News reports named gangsters who led mobs to target municipal offices in an attempt to destroy land records and other evidence of their dubious property transactions.[84] The riots ruptured the axiomatic perception of the city as the place of primary allegiance. They also breached a crucial psychological barrier, implying a qualitative lowering of the threshold of violence among the middle classes.

When the New Economic Policy was announced by the Narasimha Rao government in 1991, Maharashtra, with the largest parliamentary delegation of any state, was already nearly half a decade down the structural adjustment path. Chief minister Sharad Pawar was known in business and Bretton Woods circles as 'the man behind Maharashtra Inc'[85] and part of his grand design was the 'global city' vision of Bombay as 'one of the organising nodes of the transnational system'.[86] The illicit and copious spoils of reform through discretionary executive power and untrammelled real estate speculation had extended an already substantial parallel economy and deepened its supportive power structures. With politics effectively going underground, the 1992 municipal elections had over 40 candidates with criminal records.

The stock market crash of 1992 saw a transfer of funds from the equity to the real estate sector, stoking demand. Rent controls amidst soaring property prices led to a situation where market rents were 25–30 times the prevalent rates, and contracted violence as a means of eviction became an increasingly attractive option. The system of *pugree* or capitalised rent for the transfer of tenancy rights had fuelled a huge parallel economy and exacerbated the tenancy problem.[87] Excessive speculation created a situation where notional transactions comprised 75 per cent of exchanges in Bombay's property market in the early 1990s.[88] A range of skewed deregulation measures generated increased domestic and foreign demand, without any parallel initiatives to generate supply.

By May 1992 the state, through CIDCO, had acquired and developed 75 per cent of the private land required for the twin city development project. This resolve and alacrity were found wanting in the implementation of the ULCRA. Of the 26,000 hectares declared to be 'surplus' in Greater Bombay, by 1997 only 70.5 hectares had been physically acquired and developed for public housing.[89] In 1996, Bombay's real estate rates were, in absolute terms, the highest in the world in prime residential and commercial areas.[90] Within Greater Bombay, there was a wide variation in property prices with telling consequences on the already inequitable framework of subsidies and supplies of various urban services.

BOMBAY REAL ESTATE GRAPH - 1992 - 1999

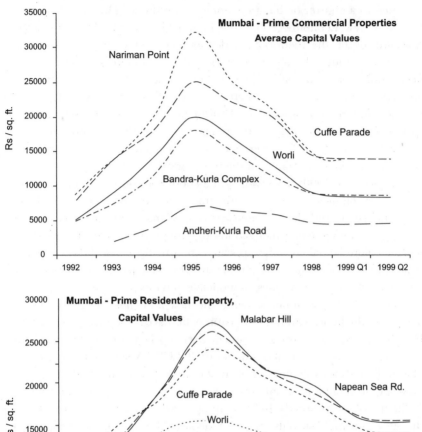

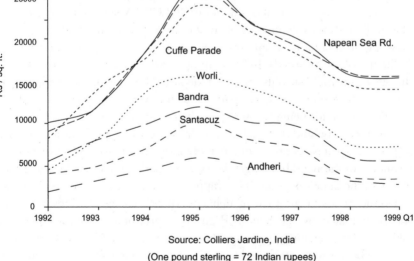

Source: Colliers Jardine, India

(One pound sterling = 72 Indian rupees)

The 74th Constitutional Amendment of 1992, proposing greater political and fiscal autonomy to local bodies, was partly a function of the central government's precarious financial position. In the second half of the 1980s, tax and non-tax revenue proportions had declined, the fiscal and revenue deficits rose alarmingly,[91] and the government's own expenditure had mounted to a quarter of the gross domestic product.[92] Drawing its rationale from the New Economic Policy, the Eighth Plan document [93] envisaged a restructuring of the metropolitan development paradigm to make it 'self-sustaining' through the mobilisation of 'internal resources'. The first major urban policy initiative after liberalisation – the mega cities progamme – attempted to shore up infrastructure in five of the country's largest cities through innovative financing mechanisms and cost recovery schemes. The spending plan for Bombay made no allocation for slum improvement, earmarking a lion's share (52.5 per cent) of the budgeted four billion rupees on cost recovery projects, mainly in the transportation sector.[94]

Moreover, the 1990s have witnessed a continuous decline in the per capita expenditure on urban anti-poverty programmes.[95] In this context, the rhetoric of 'participation' and 'decentralised governance' may be regarded as a counter-proposal to the increased mobilisation of groups vulnerable to the effects of market failure. What to some appeared 'reform by storm',[96] was actually a stealthy process of dismantling existing structures in a piecemeal manner, while unobtrusively adding new ones, to modulate and dissipate resistance.[97]

The regional governments, being the first and most pregnable lines of defence in the hybridised policy environment, have responded with ingenuity. In 1991 the Maharashtra government drew up Development Control rules that further relaxed stipulations under the ULCRA, allowing the sale of 'surplus' mill lands for the purpose of 'modernising' the ailing units. There was, however, no simultaneous attempt to erect an apparatus for monitoring sales or the use of the proceeds. By stipulating that the income generated through the sale of the mills' surplus assets be redeployed for the units' revival, the government at once appeared sympathetic to the workers' cause, while silently watching the lands being furtively parcelled away bit by bit.[98]

'The tactic,' behind such elaborate political decoys to push through reform, as Jenkins explains, 'is to accentuate fairly insignificant areas of governmental resistance to the neo-liberal agenda, even as market forces are heading inexorably in the same direction. It is wrapping the logical culmination of existing economic trends in the garb of deliberate policy change.'[99] This subterfuge was perpetuated by the Sena-BJP government when it assumed power in 1995.[100] The gangland murders of some mill owners, realtors and trade unionists have been widely attributed to rival gangs seeking a share in the lucrative construction projects by muscling themselves into the textile unions. The Sena is intimately involved in this process, and while in power is said to have evolved an understanding with the mill owners to permit the conversion of their assets into residential and commercial properties if the party's own appointees are allowed to control the unions and oversee the proceedings.[101]

The 1990s also witnessed concerted attempts to co-opt sections other than the urban élites into the reform process through populist – but stillborn – housing schemes. Ignoring equity considerations may jeopardise the economic reform process in the long run,[102] and solutions to that end were sought within the unequal urban structure reflecting the existing 'rules of the game'. The Slum Development Scheme of 1991 proposed the redevelopment of 'censused' slums on public lands through nominal contributions from their inhabitants, while the Sena government's Slum Rehabilitation Scheme of 1995 promised free dwelling units to a million poor households. 'The slum dwellers,' the policy document sanctimoniously explained, 'deserve this preferential – probably unequal – treatment to bring them into the mainstream of the social and economic fabric of this pulsating city.'[103]

Both schemes follow the logic of cross-subsidisation in which subsidies by private developers are thought to be more than adequately compensated by permitting additional floor space to be sold in the open market. Fearing the siege of their lands by a consortium of vested interests, the 'beneficiaries' have unsuccessfully urged the state for an honest transfer of a clear title to their individual plots of land and access to institutional finance.[104] The artificially inflated property prices proved unsustainable in the long run, making the schemes unattractive to private developers. The schemes also failed to enthuse the middle class market, unhappy with the idea of sharing apartment complexes with former slum communities.[105]

The political mobilisation of Bombay's vast slum populations has always been predicated upon 'votebank politics', where the logic of both demolition and resettlement find their operation. In addition to their extensive segregation along the axes of ethnicity, class and occupational status, Bombay's slum dwellers find themselves divided on the basis of tenurial rights that exist in manifold forms.[106] The threat of evictions are as high as 80 per cent among squatters and those in unregistered accommodation and 50 per cent among Bombay's pavement dwellers.[107] Particularly badly off are those in newer settlements, who have negligible amenities and few conflict-resolution mechanisms besides the local *dada*, who often serves as the political and economic intermediary.

Greater Bombay slum population

General population (millions)		Slum population (millions)		
1981	1991	1981	1991	1998
8.3	9.9	3.3	5.4	6.3

Source: Sengupta (1999: Table 7).

This criminalised and subterranean form of political recruitment and action has constrained popular initiatives to formalise their access to the state and to erect new institutional platforms from a variety of vantage points. The outcome, as embodied in Bombay's socio-spatial landscape, is a self-referential aesthetic, and an asymmetrical politics that has an ambivalent relationship to its democratic context.

4. Conclusion

The endeavour of this study has been to analyse the city as a dynamic system where spatial form and social process interact with, reinforce, and actuate one another. This has involved a review of the urban planning process as mediated through the formal political, legal and administrative entities in operation within the democratic regime, like the constitutional architecture, parties, and the bureaucratic mechanisms that set the parameters of policy and ensure its implementation. This study has also sought to focus on other regularised channels of interaction and exchange which, though not formally codified, are configured in an attempt to bridge the expanse between the official channels of 'state' and the dense networks of systems in 'civil society' that seek to negotiate their mutual terms of interaction within the centralised power. Though the formal-informal distinction is not always possible to sustain in the institutional context, the latter would include individual party leaders and their networks of influence, land and labour markets and economic arrangements like *pugree* (capitalised rent) that have evolved in response to social and political exigencies. In this amorphous zone between legality and illegality, formality and informality, are many more alternate locations and levels of power than are immediately apparent. Herein lies what Chatterjee[108] describes as the 'unestimated residue', or 'beyond' of planning, to which may be credited its disorderly outcomes.

6

UNDERSTANDING LOCAL POLITICS, DEMOCRACY AND CIVIL SOCIETY: ENVIRONMENTAL GOVERNANCE IN URBAN INDIA

Bharat Dahiya[1]

Speaking on 'The Future of Indian Cities: National Issues and Goals' at a 1960 conference organised by the University of California at Berkeley, Asoka Mehta, then a Member of Parliament, noted:

> Whether we think of patchwork improvement, of reorganisation of the cities that would involve displacement of some people and their moving to other areas, or of planning for future growth, it is patent that without widespread understanding of these objectives and the enlistment of popular interests – and, where possible, active cooperation – the major tasks will remain undone, or will be done badly. The governments and civic authorities have to discover methods of contacting, informing, and interesting citizens in the plans of change and development. A network of local organisations, neighborhood groups, and citizens' forums will have to complement a carefully thought-out program of public relations.[2]

Since then, India has witnessed wide-scale urbanisation. The urban population has grown from 61.6 million in 1951 to 285.3 million in 2001. The proportion of the urban population to total population has risen from 17.6 per cent to 27.8 per cent during the same period, and the number of urban centres has increased from 2,795 to 5,161. The populations of large cities like Kolkata and Mumbai top 10 million. Indeed, the size of the urban population of India is more than the total population of the United States.[3] According to United Nations' estimates, India will have an urbanisation level of 40.9 per cent in the year 2030.[4]

Urban centres in India are not simply significant because of their size. They also constitute a crucial aspect of the Indian economy. The contribution of urban centres to GDP increased from 31.7 per cent in 1950–1 to 60.3 per cent in 2000–01.[5] Cities and towns also act as political and administrative centres of the country. However, despite their crucial significance in Indian socio-economic organisation, these urban centres tend to suffer from problems such as poor financial condition of urban local governments (ULGs), inadequate infrastructure and service provision, increasing environmental degradation and resultant unhealthy living conditions especially with regard to the urban poor. Inadequate service provision, degrading environmental conditions and poor functioning of ULGs have contributed to the rise of civil society[6] organisations (CSOs). In light of these developments, a new understanding of the enhanced role of CSOs has been advocated in the governance of cities and towns in India.[7]

1. Democracy, Governance and Environmental Management: The Indian Urban Context

The rise of CSOs in urban areas in general and for urban environmental management more particularly has raised important questions of democracy and governance. In this essay three arguments are presented. Firstly, it is argued that, because of the colonial inheritance, ULGs constitute part of the state planning process, and are not directly related to democratic institutions from below. As a consequence, these institutions have remained bureaucratic in essence and divorced from the local population.

Secondly, in the post-colonial situation, ULGs failed to become democratic political institutions, instead remaining bureaucratic in substance. Developments that preceded and followed elections in cities and towns in the 1990s reveal an unhealthy picture of democracy at the ULG level. Democracy in some urban centres brought criminals to power who undermined these institutions rather than strengthening them. The democratically elected ULGs failed to focus on citizens' needs for basic environmental services. This was because of the lack of accountability, transparency and connections with the electorate in their constituencies.

Thirdly, in the 1990s, a new initiative was undertaken to institute democratic forms of governance (i.e. ULGs) in urban areas through the 1992 74th Constitutional Amendment Act. However, such institutions did not involve popular participation and control over local government institutions. As a consequence, a new network of social organisations evolved that may be termed civil society organisations. But while the emergence of CSOs enabled more affluent sectors of the population to develop proper environmental services at grass-roots level, poorer sections were unable to develop such organisational networks. More importantly, pressure for privatisation without consultation with CSOs tended to undermine the latter's effectiveness. Thus, the development of environmental services could not be isolated from the issue of politics and democratic forms of governance. Development could not take place through simple technocratic solutions.

The urban situation in India today thus justifies the prophetic words of Mehta quoted above. Almost four decades later, scholars and development practitioners have expressed similar views.[8] There is an increased emphasis on partnership between CSOs and the state rather than simply on public participation in urban development. However, the normative literature on urban development and management has not taken into account the political processes that operate at the urban local level. There are few studies available on the analysis of politics in urban India.[9] Further, while the urban population in India constitutes more than a quarter of total population and the process of urbanisation has been an important aspect of Indian society in the late twentieth century, it is surprising that urban issues have escaped the attention of scholars[10] in their studies on Indian politics, civil society and democracy. Instead, work on civil society[11] has focused on citizenship and democracy at the level of the Indian state, while those dealing with politics[12] have tended to restrict their purview to central and state government levels. Thus, a gap exists in the literature insofar as democracy relating directly to urban issues is concerned. It is this lacuna in current research that is addressed in this essay. In so doing, the kind of representative democracy practised in urban India, the rise of CSOs and its causal factors, and the relationship of CSOs with the ULGs will be discussed.

The lack of literature on various aspects of urban development in India, especially on urban politics and the functioning of democracy, can be attributed to a number of factors. Firstly, the fully-fledged democratisation of urban governance is a recent phenomenon. In Mehta's words, there is an 'utter paucity of analytical literature [on governance] and even good documentation to derive a generalised picture'.[13] Secondly, there are only a few institutions that focus on research in everyday urban life in India. Thirdly, since urban issues are now increasingly being covered by the media,[14] the politicisation of social, economic, environmental and institutional issues has added to the difficulty of collecting information on social, economic, environmental, institutional and political developments in a city on a regular basis.[15] Newspaper reports provide a popular picture of urban life. However, they are not reliable as they may represent the views of only a section of the society, and hence a part of the public interest. The present study is based upon field research on urban governance, CSOs and environmental services in Chennai. In addition, further examples, have been taken from other cities wherever necessary to illustrate the issues at hand.

2. Revamping of Urban Local Governments

India revamped the ULGs in its cities and towns through the 74th Constitutional Amendment Act. The Act was given the President's assent on 20th April 1993.[16] All state governments were required to enact corresponding legislation. As a result, by January 1997, 15 major states had about 60,000 elected representatives in municipal corporations, municipal councils and *nagar panchayats*,[17] the latter being areas of transition from rural to urban attributes. The 74th Constitutional Amendment Act also made provision for elections to ULGs every five years and a bi-election within six months if a ULG was dissolved for any reason (although it did not detail these reasons). Thus, another level of democracy – the local level – was instituted in the Indian Constitution, and henceforth three levels of government in India – central, state and local – were operational. The revamping of ULGs is seen as representing the devolution of power to local-level governments. This is demonstrated by the fact that the 74th Constitutional Amendment Act also added a fully-fledged Twelfth Schedule to the Indian Constitution with regard to the powers given to the ULGs (see Box 1). Here, it is important to note that, owing to the devolution of powers to ULGs, the latter form an extension of the state.

Box 1. Twelfth Schedule of the Indian Constitution
(Article 243-W)

1. Urban planning including town planning.
2. Regulation of land-use and construction of buildings.
3. Planning for economic and social development.
4. Roads and bridges.
5. Water supply for domestic, industrial and commercial purposes.
6. Public health, sanitation conservancy and solid waste management.
7. Fire services.
8. Urban forestry, protection of the environment and promotion of ecological aspects.
9. Safeguarding the interests of weaker sections of society, including the handicapped and mentally retarded.
10. Slum improvement and upgradation.
11. Urban poverty alleviation.
12. Provision of urban amenities and facilities such as parks, gardens, playgrounds.
13. Promotion of cultural, educational and aesthetic aspects.
14. Burials and burial grounds; cremations, cremation grounds and electric crematoriums.
15. Cattle ponds; prevention of cruelty to animals.
16. Vital statistics including registration of births and deaths.
17. Public amenities including street lighting, parking, bus stops and public conveniences.
18. Regulation of slaughter houses and tanneries.

Source: Gazette of India (1993).

One innovative feature of the above mentioned Act was that it made provision for a Wards Committee for cities having a population of 300,000 or more, while leaving state governments to decide the criteria and the process by which members of a Wards Committee would be selected. Potentially, it left the door open for the direct participation of people in urban local governance, if the state government so wished. Some states have legislated to involve representatives of non-governmental organisations (NGOs – e.g. Maharashtra) while others have not (e.g. Tamil Nadu).

The 74th Constitutional Amendment Act endowed the ULGs with responsibility for 'the preparation of plans for economic development and social justice; and the performance of functions and the implementation of schemes as may be entrusted to them including those in relation to the matters listed in the Twelfth Schedule.' It also gave them powers to constitute '[c]ommittees with such powers and authority as may be necessary to enable them to carry out the responsibilities conferred upon them including those in relation to the matters listed in the Twelfth Schedule.' These cover a wide variety of issues ranging from urban planning to cattle ponds and prevention of cruelty to animals. With regard to urban services and environment, it included two specific entries, e.g. entry number 6 on 'public health, sanitation conservancy and solid waste management', and entry number 8 on 'urban forestry, protection of the environment and promotion of ecological aspects' (see Box 1). Thus, considerable powers were given to the ULGs for the management and protection of the environment in Indian urban centres.

3. Representative Democracy in Urban India

Edward Craven of the British Civil Service College wrote on the public attitude to elected bodies in Great Britain in the 1970s:

> People seem to be less and less prepared to leave decisions to elected representatives who have been chosen largely by a party caucus, who are unknown to the electorate, and whose ability to control the growing apparatus of government seems to be diminishing...[18]

D'Souza correctly supposes that this 'could be repeated concerning people's impressions about our own organs of local government [in India] today'.[19] In light of this, the nature of representative democracy in urban India, the way in which ULGs focus on the needs of the urban dwellers, and in particular the failure of elected representatives to focus on the needs of urban dwellers need to be assessed. The status of service provision (solid waste management) in Chennai by the Chennai Municipal Corporation (CMC) and its implications can be taken as a revealing case study. The findings, and a survey of the literature, provide an indication of whether or not ULGs may be considered institutions of substantive democracy.

The Nature of Representative Democracy at the ULG Level

In representative democracies, the citizens elect members to different legislative bodies. In ideal terms, these elected members should represent the electorate's views as well as highlight any problem and/or issue faced by the latter. The character of the individuals elected is important, since voters are expected to develop some kind of faith in them. The question of how elected representatives perform as responsible citizens on a personal level is therefore important. A third – though less important – issue, which has often been discussed, is how representative the citizens' choice can be, if less than 50 per cent of voters support a candidate for election.

To elect a representative it is important for citizens to take into consideration the character of the available candidates. Writing about the 1992 municipal elections in Mumbai, D'Souza mentions that *The Times of India* at that time 'identified no less than 35 candidates with criminal records, some of them credited with murder, extortion, cheating or forgery. And these were only the ones the *Times* reporter could trace. There must have been many more who had covered their tracks more skilfully'.[20] It becomes difficult for citizens to select and elect their representatives from amongst such candidates. The problem is aggravated if all candidates of a constituency, for some reason or another, have criminal records. D'Souza summarises this problem succinctly:

> What kind of informed choice can you make out of a ballot paper full of such offerings? Won't you be simply helping to swap today's set of thieves and rascals for a new set, equally addicted to crime?[21]

At the national or state level, the accused candidates, including some well-known politicians, provided more acceptable candidates than themselves by asking their wives to fight the election. Surprisingly, in most cases, the latter were elected.

There would be no such questions as to the conduct of elected representatives if the latter, even at the lowest level of expectation, acted as law-abiding citizens. Such has not been the case in modern urban India. Once they have grasped the meaning of power, municipal councillors or corporators (as they are called in a number of towns and cities) engage in many types of unlawful activity. To quote D'Souza again:

> When they [the corporators] are not renaming roads…there are the regular activities of extortion, blackmail and worse to keep them busy.

A 1994 *The Times of India* report listed 13 Mumbai corporators involved in various crimes, including robbery, *dacoity*, kidnapping, and even murder. Their number quickly grew, despite a dilution of male preponderance in the council; under a new law women now numbered about a third of our representatives in the BMC [Bombay Municipal Corporation]. Arrests of Mumbai's corporators on criminal charges took place at the rate of one a week, until nearly 10 per cent of our city government had a criminal record, and women made sure that they were properly represented in this race to jail.[22]

In Chennai, where the author conducted his fieldwork, a respondent provided details of the following incident. It had become common to see the local municipal councillor – who happened to be a woman – enforcing the law. She could be witnessed stopping trucks and other goods-transportation vehicles that passed through the municipal ward, with the help of a Chennai Metropolitan Police constable, and extorting money from the drivers of these vehicles. Such examples help to shed light on the conduct of elected representatives, and many more could be found if one searched for them. If, as has been stated earlier, the character and conduct of potential as well as elected representatives constitute the basic building blocks of representative democracy, it follows that if these building blocks are not in place, it will affect other aspects of structure and practice of representative democracy.

The most common measure of the citizens' support and representation in election is the number of votes polled in favour of a candidate. D'Souza uses the case of Mumbai to illustrate how representative is democracy in urban India. In Mumbai's last municipal elections, he mentions that only 20 out of a total of 103 successful candidates of a party (*Shiva Sena*) 'won more than half the number of votes polled in their respective constituencies'.[23] The remaining 83 candidates were opposed by more voters than those who voted for them. This is in line with the scenario at national and state levels as illustrated by Basu and Das in their book on electoral politics.[24] This, some would maintain, is a general problem of democracy. However, it could also be argued that the voter-related statistics reveal important and interesting details which merit further analysis.

Focusing on Citizens' Needs

In October 1996, after a period of 23 years during which the oldest municipal government in India was kept under suspension in Chennai, new elections for the municipal council were finally held. During the period of suspension, the City was governed by the state government with the help of a Special Officer who had responsibilities equal to that of an elected mayor. Once it came to power, 'the newly elected [Chennai municipal] council wanted to establish itself as an efficient service providing agency'.[25] As a result, it took a number of steps. It initiated a programme called Madras Vision 2000 to make the City cleaner and greener. It began to build much needed storm water drains, the lack of which had resulted in annual local flooding. The CMC established litter-free zones and traffic islands at various places. This led to some improvements, but hygiene issues remained a problem.

Interviews were conducted with the heads of 25 neighbourhood organisations selected at random from two municipal zones, one in which the presence of neighbourhood organisations was strong and the other where it was weak in terms of numbers. These neighbourhood organisations were actively seeking to improve environmental conditions in their neighbourhoods,in particular to carry out house-to-house solid waste collection. Of the 25 neighbourhood organisations, 15 had been created before the municipal election of October 1996 and 10 afterwards. It was surprising to find that the elected representatives had made little impact on the working of CMC with regard to the provision of basic environmental services. All of the neighbourhood organisations had come into existence for two main reasons: irregular provision of solid waste collection service by CMC, and poor and unhygienic living conditions. The frequency of solid waste collection varied from once in a week to once in two months compared to the mandatory requirement of daily solid waste collection. It was revealed that, if pressure was exerted by neighbourhood organisations demanding proper services, the elected representatives could refuse to cooperate and/or take action to improve the situation.

ULGs as Substantive Democracy?

It is important to ascertain in the present context whether ULGs have substantive democracy or not. The term substantive democracy is taken to mean a democracy where the elected government is transparent and accountable to the electorate. Basu's study of urban industrial enclaves surrounding Kolkata[26] has demonstrated how the municipalities there came to be dominated by mill managers and government nominees in the colonial period. Democratic reforms at grassroots level were thwarted by the existence of powerful economic interest groups, such as mill managers and local landlords. Continued domination by these groups alienated the vast majority of poorer working class residents from the city's administration.

Basu[27] has also argued that historically, local governments came into existence as an extension of the state. As such, they were formulated along bureaucratic lines, which also helps to explain their failure to become democratic institutions. A certain degree of extension was undertaken – couched as administrative decentralisation – 'to satisfy the demands of self-rule, put by the national movement to the Imperial Rulers, since the local governments were touted as the training ground for larger political responsibilities'.[28] Thus, Basu concludes that the administrative decentralisation which occurred was characterised by absence of transparency and accountability of local governments to their constituencies, and hence contributed to the lack of substantive democracy.

Kundu demonstrates that on the eve of Independence, state governments controlled and supervised the ULGs directly or indirectly through district magistrates.[29] Since then, the form and structure of ULGs has remained the same or has deteriorated in large cities, where powers for the provision of infrastructure and services, and for development and planning, have been delegated to various para-statal agencies. For example in Chennai, the authority to provide drinking water and sewerage services rests with the Metro Water Supply and Sewerage Board, and that of planning and development with the Chennai Metropolitan Development Authority.[30] Although the 74th Constitutional Amendment Act has provided for the democratisation of ULGs, substantive democracy is still lacking at this level of government. This trend continues today, and whilst representative democracy has been instituted, substantive democracy (with transparency and accountability) remains a distant dream for Indian urban centres. Thus, although decentralisation has the potential to strengthen democracy at lower levels of administration, it can also strengthen higher level governments by way of patronage.[31]

The main question that needs to be asked, therefore, is how democratically elected governments in urban areas have performed and whether they have focused on people's needs. The same question can also be asked in a different way, such that one can query why there is a rise of CSOs at the urban local level. In the event that ULGs are not transparent and accountable, as has been argued above, what has been the citizens' response in redressing the problem? These questions may be considered with regard to the environmental problems faced by citizens in Indian cities and towns.

4. The Rise of Civil Society Organisations and Causal Factors

From the discussion on the nature of representative democracy, the democratic scenario looks pessimistic. From the scant literature available,[32] it can be shown that due to improper functioning of governments at different levels in India, and especially at the urban local level, a growth of CSOs in various spheres of human concern has been recorded. This has taken the form of NGOs and citizens' institutions (e.g. neighbourhood organisations). The process of the rise of CSOs is different at varied levels of operation of NGOs and other such organisations. In the British period, reform groups such as Brahmo Samaj, Arya Samaj and Ramakrishna Mission were established. These were regulated by the Societies Registration Act of 1860 which reflected the emergence of citizens' institutions in India.[33] In the post-independence period, Chatterjee argues that the process of emergence of NGOs at the national level began just after the period of Emergency. According to him, the 'dark period' of the Emergency led to a profound re-evaluation of India's political processes and to the convergence of the ideologies of Left and Right on issues of development. As a result, the dominant concepts that emerged, included 'conscientisation', 'people's participation' and 'focusing on the needs of target groups'.

The Bhopal accident in 1986 not only led to the revision of environmental laws, but also revolutionised the way in which environmental problems were viewed. The publication of *Our Common Future* in 1987[34] – also known as Bruntland's Report – led to an increased focus on environmental problems internationally. By the advent of the 1990s, the urban development scenario had totally changed. The United Nations Conference on Environment and Development[35] held at Rio de Janeiro, published the *Brown Agenda* that included the environmental issues faced by cities and towns and broad strategies. The Centre for Science and Environment (at New Delhi) has published a series of 'state of the Environment' reports on India since 1982.[36] All of these factors led to an increased awareness of urban environmental issues.

Concurrently, environmental conditions deteriorated in cities and towns in India owing to increased concentration of population, poor financial condition of ULGs, inadequate provision of infrastructure and services, and the lack of proper focus on urban problems, including those related to the urban environment. Although the ULGs were revamped through the 74th Constitutional Amendment Act, as noted earlier, they did not lead to substantive democracy. The rise of CSOs in urban areas and the kind of activities in which they engage to improve the urban environment are considered below.

Inadequate Service Provision

The major response to inadequate service provision by ULGs has been in the form of NGOs. A number of NGOs have been established by enlightened, philanthropic and visionary individuals who saw that the urban areas were on the brink of epidemics. Examples of representative NGOs include Exnora International in Chennai, the *Praja* Foundation in Mumbai and *Vataravan* in

Delhi, to name but a few. These NGOs have mobilised people living in urban neighbourhoods to get together and to begin working for local environmental improvement. They have also provided detailed guidelines to help others to set up neighbourhood organisations.[37]

It has been shown above that the revamping of ULGs did not lead to proper service provision in Chennai, especially that of solid waste management. This led the citizens to form neighbourhood organisations for the improvement of their local environment. In this process, they have received help from various NGOs such as Exnora International. A typical neighbourhood organisation is formed following a meeting of all concerned residents of a neighbourhood. They discuss the environmental issues that concern them, establish an organisation and register it under the Societies Registration Act.

In Chennai, such organisations then collect donations from the households living in a particular neighbourhood and purchase a tricycle. A 'street beautifier' is appointed who collects solid waste daily from each household of the neighbourhood and unloads it in the secondary collection bins of the CMC from where vehicles transport it to a landfill site. The 'street beautifier' is paid by the neighbourhood organisation that collects a monthly service charge from the households living in that neighbourhood. The process thus becomes financially self-sustaining, and leads to better living conditions.

Neighbourhood organisations have also become engaged in other environmental improvement works such as street sweeping, tree planting, pavement maintenance, and registering collective complaints to various authorities (such as the Metro Water Supply and Sewerage Board for proper sewage disposal). It is estimated that there are about 500 such organisations currently functioning in Chennai City and their number is growing. Similar organisations have also emerged in Delhi as *Vatavaran*,[38] and in Mumbai in the form of Advanced Local Management units.

Taking Stock of the Urban Situation

NGOs have also sought to 'take stock of the urban situation'. The Public Affairs Centre is a non-profit organisation established in the early 1990s in light of the fact that urban areas suffered from poor governance and lack of proper living conditions. The centre is dedicated to improving the quality of governance in India. Proper provision of infrastructure and services is essential to maintain healthy living conditions in urban areas. To provide these, the ULGs collect property tax from the citizens living in the administrative limits of cities and towns. Despite the fact that all ULGs collect such tax, they are unable to provide services at desired levels (e.g. solid waste should be cleared once within in 24 hours). Although it is common knowledge that the services are not provided adequately, there is a lack of proper documentation of the actual performance of ULGs. To build information on and review the functioning of ULGs with regard to their responsibilities, Public Affairs Centre developed a 'Report Card Methodology' to take stock of the provision of infrastructure and services in urban areas.[39] This approach has been used extensively in many cities in India and abroad. It has helped to highlight 'user perceptions, evolve platforms for citizens' participation in monitoring the delivery of public services and also inducing public service to redesign their internal systems'.[40]

Lack of Information on ULGs' Functions

There exists a considerable gap in information on the functions of ULGs, and ordinary citizens often do not know what functions (e.g. provision of urban services) are supposed to be performed by them and at what frequency. The Praja Foundation in Mumbai has been established specifically to address this problem. It prepared a Citizens' Charter for Mumbai City with the help of the Mumbai Municipal Corporation. This collaboration, however, was only made possible due to the presence of a welfare-minded official in this corporation. The Charter provides information on matters such as the frequency of service provision, and whom to contact if services are not provided properly or there is a breakdown in the system.

Such responses have not developed only in one particular city. Citizens in various cities and towns have come forward with a number of quite different and innovative ideas to address the issue of increasing environmental problems and the failure of ULGs to address them properly.

5. Governance of the Urban Environment

In the literature on urban development in particular, and on development more generally, there has been an increased emphasis on governance. The project of governance, led by the international development organisations, focuses on the importance of the relationship between the state and CSOs. This relationship is crucial because it constantly reflects the outcomes of the practice of democracy, the performance of governments in addressing people's needs, the response of CSOs to state functioning, and the emerging conflicts and/or partnerships between the state and CSOs. These aspects of the relationship characterise governance. There are many definitions of governance and they vary considerably. However, for the present discussion, the definition given by McCarney *et al* is employed:

> Governance, as distinct from government, refers to the relationship between civil society and the state, between rulers and the ruled, the government and the governed.[41]

The relationship between ULGs and the CSOs in India ranges from functioning partnerships, to non-cooperation on the part of elected representatives, to downright confrontation with the CSOs. Three kinds of relationships are discussed below, using examples from two cities, Ahmedabad and Chennai. It is important to note that in these cases, no effort was spared on behalf of CSOs to discuss and solve the problems related to the urban environment with the help of ULGs.

Functioning Partnerships for the Urban Environment

In Ahmedabad, slums lacked basic infrastructure and services including roads and pavements, water supply and underground sewerage link for individual households, storm water drainage, street lighting, solid waste management, and landscaping. Under a programme called *Parivartan* (literally, transformation), the environmental problems of a typical slum – Sanjayanagar – and other slums in Ahmedabad have been addressed.[42] After long and careful deliberations all partners, which included the Ahmedabad Municipal Corporation (AMC), the Sharada Trust[43], SAATH[44], the Mahila Housing SEWA Trust[45] (MHT), SEWA Bank[46] and the slum residents agreed on a set of basic rules. The UNDP-World Bank's Water and Sanitation Programme in South Asia provided conceptual design support to *Parivartan*. The AMC calculated the on-site upgradation cost of Rs.6,000 (US$150) per dwelling as per the designs of services developed for slums. It was agreed that of the Rs.6,000, one-third would be paid by each of three main partners, i.e. AMC, private industry and each community household. SAATH, MHT and SEWA Bank provided technical support. The responsibilities for on-site operation and future maintenance were left with the community. In this manner, the environmental problems of Sanjayanagar slum were addressed in a partnership approach between the ULG, the residents and the private sector. This programme is now being applied in other slums in Ahmedabad. This case shows that if properly designed, a productive institutional relationship, in fact a partnership between ULGs and the CSOs, can be established in the interests of improving urban environmental management. Such partnerships may be further utilised to mobilise private sector support for the cause.

Non-Co-operation on the Urban Environment

Since the mid-1980s, a large number of neighbourhood organisations have sprung up in Chennai owing to the poor functioning of the CMC with regard to urban services, and especially solid waste management. Exnora International has mobilised residents to form such organisations that are affiliated to the former, and call themselves as Civic Exnoras. Although Civic Exnoras provide self-help service to their residents, at times a large amount of solid waste continues to be dumped at the ends of streets owing to the presence of some commercial establishments and/or marriage halls. This additional solid waste cannot be collected by the Civic Exnoras and dumped in secondary collection points. In such circumstances, Civic Exnora members have taken their problem to the CMC officials, who have sometimes listened to the complaint and at other times sought to avoid it. If the CMC officials overlook such complaints, then the only option left with Civic Exnoras is to represent their problems to the municipal councillor (the elected representative for the smallest administrative unit called ward/division). In the majority of cases, however, the elected representatives do not pay heed to such complaints and representations. A respondent in Chennai, who happened to be one of the office-bearers of Exnora International, said the following:

'The [municipal] councillors are always obliged to the institutional machinery of the [Chennai Municipal] Corporation. They refuse to co-operate with the local organisations for instance NGO or CBO [community-based organisation] unless the NGO representative or the CBO representative has enough, I would say might to control them and have them to do the work. So this leads to a difference of opinion, and usually the elected representative's are not able to influence [the functioning of the CMC machinery] in most of the cases. This brings the hitch and then distance parts us, and many of the elected representatives refuse to co-operate when a Civic Exnora is functioning in an area.'

Thus it has been shown that elected representatives in urban India, in a majority of cases, neither represent nor work to address the needs of the same people who elect them. In light of this, it may not be difficult to imagine how efficiently people's needs would be addressed by elected representatives who themselves hold criminal records. In order to maintain healthy living conditions in cities, the elected representatives are not only required to listen to and represent people's needs. They also need to find innovative ways to address people's problems, and to work to resolve them both on an individual level as well as through the ULGs.

Conflicts and the Urban Environment

Elected councillors on a personal level, and collectively in the form of elected councils at the city level have been known to work against the CSOs that are engaged in self-help environmental service provision in Chennai. Once elected, representatives of the people engage in activities that are aimed at thwarting the efforts of CSOs to improve the local environment. To illustrate this, an excerpt from a focus group discussion held in Chennai is reproduced below. It gives an account of how local residents in Chennai implemented a self-help environmental (i.e. solid waste collection) service before the elections for the CMC, and how this service provision was affected by local elected representatives.

Participant 1 (an Exnora International Office Bearer): When we started [Exnora International in 1989], we did not have the elected body for [Chennai Municipal] Corporation. And so people themselves wanted a solution for a variety of things, for example, public urination in the streets. You are passing through a street and there is garbage lying. So in many streets which had 100 to 150 houses, for example areas like Triplicane and other places, people joined together and said let us do something about our own surroundings... They wanted to establish exclusive organisations, and through these exclusive organisations people joined together and paid a nominal fee of 2 Rupees for registration [as a Society under Society Registration Act]... They had their own elected representatives for their street... [who] collected money to run the house-to-house solid waste collection service]. Gradually in smaller places usually 100 per cent [households] paid [service charge] or at least 90 to 95 per cent paid [service charge]. As streets grew bigger and bigger, and more houses came into picture, each [house] inside had a diversity of views [for paying service charge]. So there was non-co-operation. In some areas what happened, this thing [i.e. the solid waste collection service run by neighbourhood organisations] continued and we were successful [in running solid waste collection service through neighbourhood organisations] to at least about 75 to 80 per cent. After the election of the [municipal council of the Chennai Municipal] Corporation...there was a swift fall in the functioning of...[solid waste collection] service, and now we have only 50 per cent success rate [in the formation of a Civic Exnora and its regular functioning].

Participant 2 (an Ex-Administrative Officer): Why? What is the reason?

Participant 1: Reason? For example, my own street. I had an Exnora [neighbourhood organisation] and gradually garbage was refused to be collected by the Corporation.

Participant 2: That is what I am saying. That is what I said. And the Corporation also [stopped waste collection]?

Participant 1: Not the Corporation. The lorry was stopped because the Councillor sends them. And the second problem was that the street was not swept. Things were not running, the sewage problem persisted and we regularly met this gentleman, my elected representative! He said, 'You first close down [the neighbourhood organisation], then I will [start sending the lorry for garbage collection]. Then we came to a final thing where residents started accusing us that we were stopping the functioning of the Corporation. And one fine evening at about 9:30 in the night people from our street went to the Councillor's office, and said we were closing down.

Participant 3 (an Urban Planner): The reason is that the elected representatives see the Exnora as a threat, threat to their standing.

Thus, we see that the elected representatives who collectively form the policy-making body of the CMC view the CSOs and their working for urban environmental management as a potential political threat. It can therefore be concluded that CSOs are potentially political whether they engage in political activities or not.

A second example of confrontation by elected representatives occurred at the city level where the elected municipal council took the decision to privatise solid waste collection in those administrative areas where the Civic Exnora, i.e. neighbourhood organisation movement is strongest. Chennai City's administrative area is divided into 155 divisions or wards that are grouped under 10 zones. The Civic Exnora movement in Chennai is strong in zones VI, VIII and X and weak in others. It is strong in those zones characterised by poor service provision, due to the popularity of the self-help concept promulgated by Exnora International, and the fact that residents can afford jointly to pay for a community-based solid waste collection service. Although solid waste collection is poor in north Chennai the self-help concept has not become popular there owing to the inability of the residents to pay for self-help services.

In June 1998, Exnora International gave a presentation to the Mayor of the CMC on neighbourhood based 'Zero Waste' management. The core of the concept was that most of the solid waste should either be recycled and/or reused, and only non-degradable waste should go to the dumping ground. Exnora International suggested that the bio-degradable waste that made up two-thirds of the total 2,200 tonnes of waste then generated daily in Chennai should be converted into manure by setting up micro-enterprises in the municipal divisions to harness the full potential of the Civic Exnora movement. According to Exnora International this would have many advantages: it would save on collection, and transportation costs to transfer solid waste to dumping grounds; it would provide employment; and it would generate manure, the marketing of which would make the whole process environmentally and economically sustainable. At the time of presentation, the Mayor did not take any decision, and the matter was sent for detailed investigation.

In March 1999, the CMC proposed and passed a resolution to privatise solid waste management in the same three municipal zones (viz. zone VI, VIII and X) where the Civic Exnora movement was strong. The CMC argued that by means of privatisation in these three zones, the cost of solid waste disposal (from collection to final disposal) would fall from the then present Rs. 800/tonne (US$20) to Rs. 700/tonne (US$17.5). It would thus lead to a saving of Rs. 30 million (US$750,000) per year (CMC 1999). Though a financially sound proposal, for Exnora International this constituted an attack on its work of improving the urban environment. Exnora International viewed the move for privatisation as a blow to the CSOs, their democratic organisation and their self-help service provision to keep the neighbourhoods free from solid waste, filth and sewage.

It further argued that there was no need for the CMC to privatise solid waste management in the said three zones where the citizens were engaged in environmental improvement activities. The CMC should have privatised this process in north Chennai where the level of service provision is poorer, and there are fewer neighbourhood organisations[47]. In 1999, Exnora International conducted many meetings in which Civic Exnoras participated[48]. They collectively resolved to continue with their present functioning to keep the neighbourhoods clean and green, and to act as watchdogs of the functioning of the CMC and its private contractors in relation to environmental service provision.

6. Conclusion

The foregoing shows that environmental management is inherently related to the functioning of democracy, and the process of governance in contemporary urban India. Because of the colonial inheritance, ULGs in India constitute a part of the state planning process, detached from the day to day needs of the citizens in cities and towns. After four decades of neglect since Independence, the ULGs have been revamped through decentralisation of powers through the 74th Constitutional Amendment Act in the 1990s. Their democratisation has added another level of democracy – *the local level*. However, in many cases, this has brought criminals to power who have undermined these institutions rather than strengthening them.

Evidence suggests that local level democracy lacks transparency and accountability, and in turn, substantive democracy. The ULGs are unable to provide basic environmental services adequately, which are essential for the maintenance of healthy living conditions in the fast growing cities and towns. Furthermore, there is a lack of proper information on the level of services provided by these governments. Owing to this, citizens have formed CSOs and addressed the situation in innovative ways. This has included working with ULGs in order to prepare citizen charters, and develop functioning partnerships (including the private sector) to improve the urban environment. Thus, the evolving interface between CSOs and ULGs provides opportunities to improve governance in urban areas. However, many such opportunities are lost when the elected ULGs view CSOs as a political threat.

The case of Chennai demonstrates that the ULGs do engage and may continue to engage in anti-CSO activities for the simple reason that they have the power to take such decisions; in other words, they can afford to do so. Furthermore, whether the CSOs engage in political activities or not, they are and can be viewed as potentially political organisations. This is owing to the fact that such organisations have been able to mobilise citizens for self-help activities, and that they collectively form a strong civic force. The research indicates that whether the CSOs have to build partnerships with ULGs or elicit co-operation from elected representatives, or to undertake self-help activities for sheer human survival, they will need to be vigilant and active to ensure that their 'right to life' is not breached by the malfunctioning of ULGs which are supposed to be formed by people's representatives.

7

POLITICAL INSTITUTIONS, STRATEGIES OF GOVERNANCE AND FORMS OF RESISTANCE IN RURAL MARKET TOWNS OF CONTEMPORARY BENGAL: A STUDY OF BOLPUR MUNICIPALITY

Subho Basu

1. Introduction

This essay investigates the nature of urban governance in a rural market town in India in order to understand the process of what political scientists often call the crisis of governability.[1] The choice of a rural market town in this study is deliberate, as existing studies on urban governance in India generally focus on large cities.[2] According to the 1991 census, nearly 34.8 per cent of urban dwellers in India reside in towns comprising populations ranging between 5,000 and 99,000 people. Most of these populations live in dispersed rural market towns.[3] Politically, these towns constitute the lowest nodal point of the hierarchy of diverse types of institutions of the Indian state. Even *panchayat* (rural government) offices are located in these small market towns. These institutions link rural market towns with larger urban centres such as district towns, regional capitals and finally the national capital. Economically, rural market towns act as emporia of indigenous export-import trade: exporting rural products into the vast national market grid comprising larger urban centres and importing finished industrial products for rural consumers. Thus such towns constitute the crucial interface between rural areas and large urban political, administrative and economic centres.

These political-economic links are also informed and influenced by social and cultural nexuses between urban and rural areas through rural market towns. Socially, these towns mark the crucial transitional zones where rigid social structures of villages related to complex patterns of land holdings and caste conglomerations give way to a seemingly more fluid social stratification based on the nature of labour, access to education, work and different types of housing as well as caste ranking. Culturally, such towns represent what rural people perceive as 'urban culture', including fashionable clothes, basic cosmetics, entertainment industries ranging from popular Bollywood films, to *jatra* or rural folk theatres and roving experimental theatre groups organising free shows in municipal halls. These towns are thus located at a crucial continuum between rural areas and the vast grid of urban networks in India.

This essay focuses on a rural market town in West Bengal called Bolpur. It argues that the growth of such small towns is contingent upon agrarian expansion and commercial activities on the one hand, and the proliferation of bureaucratic structures of the developmental state from the late colonial period on the other. The political culture of urban governance in these towns is conditioned by the rise of the bureaucracy-driven interventionist developmental national state that increasingly came to play a central role in all significant aspects of social and economic life. Ruling elites in such towns may be characterised as an alliance of bureaucrats employed by the state, businessmen and professionals such as lawyers, doctors and teachers who collectively identify themselves as 'middle class'. The advent of democratic political institutions such as municipal institutions at grass-roots level and the regular holding of elections in such institutions from 1978 onwards, tend to challenge and contest the bureaucratic structure of the developmentalist state at local level. Democratic political mobilisation of the urban poor, orchestrated by diverse forms of political parties – specifically, the Left Front in Bengal – have further challenged middle class hegemony and the bureaucratic political structure of governance. This mobilisation thus erodes the social premise of the bureaucratic developmentalist state, but has exerted intense pressure on [the] local business community and a sizeable segment of the middle classes. It has produced a new form of populist political reaction among the urban middle classes in the form of the Trinamul Congress, whose members have on the one hand sought to preserve middle class hegemony and on the other have developed an intense reaction to the corporatist institutionalised form of mobilisation represented by the Left Front. The clash between two politically opposite and mutually exclusive movements represents a kind of intensified class confrontation that is manifested in myriad forms in everyday life.

This essay thus asserts that what has been interpreted as the crisis of governability is actually a confrontation between democratic local government institutions and the bureaucratic apparatus of the national developmental state at local level. The institutionalisation of democracy at local level has

LOCATION OF BOLPUR IN BENGAL

raised popular expectations of redistribution of wealth in the market towns of Bengal. However, the nature of social stratification in the market towns of Bengal and the intransigence of the bureaucratic apparatus of the central government has undermined such processes of reform. This rise in expectation and the failure of the democratic machinery to fulfil its promises have created popular discontent among urban working classes in the market towns of Bengal.

2. Improved Communication, Agricultural Growth and Urbanisation in Rural Bengal: The Making of an Agricultural Market Town 1860–2000

Bolpur is located at the South Eastern corner of Birbhum district, a predominantly agricultural region of the Indian state of West Bengal.[4] Over the last five decades, Bolpur has flourished, primarily as an agricultural market town. The overriding importance of agriculture in the Bolpur region may be located in the aborted commercial revolution of the late eighteenth century. In this period, the presence of European traders in the villages neighbouring modern Bolpur led to a substantial expansion in commercial activities and the growth of indigenous products. John Cheap, a representative of the English East India Company, initiated indigo cultivation and the manufacture of sugar in the region. His attempts to procure locally produced clothes also contributed to growth in the local weaving industry. The English attempt to penetrate rural Birbhum was matched by the endeavours of a French businessman who established a silk weaving centre and a 'pig iron' manufactory in the district. Following the gradual eclipse of French influence in Bengal, John Cheap took control of the French trading centre. Despite this early expansion in commerce, two events halted the process of commercial development in Birbhum. The famine of 1770 had a detrimental effect on agriculture and destroyed many villages, while the introduction of the Permanent Settlement opened up a more secure and new avenue for investment in land revenue collection rights for Birbhum's flourishing businessmen.[5] The most important example of this transformation was the Sinha family of Raipur. This family made its initial fortune as cloth merchants supplying locally produced clothes to the English East India Company's agent. After the introduction of the Permanent Settlement, the Sinhas purchased landlord rights and became a leading *zamindari* family in the district.[6] With the slow eclipse of the company's trading role and the reluctance of Indian traders to invest in insecure ventures, commerce took a back seat in Birbhum's economy. Throughout the nineteenth century large urban centres failed to develop in Birbhum district.[7]

By the middle of the nineteenth century the establishment of railway lines through the district initiated the process of the development of new urban centres. The railway led to the realignment of traditional business centres. The Ajoy river on the Southern border of Birbhum district had been the main artery of trade. The establishment of a railway station at Bolpur transferred the main axis of trade from the riverine belt to the new railway centre. Soon Bolpur became a local export-import centre of agricultural goods. The four main urban centres in present day Birbhum district – namely Naihati, Rampurhat, Sainthia and Bolpur – were located on the same railway lines that connected Birbhum district with Calcutta, all crucial urban centres in the Indo-Gangetic plain stretching up to Delhi in the north west and in the north east to the urban centres of north Bengal and Assam. Railways thus initiated a new process of urbanisation in Birbhum district.

The establishment of the railway attracted trade to Bolpur. In the late nineteenth century, a number of displaced traders from the old riverine belt moved to Bolpur and founded new settlements.[8] Particular occupational categories were concentrated in various localities of the emerging town. One of the oldest of these was known as Sonapatti, indicating the concentration of goldsmiths there. The most crucial trading development occurred in Bolpur with the relocation of the *hat* or agricultural market to the town that attracted sellers and buyers from the rural interior on particular days in the week. The growing importance of this *hat* in the nineteenth century marked the prominence of Bolpur in the surrounding rural areas. Gradually traders from the neighbouring state of Bihar and even far flung Rajasthan were attracted to the new settlement.[9] By the first decade of the twentieth century Bolpur had acquired all the trappings of a rural market town.

Despite this expansion in the nineteenth century, the real impetus to the growth of Bolpur as a market town came after Independence. The phenomenal growth of Bolpur in the post-Independence decades may be attributed to two crucial factors: agricultural growth in the surrounding countryside; and improved communication networks with rural areas, connecting primary markets in agricultural goods with the wholesale market in the town. Throughout the late colonial period, and particularly in the early years of the twentieth century, agricultural growth in rural Birbhum remained negligible and rural communication rather limited and *backward*.[10] While the 1950s witnessed substantial agricultural growth, the mid-1960s saw a downturn in food production, and the situation did not improve until the early 1970s. But the real boom period in agriculture began in the early 1980s, reaching a peak in the 1990s. The combination of land reforms and the green revolution strategy produced unprecedented agricultural growth in the initial years of the Left Front regime. A process of healthy expansion of agro-based industries has been sustained, and marketing opportunities have created further bases for agricultural growth. Table 1 clearly indicates a link between these decadal variations of agricultural productivity and urban population growth. Indeed, a comparison with population growth in Birbhum district as a whole establishes more clearly the high rate of growth of Bolpur town.

Two factors accounted for the relationship between agricultural growth and the rise in the population of market towns such as Bolpur. The boom in agriculture ensures the steady operation of agro-based industries generating new employment in towns. For example, rice is the principal crop in the district. In Bolpur the *Aman* variety of rice occupies 82.8 per cent of rural rice cultivating land. *Aman* is sown in prime agricultural land between late July and early August, the shoots are transplanted in September and finally reaped in December or early January. The breakthrough in *Aman* cultivation in rural areas of Birbhum in the 1970s and 1980s was accompanied by expansion in other forms of rice cultivation, namely Aus and *Boro* cultivation. Between

Table 1 The Decennial Growth of Population in
Bolpur town

Year	Number of People	Growth
1921	5,896	N/A
1931	Na	N/A
1941	13,856	N/A
1951	14,802	6.83%
1961	23,353	57.78%
1971	29,636	26.89%
1981	38,436	29.69%
1991	52,866	37.4%

Source: The census statistics up to 1981 are collected from
Census of India 1981 Series 23; Town Directory Part X A
p. 60; the 1991 statistics are collected from Sauro Basu et al.
ed., *Mahakuma Parichay Bolpur Jela Birbhum* , Calcutta 1995, p.
16, table 3 row 3. If we add to the urban population also the
area under Santiniketan Sriniketan Notified Area Authority – an
analogous township centred around Vishva Bharati university
comprising 11,743 – then the total urban population comes to
64,609. Source, *ibid*, p. 34.

Table 2 Decennial growth of population in
Birbhum district per 1000

Year	Total	Growth
1921	852	–9.4%
1931	948	11.1%
1941	1,048	11.1%
1951	1,067	1.8%
1961	1,446	35.5%
1971	1,775	22.8%
1981	2,096	18.1%
1991	2,556	21.9%

Source: GK Lieten, *Continuity and Change in Rural West
Bengal,* New Delhi, 1992, p. 28.

1988–9 and 1992–3 the amount of *Boro* production of spring rice increased
from 23,311 metric tonnes to 31,631 metric tonnes, or almost a 42 per cent
increase.[11] This has serious repercussions for the rice industry in the town. In
the 1990s there were 13 rice mills. Rice mills start their operations after paddy
harvesting is over. Thus the steady operation of rice mills at the end of the
crop cycle provides a new source of jobs in urban areas, bringing mainly
Santhal agricultural workers into the town from rural areas. More importantly,
steady growth in crop production ensures regular operation of these mills.

The rapid expansion in agriculture, along with a substantial rise in marketing opportunities, ensures steady urban expansion providing a new lease of life to agro-based industries.

Agricultural growth also ensured a burst of activity in the wholesale market in these years. Established in Bolpur in 1928, the wholesale market had experienced rapid growth in the post-Independence period, reaching a height in the 1990s. The agricultural nature of this wholesale market was evident in the supply trade. In the 1990s the suppliers of commodities in this market included nearly 32 agents of rice mills, 38 licensed wholesale traders, 40 commissioned agents of larger agro-based concerns, 4 agents of various oil mills and 1 government-run agricultural co-operative.[12] According to local state bank statistics, the main items of trade are rice, wheat, potatoes, other raw vegetables, fruit, oilseed and eggs. The flourishing nature of the market is apparent from the quantity of goods that are sold in this market. In the year 1993–4, the market sold 480,000 quintals of paddy, 280,000 quintals of rice, and 70,000 quintals of oilseed.[13] More importantly, the area of the business transaction reflects this market's link with the national agricultural market grid. The market not only imports its main items of transaction from the local primary rural markets but also from Uttar Pradesh, Bihar and Nasik in Maharashtra, a radius of 1500 kilometres. It supplies goods to industrial zones centring around Durgapur in the South and to the commercial city of Siliguri located nearly two hundred kilometres north of the town. As the market has extended its area of operation, 60 warehouses and 3 cold storages have come into existence in the town.[14] Thus the entire prosperity of the town as a trading centre is crucially related to the boom in agriculture. This agrarian growth has developed through an interactive process whereby the rural population becomes far more integrated with the urban market structure. The geography of transportation centres around the town further sustains this process of integration.

The agro-based trading operation crucially depends upon the dense network of rural feeder roads that connect the town with the interior of the district. The dense nature of this road network and the transportation system is evident from the number of buses that link the town with the countryside: nearly 51 local services and 29 regional bus services connect the town with the rural hinterland. In addition, the railways carry substantial numbers of passengers. In 1993 alone 1,419,512 people used the railways for communication with both the rural interior and the outside world. More importantly, railway earnings from commercial transactions have amounted to Rs14,609,400 in the single year 1993. Apart from the railway, motorised vehicles play a crucial role in commercial expansion. In 1992, 512 heavy vehicles, mainly lorries, were registered in Bolpur subdivision, along with 389 intermediate size vehicles and 127 smaller motorised vehicles such as tempos and vans.[15] In other words, a small town such as Bolpur can become the nerve centre of rural agricultural activities and act as the main engine of market-driven growth in agricultural production.

This transformation in the nature of Bolpur and its hinterland has had an important impact on social formations and social stratification in the town. The story of this transformation has a crucial irony in it. The latest phase of agricultural growth in Bolpur region, in fact the most dynamic phase in the entire history of the town, has been partially due to the policies of the Left Front Government, which is ideologically committed to the development of a 'non-capitalist economy' in India. Yet the implementation of the policies of the Left Front, based on land reforms and expansion in small-scale irrigation measures, have resulted in capitalistic market-driven growth in the Bolpur region.[16] There also exists a contradiction in the way these economic measures have been engineered through a particular political corporatist strategy of mobilisation. This has a crucial impact upon the making of the local polity. The rhetoric of redistributive politics, the attempt to mobilise urban working classes through unions, provides a rather dramatic twist. Politics also plays a more crucial role here because of the way the town polity and its administration has come to be structured particularly in the post-Independence era within the context of a hugely expanding state-controlled bureaucratic framework.

3. The Indian State at Local Level and the Political Culture of Development

The nature of governance in Bolpur has been shaped by the development of local institutions of the interventionist developmental national state in the post-Independence era. The agricultural growth that contributed to the emergence of Bolpur as a market town has also led to the concentration of different government departments there to monitor and sustain developmental activities in the region. The process of expansion of state institutions at the grass-roots level started in the late nineteenth century under colonial rule. In the predominantly rural region of Birbhum, railways acted as the nucleus of the local administrative structure of the colonial state. While the primary purpose of railway lines was to enable rapid military movement in the country, the new railway stations soon became focal points for the administrative expansion of the colonial state in the countryside. The relationship between the consolidation of the administrative apparatus of the state in railway stations and the shaping of the urban polity is evident in the history of Bolpur. In 1871 a sub-registry office, a court and a police station were established near the railway station. In 1904 this police station was upgraded to a *thana* – the lowest unit of administration in both colonial and Independent India. By 1937 the first post office was set up in Bolpur. It was followed by the establishment of a telephone exchange in 1940.[17] Thus in the colonial period there came into existence a rudimentary administrative infrastructure which constituted the core of the local administrative apparatus. After 1947, nationalist rulers inherited the infrastructure of this state and transformed these administrative centres into outposts of the interventionist developmental state.

In colonial India, state-guided 'rural development' gathered momentum after World War 1, but the presence of an interventionist developmental state gained further impetus from the 1950s onwards, when community development became a crucial concern of the Indian state. In the 1950s, Block Development Offices were established to supervise rural community development programmes; these were followed by the establishment of the Agriculture and Irrigation Development Office, Public Works Department, Sub-divisional Information Office and Public Health Promotion Office. This growth of local government received a further boost in the Left Front period when the Sriniketan-Santiniketan notified Area Development Authority and the Office of the nationalised Life Insurance Departments were established in the town. In 1985 Bolpur was declared as a sub-divisional administrative town and further government offices opened their branches there.[18]

The post-Independence decades also witnessed the transfer of control of key economic and social institutions from private hands to the public sector, while the pressure of demand from below led to the multiplication of such public sector-run institutions all over the town and its rural hinterland. For example, Bolpur's electric power supply dates from 1916 and came under state control in 1948. This institution multiplied its branches in Bolpur's rural hinterland in the 1980s. Similarly, banks came to play a crucial role in the economy as green-revolution strategies were adopted in the mid-1960s and the banking sector was largely nationalised by a series of measures adopted by the government of Mrs Gandhi after 1969. Many of these banks adopted specific schemes geared towards meeting the needs of the least affluent segment of the rural population. As demands for banking services increased, specialised banks were established to reach the rural population. The enormous increase in the banking sector is evident in the establishment of 20 branches of 14 different nationalised banks in the late 1990s.[19] The extension of state control was also felt in the supply of essential food items sold through a government-controlled notionally fair price-ration system.

A similar transformation from private to state control took place in the sphere of education. In 1871 local 'notables' established a high school in Bolpur town. British railway personnel also started a Baptist mission and an American Methodist missionary played a pivotal role in spreading education among women in the late nineteenth century. At this time there were 4 schools in the region which were controlled by private individuals but recognised by Calcutta University. After Independence, schooling in this rural market town was brought under the control of the state government. In Bolpur town and its nearby villages there are now 5 higher secondary schools, 15 secondary schools, and 157 primary schools. These schools are mostly run by the state government. There are 8 primary schools which are run by Bolpur municipality.[20]

A similar transition from private to state initiative can be observed in the sphere of University education in the town. In the second half of the nineteenth century, railways established a close connection between social and educational movements in Calcutta and rural Birbhum. In 1860 a principal religious reformer of Calcutta, Devendranath Tagore, came to Bolpur by train in order to attend a ceremony organised by the Sinha family of Raipur. Impressed by the desolate beauty of rural Birbhum, he established a meditation centre called Santiniketan. This institution brought the region into close connection with Calcutta's new intellectual movements. By the turn of the century, one of Devendranath's sons – the well known poet Rabindranath – established an educational centre at Santiniketan. In Rabindranath's lifetime this institution, financed primarily through private donations, flourished as a radical alternative to colonial education. In 1918 this institution came to be known as Vishva-Bharati. In 1951, soon after Independence, it was recognised as a central university and thus came under the control of central government. It would be wrong to presume that private provision for education died out completely. Since the demand for privately sponsored English education has always existed among the affluent middle classes in the town, there exists a demand for private English-medium education. Recently in the Santiniketan region of Bolpur there came into existence private educational institutions such as the Naba Nalanda schools. There is also a burgeoning demand for private tuition for the children of the middle classes.

The other area in which private services flourished alongside the government-sponsored education system was the health service. It was only in 1988–9 that a government hospital comprising 125 beds was built near Bolpur town. This replaced the rudimentary structure of primary and secondary state-run health services set up earlier. In and around Santiniketan, Vishva Bharati University catered to the health needs of its members through the University hospital.[21] In the early 1990s, serious clashes between students and hospital staff members over the allegedly poor services of the hospital took place; these then spiralled into a wider confrontation between students and university employees leading to the closure of the university. Even today, basic health care in the town is very much dependent on private medical practices. Thus, while the socialistic experiments with development by the successive Congress governments in India have led to key financial and business institutions coming under state control, school education and health continue to be rely upon heavy inputs from the private sector. This has had a crucial impact on standards of health and life expectancy of the local poor.

The increasingly heavy presence of the state institutions at grass-roots level has played a crucial role in shaping local polity as well as social and economic aspirations of the local population. More importantly, such institutions employ a rhetoric of social and economic development to justify their presence and are involved in supervising developmental programmes initiated by the state government at grass-roots level. This rhetoric has made these institutions more than administrative centres. It has transformed such institutions into a source of patronage for the local population, informing and influencing their understanding of complex functions of the developmental state. Not only do these institutions constitute a conduit between a centralised state channelling its resources to grass roots level for developmental purposes, they also play a significant role in urban employment generation, providing bank loans to buy rickshaws or to start poultry-rearing enterprises, for example. The absence of transparency and efficiency in state institutions adds further complexities in their relationship with local population. The supposed impersonal nature of state institutions is mediated by powerful local brokers and political entrepreneurs whose ability to dispense state resources can both impress and disappoint.

This situation has become more complicated as bureaucrats increasingly resent the intervention of political entrepreneurs in their supposed specialised field of action. This is particularly true in the case of irrigation, agricultural and block development departments which are involved in sensitive rural development programmes. These institutions are run by individuals recruited through competitive examinationss for central and state-level administrative services. These civil servants regard themselves as specialised development personnel and act as a crucial interface between elected politicians at local and state levels. They combine a seeming concern for development with a well-documented wariness to deal with politically sensitive programmes. The bureaucrats consider themselves decision makers, planners, dispensers and custodians of local interests, and thus feel the need to maintain a distance from the local population and politicians. At the same time, these officials complain that they are overtly exposed to political pressures exerted by ruling political parties.

Market towns have become the centre of political activities and movements and thus serve as a crucial arena of politicisation of rural societies. The emergence of the government employees' federation [Coordination Committee of

Government Employees affiliated to CPI(M)], the school teachers' organisation [All Bengal Teachers' Association affiliated to CPI(M)], and several unions for low-scale employees provide the impetus for wider political movements in the town. This has also prompted the growth of unions in less financially stable private businesses such as cinema houses, electronic goods shops and rickshaw pullers. While the established unions represent lower-middle class interest groups, the new unions represent working class constituents who constitute a structurally separate domain in the town polity, and are engaged in contesting middle class hegemony over the urban political structure.

The challenge of the urban poor to middle class political hegemony is exemplified in the urban poor's attempts to establish democratic control over urban political structures in the Left Front era. Under the Congress regime, state institutions increasingly acquired the characteristics of patrons of local development initiatives, with the local population becoming the recipient client. In the Left Front era these patron-client relationships between state and local inhabitants in crucial social and economic spheres was seemingly subjected to the control of elected representatives. As a consequence, the town population came to expect far better representation than these institutions could offer. Instead these institutions remained the exclusive preserve of the middle classes due to their access to education and also because of their supposed accumulated cultural capital, which gave them superior management skills. The demand for democratisation of the structure of these institutions thus became highly politically contentious. Finally, the existence of these institutions itself gave a particular shape to the occupational structure and the nature of social stratification of these towns. The next section will explore the social stratification and class configuration of these towns.

4. Social Stratification and Class Configuration in an Agricultural Market Town

From the late nineteenth century onwards, agricultural expansion in the Bolpur countryside depended upon the gradual influx of Santhal labourers from neighbouring districts. They were also joined by local semi-Hinduised dalit groups such as the *bagdi* and *bauri*. While these groups worked mainly as marginal farmers or agricultural workers as far back as the pre-colonial era, many local peasant castes such as Sadgops established themselves as peasant proprietors. Finally, there were several powerful landholding families who also belonged to ritually poor social groups but had accumulated enough wealth and land to acquire significant social status, the Ghosh family of Taltor and the Sarkars of Surul being notable examples. Thus caste for non-dalit or adivasi[23] groups did not have much economic significance even in the early colonial era. As the urban areas started to expand, a substantial section of the non-dalit population moved towards the town, and as the town expanded it came to incorporate some of the predominantly dalit settlements. The dalit and adivasi population ultimately became concentrated between the rural and urban part of the Bolpur-Sriniketan block where Bolpur town is located. In Bolpur subdivision dalits constitute nearly 30.12 per cent of the population. Similarly, adivasis constitute 19.07 per cent of the Bolpur Sriniketan Block. However, both groups form of a negligible segment of population in the town itself.[24]

In terms of occupation it would be wrong to categorise the entire dalit community as a homogenous category. The dalit community is divided into seven different caste groups namely *Bagdi, Chamar, Bauri, Dom, Mal, Sundri* and *Hadi*.[25] Among these groups, *Sundris* – who are traditionally liquor makers – have access to higher education, own land and constitute a large number of government employees. The rest are predominantly agricultural workers and marginal farmers. In urban areas, most *Bagdi* women work as domestic servants while men are mainly engaged in rickshaw driving. In Bolpur town there are nearly 700 registered rickshaw drivers who are recruited primarily from this community, alongside migrants from Bihar. In addition there are many unregistered rickshaws and often the same rickshaws are driven by two or three men by arrangement.[26] Rickshaw driving remains the most popular profession among poorer migrants, as it requires few skills and it is not difficult to obtain a rickshaw. At one time wealthy businessmen owned the rickshaws and rented them out to drivers in return a for fixed sum of money paid every morning to the owner. From the late 1970s onwards a state bank small business loan scheme has enabled individual drivers to purchase their own rickshaws. However, gaining access to such schemes implies knowing someone, or securing the support of a wealthy patron who would act as guarantor, and finally waiting for the sanction of the loan to come through. Despite the lengthy procedures, most rickshaw drivers prefer the State Bank loan scheme. The rickshaw drivers are in constant competition, to the extent that it has become increasingly difficult for rickshaw drivers to form a union. Moreover, because the main patrons of rickshaw drivers are often individual members of the public, it is not easy for them to develop collective bargaining regarding fares. Disputes between passengers and drivers are common. Recently, an increase in the number of auto-rickshaws and buses within the town has made it more difficult for them to ply their trade at a competitive rate. Attempts to organise rickshaw drivers have been made by the CPI(M) but have been unsuccessful. On the other hand, wealthy businessmen often patronise 'non-political unions' based on personal loyalties. Control over such unions provides these figures with power in the turbulent world of business; they also enjoy an important profile in local politics. But such unions are unable to retain loyalties and often collapse due to personal rivalries among traders themselves.

As a social group, rickshaw drivers are among the poorest sections of the population, without any effective means for political organisation. Most rickshaw drivers try to run a petty shop or stall as their secondary profession, assisted by their immediate family members. They are often arrested by the police for gambling and illicit liquor selling. Attempts by town councils and local police officers to impose control over rickshaws plying their trade in the town promotes unrest and protests despite being largely ineffectual. Some educated rickshaw drivers have sought to increase the respectability of their trade and draw attention to the plight of their fellow workers by organising cultural activities including sculpture, singing folk songs and even writing poetry. These activities have generated social awareness among rickshaw drivers, which has in turn contributed to the decline of the old paternalistic ties between rickshaw drivers and their middle class patrons. Many individual rickshaw pullers have served particular households for years. Younger members express a clear disregard for such traditional relationships. Indeed most are members of local clubs which mushroomed in the early 1970s and have been held responsible for engaging in street battles with middle class youths on religious days such as *holi* and *puja*. Ganesh – a rickshaw driver – explained to me that anger takes control over their lives; rickshaw drivers are clearly aware of their social deprivation.[27]

Throughout the 1980s many bhadralok residents complained about the aggressiveness of rickshaw drivers. Many rickshaw drivers maintain a rural connection making seasonal visits to their villages. It is true that this section of the population has become increasingly militant but they lack effective means of organisation.

Another proletarian group in the town is that of the *Santhal* workers. They are mainly concentrated in rice mills and in construction work. A substantial proportion of them are women. These women workers earn lower wages than their male counterparts and enjoy less bargaining power. Ethnically different, marked out also for their gender difference in a predominantly male working world, they are socially marginalised and are often the victims of sexual exploitation. From the late 1970s onwards a number of attempts have been made to organise the rice mill workers; these initiatives were taken by a section of CPI(M-L) activists.[28] Rice milling is a seasonal industry and a competitive one given the overcrowded nature of the market for low-skilled workers. As a consequence, workers have made few tangible gains through union activities.

A second visible urban working class group is that of Muslims concentrated in the relatively higher paid skilled sectors, such as bakéries, construction and brickmaking. The bakers have organised unions and preserve their skilled position through craft associations. The construction industry employs both Muslim men and *Santhal* women. Their pay is dependent upon the construction of houses by private individuals, especially in the Santiniketan area. This group is much better paid but depends upon seasonal employment for their work.[29] It is difficult for this group to organise politically and its members tend to rely upon informal social networks to obtain employment and function as a team under a nominated head mason.

In terms of social hierarchy, roadside stallholders rank slightly above manual labourers. These stallholders generally employ family labour to run their businesses. More often than not, they exploit the services of child workers and underpaid women who do not belong to the immediate family circles to run errands and undertake menial tasks. Poor by any standard, they eke out a very meagre livelihood and are constantly threatened by the municipality for occupying state property. However, these groups can exercise their political muscle quite well. Sudden initiatives by the municipalities to clean the town often lead towards the eviction of these shop owners and stallholders; on occasion the police have evicted lawful shop owners.

The urban poor describe themselves as *garib manus* (poor people) or as *majur classer lok* (working class people). They do not constitute a homogenous social entity and tensions are quite often visible among them. Language and religion constitute a crucial marker of boundary. Affairs between Santhal women and Muslim men have been the immediate cause of intense conflicts and fights. Santhals, Muslims and Dalits live in different villages and localities and reinforce a sense of belonging through cultural activities such as *Durga puja* organised by local clubs. However, ethnicity does not create insuperable divisions between the urban or semi-urbanised rural poor, and cross-ethnic marriages are not uncommon. However, divorce and desertion is also prevalent within and between groups. The notion of belonging to a deprived urban poor social class is at least as strong as the identification with a particular locality or ethnic group. There exists a visible social distinction between these women and men and those of the more affluent segment of the population. Working class youths are well aware that they have little access to education and few chances of improving their living condition through hard labour. Babus are generally disbelieved or hated for their 'duplicity' and envied for their wealth. Anger, frustration and disregard for social conventions are increasingly evident.

However, the urban working classes cannot simply be characterised by desperate poverty and lack of organisation. The skilled workers, such as electricians, cycle repairers, ironsmiths and 'class iv' employees of government concerns, are assertive and vocal and dominate the multiplying service sectors of the economy. The agricultural boom in the late 1980s helped this group to consolidate their position. Educated up to the level of matriculation and financially far more secure than manual workers, they describe themselves as *nimna madhayabitta* or lower middle classes. They place great importance in obtaining formal education, and cultivate a sense of social honour which is constructed around employment and earning rather than caste. Their own caste origins are heterogeneous, extending from dalits to brahmins. Few women from this group are publicly employed. Marriages are generally arranged on the basis of wealth, education and the employment status of bridegroom and the ability of the bride to bring a stipulated amount of dowry. The skilled workers are highly unionised and constitute the backbone of different political parties, playing an active part in processions and public meetings. The opportunity for social mobility is higher among these groups but the immediate evidence of cross-generational mobility is not always very large. They have greater roots in urban society and are much more divorced from their rural origins.

The clerical employees of banks, government establishment, railways, schoolteachers, college lecturers and non-teaching employees of the colleges also fall into this category. These groups are well established, obviously conscious of their rights, and regard themselves as the guardians of civic life. They possess superior access to government resources, dominate the local political structure and enjoy substantial opportunities for social mobility. Education is considered a valuable asset, many studying for university degrees, and there tends to be resentment towards those from further down the social scale who seek access to their ranks. Marriages across caste, locality and even religion occur, and decisions tend to be made through mutual consent, with youths independently entering relationships and subsequently seeking the approval of their parents, which in most cases is granted after certain negotiations. Though dowry is common in this social group, it is often taken in kind rather than cash, and there is increasingly vocal opposition to dowries and all forms of arranged marriages. Local middle-ranking bureaucrats and the intermediate level political elite of the town are generally recruited from this group.

There is however a sharp division between political, commercial, academic and bureaucratic elite groups within the middle classes. The commercial elite is recruited from larger shop owners who often come from trading, or prosperous peasant castes. Many of them are from large landowning families who have moved into trade and commerce and run large shops and agro-based industries. Education beyond school level is not generally sought after; highly conservative in their social life, women tend to remain within the household while caste rituals are scrupulously observed. They constitute the mass base of the Congress/Trinamul Congress organisations, though a substantial minority tend to support ruling parties irrespective of political colour. As agrarian prosperity developed in Bolpur, this group has benefited substantially. For the last two decades commercial families have moved out to new business areas and invested substantially in selling electronic consumer items, house-building material and other non-traditional goods. These groups remain dependent upon the support of political and bureaucratic elites as the latter act as the gatekeepers of the licensing system and the distribution of business loans by banks crucial for their survival. Radical political rhetoric and union activities are often directed against such groups.

Finally, there exists a powerful stratum of academic elites based in Vishva-Bharati University, which remains a separate enclave within the town outside the jurisdiction of the municipal authorities. These elites receive direct benefits from the central government and enjoy a high level of salary and research grants, and remain generally aloof from local politics, though they tend to support the liberal wing of the former Congress party and present Trinamul political formation. Their economic interests are secured through privileges accorded to central government employees, and they retain close contact with local bureaucratic elites. This group is by turns ridiculed, envied and criticised for their perceived elitism and snobbery, despite their championing of liberal values. They supposedly oppose religious, caste and regional exclusiveness while laying claim to a superior culture. They have their own clubs, associations and charitable organisations, and often participate in the activities of local Rotary and Lion clubs along with commercial and bureaucratic elites.

Bolpur town is ruled by a segment of specialised bureaucrats and technocrats. They are temporarily posted, transferred after three years and recruited from the higher echelons of the West Bengal Civil Service, or more rarely from the Indian Administrative Service – the prestigious all-India level service. The head of the local administration is a Subdivisional Officer who runs the civil administration and is assisted in his task by the local SDPO (Subdivisional Police Officers), Block Development Officer (BDO), Subdivisional Information Officer (SDIO), the Judges of the subdivisional court and an Irrigation and Agricultural officer. The occupants of these transferable offices maintain little connection with local politics but jealously guard their status as bureaucratic elites. Bank managers, doctors, headmasters of schools and principals of the college constitute the remaining elements within the bureaucratic elite. These are powerful local elites with a definite position within the bureaucratic map of the Indian state.[30] Caste remains an insignificant element in determining their social position, though the overwhelming majority of government employees, despite reservation for SC and ST communities, belong to a non dalit-adivasi background.

Class configuration and social stratification in Bolpur town is highly complex, but this does not preclude the existence of a deep social divide between those who claim middle class status and those who self-consciously belong to the working classes. While the city's commercial, bureaucratic and academic elite generally meet in the Lion or Rotary clubs – set up in the town in 1970 and 1977 respectively – the city's poor have their own social organisations, dominated by local youths from clerical or class IV employments , and bearing typical Bengali names such as Mahamaya Sangh, Adyashakti club, or locality markers such as the Bhubandanga Youth Society, and incorporating many of the poorer youths of the town. Santhals and other social groups have more ethnicised social organisations such as adivasi *kalyan samity* (Aboriginal Welfare Society), *harmarshal gaonta* (Organisation of Santhal Villagers) or even their own cultural organisations that often fulfil the role of both a centre of recreation and a pressure group.

The other most significant marker of class remains the absence of opportunity for social mobility, something which is reflected in family life. Marriage breakdown and neglect of children and elderly parents remains a problem among the poorer classes, who face an intense battle for survival. Lack of financial and job security, remain a constant source of worry for the poor. Precarious living standards take a heavy toll on health and there exists very little scope for escaping the limitations imposed by grinding poverty. Economic growth may ensure a few more jobs, and offer a slightly better hope for the future but it scarcely affects the daily life of the poor. For the middle classes, family welfare and status occupies a central position. Family is used to push forward the career of a son, or marriage – and even career – of a daughter, provides a sense of belonging and hope and opens up life chances for them. Education and economic improvement thus take place through family connections. In this manner, the prominence of family as a form of social and economic stability further separates the various social groups.

The connection with the villages is another social marker between classes. The poor retain greater ties with rural areas, while the middle classes, excluding commercial elites, are generally divorced from rural society. Dalit social groups often use their urban incomes to strengthen their meagre rural resources. The classic notion of an urban proletariat divorced from rural roots is obviously not applicable to these groups, though they belong to the rural landless agricultural workers' categories. Commercial elites have to maintain close connections with the rural market and to cater to rural clientele, and hence economic and political reasons keep them in touch with rural bases. Bureaucrats, academic elites and the city's organised skilled workforce have little connection with the land. Many of the latter groups are refugees from East Bengal with little notion of rural roots in West Bengal, and the second generation constitutes an urban population with no rural memory except for reified images of East Bengal villages in vogue among their parents. Class therefore constitutes a significant marker of the degree of urbanisation, even in a small market town in rural West Bengal.

The most important issue here is the conventional idea of the economic relationship between these social groups. These economic relationships are generally characterised by a culturally defined notion of sense of duty. Thus the rickshaw driver would try to assess how to define the bargaining process with his passengers, a shop keeper may offer certain specific credit limits to his workers or poorer neighbours in return for particular services. Credit will be offered by cycle repair men to a supposedly student clientele. All these take place within a personalised world of economic transactions. Even purchasing daily items from a particular shop depends upon the personal relationship with the shop owner. For example ration-shop owners keep the ration cards of their poorer clientele and offer cheaper credits on their rations in return for the shop owner being allowed to sell parts of their ration quotas at a dearer price (or black-market rate) to their more affluent middle class customers. Domestic servants expect food, new clothes during *pujas* and the right to watch television in the evening in their employers' houses. While most of these dealings are made on a personal level, the institutions and mechanisms of the state are looked upon as the ultimate determinant of everyday economic life. Thus a bazaar economy, based on personal relations and local conventions, is ultimately regulated by the institutions of state. In the wholesale market the state controls many of the warehouses and cold storage facilities. The state also regulates the supply of rationed articles in the retail trade. Prices of train tickets and prices of petrol are regulated by it, and the access to state resources remain the crucial marker of real power in the town. This is where the dynamics of politics becomes critical in terms of understanding local social and economic relationships.

5. The Transformation in the Polity Under the Left Regime: Centralised Decentralisation and Orchestrated Democratisation

The coming of the Left Front to power is a crucial landmark in Bengal's politics. It initiated radical changes in the polity, both in terms of intense polit-ical mobilisation and institutional structure. The intensity of this political transformation is marked by a duality inherent in Communist mobilisation in an open democratic context. On the one hand, the Left attempt represents the most bold effort to reorganise the polity at grassroots level; on the other hand it imposes a very impressive degree of political control by the party over the myriad forms of political activities planned by the constituents of the Front and their mass organisations. On the other hand the left attempt democratises the polity, institutionalises the principle of democratic political competition at grassroots level and erects a structure of participatory democracy; on the other, the centralised party organisation becomes the pivotal feature of everyday political life. The powerful corporatist structure of the organisation of the Left Front provides it with the opportunity to intervene, partially restructure the rural power relations and reorganise the economic mechanism of growth.

While the Left Front's constant mobilisation and the institutionalisation of the polity makes the notion of democratic rights a significant feature of every-day social life, at the same time its organisational structure stifles individual initiative. To understand this we have to explore the Left Front's political and economic strategies, and their implications, more closely.

The Left Front Government came to power in West Bengal in 1977. Soon afterwards, it sought to reorganise the polity at grass roots level by installing Panchayati Raj in villages through the implementation of the Congress Government's *Panchayat* Act of 1973. While the Congress, true to its political tradition, enacted the law as a mere token – a gesture of goodwill to the rural population, with little chance of implementation – the new Left Front used the act to hold regular elections in the three-tier *panchayat* structure in rural areas on a party political basis. In 1978 a new Panchayati Raj came into existence in rural areas. The Left Front Government then used old municipal legislation to hold elections to municipalities. For example, Bolpur municipality was formed in 1951 but experienced proper regular elections only from 1981. Municipal elections from then onwards have been held through the state at the same time; the last being held on 28 May 2000. Then the election of Calcutta corpora-tion is institutionalised in 1985. The Left Front also changed laws in the University to hold regular elections for the University senate and syndicates comprised of representatives from students, teachers and non-teaching employees of the University. Similar elections were held for school boards.

If we look at the implication of these changes for the polity we have to look at what changes these elections brought about in Bengal. Let us take the example of the second Left Front government's period from a voter's perspec-tive. In 1982 our putative voter voted for the assembly election; in 1983, he voted in rural panchayati elections all over Bengal; he would again vote in the Loksabha election in 1984. This rural voter, let us assume, had moved from his village to a nearby market town such as Bolpur, in which case he would then vote in the municipal election of 1986, and would witness the drama of Calcutta corporation's election on radio in 1985 or – if he has access – on television and – if he could read – in the newspaper. He would again cast his vote in the assembly election in 1987. In West Bengal electoral mobilisation has been a central feature of everyday political life. Moreover, all these elections are contested along party political lines. More importantly, there exists the corpo-ratist structure of this mobilisation. The CPI(M), the principal constituent of the Left Front, has five major mass organisations: the Student Federation of

India; the Democratic Youth Federation; the Democratic Women's Association; Kisan Sabha; and the Centre for Indian Trade Unions. These organisations issue propaganda in almost every aspect of daily life. We can safely assume that our putative voter is now saturated with constant party political propaganda and has already realised the importance of his vote as an instrument of political change. More importantly, as my interviews with 24 employees of rice mills, 12 construction workers and 8 rickshaw drivers reveal, there has developed a deep notion of democratic rights and egalitarian political culture, irrespective of political affiliation. Not only has such democratisation created a tradition of participatory democracy but it has instilled a sense of the administration's accountability to the public. At the same time, expectations of the poor have increased substantially; this is due particularly to the progress of the Panchayati Raj in rural Bengal.

Electoral mobilisation by the Left Front in Bengal has been accompanied by a drive for land reforms, which – particularly the registration of share croppers – became a mass movement in rural Bengal. However, the principal legacy of the *panchayat* is not simply the land reforms programme. The fact that accelerated agricultural growth in the state during the 1980s coincided with the Left Front agrarian reforms has provided some scope for speculation about the possible effects of reforms on productivity.[31] There are some studies that suggest a positive link between the Left Front reforms and agricultural performance,[32] and I agree with Harriss, that technological developments (such as the wide adoption of High Yielding Variety seeds for *aman* crop and an extensive increase in irrigated *boro* cultivation) and farmers' response to relative price changes through an increased consumption of agricultural input have played a crucial role in agricultural growth.[33] The dichotomisation of the explanations for recent agricultural growth in West Bengal in market versus non-market innovations is problematic. After all, private agents operate within an overall economic context that is conditioned to a great extent by the distribution of assets as well as political power. The agrarian reforms introduced by the Left Front government have possibly built up confidence among rural producers and hence created greater incentives for them with regard to investment in land.[34] Most importantly, the effective operation of local-level governments has played a positive role in the flow of information, the general functioning of input delivery systems and the execution of rural infrastructure development schemes. Indeed, the access to urban markets through a gradually expanding dense network of feeder roads constructed by Jela Parishad has played a crucial role in sustaining agricultural growth and consequent urban expansion.

Peasant mobilisation on the issue of land reforms also had enormous repercussions on urban politics. Every day, large processions gathered in front of several government offices in the town. Often peasants encircled BDO and

SDO offices and the agricultural office in an effort to obtain better information. Bank officials and bureaucratic elites were forced to attend peasant meetings to discuss rural development issues. These events impinged on the urban working classes. As several rickshaw drivers and flower-mill workers testified, they then believed that their turn would come soon. By the mid-1980s agricultural growth had contributed substantially to the expansion of urban agro-based industries. Attempts were made to float new unions in all segments of the urban population. Two important segments of population experienced the steady progress of unionisation among themselves: the employees of the government offices and concerns. Indeed, in the absence of an industrial proletariat, government employees functioned as a surrogate working class for communist mobilisation in urban Bengal. The Coordination Committee of the government employees became a formidable union. Similarly, schoolteachers were grouped into several teachers' organisations, while West Bengal College and University Teachers' Association also established a powerful foothold among Lecturers of the University. In Vishva Bharati, the Adhyapak Sabha Association of University Teachers was set up. Yet the poorest segment of the urban working classes – namely rickshaw drivers, employees of seasonal industries and construction workers – remain significantly outside the purview of this new drive towards unionisation. The need for unionisation and the protection of minimum wages is surely greatest among this segment of the population.

The drive for the unionisation of workers in small industrial concerns, such as rickshaw drivers, came from workers themselves. The union that claimed to have led the rickshaw drivers was organised by a local trader with no known political affiliation. Such unions are run as private enterprises and rickshaw drivers generally remained unorganised. Two strikes were organised in the early 1980s that were marked by clashes between the rickshaw drivers themselves. Moreover a rickshaw strike caused wider resentment among the passengers from various segments of the middle classes. When a segment of the Left Front formed the municipality board in 1981, it was forced to impose new control over rickshaws plying their trade in the town. Indeed, this time the CPI(M)'s own union made an effort to further the cause of rickshaw drivers. Again, the strike turned out to be a partial success. A section of CPI(M-L) groups then made an attempt to organise rice-mill workers and employees of the high-street shops known as *path parsastha dokan karmachari samity*.[35] This union collapsed, as it rapidly became clear that the high-street shops would prefer to dismiss their employees rather than accept the demands of the unions. Rice mills similarly accepted the existence of unions but refused to abide by the negotiations. Even cinema-hall employees have tried to establish unions in the town's growing number of cinema halls, but these proved rather inefficient. On most occasions, it appears that the combination of employers is far more powerful than workers of such seasonal industries. Strategies of collective bargaining turn out to be more problematic and can contribute towards complete closure and immediate lock-outs. Thus there exists little planning for meaningful economic redistribution in the economy through political mobilisation or collective bargaining.

Municipalities were resurrected by the Left Front as urban self-government institutions. But they have little power to raise extra resources. When the Left Front came to power the working classes voted for several Left candidates, particularly in the poorest localities. In fact, Bolpur municipality came under the sway of an alliance between a section of CPI(ML) and CPI that dominated the urban municipal board till 1991. However, despite some rudimentary developmental programmes, such as street lighting and improvements to the supply of drinking water, the municipality remained basically an institution deprived of power. In fact, the resurrected municipality pressurised the poorest section of shop owners for taxes, yet could raise little from its richer inhabitants. Few efforts were made in that direction, while pressure mounted upon municipal councillors to reorganise municipal affairs. Resource-poor and financially insolvent, the municipality hardly turned out to be an agency for radical redistribution, despite the sincere dedication of its members. So powerless did the municipality appear to be that it soon faced strikes by its own employees, mostly dalit cleaners employed in the sanitary department. The strike was particularly directed against the reputedly '*naxalite*' Vice Chairman of the municipality. Ward representatives had to tread a very thin line to balance the demands of the urban poor with those of their middle class constituents. More importantly, as we have observed, the fundamental premise of privilege in urban Bengal is the connection between state institutions and various educated elite groups. This connection could have been meaningfully challenged through effective strategies to spread education and create a democratic condition for the governance of these institutions, which would diminish the hold of privileged classes and lessen bureaucratic controls in urban Bengal. It did not happen.

Interestingly enough, the political climate increasingly started changing in these municipal towns from the late 1980s onwards. On the one hand, the old notion of the personalised relationship between employers and employees eroded rapidly. The old relationship was shaken by two factors. First, the notion of employers acting as the custodians of workers' interests was steadily eroding as the political culture of collective bargaining asserted its presence, and secondly, the absence of a commensurate increase in the salary of the workers also played a role in the erosion of personalised political culture. Yet growing political consciousness in the absence of a sustainable trade union movement has led to the unpredictable, and to violence in the political culture of urban Bengal. Unlike the early 1970s, when large-scale political violence was characteristic of everyday life, this violence takes the form of street fights, local gangsterism and organised criminal activities under the protection of leaders of political parties. Militancy has also acquired the form of continuous road blockades, attacks on buses, beating up of doctors and setting fire to vehicles involved in the accidents. All these stray incidents of violence are endemic in the urban areas of Bolpur. Political assertiveness had acquired the notion of instant justice.

The notion of instant justice has developed through the regular viewing of commercial movies. The four cinema halls and numerous video parlours are frequented by the poor city dwellers themselves. Movies in the 1980s emphasised individual heroism as a solution to social ills. They depicted a liaison between corrupt police, trade-union leaders and public officials. On the other hand, they sometimes glorified ordinary urban working class youth action, but on an individual basis. The ability of silver-screen heroes to find instantaneous solutions to everyday problems, and particularly to the complex problem of slum eviction in the larger cities, impress the urban working classes greatly. Young male workers told me without qualification that they prefer their movie heroes to real life political bosses. There is now a different form of rebellion against any form of incumbent power. It is not that the CPI(M) has lost its political foothold among the urban working classes, but rather that the working classes are increasingly reluctant to express their active support. Instead, populism with instantaneous solutions appeals to them: road and railway blockades, burning of tyres and the culture of instant protests demanding instant solutions from the town administrators. This partially explains the new popularity of the Trinamool Congress among urban working classes. The populist appeal of Mamata Banerjee, her spontaneous, aggressive approach with its thinly-veiled threat of violence, gained political legitimacy in urban Bengal.

The failure of unionisation has been capitalised on by traders in Bolpur. They had resented the radicalism of the early 1980s and the growth of labour militancy at grassroots level. There is a new resentment among all segments of the middle classes against the erosion of the culture of obedience and respect for employers among the working classes. The constant complaint in middle class households is of the insolent behaviour of domestic servants. The emphasis placed by domestic servants on a negotiated employment, based on a day off, the right to watch television, periodic increase in wages in accordance with price increases, gifts during the time of festivities, together with their frequent absence, is widely disliked by employers. More importantly, middle class house owners complain about the reluctance of young women and men to take up domestic service, which is now looked down upon by many young members of working class households. Thus the democratic revolution in Bengal, initiated by the decentralisation of polity and electoral mobilisation, has created a situation of class conflict without any clearly formulated strategy for redistribution of wealth or any sustainable basis for the creation of better life chances for urban workers.

6. Conclusion

The nature of the transformation of urban politics throws light upon three crucial factors as ingredients for urban political changes: the economic organisation and the nature of class configuration in a town; the institutional structure of politics; and the nature of political mobilisation and language of politics. In Bolpur, an economic model for growth was premised upon market-based structure and technological innovation combined with democratisation of rural administration and land reforms. However, in the urban context such growth did not provide the sustainable basis for an urban redistributive strategy. Democratisation of institutional reform remained limited, while political mobilisation in an environment of democratic upsurge moved far ahead, firing the imagination of the urban population. The crucial corollary of that political movement has been the demoralisation of the urban working classes and a situation of political instability without a clearly defined programme of political action. In urban Bengal, Left mobilisation assisted the relatively affluent organised sector of the workforce employed in government concerns. The democratic upsurge thus paved the way for the first rudimentary level of urban political reorganisation, where the state institutional structure still controls and dominates the economic life of the town and constitutes the fundamental premise for institutional forms of social privilege. By highlighting the notion of social class, this essay asserts the crucial importance of a redistributive political and economic solution to urban poverty in Bengal.

8

ACTION, AUTONOMY AND POLITICAL RIGHTS: TOWARDS A THEORY OF 'POLITICAL LITERACY'[1]

Sumi Madhok

This essay focuses on particular aspects of 'public individualism': autonomy and political rights. It analyses the significance of political rights in conditions of subordination and argues for a non-individualist formulation of moral agency.[2] By 'public individualism', I refer to the public view of the person that informs the functioning and maintenance of political institutions that defend or guard specific rights of the individual. Political institutions informed by public individualism presuppose the autonomy of individuals or of (public) citizens who are expected to exercise the 'rights' maintained by these institutions and be responsible for the choices that they make. However, this public individualism is often in conflict with social doctrines that sanction private freedoms. There is thus a tension between individualism as a public view of the person informing the rights of persons, and the narrow agreement on social freedoms that characterise the private person.

Feminist theorising has shown the inadequacy of conventional philosophical conceptions of autonomy for both feminist philosophical practice as well as feminist politics, and has offered reconstructed accounts of autonomy. This essay builds on these reconstructed understandings while contributing an additional argument. It asks how we can understand agential capacities of persons within conditions of subordination. It suggests that 'free action' accounts of autonomy, i.e. the accounts of autonomy that privilege an agent's ability to commit free action, constitute the principle obstacle to this exercise. We argue that action does not exist in a social vacuum, and that there are reasons why people act in certain ways which are not always expressive of one's preferred judgements.

It is beyond the ambit of this essay to explore the 'value' of autonomy and its desirability. It is sufficient to say, however, that some notion of autonomy is important for understanding political and moral agency and is also essential for feminist epistemological practice. We need a conceptual language which can adequately capture the attempts of persons to introduce change in their lives. The language of autonomy – suitably modified – can, I believe, usefully serve this purpose.

To begin, I shall first examine the tension between the public and the private view of the person by examining rural Rajasthani women's encounters with political rights. Through their engagement, it is possible to identify the forms as well as the functions assumed by political rights as embodiments of this public individualism. These engagements with political rights take on two different forms that correspond with and reflect two different understandings of the self that are expressed as a result of these engagements. The first acknowledges the self as a possessor of rights; the second reflects a primarily relational, embedded self.[3] More often than not these two forms intersect, revealing a complex self, accommodating different moral pressures and demands. The engagements with political rights and the reformulation of meanings that accompanies these are, I shall argue, indicative of their particular capacities, and more specifically, of their moral autonomy.[4] Finally their articulation of and commitment to political rights, which is not always evident in their action, compels us to look for ways in which we can capture conceptually their capacities and the ensuing particular skills. I shall refer to these skills as 'political literacy'.

In order to illustrate my argument I will examine the moral encounter with the idea and language of rights of a group of rural women known as the *sathins*,[5] who are involved in a state-sponsored development program for women in the North Western Indian State of Rajasthan. The *sathins* are largely illiterate or semi-literate, and generally belong to the lowest castes. The fieldwork was conducted in the districts of Jaipur and Ajmer over a period of eight months, between September 1998 and April 1999.

The negotiations of the *sathins* with political rights take the form of an interpretative exercise that results in new meanings, both moral and linguistic. Some of these meanings are born out of a desire to weave newly acquired values within an existing moral framework. The linguistic meanings are essentially efforts – both practical and intellectual – to increase the comprehensibility of rights-based ideas within their existing moral framework.

1. Moral Autonomy and the Individual

Questions of moral agency have traditionally involved establishing the responsibility of persons for actions emanating from freely chosen rational principles. The most general formulation of a person considered to be morally autonomous has been when, and only when, his or her moral principles are entirely his or her own. But what does it mean to be the self-originators of our moral principles? According to Gerald Dworkin, these might mean 'if one is the author of one's moral principles, if one chooses these, if the ultimate source of these principles is our will, if one decided which moral principles one would be constrained by, if one refuses to accept others as moral authorities, etc'.[6] Moral autonomy is then largely constructed as a capacity that makes for self-regulation. According to this view, morally autonomous persons contain the grounds of morality within themselves and possess the ability to ascertain moral requirements. Increasingly, however, moral theorists have come to accept the social character of these moral principles and to argue that moral autonomy does not always imply that we become the 'self originators' of our moral principles.[7] This revised position does however insist that we project an affinity with these principles. But what does such identification entail? Can our actions always be explained in terms of reference to our identified beliefs? I regard these to be two separate problems. We identify with our principles if we can provide reasons for these being our principles, our beliefs. Whether we allow these beliefs with which we purport to identify, to motivate our conduct is determined to a large extent by prevailing social and moral compulsions. Not only do we not always express what we truly desire in our actions, we do not always value what we desire.[8] Therefore our actions cannot always be explained in terms of reference to our beliefs.

Feminist philosophers have unmasked the excessive individualism underlying this conception of moral agency and have consequently presented reconstructions of the concept. These reconfigurations have focused on and drawn upon women's moral experiences as 'caregivers' within the family and community and their 'oppositional agency' in the face of social, economic and political marginalisation.[9] This paper introduces a further category. It addresses the question of moral agency of persons in circumstances where there exist a number of constraints, both social and moral, on certain kinds of action by considering three factors. The first defines what we mean by 'moral agency', the second establishes its 'starting point' and describes the nature and capacities of 'moral agents' and the third specifies the social conditions within which this agency of persons can be observed. Conventional understandings of moral agency offer explanations for all three. These conclude that moral agency involves responsibility for freely chosen actions and goals by persons who are equal and free from encumbrances and interferences in making these choices, and finally, that these choices cannot be fulfilled in conditions other than those of 'negative' freedom. While feminists have taken the first two of these accepted generalisations to task, there is a general concurrence within feminist scholarship that certain conditions of 'negative' freedom are essential for the exercise of individual autonomy. It is this third contention that forms the focus of this paper. The failure to explore conceptually the moral agency of women within conditions of subordination has led to two widespread generalisations, especially within the literature on 'the third world woman': a) that these women are passive and lack agency and b) are a construction of a 'victims' discourse in relation to women in the developing world.

This essay aims to recognise the autonomy of persons through a standpoint of interdependence and community.[10] It defines autonomy as a capacity to question aspects of existing morality. The modifications in the language of autonomy that I propose are two-pronged. To understand autonomy in terms of a capacity and to shift the site of its recognition from action to identifying the ideas that lie behind action itself. Speech practices are a possible site for recognising this ability. I suggest that the moral engagements with political rights that I describe are indicative of these women's autonomy. By challenging the inconsistencies that abound in their existing moral frameworks they seek to formulate not only an alternate system of ideas, but also to produce a vocabulary through which this system might be articulated and justified. The paper seeks to examine through these speech practices not only how society shapes its members in moral terms, but also the nature of morality itself.[11]

The examination of these engagements is intended to develop a case for a wider and a more nuanced conception of autonomy, one which involves recognition of a person's capacity to introduce change, to challenge the moral repetitiveness of their lives, their ability to reorder existing moral priorities and to engage with moral rules and preordained social roles. Autonomy is thus defined as a capacity to imagine alternative moral rules and social roles.[12]

2. Political Rights and 'Recognition Respect'

Why are political rights significant in a moral economy marked by lack of sociological individualism?[13] In the particular case of the *sathins*, political rights are considered very important. These perform a moral as well as a practical function. The moral function of political rights here is to make accessible the language of 'moral worth' and respect. I am here referring to the respect that accrues to persons on account of being primarily bearers of rights. Since rights are not available either in the form of a moral language or because of institutionalised denial of these rights, the fundamental provision of self-respect in society becomes unavailable.[14] The moral community becomes the domain of the few considered to possess 'moral worth'.

Citizenship is generally held to be distinct from social membership.[15] However, in the case of the *sathins* and many members of their women's group, citizenship rights are used to gain inclusion into the moral membership of the community/village/*panchayat* etc. The language of political rights is employed to secure their inclusion within the community, especially of participation in its deliberative activities, for example through attendance and participation within the *Gram Panchayat*, or *Jati Panchayat* etc.[16] Political rights, therefore, provide a language of self-respect and a vocabulary in which to claim it. I shall refer to this respect for oneself as 'recognition respect'.[17] There are different philosophical understandings of what constitutes respect for persons and what is meant by 'treating persons as persons'. The common assumption underlying these differing understandings is that they all recognise that an important constituent of treating persons as persons is to acknowledge that they are right-bearing individuals and to treat them as such. According respect to persons involves (amongst other things) a focus on a person's status as a full and equal member of a moral community and as a bearer of certain basic moral rights.[18]

The respect due to persons on account of their being rights-bearing agents is but one way of viewing them as self-respecting individuals. Also known as the 'objectivist' position on self-respect, it requires respect to be rendered to persons on the basis of certain 'morally significant features' considered as objective standards of worthiness. As opposed to 'objectivist' positions, 'subjectivist' positions on self-respect endorse positive beliefs about, and attitude towards, oneself 'without reference to any independent standard'.[19] Feminists have voiced a concern over 'objectivist' positions on recognition respect, believing them to be informed by an abstract and essentialist conception of person, the 'neo cartesian model of the moral self, disembodied, autonomous, separate, isolated, indistinguishable from every other self'.[20] Staking our claims to personhood on the basis of being essentially right-bearing agents then makes it difficult to envision a connected and relational view of the self. They argue instead for a more connected subjectivist vision of self-respect that values our individual circumstances, in particular the subordinating circumstances of women's lives.[21] While there are obvious problems with the androcentric characterisation of 'recognition respect', it must be stated that the erasure of differences which recognition respect involves does have an empowering effect in a polity marred by rules of segmentation, where difference is held to be responsible for one's disenfranchisement from the membership of the 'moral community'.[22]

3. Sathins and the Discourse of Rights

Political rights perform not only two important functions but also assume two different forms or interpretations. These interpretations are reflective of the two ways in which the self comes to be understood and defined in the narratives of the *sathins*. The first of these two interpretations uses political rights to claim 'recognition respect' on the basis of one's personhood, defined principally by the possession of individual rights. The second interpretation of the self, as a result of these engagements with political rights, employs a more relational view of 'recognition respect', one which is marked by the creation of the new rules regularising behaviour of the emergent 'public person', in this particular case, the newly emerging 'public woman'. This challenges the linear narrative of rights discourse as one presenting an opportunity to succeed in conventional, male-defined terms.[23] In other words, in the narratives of the *sathins* the 'public' is not defined as entirely male.

In the following two sections, I shall seek to show the intersection between the ideas of the self as a right-bearing agent and those which describe the self in relation with others in the speech practices of the *sathins*. The self-authorship that occurs as a result of these engagements is interactive and situated between the categories of the 'separate self' and the 'relational self'. Therefore, while upholding rights as the basic social provision for self-respect, the *sathins* also fashion their self-portraits according to moral and social commitments informed by doctrines other than rights, for example, by the role of certain traditions considered as inalienable.

Before we look at the two forms assumed by political rights and consequently by 'recognition respect', let us first look at the process through which the *sathins* acquire and identify with the moral language of rights. The process has within it both a linguistic as well as a moral dimension. The moral process comprises a dynamic ethical reflection, which occurs when they come in contact with rights-based ideas. This leads to attempts not only to rethink many of the moral rules informing their own moral frameworks, but also selectively to absorb many of these 'new' ideas in ways which do not clutter their existing moral priorities and commitments.

The linguistic exercise takes place when the moral ideas encountered and selected need justification in a language that is both acceptable and comprehensible. In other words, when the conceptual language of rights comes in contact with the natural language[24] (Hindi/ Rajasthani/Urdu in this case), it results in a considerable amount of linguistic dislocation and turmoil. I am not referring here to the problem of translation and linguistic correspondence but to the problem of moral justification of ideas in language. This moral justification involves using a conceptual term of high moral ranking within the vernacular for the new moral idea we want to introduce within our moral repertoire.

An examination of the narratives of the *sathins* revealed a process bearing three clear stages in their thinking on rights over fourteen years of participation within the WDP (women's development program). Only 2 of the 70 *sathins* interviewed identified sources other than the state as their first point of contact with the discourse of rights.[25] The initial contact with rights-based ideas produced in its wake moral dissonance, and led to them being received by the *sathins* with considerable suspicion. This moral dissonance gave way in time to a 'new-found faith' in the discourse of rights as upheld by the state. The notion of rights in the second stage was marked by the legitimation of the rights discourse in a language that is state-dependent. The final stage in the *sathins'* thinking about rights occurred when they began to weave their own theoretical and practical defence of the idea of rights independent of the state. The state is no longer used to legitimise the upholding of women's rights. The new vocabulary of the sathins rests its intellectual defence of rights on the notion of 'truth'. Women's rights now come to be justified in the name of truth.

Here, it would be useful to examine the literal terms used in the vernacular to connote the idea of rights. The idea of possessing rights is denoted by the employment of the Urdu term *haq* and the Hindi *adhikaar*. However, the latter is used in a more formalistic manner and often interchangeably with 'power'.[26] The change from state-dependent definitions to a reference to truth may be explained in terms of the intimate connection existing between the terms for 'rights' and 'truth' in the vernacular. Rights in the vernacular usage is denoted by the term *haq*[27] whose other meanings include *sach* or truth.[28]

The architecture of this conception of truth is an intellectual as well as a practical one, drawing upon certain 'ideal' and uncorrupted aspects of social life. While this idea of truth draws upon notions of purity, it is in terms of certain social behaviour that are considered immoral and in violation of this pure ideal that 'truth' or 'truthfulness' as a particular social practice comes to be defined. There are three kinds of practices that come to be upheld as the embodiments of truth: morality in public life seen in terms of non-corrupt dealings while occupying public office, the upholding of equal rights of women, and the espousal of justice.

Recourse to the truth argument becomes essential in altercations with disbelieving and often hostile villagers, who see them as posing a threat to established norms.[29] The popular notion that women are not to be believed and that their word is not weighty enough in part explains the appeal to 'truth'.[30] It is also employed to ward off those who question their 'moral character',[31] as well as to support their raising issues which are generally considered best left alone. The injustices cited by the *sathins* are often references to the rights that they believe women possess but are unable to exercise, or in the case of development schemes or relief measures, unable to benefit from. These rights often revolve around women's property rights,[32] education, child marriages, the practice of sending women forcibly into *nata*,[33] women's right to vote and to political office, equal wages, the practice of untouchability, and so on.

4. The Evocation of Rights – Case Studies

Let us now bring back into discussion the two forms that political rights assume. The first, as I said earlier, is to claim 'recognition respect' through claiming one's right-bearing status. Let me give an exceptional example to illustrate this point: not an exceptional case in terms of the language used but in terms of the initiative taken. It is an instance where action can be explained in terms of one's 'preferred preference'. It also serves to highlight the political exclusion of women from public spaces and the context under which rights are espoused. While offering a reading of the near absence of concepts such as rights in the lives of the vast majority of rural women in India, in a way it also reemphasises the potential of rights to make meaningful interventions in people's lives, subject to there being effective support mechanisms, to provide redress of those rights claims.[34]

Mohan Kanwar of *Dosara Panchayat*[35] decided to contest the *panchayat* elections at the behest of some of the villagers. The *panchayat*, comprising eight villages, had a reserved seat for a woman *Sarpanch* under the provisions of the 73rd amendment to the constitution.[36] Two groups of influential castes, the *Jats* and the *Gujjars*, got together and proclaimed their opposition to the reservation of seats for women in the *panchayats*. These men had decided that they would boycott the election for the women's seat in the *panchayat*, and one effective way to oppose the election was to make sure that no woman contested. The men openly denounced the reservation of seats for women and wanted to make Dosara *Panchayat* an example of this opposition. They announced that there was going to be no contest. However, about eight days before the voting was to take place, when it had become abundantly clear that elections were in fact going to take place, the *Jats* and the *Gujjars* of Dosara *Panchayat* declared that they had reached a consensus: they had elected a *Sarpanch* unanimously and therefore there was no need for women to go out of their homes and contest the elections. Their consensus candidate was a Jat woman of 65 years, who was publicly garlanded and declared to be the 'consensus *Sarpanch*,'[37] elected uncontested. Following this, *jaggery* (unrefined sugar) was distributed in all the eight villages of the *panchayat*.

Mohan Kanwar's account of the events is as follows:

> This party [referring to the group formed by the *Jats* and the *Gujjars*] wrote a letter to the election commission saying that they did not want an election to take place as they had already elected a consensus candidate without opposition hoping that the election might be called off. Some people opposed to this group of *Jats* and *Gujjars* asked me to stand for elections. I refused in the beginning, as I am very poor and knew that these people might forsake me in the end. Anyway, when I heard that this 'party' had created such a terror around women's reservation and women's seat in the *panchayat*, I decided to contest the elections. Whether I lost or won now ceased to be of much concern to me, even if I only got 4 votes still, I was ready for it. I was contesting. People started offering

me money, 20,000, 40,000 rupees if I withdrew my decision to contest. I refused. I hired a tractor and went into the villages and spoke with the women. The *Jats* and the *Gujjars* issued threats that if any tractor came into the village for the purpose of campaigning for elections, the people in the tractor would be killed. I went to the villages and told the women that it was our right to contest elections and that even they should come forward and contest the seat along with me. I kept saying that it was a woman's seat which had come in our *panchayat* and that we must take full advantage of it and bring women forward to contest the elections. The group of *Jats* and *Gujjars* started campaigning against me and threatening everyone especially the women not to vote for me. For they felt that I was *padhi likhi* [Mohan Kanwar is semi literate, but she regards herself as politically literate and believes that other people regard her as such] and that if I won I would do as I please and upon electing the Old woman they would be able to do as they pleased. I am not upset about losing. I just feel content in knowing that the election did take place. When the votes were counted I polled 765 votes out of a polling list of 1700 voters. Obviously, the women of my *panchayat* voted for me other wise how could I have got 765 votes and lose by only a hundred? However, importantly, an election took place for the women's seat, we did not just give away our right to political office without a contest.'

In the above narrative, Mohan Kanwar makes two points which deserve attention. Her evocation of formal principles of rights is very powerful. She employs these formal principles to articulate her self-descriptions and to describe the denial of rights in the general social treatment of women in her *panchayat*. Her knowledge of these formal principles contributes to and is reflected in her portrayal of herself as *padhi likhi*, or literate. She highlights the indifferent impact of progressive law reform on gendered identities within the popular imagination, particularly in villages where this disregard of women's rights often escapes the focus of the state and its institutions. Both observations bear on broader concerns: the first on the rights debate within feminist theory and the second on the nature of legality and the penetrative capability of the state. The evocation of formal principles of rights has important implications for feminist theorising and feminist politics. It raises the larger question of the importance of rights-based discourse in the lives of women in subordinate circumstances, and the impact of these experiences in informing the debate within feminist theory on the relevance of rights within feminist politics.

The second form that political rights assumes is a relational[38] one. By relational I mean that people develop as a result of their embeddedness within particular social, cultural, and historical contexts and that their identities are formed within the 'context of social relationships and shaped by an intersection of cultural determinants...'[39] Political rights assume a relational form when they are employed in a manner which carefully accommodates their other identities and connections within the family and the community. This careful weave of their new public identities with their pre-existing roles leads – among other things – to the creation of new public and private rules. Rather, the rules which govern the conduct of private persons, by whom I mean persons who do not engage in the 'public/political' life of the community/village/*panchayat*, are renegotiated and revised in order to suit the demands of public/political life. There were many examples of this kind of selective absorption that occurred but perhaps one of the most interesting negotiations resulted over the observance of the *purdah*, or veil. Let me illustrate the creation of these new rules by a narrative that runs as follows.

Salma, a ward *panch* in the village of Gegal in Ajmer district, was campaigning for a selective abandonment of the *purdah*. *Purdah* is often used metaphorically to invoke the notion of silence as well as of invisibility.[40] Observing *purdah* as a mark of respect is considered important; however, its observance in places where the 'rules' are different, she suggests, is not necessary. A reservation is expressed in respect of observing *purdah* in the performance of one's public duties, although its observance within the family is regarded as a mark of respect:

The other ward *panch*[41] who has been elected sits there with her *ghungat*. She used to sit outside the *panchayat* earlier. I had to pull her inside by saying was she holding a meeting outside or inside? Now, slowly I have been able to persuade her to sit inside with everyone. She keeps whispering in my ear *bai ji ek kam kiyo ji* (sister, please do me a favor) the hand pump in my village is not working. Will you please tell them that it needs to be repaired, please tell them. She always whispers to me from underneath her *ghungat*. I keep telling her that she must lift her *ghungat* while sitting in the *panchayat*. She however, refuses to remove her *ghungat*. I don't observe a *Purdah* as I live in my *maika* (natal home). The women still keep the *ghungat* but it is much shorter now. *Ghungat* means *adab*. You are respecting your brother in laws, your father in law. The ward *panch* should not keep *ghungat*, if you observe such a long *ghungat* and keep quiet how will you reach the issues of the village to the proper authorities if you do not talk or 'speak.'[42]

Implicit in this narrative is an argument of distinction between the public and the private, wherein a particular social custom needs to be redefined according to the nature of the space or realm in which it is being invoked. (I use private here very cautiously, using it to denote spatial boundaries rather than to any reference to 'privacy' or individuality.) Abstract principles of rights are imaginatively applied, reflecting both a critical engagement and appreciation of such moral principles, as well as the existing social agreements on 'proper' comportment of women. *Purdah* is discouraged, especially when its accompanying connotations or meanings are employed without discernment of the changed context as well as the new demands/roles. Hence, the observance of *purdah* within the home is not a subject of criticism, as it is a symbol of respect as well as of modesty or *do aakhon ki sharam* (feminine virtue as displayed in modest/downcast eyes).[43] However, its observance in public spaces under different obligations – to be silent and not participate openly and unhesitatingly – is something to be denounced.

5. Sathins and Election Problematics

Despite the obvious capacities of the *sathins* for political action and their commitment to women's entry into the public sphere, very few of them contest elections to local government bodies. Although some of the difficulties associated with the failure to contest elections is unique to the *sathins*, their failure to contest elections can be used to find some general reasons why rural women fail to come forward as potential candidates. It also leads us to examine why women who consider themselves to be able candidates shy away from publicly putting themselves forward. *Sathin* Mohini Devi of Nayla village sums up what according to her are the many problems facing women *Sarpanches*:

Very few *sathins* stand for the election of the *Sarpanch. Yeh to 'jhagre ki jhopdi hai'*, [It is a house of conflict] there is so much pressure and opposition and all the party politics. [The party politics here refers to the groups that are formed during elections mainly around caste affiliations, not to political organisations such as political parties] Some village people want us to contest, however, that is possible only in the event of there being a reserved seat in the *panchayat*. I am already burdened with work, I have to work at home, look after the children, and work for the women's programme, and I do not have any time to run around the *panchayats*. A *Sarpanch* does not get any salary, we are poor and have to work to feed ourselves, being *sathins* we always stand up for the truth which means we cannot indulge in corrupt activities or even demand money in return for an official favour. Anyway, my household would face a sure ruin if I became a *Sarpanch*. There would be a lot of hostility all around and my family would become targets of people's ill will. Furthermore, if women are illiterate they face a lot of difficulty in doing the work of a *Sarpanch*. Men are also illiterate, however there are ten men around him who are literate'.

The narratives of the *sathins* reveal three kinds of difficulties associated with women contesting political office. I shall categorise these as financial, occupational and moral. The first kind of problems are linked to structural positioning and the general lack of ownership of financial assets, which means that in most cases women do not possess the financial ability to contest elections.[44] Contributing to and resulting from their structural position is the problem of violence.[45] Their subordinate circumstances result in the voices of women being seldom heard on political matters. The whole process of nominating persons to contest elections is still controlled by men. The typical manner in which a woman is nominated as a candidate for election is usually through the prior consent of the male elders in her family. One of the *sathins* who stood for elections confessed that she was informed of the impending electoral contest days after she had put her signature on the election form.

The second category of problems is associated with the actual manner of functioning of the *panchayats*. Apart from the threat of or actual violence associated with the work of the *Sarpanch*, the other barriers perceived by rural women are those of illiteracy and corruption. They fear that they would be coerced into approving schemes and loans in favour of the dominant few, either through violence or other forms of intimidation. The discomfort and even fear of being the lone woman in an all-male *panchayat* fills many with apprehension. Being outnumbered by men was linked to the observation that women were not allowed to play any reasonable role within the *panchayat*, especially in its financial deliberations.[46]

The final set of problems is representative of the moral dilemma facing these women in their new public roles. There are moral issues regarding what constitutes 'respect and respectful conduct' and of renegotiating 'proper womanly' behaviour within 'a shared public space'.

6. Political Literacy and the Sathins

After we recognise the capacity of *sathin* women to reflect upon and creatively engage with 'second hand' moral principles[47] in ways which fit in with their other moral and social commitments and responsibilities, we still are faced with another task. We still have to find a conceptual language that will describe their specific skills. I am here drawing a distinction between capacities and skills. Capacities are to do with particular abilities, physical or cerebral. Skills relate to expertise in any specific area. I am referring to their particular abilities, which include exhibiting political choice and opinion, knowledge of one's rights, knowledge of state institutions, hierarchies and procedures. In other words, knowledge not only of institutions but also of the rules that govern their functioning. These skills I shall collectively refer to as 'political literacy'.

There are two reasons why 'political literacy' is an important conceptual tool. It draws attention to the ways in which women in non-literate social contexts describe their social world and their roles within it. When they speak of the dissemination of knowledge and even development of capacities, schooling is given pride of place. It is widely held that formal schooling leads to the development of certain cognitive capacities that can have a bearing on social life.[48] Schooling is in itself a socially sanctioned good, but educational opportunities are not available to many women. 'Political literacy' does not necessarily rest on literacy skills; indeed, it can supplant or even make up for their absence. It refers to particular kinds of knowledge, which need examination, particularly in non-literate social contexts. This makes it imperative for us to go beyond the literacy skills of women in order to recognise their capacities and skills. 'Political literacy' becomes an important indicator of autonomy within conditions of subordination.

Second, 'political literacy', in weaning attention from an emphasis on literacy, also directs attention to aspects of women's lives not conventionally considered as 'women's activities'. Much of the scholarship on women tends to limit itself to particular activities regarded as 'women's activities'. This is particularly true of studies focusing on what are termed as 'women's position, roles and status'. The political activities of women, or indeed their political interests, are often sidelined or are only given secondary mention.[49] While politics here is defined in the broad sense, where the 'political' includes all aspects of life that generate debate and conflict, 'political literacy' is specific in its scope. In so far as it involves the capacity of persons to fashion responses to conflicts and debates, these debates pertain to the activities and issues surrounding the inclusion and participation of women within the decision-making and deliberation activities of other groups within the village or community. 'Political literacy' can be examined through the following: 1) an awareness of the activities and institutions of the village deliberating body, their powers and jurisdiction; 2) an opinion on the deliberative process and outcomes; 3) knowledge of particular plans and policies including government schemes offering benefits to women or the rural poor; 4) participation in the activities of the village council or other informal groups within the village.

'Political literacy' has close connections with:

a) Autonomy through ability, as evidenced in the ability to form a political choice, which involves some degree of engagement and identification with the reasons for endorsing that choice. Autonomy is thus primarily concerned with capacities of self-reflection and the expression of these reflexive capacities in conversation. It lays emphasis not only on actions – or the lack thereof – but also on the process through which persons arrive at the decisions or opinions about issues confronting their lives within the community.

b) Citizenship concerns and participation. 'Political literacy' is linked to citizenship concerns and even with participation (though the latter does not always follow). Knowing one's rights as well as expressing an opinion on the affairs of the village and the larger political community are important indicators of this skill.

c) With particular forms of knowledge. While there have been longstanding linkages established, particularly within the philosophy of education, between education and autonomy[50] and more recently between these and democratic citizenship, the knowledge that I am referring to is different from the education designed for democratic citizenship.[51] There are three differences: 1) it does not have an association with schooling; 2) the autonomy that it seeks to recognise within specific knowledge skills of persons is different from the autonomous citizen that educational environments want to develop; and 3) the attributes of the citizen are different from those of politically literate citizens within conditions of subordination. This difference is articulated on the premise of autonomy, which does not insist that persons act on their beliefs, but that they choose to act in a specific way for particular reasons. The knowledge, or *Jaankari*, described by the *Sathins*, includes information about their political, social and property rights, government rural development policies and income-generating schemes, especially those concerning drought relief and food for work programmes, rural administrative structures and the powers of the local elected councils or panchayats.

'Political literacy' may be of two types: effective and minimal 'political literacy'. Effective 'political literacy', in contrast to minimal 'political literacy', means more than exhibiting awareness of political choice. It displays itself not only in the knowledge of the functioning of the bureaucratic and developmental apparatus but also in terms of voicing expectations, not only from the state but also from the local social environment. It means taking an active interest in the affairs of the *panchayats* and playing an active role in their deliberations and discussions. The *Sathins* are politically literate in an effective sense because of their active involvement and role in raising women's issues (at least in the initial phases of the programme) and the espousing of these issues in various state forums, especially in the offices of collector and BDO (block development officer). They are therefore very skilled in taking up matters with the relevant government officials. The difference between effective and minimal 'political literacy' is thus more than a matter of degree. The difference manifests itself in the kind of practice effected. An example of this 'political literacy' is as follows:[52]

> After becoming a *sathin* I have got so much information, knowledge as well as strength to go to the *panchayat* meetings, talk to the other women and

have even distributed this knowledge to the other villagers [men]. For instance, in the event of rape I tell the women in my group that we must get a report filed with the police. We have to go to a *thana* (police station) and if the woman is illiterate she must dictate her report to the policeman, if she is literate then she must write out the report herself. One must keep the photocopy of the report. We must not wash out the clothes, which we were wearing at the time of rape. If the police station is not giving us a hearing or if some one has paid money to the *thanedaar* (Police constable) we must go to the SP (Superintendent of Police), if he is also not receptive then we must go to the collector and leave him a written application. And if there is no one to hear us out even then we must go to the Chief minister.

'Political literacy' is an important analytical tool for recognising the autonomy of women where there exist very narrow agreements on social freedoms, especially when it comes to rules regulating women's behaviour. These rules of 'proper behaviour' might for instance place curbs on girls attending schools, or be manifested in a refusal to enter the names of unmarried girls over the age of 18 into the electoral register, thereby effectively disenfranchising them. Of late, there have been a number of studies, particularly in what has come to be known as the 'demography of women', involved in measuring the autonomy of women in the developing world using a number of autonomy 'indicators'. These are purported to be quantifiable and are measured against certain actions considered *a priori* to be autonomous. Autonomous actions in this literature then typically consist of, among other actions, a control over one's fertility, which is recognised through small family size or a high marriageable age. While these projections on women's autonomy, often made on the basis of correlation analysis, may be indicative of a number of findings – for example, with respect to a woman's fertility – they do not reveal whether the decision to have a small family was the woman's or her husband's, or indeed that of the woman's extended family.

While women's subordinated circumstances constrain their abilities to exercise autonomy, this does not always imply that they are incapable of formulating preferences. I propose that in order to make conclusive arguments about women's autonomy we must be able to ascertain their ideal preferences rather than those which they display through their actions. Such an exercise will lead towards recognition of women's ability to reflect upon their choices and the reasons for their inability to translate these into actions. The low ranking of freedom in these societies presents difficulties in the employment of standard measures of autonomy, but that constraint cannot be used to draw conclusions about the abilities of persons to form preferences. The challenge, therefore, is to find a way in which there is not only a recognition of the social and moral contexts within which people live their lives, but also of the possibilities and capacities they might possess for self-transformation.

'Political literacy', an indicator recognised primarily in speech practices, enables us to locate the reasons underpinning the political choices women might make. It recognises not only the skill involved in forming the choice but also that the reasons for acting are sometimes at odds with the choice formed. This leads us then to go beyond action itself into the reasons for why persons act in the way they do. Let us recollect the case of Mohan Kanwar. Her action stands out spectacularly but it is also important to note that these actions are led by a set of ideas which have a significance of their own. Moreover, the action of the women of her *panchayat* who voted for her despite intimidation also needs to be captured in conceptual terms. These women voted for her, safe in the knowledge that the secret ballot would not expose their actions in ways that might make them the targets of the wrath of their families or others. 'Political literacy' captures both the action and the ideas behind Mohan Kanwar's action as well as the women of her political constituency who voted for her.

The important point that the idea of 'political literacy' seeks to make is that evidence of autonomy ought to be made on the basis of an examination of the ideas that lie behind actions. In so doing the language which is used to give form to these ideas becomes important, and not only reveals the kind of ideas which may be considered important, but also certain compulsions which prevent these ideas being expressed in action. However, in order to recognise agency in the absence of congruence between belief and action, we need to be able to accord a theoretical significance to beliefs not always expressed in action.

7. Conclusion

In this essay, I have proposed that we should move away from conceiving autonomy in terms of free action towards an examination of the ideas that lie behind action. The examination of ideas that may not be expressed in action is important in order for us to account for certain capacities, and indeed ideas, which may not be evident in action. Analysis of the moral engagement of the *sathins*, a group of rural women with political rights, reveals a dynamic process of reflection that in turn leads towards not only a creative moral but also a linguistic activity. It has been suggested that the *sathins*' moral autonomy lies in their ability to engage with and selectively absorb and identify with many of the rights-based ideas with which they come into contact. However, this moral identification with rights, and more specifically with political rights, does not always find expression in action. In the case of the *sathins*, their action was to a large extent circumscribed by prevailing social and moral compulsions. However, while these compulsions go some way towards explaining sathins' lack of freedom, they cannot entirely account for sathins' lack of autonomy. These narratives also reveal the difficulty that rural women have in coming to terms with the excessive individualism underpinning not only the access to but also participation in political institutions. Creating spaces for women within political institutions through public policies of positive discrimination/ reservation quotas are really the first steps towards the gendering of the public and of the public space. Agreements on important questions of respect, dignity, equality – all constituents of a social principle of freedom and rights – need to evolve and mature before we can bridge the gap between formal and actual access to political institutions.

Sathins Elected to the *panchayat* Institutions in 1995

Name of district	No. of *sathins*	No. elected to *panchayat* institutions	Elected post
Jasota, district Dausa	5	1	*Sarpanch*
District Jodhpur	93	13	*Sarpanch*: 1 Member of *Zilla Parishad*: 1 Ward *Panch*: 10
Banswara	83	7	Member of *panchayat Samiti*: 3 Ward *Panch*: 3 Deputy *Sarpanch*:1
Ajmer	80	7	Member of *panchayat Samiti*: 2 Ward *Panch*: 5
Udaipur	78	9	Ward *Panch* 6 *Sarpanch* 2 Member of *panchayat samiti* 1
Baran	6		
Bhilwara	60	Figures unavailable	
Dungarpur	26		
Jaipur	68		
Jodhpur	93		
Kota	21		
Rajasamand	6		
Sikar	40		
Udaipur	78		
Total no. of *sathins*	566		

Source: The department of Women and Child and Nutrition, Government of Rajasthan, 1999.

9

THE DEVELOPMENT OF PANCHAYATI RAJ IN INDIA[1]

Crispin Bates

1. Introduction

In the years after Indian independence, the concept of Panchayati Raj seemed to have disappeared permanently into the mists of India's romantic past. In the late twentieth century, however, the notion has returned once more to the political agenda, for a variety of reasons: strategic, practical, economic and ideological. This essay briefly traces the origins of the concept of Panchayati, offers some historical examples of the *panchayat* in use, and attempts an explanation as to why it should once again have assumed importance in the minds of politicians, NGOs and administrators.

To begin with, we need to ask about the etymology of '*panchayat*'. On doing so, one discovers that despite its apparent place in Indian tradition, the meanings of the term have their origin in orientalist thinking. Using inscriptions and other sources, historians have identified patterns of association and resistance among peasant communities in both north and south India. The terms used to describe such communities include the *bhaiband* or 'brotherhoods' in the villages of the Bombay Deccan, and the *nurwa* and *patidar* in Gujarat. Further back in time, the *gana*, *sabha*, *samiti* and *parisad* in the north, and the *nadu*, *brahmadeya* and *periyanadu* in southern India, refer to equivalent political or social communities, while anthropologists have observed the functioning of caste panchayats in the present day.[2] To a large extent, however, the modern idea of the *panchayat*, its nature and its functions, derives from the image of the Indian village community conjured up in the writings of Sir William Jones, Hector Munro, Mountstuart Elphinstone, John Malcolm and a variety of other colonial authors in the late eighteenth and early nineteenth centuries.

References to *panchayats* and *janapadas* in ancient Vedic texts, translated into English for the first time by orientalist scholars, played a part in persuading

British officials that here was to be found an elemental unit of Indian society and politics. Its most succinct and influential expression may be found in Charles Metcalfe's defence of the *mahalwari* system of revenue settlement adopted in the newly ceded and conquered territories of the North-Western Province (later UP). Describing the fortified villages which sprung up around Delhi in the years after the collapse of Mughal power in 1761 Metcalfe wrote to the 1832 Select Parliamentary Committee on the East India Company's charter in brilliantly evocative terms:

> The village communities are little republics, having nearly everything they can want within themselves and almost independent of any foreign relations. They seem to last where nothing else lasts. Dynasty after dynasty tumbles down; revolution succeeds to revolution; Hindoo, Pathan, Mogul, Mahratta, Sikh, English, are all masters in turn; but the village community remains the same... This union of the village communities, each one forming a separate state in itself, has, I conceive, contributed more than any other cause to the preservation of the people of India through all the revolutions and changes which they have suffered, and is in a high degree conducive to their happiness, and to the enjoyment of a great portion of freedom and independence.[3]

The same description was picked up by Karl Marx and used to describe what he saw as one of the characteristic features of the societies that existed under 'Oriental despotism'.

The idea of the village community, and of the *panchayat* or village council, subsequently assumed enormous importance in the writings of Henry Maine, who, in an effort to contradict the Roman school of law, represented by Austin, sets out to describe in his influential *Ancient Law* (1861) the historical evolution of legal systems, linking these systems to what he saw as the various stages in the progress of Civilisation. This theory was later underlined in the writings of Baden-Powell and others (*The Indian Village Community*) and became one of the backbones of the theory of indirect rule developed in India in the second half of the nineteenth century, as well as extending elsewhere into other British colonial territories.

In the hands of these later colonial administrators, the main purpose of the idea of the village community and of its *panchayat*, or council of elders, was that it purported to be a natural and customary source of authority upon whom the government could legitimately devolve certain responsibilities, thus obviating the costs of a minute and detailed system of policing and of law, whilst at the same time avoiding the time-consuming and controversial business of holding elections and setting up local authorities to deal with matters such as street cleaning and petty theft. In time, a measure of democratic local government was also introduced, beginning with Municipal Boards in 1882, which were set up to administer those towns large enough to have a magistrate. However, the village community and its *panchayat*, remained a first resort in case of dispute, practically at least if not juridically, over large parts of rural India.

The problem with this was that lineage, locality and caste were the main determinants of traditional village tribunals, and the so-called village panchayats were often no more than caste panchayats (which were and still are widespread). This was a poor apparatus upon which to heap the burden of jurisdiction and the legal standards expected of a British-style system of justice.[4] Furthermore, despite the best efforts of Elphinstone in Maharashtra, Munro in Madras and the Lawrence brothers in the Punjab, no matter how hard they were pressed, British district collectors were always reluctant to devolve much of their power to a lower level.

At the same time, the parallel development of the British court system meant that villagers were becoming increasingly reluctant to submit their disputes to the informal jurisdiction of a group of elderly high caste males, and when they did so, would often request the local British magistrate to overturn a judgement they had just received if it were not to their liking. The real authority of the village *panchayat* therefore, where it existed, was thus steadily eroded.

Despite this, by the later nineteenth century the ideal of village self-rule had become firmly entrenched in the minds of most colonial officials, and indeed that of the wider public. After all, were not such 'communities' the origin of democracy in Ancient Greece and, transmitted to Britain via the Teutons, the fount of democracy in British society itself? With the rise of a substantial middle class in towns and villages in the UK, the development of local self-government became a major theme in British society and politics in the late nineteenth century. Magnificent town halls were constructed, parish councils were vested with new powers, and Rotary societies flourished (perhaps to subvert the growing influence of popular democracy at the centre), while the village community and its leitmotif, the *panchayat*, was enshrined in the orientalist imagining of India.[5] Within that vision, it had a similarly defensive political role to play, the village and the sturdy peasant being always perceived as loyal to the British regime, no matter how hard the wily Congressmen and educated elites might attempt to mislead them.

It was no great surprise that, in the wake of Lord Ripon's enthusiasm for local self-government in the 1880s, attempts were made by William Wedderburn in Bombay, Elphinstone's former province, and by others, to revive the village *panchayat*. 'On the platform under the tree in the village',

Wedderburn wrote, 'truth is spoken, but not often in the law courts...'[6] Unfortunately, just as many were suspicious as were enthused by the idea of village committees, arguing that they were liable to corruption and were so irrevocably faction-ridden as to make them incapable of impartially administering any form of justice, no matter how trivial the limits of their authority may be.

In 1920, however, following the report of the Royal Commission on decentralisation and the Montagu-Chelmsford report of 1918, the nettle was grasped again, and village panchayats were formally vested with legal powers in no less than five provinces, including the Punjab, Central Provinces and UP. There were sound practical motives for this course of action: most official commentators accepted that by this date the 'ancient' village communities of which Metcalfe had written, if they had ever existed, were all but extinct. And should anyone doubt it, reference could be made to the 1911 census, in which particular efforts had been made to track down and enumerate village committees. The census concluded that the 'myth' of their existence had 'probably arisen from the fact that a village is generally, if not invariably, formed by members of the same caste', and that castes often had their own panchayats, even though the village might not.[7]

Nonetheless, the various provincial administrations went ahead and formally invested village committees with a combination of administrative and judicial powers. Economy was a strong motivation: it was hoped that the panchayats might relieve pressures on the overstretched district and provincial courts. There was also the desire that by conferring powers upon villages, and cutting out the overeducated (and increasingly troublesome) class of collaborators upon whom the British depended for much else in their administration, the white rulers might further cement the bond between themselves and their loyal subjects.

The composition of these village committees and the powers they exercised varied enormously from province to province. Most were democratically elected, although in the UP all elections by the *gaon sabha* had to be approved by the local magistrate. Although hardly a 'traditional' method of selection, this procedure at least had the merit of locality combined with some sort of oversight. Nearly all of them were constituted primarily to carry out judicial business.[8] In Punjab, Bombay and the Central Provinces the panchayats covered about one-tenth or one-fifteenth of the countryside; in UP a quarter of the province was brought under their jurisdiction; and in Bengal and Madras presidencies panchayats were set up throughout the length of the country.[9] While initially enjoying some measure of success (the Bengal panchayats disposed of some 122,760 cases in 1925), the picture thereafter was one of steady decline, partly because, as previously stated, their jurisdiction was all too easily subverted by resort to a British court.

Ironically, it was during this same period, when the British were somewhat cynically encouraging the Panchayati system and putting its role into statute, that the idea of the *panchayat* also entered into nationalist discourse. To nationalists, however, the *panchayat* was not simply a cheap and easy means of indirect rule. Rather it was a symbol of the type of democratic government which Mahatma Gandhi and others wished to see supplanting that of the Europeans post-independence.

Gandhi of course was well educated and deeply influenced by a variety of western writers, including Leo Tolstoy, whose vision of a self-sustaining community he absorbed. He was also strongly influenced by his reading of Sir Henry Maine, using Maine's *Indian Village Communities* as one of the principal items of evidence in a petition to the Natal Assembly in 1894, in which he argued that the franchise should be extended to members of the Indian community. A key passage in the Petition reads as follows:

> The Indian nation has known, and has exercised, the power of election from times prior to the time when the Anglo-Saxon races first became acquainted with the principles of representation... In support of the above, your Petitioners beg to draw the attention of your Honourable Assembly to Sir Henry Summer Maine's *Village Communities*, where he has clearly pointed out that the Indian races have been familiar with representative institutions almost from time immemorial. That eminent lawyer and writer has shown that the Teutonic Mark was hardly so well organised or so essentially representative as an Indian Village community until the precise technical Roman form was grafted upon it.[10]

Gandhi went on to quote Chisolm Anstey in a speech delivered before the East Indian Association in London, in which 'the East' was described as 'the parent of municipalities', and it was said that 'local self-government in the widest acceptation of the term' was 'as old as the East itself'. Gandhi himself then insisted, somewhat imaginatively, that

> Every caste in every village or town has its own rules and regulations, and elects representatives, and furnishes an exact prototype of the Saxon Witans, from which have sprung the present Parliamentary institutions.

He warmed to this theme again in a letter addressed to 'Every Briton in South Africa', published as a pamphlet in 1895:

> To say that the Indian does not understand the Franchise is to ignore the whole history of India. Representation, in the truest sense of the term, the

Indian has understood and appreciated from the earliest ages. That principle – the *panchayat* – guides all the actions of an Indian. He considers himself a member of the *panchayat*, which really is the whole body civic to which he belongs for the time being. That power to do so – that power to understand thoroughly the principle of popular government – has rendered him the most harmless and docile man on earth.

His argument was threefold: firstly that the Indian people were as civilised as any other and therefore entitled to vote; second that they were long accustomed to the concept of representative democracy and indeed enjoyed the powers of voting – at least some of them – for members of municipal councils and provincial assemblies in India, and thirdly, that the Indian community was not at all political and that if given the vote they could be relied upon more often than not never to exercise it or, when doing so, to confine their support to modest and conventional candidates who would uphold the status quo.[11] For good measure (and perhaps with some cunning) he reassured his readers that Indians were rarely ever likely to stand for election, as few of them were sufficiently well educated in English to be able to keep up with the level of debate in the assembly chamber.

In later years Gandhi's supporters perceived in village-based action not only the means to *swaraj*, in a personal sense, but also the means towards a national awakening and wholesale programme of social and economic reconstruction. Gandhi himself was rarely so radical in his own writings on the subject; indeed, he does not even mention the idea of village self-government in *Hind Swaraj*, his erstwhile nationalist manifesto, published in 1910. He nonetheless insisted that it was a good Indian tradition to subordinate self-interest to the collective decision of a *Panch*, and often described the Indian National Congress central working committee as one such *Panch*: a sort of elected oligarchy to which unquestioning obedience was expected.[12] At the same time, he freely admitted that the practising institution of the Village *panchayat* was rarely if ever likely to be found in effect. And although he expressed the hope that it might be revived, he clearly did not expect it to happen in a hurry. When asked in 1925 what should be done with those who borrowed capital from khadi boards and then failed to return it, he answered that in an ideal world they would submit themselves to the judgement of a *panchayat*, but that since the idea of the *panchayat* is 'as good as non-existent now', it would be best just to take them to court.[13] And in 1931 he wrote in *Young India* as follows:

... we may not replace trained judges by untrained men brought together by chance. What we must aim at is an incorrigible, impartial and able judiciary right from the bottom. I regard village panchayats as an institution by itself [sic]. But thanks to the degradation of the caste system and the evil influence of the present system of government and the growing illiteracy of the masses, this ancient and noble institution has fallen into desuetude, and where it has not, it has lost its former purity and hold. It must, however, be revived at any cost, if the villages are not to be ruined.[14]

Gandhi was thus a believer, but hardly an unequivocal champion of village self-government, and he fully accepted the practical limits to such a scheme. Others however were more enthusiastic. The idea of village development through self-regulated councils was in fact first deployed politically in India, not by Gandhi, but by Rabindranath Tagore as early as the 1900s, and it became a major issue during the *Swadeshi* movement in Bengal between 1905 and 1910.[15] CR Das, the Bengali *swadeshi* campaigner, was amongst those who supported it. Like Gandhi, Das was a student of law, cognisant of the writings of Maine and Baden-Powell, and he shared the same thoroughly orientalised and idealistic view of rural India, although in many ways more radical and politically ambitious. Thus CR Das spoke on the issue during his Presidential Address to the Bengal Congress in 1918, advocating the growth of village councils as a means of economic development. The policy was later written out of the manifesto of the Bengal provincial congress following pressure from the Zamindar lobby.[16]

In 1922 CR Das became President of the Indian National Congress, and in his Presidential address he again urged, as a requisite of *Swaraj*, the 'organisation of village life and the practical autonomy of small local centres'. 'Village communities must not exist as disconnected units', he argued, but be 'held together by a system of co-operation and integration'. He concluded: 'I maintain that real *Swaraj* can only be attained by vesting the power of government in these small local centres', and he advised the Congress to draw up a scheme of government based upon these proposals.[17]

As a result of this an *Outline Scheme of Swaraj* was drawn up by CR and Bhagavan Das, presented to Congress in 1923 and adopted as party policy. This plan recommended a massive decentralisation of government after independence, the higher centres of governmental power being reduced and the organ of administration becoming the *panchayat*, organised into village, town, district, provincial and all-India units of government. The purpose behind this idea was the upliftment of India's villages and, as the memorandum put it, the 'spiritualising of India's politics by changing the whole culture and civilisation of society from its present mercenary to a missionary basis'.[18]

Gandhi and the Indian National Congress were not the only advocates of panchayats. The enthusiasm for the village, for co-operation and for local self-government, was shared by a variety of liberal colonial officials – particularly members of the government's revenue and agricultural departments, who saw the 'intermediary classes', whether moneylenders or lawyer-politicians, as a drain upon society and a barrier to progress, particularly in the progress of the revenue receipts. Neither Gandhi nor the British advocated anything so radical as land reform – this would be too revolutionary, but both expressed enthusiasm for the possibilities afforded by cooperation, the cooperative movement being increasingly encouraged by the British in the 1920s as the idea of the *panchayat* was taken over by the nationalists. A particular influence here was another 'friend of the peasant': 'Punjabi' Malcolm Darling.

As the nationalist struggle progressed, Gandhi became more ambitious for the idea of village self-government. His clearest and most often quoted exposition of the idea dates from 1942, when he wrote of 'village *swaraj*', in words that closely echoed those of Metcalfe:

> My idea of village *swaraj* is that it is a complete republic, independent of its neighbours for its own vital wants and yet interdependent for many others in which dependence is a necessity... As far as possible every activity will be conducted on the co-operative basis. There will be no castes such as we have today, with their graded untouchability. Non-violence with its technique of satyagraha and non co-operation will be the sanction of the village community... The government of the village will be conducted by a *panchayat* of five persons elected annually by the adult villagers, male and female, possessing minimum prescribed qualifications... Since there will be no system of punishments in the accepted sense, this *panchayat* will be the legislature, judiciary and executive combined to operate for its year of office... Here there is perfect democracy based upon individual freedom. The individual is the architect of his own government. The law of non-violence rules him and his government. He and his village are able to defy the might of a world. For the law governing every villager is that he will suffer death in the defence of his and his village's honour...[19]

Later on, Gandhi described his vision more poetically still in an interview given just two years before his death:

> In this structure composed of innumerable villages, there will be ever widening, never-ascending circles. Life will not be a pyramid with the apex sustained by the bottom. But it will be an oceanic circle whose

centre will be the individual always ready to perish for the village, the latter ready to perish for the circle of villages, till at last the whole becomes one life composed of individuals, never aggressive in their arrogance but ever humble, sharing the majesty of the oceanic rule of which they are integral units.[20]

Jawaharlal Nehru also warmed to the idea, asserting in *The Discovery of India* that in ancient times 'the Village *panchayat* or elected council had large powers both executive and Judicial and its members treated with great respect by the Kings officers.'[21] However, this was little more than a fit of historical imagination, with few practical implications as far as Nehru's Congress policy was concerned. Soon after writing it he was indeed engaged in discussions with P Thakurdas, GD Birla, JRD Tata and others, which led to the drawing up of the famous Bombay Plan of January 1944, setting the framework for India's social and economic development post-independence: a world of industry, urbanisation and of partnerships in development between government and the national bourgeoisie.

2. The Resuscitation and Revival of Panchayati Raj

Following Gandhi's death, the possibility of a continuing judicial and administrative role for the village *panchayat* was considered, criticised and rejected by the Indian Constituent Assembly: the view being held, as by the British previously, that such local organisations were prone to corruption. Ambedkar's experience of the suffering of his Mahar community gave him particular insights into this problem, according to one source.[22] Consequently, the only reference to panchayats at all in the Indian Constitution adopted in 1951 is in Part IV (in the Directive Principles of state Policy), which is non justiciable, and which merely stated that 'the state should take steps to organise village panchayats and endow them with such power and authority as may be necessary to enable them to function as units of self-government'. The same fate befell the cooperative movement. After a brief flurry of enthusiasm in the 1950s, cooperation was found more often than not to be sham in practice, and the cooperative ideal, together with the panchayati ideal, was shelved by most government departments.[23]

One important source for this article, the 1994 report of the Indian Social Science Institute, asks the rhetorical question: 'Why did the panchayats not come under the legally enforceable section of the constitution?... The answer is [it states] that 'the urban and the rural elites, their representatives in politics (from the time of the national freedom movement onwards), and a bureaucracy conditioned by its class character, had a disdain for *panchayat*, and has ever since remained intact.'

This disdain seems real enough. In what has become a famous quote, BR Ambedkar wrote: 'what is the village but a sink of localism, a den of ignorance, narrow-mindedness and communalism'.[24] If men of this ilk monopolised political decision making in the 1950s, what has changed since to bring the idea of Panchayati Raj back into fashion? One explanation points to the same sort of financial pressures that first brought the Panchayati experiment seriously into vogue in the 1930s. These pressures began to make themselves felt soon after the launch of the first five-year plan. With the concentration of development resources on the industrial sector in the first, and particularly in the second five-year plan, it rapidly became apparent that there were not the means available to carry into effect the rural arm of the government's development programme.

These shortcomings were manifested in the Community Development and National Extension Service programmes, both of which were the subject of an enquiry by a national planning committee study team led by Balwantrai Mehta, a member of Parliament, in 1957. The study team concluded that if these programmes were to be effective, and affordable, and if repeated interventions by officials were to be avoided, there was a desperate need for an agency at the village level 'which could represent the entire community, assume responsibility and provide the necessary leadership for implementing development programmes.'[25] The case for governmental decentralisation was later affirmed by the National Development Council, and once again panchayats came back onto the political agenda. The phrase 'panchayati raj' came into fashion: zealots even claiming that it was coined by Jawaharlal Nehru, although it had obviously been previously used by Gandhi and many others.[26]

Rajasthan was the first state to pass legislation authorising the constitution of a new style of *panchayat*. The first, assuming largely administrative powers, was established at Naguar, about 260 kms from Jaipur, the state capital, in October 1959. Another was soon set up at Shadnagar in Andhra Pradesh, and by 1959 every state had passed a Panchayati Act and some sort of *panchayat* was thereafter established, in theory at least, in nearly every village.[27]

It seems likely that the concept of Panchayati raj was both a response to financial exigencies and to the emergent conflicts between the Congress government's espousal of equality and welfare for all, and its heavily urban and industry-biased development planning. These conflicts heightened social and political tensions, and it is likely that Jawaharlal Nehru espoused the *panchayat* ideal for the same reason that in 1963 he espoused the so-called Kamraj Plan, which called upon Congress politicians to resign from office and devote themselves to grassroots work in the rural areas. Both could be seen as an attempt to undermine the influence of powerful and reactionary landed and bourgeois state level politicians and to reaffirm his party's links with the rural masses – just as the British had sought to do some forty years earlier. There was also strong support in favour of the Panchayati ideal among opposition groups. Jai Prakash Narayan, for example, was a great advocate of panchayats in the late 1960s and early 1970s, his vision being quite a radical one, championing the notion of partyless democracy.

The problem was that these panchayats were set up largely, as already stated, for developmental reasons, and although constituted at village level (always including a certain number of women and Scheduled Castes/Scheduled Tribes), the executive powers usually lay at block level, where a block *Samiti* was constituted by delegates from a number of villages. Executive powers here were effectively shared with the government block development officer, and of course above the block there were also Zilla Parishads playing a supervisory and coordinating role. There was thus very little continuity with the primarily judicial panchayats of the 1920s, let alone with Metcalfe's or even Gandhi's idea of little village republics. Where they functioned at all, they served as a channel for developmental and improvement works, and when in the later 1960s these programmes flourished, the village level panchayats played little part in administering them. This deficiency in community involvement was hightlighted in RC Jain's 1985 study *Grass without Roots*.

With the shift of government expenditure away from industrial projects and into rural development after 1966, funds were made available to train and appoint officials to carry on the business of project implementation and management. The Block Development Officer therefore flourished, and was soon joined by a variety of other specialist teams sent by different ministries, each of which set up their own committees and other means of consulting with villagers, and none of whom were willing to entrust their pet projects to the control of villagers themselves.[28]

Even as early as 1964 these problems were publicised in a seminar held by the All-India *Panchayat* Parishad, a voluntary association of *panchayat* organisations across India, presided over by Jayaprakash Narayan.[29] The rapid deterioration of the panchayats constituted in the late 1950s and early 1960s was further underlined in the report of the Asoka Mehta Committee on Panchayati Raj institutions which was set up in December 1977, and included such luminaries as EMS Namboodiripad and MG Ramchandran among its membership. The Committee observed that the activities of the Panchayati Raj institutions, even at block level, were meagre, their resource base limited, and that they had been stagnating, if not declining, since 1965. They further noted that the panchayats were mistrusted by state government officials, and that a growing range of developmental activities, such as the Small Farmers Development Agency, the Drought Prone Areas Programme and the Intensive Tribal Development Project, were not being brought under the purview of the elected Zilla Parishads in states such as Gujarat and Maharashtra. The Panchayati Raj institutions were also dominated, it was said, by economically or socially privileged sections of society, 'and have as such facilitated the emergence of oligarchic forces yielding no benefits to the weaker sections'.[30]

The solution, and key recommendation, of the Asoka Mehta committee was that the panchayats be brought closer to the people by putting executive powers in the hands of 'Mandal Panchayats', which grouped together villages of 15,000 to 20,000 inhabitants, with a single tier of district level panchayats above them. Although a contrast with the system adopted in the 1960's, this hardly equated with the orientalist dream of village self-government, the foundation of '*Swaraj*', as noted in a dissenting minute to the report by Siddharaj Dhadda.[31] The idea of further reform was in any case shelved at a meeting of (mostly Janata) Chief Ministers in 1979 – presumably already confident of their democratic credentials.

This then effectively remained the situation for the next few years. Panchayats were constituted in many villages, but had few responsibilities beyond village drainage, street lighting, sanitation and the arbitration of petty disputes. Development money was dispersed at the block level and remained largely in the hands of officials. A rare exception to this pattern is perhaps the experience in West Bengal, where village panchayats have been elected by universal suffrage since 1978, and where they are seen as both successful and egalitarian: the Food for Work programme, for example, has been organised through these local bodies; turnout at election time is often of the order of 75 per cent; and significant amounts of surplus land have been redistributed to poorer *Scheduled Caste/Scheduled Tribe* peasants through a land reform programme (Operation *Barga*) administered by elected panchayats.[32] Other exceptions include Orissa, where the driving force of Biji Patnaik's personality has kept Panchayati Raj on the agenda almost uninterruptedly since the 1950s, and Karnataka, where it has been reported that democratic decentralisation in the 1980s led to a major improvement in the performance of village teachers and health workers. It is further claimed that in Nagaland, Village Development Boards have achieved a great deal. These exceptions, however, tend to prove that the opposite was generally true: that decentralisation and agrarian reform rarely went hand in hand.[33] In these cases, further important qualifications need to be noted. At the same time as promoting Panchayati Raj in Karnataka, the Janata Dal state government, led by Ramkrishna Hegde between 1980 and 1984, simultaneously raised land ceilings, indicating that an important motivation was the attempt to increase electoral support among the richer, landowning peasantry. There are parallels here with Charan Singh's vigorous support for Panchayati Raj in UP, at a time when, post-Green revolution, the rich peasantry were achieving political ascendancy. In Gorkhaland, the demand for greater political influence even led to violence – Subhas Ghising's Gorkhaland agitation – supported by disappointed rich peasants and other local elites when the CPI (M)'s proposals for an autonomous Hill District Council were shot down by the central government in the early 1980s. Even Bengal's agrarian programme has been criticised, amongst other things, for its gender bias.[34] It should be noted, furthermore, that Bengal's advances in land reform and agricultural production have not been matched (as they have in Kerala) by advances in education – hardly surprising, since local primary and secondary school teaching positions are often used as sinecures for loyal CPI (M) party members and activists. Although political activism has been apparently a key factor in the success of land reforms and the development of panchayati raj, questions have been raised about the potential conflict between the ideals of democratic decentralisation that lie behind the panchayati movement and the democratic centralist philosophy of the CPI (M), which requires every decision to be approved by local party cells.

This mixed and generally unsatisfactory state of affairs began to change dramatically in 1985, soon after Rajiv Gandhi became Prime Minister, when two committees were constituted. The first, under GVK Rao, was established to review the arrangements for rural development and poverty alleviation. It recommended the revitalisation of Zilla Parishads, with the appointment of a District Development Commissioner as Chief Executive of the *Zilla Parishad*. The second committee, chaired by HM Singhvi, proposed the reorganisation of Panchayati raj institutions and the setting up of effective village-level committees. Following this report the Sarkaria Commission on Centre–State relations and a Parliamentary Consultative Committee also recommended that there should be a significant strengthening of Panchayati raj institutions.

After consultations with Collectors and District Magistrates, and representatives of existing panchayats, a special meeting of the All-India Congress Committee was convened to consider the matter. This obviously included the political implications of a program of administrative decentralisation, but with the popularity of Rajiv's government by this stage sinking in the polls there was clearly nothing to lose by it. A bill proposing an amendment to the Constitution, the 64th, was therefore finally drawn up and presented to Parliament in May 1989. This bill proposed to make it legally binding upon all states to establish a three-tier system of panchayats at village, intermediate and district level, each of them to be appointed by direct election and to enjoy a fixed tenure of no more than five years. At the first attempt, the bill was passed by the *Lok Sabha*, but rejected by the *Rajya Sabha*, following which the Congress called an election. The bill was eventually passed after it was reintroduced (as the 74th amendment bill) for the second time in 1991. It was passed by the *Lok Sabha* on 22–23 December 1992 and, following its ratification by half the states, it achieved Presidential assent in April 1993 as the 73rd Amendment to the Constitution. Along with the requirement to establish elected panchayats, it further required that one-third of municipal and *panchayat* seats should be reserved for women.

Following the passage of the 73rd amendment into law, in some cases the states introduced radical measures, which delegated significant powers and responsibilities onto panchayats. Rajasthan was once again amongst the first to respond, with legislation passed in 1994 and elections in 1995.[35] Some states, notably Andhra Pradesh, jumped the gun and evolved legislation extending Panchayati raj into scheduled (i.e. adivasis) areas as well, though not always on favourable terms. The AP Panchayati act was in fact struck down by the Andhra Pradesh High Court after agitation by adivasi groups. In 1996 therefore the *Lok Sabha* passed a bill extending the proposed Panchayati system of the 73rd amendment into all Scheduled (i.e. adivasi) areas. The Act requires state governments with scheduled areas in Andhra Pradesh, Himachal Pradesh, Bihar, Maharashtra, Madhya Pradesh, Gujarat, Rajasthan and Orissa to devolve responsibility in key areas onto elected panchayats in tribal areas, no fewer than half of whose members should be Scheduled tribes. Every village was to have a *gram sabha*, whose mandatory responsibilities were to include preservation of the traditions, customs and resources of the community, and which was to be empowered to approve plans and projects for social and economic development. The gram sabhas were to have the right to be consulted in matters of land acquisition and in the exploitation of mineral resources. State Governments were also directed in section 4(m) of the Act to devolve to the gram sabhas' powers which would enable them to become effective institutions of self-government, including control over prohibition, ownership of minor forest produce, the ability to prevent alienation of land, the power to manage village markets, to exercise control over moneylending, social services, local plans and development resources. Above all, the Extension Act recommended that the powers of the gram sabhas be protected so that panchayats and state institutions at a higher level could not overrule them and assume their responsibilities, and that their devolution of responsibilities should be in line with the 6th schedule of the constitution – in other words, that they should have legislative, administrative and judicial responsibilities.

Altogether, the 73rd constitutional amendment and the 1996 Extension Act proposed a radical upgrading of the juridical position of the panchayats, with which state level administrations are now only beginning to come to terms.

Thus far, it is difficult to draw conclusions, but the early signs are not so promising. Earlier successes in Bengal, and arguably also in Karnataka, were only achievable because of systematic political activism at the local level.[36] Where this is absent, or where there is extreme social and economic inequality, the chances of success are more limited. In UP, there is already evidence that the institution of elections under the new Panchayati scheme has fared no better than attempts at democratic decentralisation in the early years of zamindari abolition.[37] Meanwhile in Karnataka, while in the late 1990s the gram sabhas successfully combated the Devdasi (temple prostitute) system that prevailed in 167 districts of Belgaum district, it is nonetheless alleged that the Panchayat Act of 1993 significantly erodes the powers of elected panchayats when compared with their original status in the path-breaking Karnataka Panchayat Act of 1983: defining them as no more than bodies 'for the effective implementation of rural development reforms' rather than real units of local self-government. The powers of the panchayats over local officials (including the police) are thereby, it is alleged, effectively withdrawn, and what powers they do possess can at any time be suspended by notification in the gazette.[38] In Rajasthan, while the panchayat elections were overwhelmingly popular, 76 per cent of panchayat members felt that their new powers were resisted and resented by officials.[39] At the same time, the collapse of the Women's Reservation Bill in the Lok Sabha in July 1998 caused some doubts about the constitutionality of the 73rd amendment. Therefore, the silent gender revolution anticipated by the legislation may well be stillborn.[40]

Perhaps most disappointing of all is the legislation enacted by the state governments in regard to the Scheduled areas. In most cases the state governments have conspicuously avoided devolving the powers recommended by the 1996 Extension Act. In many instances, they have exploited an ambiguity in the Act, and powers have not been devolved to the gram sabha at the village level, but remain largely with an elected panchayat at a level coterminus with electoral constituencies (the gram sansad in Bengal) or even a non-elected state government authority. Elections are postponed by the state government on one pretext or another. Crucially, furthermore, not a single state Panchayat Act, or any of their subsequent amendments to date, have included a clause making panchayats or gram sabhas at village level into effective Institutions of Self-Government. In only two states – Kerala and Madhya Pradesh – are the advice and suggestions of the village-level gram sabha binding on the gram panchayats. Mostly, elected panchayat members do as they please, meetings are rarely quorate, and decisions are thus made by just a handful of individuals. Even where powers have been devolved, for example in control over minor forest produce, the state government has retained the right to assume their powers and authority and to overrule the panchayats and gram sabhas at any time. In the view of Mahi Pal, in one report the majority of the states have completed the formalities with regard to devolution of powers in scheduled areas, but with the exception only of Maharashtra, Orissa, and to some extent MP, they have entirely avoided the spirit of the legislation.[41]

This begs the question of whether the new enthusiasm for Panchayati rule is likely to fare any better than those that have gone before, and whether it is a long cherished dream finally come true or merely the latest twist in a struggle for power and control over government expenditure between central and state governments and newly emergent village elites. Given the signs of a backlash against some of the more radical implications of the legislation, and the evidence of serious attempts at foot-dragging by state governments in the manner of its implementation, it is tempting to conclude that the latter is most likely. In all this, though, the agency of ordinary Indians should not be underestimated. It is equally possible that the legislative shifts and controversies have played a part in further politicising the Indian masses, making them aware and willing to fight for their new-found rights. How this will work out in practice is something that only time can tell.

10

POLITICAL REPRESENTATION AND WOMEN'S EMPOWERMENT: WOMEN IN THE INSTITUTIONS OF LOCAL SELF-GOVERNMENT IN ORISSA[1]

Evelin Hust

1. Introduction

At the beginning of the new millennium democratic states are facing some pressing problems. Among these are a more just representation of the different groups in society, be it ethnic minorities or women, and the decentralisation of the political decision-making process, which becomes increasingly important in a globalising world. The exclusion of women from positions of political power is especially widely lamented, and has emerged as a contentious political issue. Interestingly enough, India, otherwise classified as a 'developing' or '*backward*' nation, is – at least from a constitutional point of view – at the forefront as concerns inclusion of marginalised groups in the political process and the devolution of political power.

The passing of the 73rd Amendment of the Constitution in December 1992 is considered by many as a milestone in the history of women's political participation in India. Besides providing the basis for the mandatory introduction of a system of rural local self-government in all Indian states, it laid down a reservation of seats and offices for women of not less than 33 per cent. Additionally, there is provision for a proportional representation of women in the existing Scheduled Castes (SC) and Scheduled Tribes (ST) quotas. This system of local self-government, called Panchayati Raj ('rule of the five'), was introduced in the 1950s, but lay dormant in most of the states. Since the ratification of the Act by the state Legislatures on 24 April 1994, all Indian states except Bihar have held elections, and in March 1997 there were 716,234 women representatives in office.[2]

The question which will be addressed in this essay is how far the mere passing of an Act will really lead to the empowerment of women. We have to bear in mind that in many states of the Indian Union, especially in rural areas, freedom of movement as well as of decision-making is very circumscribed for women. One symbol of this is the practice of *purdah*, still found in many parts of North India. Critics of the 73rd Amendment argued, therefore, that only proxies would be elected under the women's reservation. However, before we start to conceptualise political representation and empowerment, and turn to the case study from the eastern state of Orissa, we will first make a digression to ask how reserved seats for women made it into legislation in the first place.

2. The Background to the 73rd Amendment

After Independence, Panchayati Raj had no compulsory status, but was only incorporated into Article 40, part IV of the Constitution of India (Directive Principles), which left the initiative to implement it to the state Governments.[3] Unsurprisingly, most states did not bother seriously to enter into a system of local governance. The first influential document addressing this malady was the Balwantrai Mehta Report in 1957, which came to the conclusion that the main problem was the absence of local initiative and interest, now seen as the *conditio sine qua non* for rural development. The Committee accordingly recommended the set-up of a three-tier structure of elected self-governing bodies, the Panchayati Raj Institutions (PRI). The circumstances of rural women were considered and the conclusion reached that they should be assisted to find ways to increase their incomes and improve their children's condition.[4] The Committee was also particular about the fact that women should be represented in the rural political institutions, and recommended the co-option of female members.[5]

The next landmark in the development of local government was the Report of the Committee on Panchayati Raj Institutions in 1978, popularly known as the Ashok Mehta Report. This was set up by the Janata Government to look into the workings of local self-government in various states, as it was felt that the situation was not satisfactory. Concerning women, this Committee laid special emphasis on the need to strengthen their decision-making capacity and managerial roles. Apart from measures to improve the economic standing of women, they focused on the effective organisation of *Mahila Mandals* (women's groups) as an important component of rural development programmes.[6] The Report recommended that two seats should be given to the women who secured the highest number of votes in the *panchayat* elections or, in the event that none succeeded in the elections, to co-opt women.[7] At *Samiti* level there should also be a committee with all women members of the *panchayat* represented on it [which] would also ensure that decisions are made by women themselves on priorities and choices in welfare and development programmes specifically for women and children.[8]

In a major departure from the Balwantrai Mehta Report, it also suggested the creation of a two-tier instead of the three-tier system.[9] These two reports were the principal documents for shaping and evaluating the Panchayati Raj Institutions prior to the constitutional endeavours of the late 1980s and early 1990s.

The discussion about the reservation of seats for women began before Independence. In 1917 women demanded enfranchisement and eligibility for the legislatures before the Montagu-Chelmsford Committee. The request for reservation in the legislatures came up in the second phase of the women's movement (1928–37), when the salient issues were liberalisation of the terms of enfranchisement and increasing female representation in the legislatures.[10] The women's movement was divided into two distinct camps: the 'equal rights' and the 'women's uplift' factions. In the early 1930s members of the latter group testified before the Simon Commission and demanded enfranchisement of literate women and reservation of seats for them. It was believed that enlightened female legislators would work for the cause of all women, and that without reserved places women would not be able to capture seats in the legislatures. The 'equal rights' faction, on the other hand, argued for universal adult franchise, which would create a progressive electorate since it would not be constituted only of the propertied and landed elite, and would, it was thought, automatically elect a reformist legislature. This faction was against the reservation of seats, preferring equal treatment of men and women. The Simon Commission finally recommended reservation of seats for women under limited franchise, and the 1937 Provincial Assembly Elections took place, with 1–4 per cent of the seats reserved for women.[11] After Independence the ideals of the equal rights faction were incorporated in the Constitution, which gave suffrage to all adults and opened public office to everybody irrespective of gender, sex, caste and race, but recognised no special reservation of seats for women. Reservations for the Scheduled Castes and Scheduled Tribes were made in various fields, including politics, which shows that reserving legislative seats as a means of social engineering was accepted by the framers of the Constitution. Over the years the population became used to the principle of quotas for the advancement of specific marginalised social groups. This differs significantly from Western democracies like Germany, where affirmative action is very difficult to implement from a constitutional point of view.

More than two decades later the need was felt to investigate how far the status of women had changed since Independence. The result was the pioneering and influential Report of the Commission on the Status of Women in India (CSWI), prepared between 1971 and 1974.[12] The findings were shocking to many, as they revealed that the status of women had actually declined in several areas (it is perturbing to note that many of the Commission's findings are still valid today). Chapter 7 dealt with the political status of women. Even though it was observed that some positive developments had taken place – for example, an increase in female voting turnout – it was felt that a great deal remained to be done. The reservation of seats in the legislatures was proposed as a remedy to the Committee by women delegates as well as by social scientists, and it is interesting that the figure of 30 per cent is already mentioned in this early document.[13] Yet strong opposition was voiced by political parties and most women legislators, and the writers of the report finally found themselves unable to recommend reserved seats for women in the state Assemblies and the Parliament.[14] This decision was not taken unanimously, which was rather rare for this Commission, pointing to the differences in the women's movement concerning this difficult issue.[15] In regard to Panchayati Raj Institutions, they noted that the necessity for women's representation had already been accepted, and that a system of co-option or nomination in these bodies existed in most state legislations. However, they regarded it as mere 'tokenism', and argued that the views of women were generally neglected in the Panchayati Raj Institutions.[16] Thus, the main recommendation regarding the strengthening of women's roles in local politics was the constitution of a separate body exclusively for them, which would have an integral connection to the other bodies of the PRI:

> We therefore recommend the establishment of statutory women's panchayats at the village level with autonomy and resources of their own for the management and administration of welfare and development programmes for women and children, as a transitional measure, to break through the attitudes that inhibit most women from articulating their problems and participating actively in the existing local bodies.[17]

A quota was only advocated as a transitional measure at the level of municipalities.[18] Thus we see that reservation for women in legislative bodies was fervently discussed in the mid-1970s but neither advocated nor implemented.

The recommendations concerning women in local governance lay dormant in the decade which followed. From 1976, the National Plan of Action, which was the major outcome of the CSWI Report, hardly mentioned the political participation of women.[19] Still, the need for greater efforts for the emancipation of women was felt especially after 1975 (International Women's year), and a chapter on Women and Development was included in the Sixth Five-Year Plan (1980–5).[20] In 1985, the Congress Government under Rajiv Gandhi indicated that it wanted to give a greater priority to women's issues.[21] Soon after, a core group was constituted to prepare a long-term policy document for the empowerment of women. The result was the National Perspective Plan for Women, 1988–2000, Chapter 7 of which dealt with 'Political Participation and Decision Making'.[22] On the subject of women in local government, the Committee came to the conclusion that the co-option of women recommended by the Ashok Mehta Report had not brought any perceptible impact on women's participation in the PRI.[23] The states of Karnataka and Andhra Pradesh were praised as positive examples for enhanced representation, as they supposedly had introduced a reservation for women of 25 per cent and 30 per cent respectively.[24] Thus the Commission recommended that

- 30 per cent of *panchayat* seats should be reserved for women at *zilla parishad* level and in local municipal bodies. Wherever possible, higher representation of dalits/ tribals, women of weaker sections should be ensured.
- 30 per cent of executive heads of all bodies from village *panchayat* to district level and a certain percentage of chief executives of panchayati raj bodies at lower, middle and higher levels must be reserved for women.[25]

Rajiv Gandhi followed these recommendations in the formulation of the 64th Amendment Bill of 1989, which was the first attempt to give a constitutional status to the institutions of local government and to introduce a substantive quota for women. This document provided for a reservation for women at all levels for 'as nearly as may be' 30 per cent, including inbuilt quotas for the seats reserved for the Scheduled Castes and Scheduled Tribes. The Bill did not pass the *Rajya Sabha* for various reasons, which were however not related to the question of reservation for women.[26] The Bill re-emerged after three years in a slightly modified form as the 73rd Amendment Bill and was enacted under the Government of Narasimha Rao on 22 December 1992, about two weeks after the demolition of the Babri *Masjid*. With the attention of the public and media thus occupied, the Amendment was quietly ratified without much discussion by Parliament in April 1993, with the provision that the states had to amend their Acts accordingly by 24 April 1994.

It is baffling that the provision for the reservation of seats for women did not lead to major debates in the late 1980s and early 1990s, when the 64th and 73rd Amendment Bills were tabled, whereas it emerged as a bone of contention in the discussion about the reservation of seats in the Parliament and state Assemblies. Observing current discussions, one is amased that the reservation of 33 per cent for women with inbuilt quotas in the Panchayati Raj Institutions made it into legislation at all. Women activists claim that it is due to the prolonged struggle of the women's movement (though it was never unified on this issue), whereas others see it as an election gimmick initiated by Rajiv Gandhi and followed up by Narasimha Rao to attract women's votes. A further reason for the absence of a heated debate in Parliament, one could speculate, is the fact that the reservation of seats at the lowest level of government does not endanger the prospects of the sitting MLAs and MPs who enacted it (the majority being male), whereas a reservation of seats for women in the state Legislatures and Parliament would considerably affect their chances, as they run the risk of losing their constituencies to a woman.

3. Political Representation and Women's Empowerment

In the foregoing discussion we have seen that the political representation of women figured on the agenda of the women's movement right from the beginning of the nationalist movement, and this was reflected in various reports on the Panchayati Raj Institutions. Reservation of seats as a means to this end was finally made concrete by the 73rd Amendment. It was also recognised quite early that the political presence of women is important in order to secure their specific interests. However, to what extent women do indeed form a group with particular interests is still a highly contested issue. Nevertheless, even when one does not follow an essentialist line, one can argue, that some interests are gendered (for example, issues concerning childbearing, unequal access to education, to the labour market, or to inheritance), even though women might not share the same views on all issues. The argument that these specific interests may be overlooked by political decision-makers is one justification for a call for women's inclusion into politics.[27] Apart from this there is the hope that the enhanced representation of women will also lead to their empowerment.[28] The problem with this notion is that, theoretically speaking, there is no proven direct road leading from one to the other. Whereas the inclusion of women in political decision-making bodies is a top-down approach, the concept of empowerment is essentially a bottom-up view, supposed to be taking place at the grassroots. Creating an awareness and understanding of the systematic forces which have led to women occupying a marginal position is regarded as the starting point of empowerment, and ultimately the restructuring of all power relations.[29] Yet the term has recently been expanded to include institutional strategies, especially by development agencies. The most obvious link between the concept of political representation and empowerment is the bringing of women into positions of power. Jo Rowlands argues that the dominant perspective of empowerment held by western development experts is to give women the chance to occupy positions of 'power', in terms of political and economic decision-making. [...] The difficulty with this view of 'empowerment' is that if it can be bestowed, it can just easily be withdrawn. In other words, it does not involve a structural change in the power relations.[30]

Rowlands' warning concerning the lack of change in power relations, which is the stated goal of empowerment, is very important for our case. She argues that this notion of empowerment stems from the dominant understanding of power as being 'power over', in the sense of command and control over resources and values. In this world view, power is in finite supply, and the empowerment of one group, i.e. women, is at the expense of the other group, i.e. men, leading to a possible backlash or at least protest by the latter. In contrast, therefore, she argues for a 'feminist model of power', which draws on the Foucaultian notion of power as productive and bound up with knowledge and therefore not finite. Yet, this view has to be enhanced by a gendered analysis of power:

of how 'internalised oppression' places internal barriers to women's exercise of power, thereby contributing to the maintenance of inequality between men and women.[31]

Here cultural norms and societal structures of gender relations become a fundamental framework of analysis. The exercise of power is assumed to be circumscribed to a considerable degree by structural determination. The focus of the feminist approach thus lies in gaining productive power, wielding 'power to',[32] challenge the existing power relations. The concept of empowerment now encompasses women moving into positions of 'power over', but also embraces their movement into 'power to', understood as power to formulate their own preferences and to be able to change society by negotiating gender relations. In respect of the latter, some proponents of the empowerment approach remain sceptical over how far merely bringing women into the political process will lead to their empowerment, if not combined with processes of raising awareness. For example, a strong women's movement outside the institutional framework would make the elected members accountable to the female constituency.[33] In order to answer the question of empowerment, therefore, one has to distinguish between the empowerment of women who become included in the formal political process and that of women who remain outside the system. An extensive discussion of broad-based definitions of empowerment is impossible here; nevertheless, it is important to distinguish the several aspects and understandings of empowerment. The bringing of women into positions of power is one aspect, and this was formally endorsed through the 73rd Amendment. However, we must ask whether women actually came forward to contest these seats, and to what extent were they able to participate fully. If we can answer these questions positively, we have to go a step further and look at the nature of their participation. Were these women equipped with sufficient knowledge to formulate and defend their own preferences and interests? Were they agents of their own destiny? It is also important to look at the space which is accorded to women in the public sphere by societal norms. These vary from place to place, and also in respect to caste, religion and lifecycle of the women. These conditions determine to a certain extent the scope of how far women can and are using the new political space which has suddenly opened up for them. A final issue is to distinguish between women elected to political institutions and those who remain outside the formal political process. Does bringing some women into the political process really lead to empowerment of all women? As the process of empowering women can only be understood in contextual terms, a case study offers the most rewarding method to deal with this complex matter.[34]

4. The Case Study

As one of the most *backward* states in economic and social terms of the Indian Union, Orissa was selected for this case study.[35] In such an unconducive 'patriarchal' setting, one might expect women not to participate at all. As we are interested in whether the legislation has empowered women, a 'worst case scenario' can give important clues. If the political representation of women leads to empowerment here, we can assume that it also leads to empowerment elsewhere. In order to have a variation in the factors which are assumed to influence women's participation, two areas for study[36] were selected from two districts. These are Balipatna from coastal Khurda and Gania from the more hinterland Nayagarh District, which belonged to the princely state of Daspalla. Hence there is a distinct difference between the two chosen areas in the historical evolution of local self-government and political culture of each. More importantly, there remains a marked variance in economic development, infra-structural facilities and gendered literacy rates, which could be labelled more 'advanced' in Balipatna than in Gania. Additionally, exposure to urban life is much higher in Balipatna, as it is only 30 km from Bhubaneswar, whereas in Gania, 100 km away from the capital, some of the Gram Panchayats are inaccessible by car or motorbike.

Before we start with our analysis we will first have a look at the socio-economic profile of the people elected in the PRI in these two areas.

Age, educational level, and annual income are seen as important determinants for political participation.

Who are the Elected Women and Men?

A sample of 105 women was interviewed, mainly at the level of the *Gram Panchayat* (82 ward members, 7 *Sarpanches*, 12 *Naib-Sarpanches*) and very few at the *Samiti* Level (2 *Samiti* Members and 2 *Samiti* Chairpersons, whose positions were reserved in both blocks for *Scheduled Caste* Women), presenting a more or less full sample of women elected in these two blocks.[37] Additionally a random sample of 80 men were interviewed.[38] The *Zilla Parishad* level was not investigated.

Age

Before elections took place under the new legislation, there was a widespread belief that mainly older women past their reproductive age would come forward. This perception was based on the assumption that these women have fewer household duties because their children are grown, or they already command daughters-in-law (*bahus*) who manage the bulk of household responsibilities. The second reasoning was that they have a different status to young women in the village community, which gives them greater freedom. For example, from a certain age (usually in their fifties onwards) women decide to stop putting the end of their Sari over their eyes, and only cover their hair when they go out. Higher age also stands for experience and maturity, which is greatly valued in rural society; additionally the position of a mother of sons and mistress of *bahus* further elevates a woman's status. Surprisingly, in studies of other regions as well as in Orissa, it was found that this was generally not the case, and rather that younger women came to the fore.[39] During the survey we found that the majority of women were still in the 'reproductive age' bracket. The largest group, with nearly 42 per cent, were between 31 and 40, when household responsibilities are still quite substantial, and more than 62 per cent were younger than 41 years. The mean age of women was 37.7 years.[40] It could be interpreted as positive that only very few women above 61 had been elected as compared to findings for example in Haryana,[41] because they are often not capable anymore of being very active. In regard of the assumptions given above, this age pattern is remarkable and not readily explained. We will give some possible interpretations later. Interestingly, the men tended to be older than the women. Only 50 per cent were younger than 41; however, here again the largest group was between 31 and 40 (28.75 per cent), but an only slightly smaller group were aged between 41 and 50 (26.25 per cent). Men's mean age is 41.3 years; thus they tended to be on average 2.6 years older than the women.

Education

Education is considered to be one of the most important independent variables for participation and effectiveness in politics. Lack of education is frequently bewailed by ordinary villagers, as well as social scientists, as making the concept of women's representation within political institutions a farce. Illiteracy definitely restricts a person's access to information and makes her dependent on others. Especially in higher positions, literacy is essential in order to be able to read and understand the orders, rules, and regulations. Education normally also enhances the personal feeling of efficacy, and lack of it can contribute to a low self-esteem.

We found that the women we studied had little access to formal education. The majority of those interviewed only made it up to primary level, and among these many dropped out after their second or third year. Thus they can hardly be rated as literate in a functional sense. 19 per cent never went to school, although most of them have learned to sign their name, the minimum prerequisite for a position in the Panchayati Raj Institutions. Yet, to perform well as a ward member, few literary skills are necessary. The women who have been elected as *Sarpanches* or *Samiti* Chairpersons normally have a higher education.[42] Interestingly there is no marked difference between the educational level of women in the political institutions of Gania and Balipatna, even though this is quite notable in the general population.[43]

Men in the PRI are generally better educated than the women, which complies with the wider pattern of the population. All of them went to school, though the majority also attended only up to primary level. Here, it is interesting to note the marked difference between the men in Balipatna and in Gania. The educational level in Gania is considerably lower than in Balipatna. More than half the men here went to primary school only, whereas in Balipatna the majority went to secondary school, while a substantial number are even matriculates and above.

Income

The last variable we will look at is income, always considered as significant in the political sphere. Traditionally, the PRI were manned by the propertied and landed elite. Most people believe that for election to higher positions money is needed for entertainment of voters, bribes, and so on. One has to keep in mind that cash income is very difficult to assess in rural Orissa, as most people still live a life of subsistence agriculture. Often women do not have much idea about the cash-position of the household, and the answer was frequently given by the husband, or calculated by knowing the assets of the family. Thus the income given also takes landed property into account. However, the figures can not be taken as absolute, as there is a tendency – especially in the richer section of the population – to underestimate income, but it still gives a rough idea about the financial position of households (see Table 1, below).

Keeping this underestimation in mind, the figures do reveal an interesting trend. The Indian Poverty line is Rs 11,000 per annum;[45] we thus find that more than 40 per cent of our sample is below the poverty line. This is quite remarkable when we remember that the Panchayati Raj Institutions were traditionally dominated by the rural elite. As expected, there is a difference between the economic position of women in the two sample areas. In Gania, more than 65 per cent of the women are below the poverty line, compared to around 39 per cent in Balipatna. In addition, it is worth noting that there are more middle income groups in Balipatna. Men's incomes are compared in the table below.

We can see that the men generally fall into higher-income groups. One reason for this seems to be the fact that families from higher economic strata are very

Table 1 Total Family Income per annum of female respondents (in rupees, percentage of population in brackets)[44]

	<5,000	5,000– <10,000	10,000– <20,000	20,000– <50,000	50,000– <100,000	100,000 and above	Total
Balipatna	12 (22.2)	9 (16.7)	13 (24.1)	16 (29.6)	3 (5,5)	1 (1.8)	54* (55.7)
Gania	6 (14.0)	22 (51.2)	7 (16.3)	5 (11.6)	1 (2.3)	2 (4.6)	43 (44.3)
Total	18 (18.6)	31 (32.0)	20 (20.6)	21 (21.6)	4 (4.1)	3 (3.1)	97 (100)

Key: Percentage in rows for Balipatna and Gania are calculated for each sample separately
*8 women could not give their financial position and other family members were not available. Thus they have been deleted from the sample.

Table 2 Total family income per annum of male respondents (in rupees, percentage of population in brackets)

	<5,000	5,000– <10,000	10,000– <20,000	20,000– <50,000	50,000– <100,000	100,000 and above	Total
Balipatna		9 (22.5)	15 (37.5)	11 (27.5)	1 (2.5)	4 (10)	40 (50)
Gania	3 (7.5)	14 (35.0)	13 (32.5)	6 (15.0)	2 (5.0)	2 (5.0)	40 (50)
Total	3 (3.75)	23 (28.75)	28 (35)	17 (21.25)	3 (3.75)	6 (7.5)	80 (100)

Key: Percentage in rows for Balipatna and Gania are calculated for each sample separately.

reluctant to encourage their womenfolk to join politics. Women from lower economic strata are already more exposed, as they might be working outside the house. The sample is also biased, in so far as more Scheduled Castes are represented in the female sample than in the male sample. There are only three men whose income is below Rs 5000 per annum, and all in all there are 32 per cent of the men below the poverty line, as compared to more than 40 per cent of the women. Among the men we also find a marked difference between the levels of income in Gania and Balipatna, revealing that 43.5 per cent of men in Gania are below the poverty line, whereas in Balipatna the figure is about 22.5 per cent. One can conclude that it is mainly people from modest back-grounds who have been elected to the institutions, yet as Orissa is a very poor state, there are in any case relatively fewer wealthy families. Additionally, the position of a ward member, which forms the majority of this sample, holds little attraction for the rural elite. Not surprisingly, we can establish a positive correlation between the position in the PRI and income: the higher the posi-tion, the higher the income.[46] After having ascertained who the representa-tives are in terms of their age and socio-economic status, we can look at the extent to which they participate in the functioning of the PRI.

The Extent of Participation

The basic indicator for a minimum of political participation is the attendance of the monthly *Gram Panchayat* or bimonthly *Panchayat Samiti* meeting. Most representatives stated that they participated in every *panchayat* meeting, and there was no marked difference between the two sample areas; moreover, the difference in attendance between men and women was not significant. A variation between the women and men becomes more salient in the answers to the question concerning their participation in the decision-making. Here, we found a gap between the female and male members of the Panchayati Raj Institutions. Less than two thirds of the women claim to have participated in every decision, as opposed to 90 per cent of the men. Slightly more than 11 per cent of the women said that they participated in no decisions, while around 14 per cent stated that they had participated in only a few decisions.

An even more pronounced variation revealed itself when we turn to the question of the amount of time spent on the work of the *panchayat*. The majority of women (59 per cent) did not spend more than 5 hours a month, which is basically the time taken in attending the meeting. A fifth spent between 6 to 10 hours a month. The average time spent was 17.03 hours in Balipatna, and 10.14 hours in Gania, adding up to 14.21 hours as a total aver-age spent by women in the PRI per month. The gap between Balipatna and Gania is quite prominent. Yet, if we subtract two high-profile women who spent more than 100 hours per month (a very active *Sarpanch* and the *Panchayat Samiti* Chairperson), the average was reduced to 11.93 hours in Balipatna. Even though this does not look very impressive, we should keep in mind that the women do at least attend most of the meetings. In other states, especially in the 'Hindi belt', we hear of husbands attending the meetings, and of registers sent home to be signed by the women in *purdah*. The main problem is the fact that women have not been relieved from their household duties. One could argue that women's entrance into rural politics encumbers them with a triple burden – domestic work, outside work and politics. Most of the women said that they get some help when they attend the meetings – mainly from other female household members – but basically the amount of work to be done remains the same. These remarks are very familiar to women in the West, where most working women have either not been relieved of their domestic duties, or the burden has been transferred to other females.[47] In rural India it is often difficult for women to cope in a nuclear family with young children, as they have only the husband to help. Asked whether her husband was supporting her in the household now that she is busy with *panchayat* work, the answer of a young *Sarpanch* in Gania block was:

> Being a woman I am used to work hard. I can not ask my husband to do household work – I would feel ashamed! I rather get up early and do all the work alone before I leave for the office. Normally I do take my children to office. But when I have to go to the Block Office I can not take them with me. My husband does care for our youngest daughter when I am away and can not take her. When we are entertaining guests I have to stay at home as I am the only woman in this household.

Men spend much more time on *panchayat* work than women. The biggest group (27.5 per cent) spends between 26 and 50 hours on work for the PRI, with less than 20 per cent just attending the meetings. The average number of hours spent by men is 51.95 in Balipatna and 49.19 in Gania, amounting to 50.53 altogether. Thus we see that the difference between the two sample areas is more prominent among the women than among the men, and that men spend around five times as many hours per month than do women.

Another interesting question is the attendance of women in the Grama Sabha. This is the village parliament where everyone on the electoral register in the specified area meets at least twice a year to discuss and approve the budget of the *Gram Panchayat*. The real decisions are supposed to be made here, and the *panchayat* members should implement the resolutions of the Grama Sabha. Compared to the *panchayat* meetings, which are attended by elected members only and which have an exclusive atmosphere, Grama Sabhas are public meetings which often take place in schoolbuildings or open spaces. Nearly all men said that they go to the Grama Sabha. It is interesting to note the large difference between the attendance of women in both areas: 52.4 per cent of the women in Gania – as compared to 83.1 per cent in Balipatna – claimed that they attend the village meetings. In Gania a frequent answer to the question was 'I am a *bahu*', which translates more or less as 'Why are you asking me such a stupid question, as a daughter-in-law I can not attend a public village meeting.' It seems that the *panchayat* meetings are considered as a kind of 'private' space where women do not face men from their own village, with whom they have fictive or real family relations that traditionally prohibit social intercourse. The Grama Sabha, on the other hand, is a public meeting, attended by men from the village. One ward member observed that

> I have no problems to speak with men in the [*panchayat*] meetings. They do not belong to my village. I do speak to them like I do speak to the women. Outside the *Panchayat* Office I do not speak to the men. After the meeting I go home immediately and stay in the house. [...] I do not go to the Grama Sabha. My husband attends the Grama Sabha. I am a *bahu* of the village.

It is interesting to note that women normally attend the *panchayat* meetings as part of their legitimate role as elected members. A commonly held perception in Orissa is that only elected members can attend the *panchayat* meetings; this is not the case everywhere. In some cases, husbands were treaded as ward members or the *Sarpanch* during the survey (people directed us to them when we asked for the representative) and these men claimed that they could answer the questions much better than their wives, who did not know anything. Nevertheless, these women normally do attend the meetings, accompanied by their husband or sons. But total control by male family members did not seem widespread in the areas investigated. Still, work outside of the *Panchayat* Office, like solving disputes among villagers or supervising the implementation of development works, are generally done by male relatives. One husband of a tribal ward member formulated it like this:

> I am not going to the meeting. She is the ward member, I am not. Imagine I will go to the meeting and they will not recognise me and will say there is no ward member from N* and will not offer me a chair. I will feel insulted! But I am the one who goes to solve the village problems and supervise[s] the development work.

Still, it is important to see that many women, *bahus* included, do go to the Grama Sabha. The attendance of women has gained some legitimacy, but it is mainly bound to their position in the PRI. This can be seen in the revealing statement made by a young *bahu*, who is not in the PRI, but wishes to participate in the next election:

> I am interested to become *Sarpanch* in the next election. I want to serve the people. No, I have not been to the Grama Sabha. I am a young *bahu*. When I will be the *Sarpanch* I will go, but not as an ordinary woman.

The above statement was also confirmed when I attended three Grama Sabhas. There were mainly men, and most of the few women present were PRI representatives.

So far we have established that women normally attend the *panchayat* meetings, but most of them do not do much more than this. Women did not generally show up at public village meetings like the Grama Sabhas, where the main decisions are determined, nor supervise the implementation of development works, nor go out to settle village disputes. Crucially, it is normally not approved of within rural society for women to travel alone. However, here again there is a difference between the two sample areas. In Balipatna we see more young girls and women on bicycles, one bold *Sarpanch* even driving a motorbike. Here more women come to the *Panchayat* Office without male company (69.8 per cent as compared to 41.9 per cent in Galnia), because they are not so dependent on means of transport. In Gania, on the other hand, villages are so small and dispersed that members have to cover distances up to 15 km, often through forest areas which are not considered safe for women. Thus most of the women here are accompanied by male relatives while attending the meetings. The results of the preceding analysis are better understood when we look at the way the women came to be elected.

The Election

How did these women come to be elected? Why did they enter the arena of local politics? Were they motivated by their own interest in politics, or were they pushed? In a Western democracy like Germany it would be very difficult suddenly to fill a quota of this magnitude. However, in India the more entrenched patriarchal values do act as 'facilitators', as most of the nominations were filed by husbands or fathers-in-law, often even without informing the women in question. Later when they were told they nodded in assent, like dutiful *pativratas*.

Table 3 How was your decision formed to participate in the election (percentage in brackets)?

	Own decision	Husband	Other family members	Village leaders	Villagers	Caste/ tribe	Other	Total
Fem. (Balipatna)	12 (19.3)	3 (4.8)	11 (17.7)	8 (12.9)	42 (67.7)	1 (1.6)	–	62
Fem. (Gania)	5 (11.6)	9 (20.9)	4 (9.3)	–	36 (83.7)	–	1 (2.3)	43
Total	17 (16.2)	12 (11.4)	15 (14.3)	8 (7.6)	78 (74.3)	1 (0.9)	1 (0.9)	105
male (Balipatna)	22 (55)	–	–	1 (2.5)	18 (45)	–	3 (7.5)	40
male (Gania)	7 (17.5)	–	2 (5.0)	1 (2.5)	29 (72.5)	–	5 (12.5)	40
Total	29 (36.2)	–	2 (2.5)	2 (2.5)	47 (58.7)	–	8 (10.0)	80

Key: Multiple answers were possible; percentages calculated according to number of persons interviewed in each category; does not add up to 100 per cent.

We see that far fewer women than men claim that it was their own decision to participate in the election, and we can assume that the actual figure is even lower. Still, we can assume that the difference between Balipatna and Gania is real and that more women in the coastal area have made their decision with a measure of independence. Important to note is the high percentage of answers stating that local villagers had encouraged the women. But in the case of both women and men – especially in Gania – many have been influenced or persuaded by villagers. In some instances, the villagers had to win over the erstwhile reluctant husband to nominate his wife. Sometimes the husband had already been selected as the ward member, and when the ward became reserved for a woman she became the ward member automatically. This could be one factor in the remarkably young age of the women, as wives tend to be younger than their husbands. A majority of women ran uncontested: 41 (65.1 per cent) in Balipatna and 26 (60.5 per cent) in Gania. This has partly to do with the reluctance of many families to let their womenfolk contest. However, despite the assertion of many critics that women would never contest seats, 35–40 per cent did compete with other candidates to fill their posts. And we should be aware that many men's seats were also not contested: 14 (35 per cent) in Balipatna and 15 (37.5 per cent) in Gania. The high percentage (more than a third) of uncontested men's seats gives a hint of the traditional value of unanimous decisions within village communities, regardless of the gender of the representative. Electoral competition is perceived as dividing the village community, and villagers are proud to show that there is harmony in their village.[48] Another important point to note is that the influence of the village community is more salient in the more 'traditional' Gania.[49] But who are the villagers who make these unanimous decisions? These are normally the male elders of the village community. Meetings were conducted in the constituencies of women to find out what villagers think about their female representatives, and how they decided whom to elect. These meetings were only attended by men. They were asked why they had elected a woman. The first answer was normally: 'We were forced to do so!' Asked whether they were happy with the reservation for women, some stated initially that they were proud to have a woman representative. Asked more provocatively, most of them confessed that they tried to evade their bad 'fate'. Some even went to the Block Development Officer (BDO) to protest against the decision, and wanted to have it changed. There is a marked difference between a general acceptance of the reservation for women ('It is good to give them a chance – they will advance', 'Now they get the opportunity to go out and learn something'), and the reservation of one's own ward or *Gram Panchayat* for a woman ('She is not educated', 'She is shy, look at her, she can not speak', 'There are no educated women in our village, so it is bad to have a reservation here'). Asked further about why they had elected the specific woman, different criteria emerged.

The most important issue was the willingness of the woman, or rather her husband's/father-in-law's willingness to nominate her. Another point was the level of education: they wanted to choose the most educated woman available. This could be another reason why many young women came to be elected, as they tend to be more educated than the older women. Generally men lamented the fact that their womenfolk were not educated, often pointing at me or my assistant as being the right women to elect to a public office, as we are educated and can express our views more clearly. Asked about their willingness to give education to their daughters, the answers were, however, quite defensive: 'They will go away. Why should we water a foreign tree?'[50] Another frequent argument was the distance to the next higher school and the work done by girls:

> Yes, education is important and can change things, but we will not educate our girls. There are so many things to do here, like grasing the goats and household works. Who will do this when the girls go to school? In our village not even a single boy has passed the 10th standard, so why should we educate the girls? And the middle school and high school are far away. 10–15 years back our village was surrounded by jungle, so even men did not go to higher school. It was too difficult to get there.

A repeated complaint was the shyness of women, their inability to speak in public. In order to evade this problem one can detect a definite preference for the married *gaanjhia* – the daughter of the village. Marriage is an important consideration, as we have seen that much work outside the *panchayat* meetings are done by the husbands, and villagers want to be sure that these things really get done. It is not by chance that the sole three unmarried women interviewed are in Balipatna, the more 'progressive' block. Men often remarked that they had selected the specific woman because her husband is active and they know that he will do good work. If women were born in the respected village it was seen as an advantage, as due to cultural norms *gaanjhias* are less inhibited in their social intercourse. They do not have to cover their face when they go out of the house in their native village; they can move relatively freely and have a good relationship with most villagers. It is interesting to note that there are several *gaanjhias* in the PRI, even though it is not a dominant social custom. In Orissa, as in the rest of North India, women normally leave their native place to get married. But it became obvious that there is a preference for selecting *gaanjihias*, as both villagers and the elected women themselves were aware of this being a consideration.[51] Another issue is where the woman lives. A ward often comprises up to four villages, or in bigger villages several *Sahis* (parts of the village mostly inhabited by one caste-group). People are keen to vote for a woman from their own village, because they feel that they will be better represented. The same holds for bigger villages, where several *Sahis* make up one ward. Here people want to elect a woman from their *Sahi*. Thus women were generally elected from whichever village or *Sahi* was the biggest. Obviously the same consideration holds for men as well.

Last but not least caste does play a role. One has to remember that the choice of the electorate is limited: seats are reserved for Scheduled Castes and Scheduled Tribes proportionally; additionally 27 per cent of the seats are reserved for OBCs. At the level of ward member, caste plays a role mainly because caste-groups are concentrated in different localities. As the wards consist often of different communities, the ward member will either come from the majority community or the biggest *Sahi* or village, and thus be of a specific caste. When the position is reserved for *Scheduled Caste, Scheduled Tribe* or OBC, the choice is limited. Villagers voiced the strong preference that if they had to vote for a *Scheduled Caste*, they at least wanted at least for a 'touch-able' *Scheduled Caste*. In Gania these *Scheduled Caste* candidates come from the Keuta community (traditionally fishermen or producers of puffed rice [*Chuda*]). This community has been included in the *Scheduled Caste* category, but is 'touchable'. The preference for *Scheduled Caste* candidates from this community was generally voiced by villagers, and one meets a high percent-age of Keutas in the Gania PRI. Again, the same considerations hold for men as well.

The Political Dimension

We have seen that very few women were elected as a result of their own interest in politics or public service. Traditionally, politics was not considered a 'proper' domain for rural women, and women were normally not informed or consulted about political matters. However, knowledge is an important prerequisite for exercising power and for participating in a meaningful way. As we have seen, formal education is rather thin on the ground for both men and women. We need therefore to establish what the elected representatives actually know about their political environment. Concerning knowledge of the formal system, the elected members were asked several questions during the survey: whether they know the name of the BDO, of the ruling party in Orissa, and of the MLA. Additionally they were asked about their knowledge of the 73rd Amendment and Government schemes.

With regard to the first three questions, we found that women have much less knowledge than men about formal politics. The name of the BDO was known by 13.3 per cent of the women, and by 40 per cent of the men; the name of the ruling party by 34.4 per cent of the women and 88.8 per cent of the men; and the name of the MLA by 47 per cent of the women and 95 per cent of the men. We can also find a knowledge gap between Gania and Balipatna: people in the latter were more knowledgeable. This difference becomes even more significant when we compare how many of those interviewed could answer all three questions correctly. Among the women, in Balipatna 5 (8.1 per cent) could do this, in Gania only 2 (4.7 per cent); among the men, 17 (42.5 per cent) in Balipatna and 14 (35.0 per cent) in Gania. One could argue that it is not too important for ward members to possess this kind of knowledge, but it gives some hint of their political interest and involvement. Knowledge about the existence and content of the 73rd Amendment is perhaps more important for local-level politicians. Yet we found that it was basically nil in both genders: only the *Sarpanches* and *Samiti* Members could give some response – and in most cases this was not very detailed. Among both sexes only 3.8 per cent of either sex had more detailed knowledge of specific features of the amendment on which the institution they are serving in are based. Another important area of information concerns the government schemes, which are supposed to be implemented by the PRI. Around 25 per cent of the women were unable to name any scheme; the others mentioned up to 10 schemes. Among the men only 2 were unable to name any scheme, and generally they were more knowledgeable. We can assume that the 25 per cent of women who were unable to name any programme have not been very involved so far in the *panchayat* work. In respect of the representatives who could give some response, the mention of schemes was notably gendered. Women more often mentioned the Old Age Pension and the Widow Pension, as well as the Ballika Samrddhi Yojana, which gives incentives to keep and nurture female children, while men more frequently named schemes for obtaining loans for productive purposes. Men were better informed than women in all areas except specific knowledge on the 73rd Amendment, and people in Balipatna were generally better informed than those in Gania.

As we have seen, there is a slightly gendered pattern in knowledge of government schemes, which points to different preferences between men and women. Does this also translate into different preferences voiced for works to be conducted by the representative? It would be important to establish whether or not women do indeed introduce different issues or focus on different areas. We asked the representatives what they want to do in their constituencies. The most frequent response by women and men in both areas was the improvement of infrastructure, mainly roads, and also irrigation facilities. Next came issues like health, community development through building of community halls or temples, economic development, improvement of education and implementation of government schemes. No clear gendered pattern emerged from this data. Thus, responses were additionally coded as to whether respondents mentioned something in particular for women. That could be remarks like 'I want to do something for widows' or 'I want to see that a *Mahila Mandal* (women's group) gets established in our *panchayat*'. Here one could find a distinct gendered – and also regional – pattern. In Balipatna 21 per cent of women voiced that they wanted to do something specifically for women, whereas in Gania no woman made such a statement. Among the men, 2.5 per cent in Balipatna, and 7.5 per cent in Gania claimed to have a special concern. It appears that women in Balipatna are more gender-conscious than women in Gania, and that there is generally a noticeable distinction between men and women. Thus we can find some indication that the introduction of women into the political process will shift policy priorities, at least in the longer term.

We will now turn to the question of the empowerment of women serving in the institutions. We are mainly looking here for 'process,' for example the gaining of knowledge and political interest, of status and of confidence.

Prior to their election, most of the women were not interested in politics. The reason given was that there was no scope in politics for women, so why should they be interested? Nevertheless, after having been in the *Panchayat* Institution for quite a while, they gained more knowledge and many of them now showed an interest in politics. One could detect also an improvement in political interest and awareness in the second round of fieldwork, which took place a year after the first.

One ward member in Balipatna formulated it like this:

Before I became ward member I was not interested in politics at all. This started only after my election. I learned a lot of things, because everybody is talking about politics in the meetings and there are discussions in the *Panchayat* Office. Now I am interested in politics and I also campaigned in this MLA election [in February 2000]. I have also learned a lot of other things. Now I get to know everything about different government programmes, and I even get information from the Collector. So I am learning a lot.

A female ward member from Gania observed that

Before the election I had not the slightest idea about politics. But now I am a political person. The Panchayati Raj Institutions are political, even if the elections do not take place under party symbol. I know that the *Sarpanches* or ward members do support their party people or the people who have voted for them.

A *Naib-Sarpanch* from the headquarters *panchayat* in Balipatna said:

Even before my election I was interested in politics. I have seen other people standing for election and I also wanted to become a ward member. My husband was a ward member, you know. So I have seen things, but I did not know very much. But I was very interested and determined to learn. I thought that first I will become a ward member and when I have learned enough I will maybe become a *Sarpanch* later. Now I am reading the *Panchayat* Manual in Oriya. I am also interested in state Politics and do watch the news. At the moment I follow the parliamentary session in TV.

In these statements, one can see that some women definitely gained knowledge and interest in politics through their election, which would presumably not have happened without a reservation for them. One can speculate that this trend will be enhanced, term of office is increased serve longer in the PRI than just two years.

Another interesting issue is whether the elected women perceive that their status has changed in the family. During the quantitative survey, 42 per cent of the women answered that their status in the family has improved due to their position in the PRI. They mentioned instances of now being consulted by family members on certain matters. They also benefited from increased status in the village community. Many have acquired an independent identity through their position in the PRI. One *Sarpanch* told us: 'I feel good in Gania. People know me now, know that I am the *Sarpanch*, and they respect me. Before I became the *Sarpanch* they did not know me.' This is not a trifling development: women in rural Orissa are normally not known by name and only addressed in a relational context as daughter, sister, mother, *bahu*. This is, for most of them, the first time that people notice them as a person in their own right, though their familial ties still play a dominant role. Even in cases where women are mere proxies, they have also gained visibility in the village community.

The women's interest in what they are doing, and their confidence in their own abilities, is revealed when asked about their future aspirations within the Panchayati Raj Institutions:

The figures are quite amasing. Nearly 70 per cent of the women would not only like to remain in the PRI, but more than half of them aspire to a higher position. Interesting to note is the huge gap between Balipatna and Gania concerning 'going up' (Indian English for promotion). It seems to suggest that women are more assertive in the more developed block, as well as more self-confident. There is also, naturally enough, also a good dose of vanity. In a group meeting with all women representatives of a *Gram Panchayat* in Balipatna, they said: 'We are happy to be ward members, because we get high-lighted now and have more prestige. Actually we would like to have 100 per cent Mahila Seats!' Generally the reservation has given a boost to their self-image of their capabilities. Asked why they aspire to a higher post, more women in Balipatna named increased power to do more work and the wish to do more for the people. Thus they perceived their present post as insufficiently power-ful to do what they would like to do. The ones who want to get out of the PRI are often more aware of the difficulties which are involved with this post. Some of them were frustrated because they had not yet achieved anything, so they regarded it as a waste of time to remain in the institutions much longer. Some women also said that they had too much household work to do and could not afford to spend so much time for the PRI; others were simply disinterested.

One can conclude that some modest empowerment has already taken place, and that women in Balipatna are more confident, assertive and – as we

Table 4 Do you have any future aspirations in the Panchayati Raj (percentage in brackets)?

	Getting out	Running for the same post	Going up	Can't say, don't know	Total
Women in Balipatna	9 (14.5)	18 (29.0)	27 (43.5)	8 (12.9)	62
Women in Gania	10 (23.3)	15 (34.9)	12 (27.9)	6 (13.9)	43
Total	19 (18.1)	33 (31.4)	39 (37.1)	14 (13.3)	105

have seen concerning their project preferences – also more gender-aware. There is, however, no indication that gender relations have changed, as women are still very much dependent on male household members.

How does it look concerning the empowerment of women outside the PRI? In Gania it was quite difficult to talk to women and get informed statements, as there were no functioning women's groups there. In one village I met some old and very young women, because the others were working in the fields. I asked them about their female ward member. One old lady responded:

> We do not know anything. We know the ward member, but we cannot say whether she is doing a good job or not. You have to ask the men, if you want to know. I have not talked to her since she is the ward member. In case the ward member wants something she is calling a village meeting and the male villagers go. So we women do not know what she wants and what she is doing.

A similar remark came from women in a very remote tribal village. They told me: 'Our ward member comes and speaks with the men. She has not organised a meeting with us or asked us any questions.'

In both these cases it seems that the women who became ward members have somehow crossed a line, separating them from the female world, and the village women regard them now as part of the male world of politics. Still, even in Gania we found also positive remarks. Asked more generally how they view the fact that there are now women in the PRI, most village women welcomed the inclusion. A main reason for this can be found in the gender-segregated nature of Oriya society. Prior to the election of female representatives, village women had no access to elected representatives, since they could not go and speak to men. Now they can imagine placing their demands in front of the female ward member, *Sarpanch* and *Samiti* Chairperson. Some young women, again in another *Gram Panchayat* in Gania, said: 'We are happy with our ward member. She is a woman and we can now place our demands.' This was also confirmed by the ward member in question, who claimed that the women really do come to her.

The situation in Balipatna looks somewhat different. Here an NGO has organised several vibrant women's groups around micro-credit.[52] The women in these groups are quite vocal and all of them were very positive about the fact that there are now women in the PRI. In one group meeting they said:

> It is good that there are now women in the Panchayati Raj Institutions. It is good because now the women are coming out of their houses. Before women were not participating, but now we get the chance to

participate at different levels. Our daughters might participate in the next election, when there is again a reservation for women. We want to stand on our own feet, but sometimes we are dependent on our husbands. In our *panchayat* the female representatives are doing the work and they are all participating in the meetings. They also go out and supervise the work.

In another *Gram Panchayat*, members of a women's group made observations that echoed the arguments of the young women in Gania:

We are happy that there are now women in the panchayats. Because we can put our demands and requirements in front of the women, we can not do this in front of the men. We women are not independent here, and before we could not talk to the Panchayati Raj people, because they were all men.

From these remarks we can see that the situation is not straightforward. In Gania, it seems that the female representatives have crossed a line, separating them from the village women. In Balipatna it seems that the village women have also gained some pride from the fact that there are now elected women in the institutions, and think about encouraging their daughters to involve themselves as well. However, they were mainly critical in terms of the extent to which the inclusion of women has changed their lot thus far. But one should not underestimate the power that the symbolic recognition of women has for all women. The gender-segregated nature of society here is an additional argument for an inclusion of women in local governmental decision-making in the Indian countryside. How far it will really lead to major changes in the situation of women in general still remains open to speculation, but it seems that an important step has been made through the reservation of seats for women, giving other women access to their representatives and, through them, to the sphere of politics for the first time.

5. Conclusion

In this essay I asked whether the 73rd Amendment has really led to the empowerment of women. For this purpose I distinguished between empowerment as bringing women into formal positions of power, and enabling women to wield power to achieve qualitative change within society. We have found that empowerment, in the sense of coming into positions of power, has been established through the legislation. The women are really there. India has reached a stage in the quantitative participation of women in politics after

50 years of Independence that many so-called 'developed' countries have not yet reached. In this respect we can consider the effects of the 73rd Amendment as no small success. But when we go further and look at the quality of women's participation, the situation is less promising. Very few women have decided independently to participate in politics; they contribute much less to the decision-making process than men; they devote less time; and they rarely take part in activities outside the confines of the *panchayat* office. It is especially significant that they do not usually participate in decision-making on real issues, while the 'villagers', synonymous with the male elders, still formulate village priorities. Additionally, women do not have much knowledge about formal politics and are very dependent on outside help. There is furthermore little evidence that the power structure within families has changed, as the load of household duties has basically remained the same, even though women perceive that their status within the family has improved. The question therefore remains: is the empowerment of women through the 73rd Amendment after all only an illusion?

The answer to this question depends on one's expectations and timeframe. We have to remember that the women interviewed in Orissa have been in office for just two to three years. We cannot expect rapid change, nor that political novices will start acting confidently and gain the necessary skills and information straight away. To hope that society will change rapidly to accommodate the new role for women is naive, to say the least. There are many obstacles in the way, the major one being the traditionally perceived roles for women. Still, it should be encouraging to see that some attitudes have changed already. It is now a respected fact that women do participate in the *panchayat* meetings, even though villagers might not be very impressed by their performance. Their participation in public village meetings is also partly respected. Some well-performing women were able for the first time to have the chance to prove themselves, which would not have been possible without the quota for women. Most women in the PRI gained in confidence and knowledge, and most would like to remain in positions of power. Women in Balipatna seemed to have gained more self-confidence and more gender-consciousness. Concerning the empowerment of women outside the institutions, the pattern is mixed. Again, it seems that the women in Balipatna have gained most, at least from a psychological point of view. But the symbolic recognition of women and their new access to the elected representatives were seen in both Balipatna and Gania as positive effects of the legislation.

One can conclude therefore that the magnitude of the effect of the legislation is on the one hand a function of time, but also depends substantially on socio-economic environment. In Balipatna, where women are already more advanced in matters of mobility, and where exposure to urban values is greater, the impact has been more noticeable. In this respect it becomes obvious that what is supposed to be gained through the inclusion of women in the political process is to a certain extent also a precondition, presenting the situation as a kind of vicious circle. We have to keep in mind, however, that Orissa was selected as representing a kind of 'worst-case scenario', and Gania is definitely very *backward* in many respects. Yet even under these very difficult circumstances we find some positive impact of the legislation on the position of women, albeit to a lesser degree than in Balipatna. When we try to imagine the situation in other Indian states where women are already more empowered, like in Kerala, one is inclined to believe that the advances there should be greater.

In conclusion, I argue that the political empowerment of women through the 73rd Amendment will be a long process and that some of the expected gains are already a kind of pre-condition. There should therefore be policies in place, such as the promotion of women's groups, in addition to the inclusion of women into the political process. It will be very difficult to induce women representatives to work in the interests of women if there is no sizeable pressure from their female constituency. It also remains open to debate whether the 73rd Amendment is the most conducive measure for empowerment, if this is understood more in the traditional sense of gaining the ability to understand the systematic forces behind women's oppression and becoming psychologically empowered. We should not forget that other measures, like literacy campaigns, awareness building, or the granting of economic rights to women, might be equally important. In order to reach the goal of women's empowerment, such policies must be implemented in tandem with the inclusion of women in decision-making bodies. As long as women are dependent on male relatives to fulfil their public duties, as long as they are not relieved from domestic work, and as long as they do not participate in institutions like the Grama Sabha where the real decisions take place, it will be very difficult for them to formulate and follow their own preferences and thus be truly empowered to contribute to social change. Still, this study shows that a seed has been planted and will grow, even if it will need patience and nurture to blossom truly.

NOTES

Introduction

1 For details regarding the conflict on Babri Mosque and its consequences, see T.B. Hansen, *The Saffron Wave: Democracy and Hindu Nationalism in Modern India* (Princeton NJ: Princeton University Press, 1999). A. Vanaik, *The Furies of Indian Communalism: Religion, Modernity and Secularisation* (London: Verso: 1997).

2 The Indian police force witnessed nearly 87 per cent increase between 1953 and 1983. This apparently approximated nearly 89 per cent population growth in the given period. These numbers, however, do not include paramilitary forces and armed forces which a decade back in 1992 stood at 449,800 and 1,265,000 respectively. P. Brass, *The Politics of India since Independence* (Cambridge: Cambridge University Press, 1997). pp. 57–59.

3 The number of bureaucrats in India increased from four million in 1983 to 18.5 million in 1988. *Ibid*, p. 56.

4 The existence of a number of special ordinances to arrest and detail people without being produced in the court indicates this. These ordinances include the Essential Service Maintenance Act, National Security Act, Terrorist Detention Act and Prevention of Terrorists Act and their several variations at the state level.

5 Hermann Kulke (ed.) *The state in India, 1000–1700* (Delhi; Oxford: Oxford University Press, 1995).

6 Cambridge based historians between the late 1960s and early 1980s have analysed the functioning of the colonial state. A crucial and collective intervention in this regard was John Gallagher, Gordon Johnson & Anil Seal (eds.), *Locality, province, and nation: essays on Indian politics 1870 to 1940* (Cambridge: Cambridge University Press, 1973).

7 Gunnar Myrdal, *Asian drama: an inquiry into the poverty of nations* (Harmondsworth: Penguin, 1977).

8 Pranab K. Bardhan, *The political economy of development in India* (Delhi; Oxford: Oxford University Press, 1998). Also see 'Dominant Proprietary classes and India's Democracy'. In A. Kohli (ed.) *India's Democracy: Analysis of Changing State – Society Relations* (Princeton; NJ: Princeton University Press, 1988).

9 Lloyd I. Rudolph and Susanne Hoeber Rudolph, *In pursuit of Lakshmi: the political economy of the Indian state* (Chicago: University of Chicago Press, 1987), pp. 211–220.

10 Atul. Kohli, *Democracy and discontent: India's growing crisis of governability* (Cambridge: Cambridge University Press, 1990).

11 A. Seal, J Gallagher and G. Johnson *Locality, Province and Nation* (Cambridge: Cambridge University Press, 1974).

12 With the decline of central control and greater autonomy allowed to the regions, some state governments have in turn become heavily indebted to foreign lenders and in 2002 at least three state governments were having their budgets virtually set by the Asian Development Bank, as the effective lender of last resort.

1. Stages in the Success and Failure of Economic Reform in India: A Review of the Literature

1 An earlier version of this paper was presented during the 16th Conference of the European South Asian Association, Edinburgh, 5–8 September 2000, where useful comments were made. A longer version of this paper has been submitted to the *Economic and Political Weekly* for publication.

2 Ahluwalia 1999; Joshi and Little 1997.

3 Currie 1996, p. 795.

4 Bhaduri and Nayyar 1996; Currie 1996.

5 Rajiv Gandhi, quoted in *Times of India*, 6 January 1986. Quoted in Kohli 1989, p. 312.

6 Kohli 1989.

7 Varshney 1999, p. 239.

8 Jenkins 1995a, p. 37.

9 Shastri 1997, p. 51.

10 Ibid.

11 Jenkins, 1999, p. 3.

12 Kohli 1989, p. 307.

13 See also Shastri 1997, p. 36.

14 Kohli 1989, p. 307.

15 Patnaik 1986, p. 1015.

16 Ibid.

17 Op.cit., p. 1017.

18 See Harriss 1987 and Rubin 1985.

19 As analysed by Bardhan 1984.

20 Rubin 1985, pp. 942–3.

21 Kohli 1989, p. 312.

22 Manor 1987, p. 42.

23 e.g. Sridharan 1993, p. 14.

24 Harriss 1987, p. 38.

25 Kohli 1989, p. 324.

26 An exception is Pani (1994) who emphasised the conservatism of the reforms, rather than the fact that they went ahead. Another exception is Denoon (1998) who stressed the cyclical character: since the mid-1960s, he argued, there is 'an oscillation between controls and a more open economy' (Denoon 1998, p. 55).

27 Jenkins 1999.

28 Why this assessment of political reality is termed 'incentives' is not clear to me. Indeed, when politicians have this confidence, they may not oppose reforms because they think they will not lose much. But that cannot be defined as an incentive.

29 Jenkins 1999, pp. 83–118.

30 Jenkins 1999, pp. 119–51.

31 Jenkins 1999, pp. 151–68.

32 Manor 1995; Panini 1995; Shastri 1997.
33 Panini 1985, p. 43. He is referring to two other interpretations: George, Susan, 1994, 'The Bretton Woods institutions at 50 years: a critical appraisal', in Janet Bruin, ed., *The South and Bretton Woods Institutions*. Sub-Committee on the South, Special NGO Committee on Development, Geneva, pp. 5–23; and Oommen, MA, *The Political Economy of Globalisation*, Discussion Paper II of Institute of Social Sciences, New Delhi.
34 Manor 1995, p. 348.
35 Op. cit, p. 352.
36 Shastri 1997, p. 51.
37 Shastri 1997, p. 38.
38 Shastri has surprisingly little eye for the fact that there may be several discourses existing at the same time. Although she does acknowledge the gap between discourse and real policy (1997, p. 50), she neglects the ongoing importance of the old discourse. Perhaps she is right that the ideological orientation of the bureaucratic elite has changed in definitive ways, but this is certainly not true for the whole of Indian society.
39 Jenkins 1999; Panini 1995; Sachs, Varshney and Bajpai 1999.
40 Panini 1995, p. 48.
41 Op. cit., p. 50.
42 Varshney 1999.
43 Varshey 1999, p. 222.
44 Varshney makes a distinction between elite and mass politics. 'Elite politics is typically expressed in debates and struggles within the institutionalised settings of a bureaucracy, a parliament, a cabinet. Mass politics takes place primarily on the streets. Touched off by issues that unleash citizen passions and emotions, the characteristic forms of mass politics include large-scale agitations, demonstrations, and civil disobedience: riots and assassinations are also not excluded" (Varshney 1999, p. 223). The difference between elite and mass politics is thus one of: a) interests affected; b) the arena of the debates and struggles, and the form that these debates and struggles take; and c) the participants in these political contests.
45 Varshney 1999, p. 247; italics in the original.
46 Varshney 1999, p. 248.
47 Varshney 1999, p. 249.
48 Varshey 1999, p. 223.
49 See Bardhan 1998.
50 Bardhan's reaction to Jenkins is ultimately a functionalist one. He claims that diffusion of resistance (as Jenkins describes) can only happen in some instances, and that allowing illegal things to happen has its drawback: 'In general, reforms, if they remain clandestine, may strain credibility in the medium and long term' (Bardhan 1998, p. 127). This may be true, but it is not an argument against an analysis of an empirical reality in which these things may of course happen. There is no reason to assume (as Bardhan seems to do) that reforms should always take a form that enhances their credibility in the medium and long term.
51 Bardhan 1998, p. 127.
52 Bardhan 1998, p. 130.
53 Bardhan 1998, p. 132.
54 Bardhan 1998, pp. 134–5.
55 Bardhan 1998, p. 137.
56 Bhaduri and Nayyar 1996; Patnaik 2000; Patnaik and Chandrashekar 1995.

57 Patnaik 2000, p. 234.

58 Patnaik 2000, pp. 235–6.

59 Patnaik 2004, pp. 238–9.

60 Patnaik 2000, p. 245.

61 Patnaik 2000, pp. 248–9. In another paper written half a decade earlier (Patnaik and Chandrasekhar 1995), more weight is given to the domestic political economy to explain the reforms (although the role of the Bretton Woods institutions is also highlighted). In this paper, it is argued that the Nehruvian *dirigiste* policy regime had produced several internal contradictions, namely: a) the fact that the Indian state had to invest/spend in order to increase the domestic market (especially given the socially narrow base of this market), while at the same time it was the main instrument for 'primary accumulation' of capital (through its large-scale transfers to capitalists and proto-capitalist groups); b) the fact that the state was unable to impose a minimum of discipline and respect for the law among the Indian capitalists, although this is necessary for a further development of capitalism; and c) the fact that the domestic industries could no longer meet the consumer desires of the affluent sections of society. These three contradictions, it is argued, led to dissatisfaction and pressures to dismantle the *dirigiste* regime.

62 Guhan 1995, p. 73; see also Weiner 1999.

63 Weiner 1999, p. 287–8.

64 Currie 1996, p. 798.

65 Currie 1996, p. 802.

66 Jenkins 1995a, pp. 37, 47.

67 Bardhan 1998, p. 132.

68 At an early presentation of this material, some people in the audience took issue with Bardhan's interpretation, and remarked that statistical figures do not support the claim that lower caste representation within the bureaucracy has increased. This may be true, but it is not significant as far as the argument is concerned. Whether or not there is a higher low-caste representation in the state bureaucracy, the high-caste perception may be that there is – and it is this perception that matters for Bardhan's hypothesis.

69 For elaboration of this argument, see Milner and Sahay 1997.

2. The Temptations of Presidentialism: An Explanation of the Evolving Political Strategy of the BJP

1 See Sumit Mitra, Farzand Ahmed and Javed M Ansari, 'Review rift', *India Today*, 14 February 2000.

2 At present, the BJP heads a multiparty coalition Union government. However, the analysis which follows restricts itself to the politics of the party, and more widely the Sangh Parivar, from the campaign for the Eleventh General Election in April–May 1996 to the defeat of the second BJP coalition Union government in April 1999.

3 The most powerful exponent of such a position is Paul Brass, *The Politics of India since Independence*, 2nd edition, Cambridge: Cambridge University Press, 1994.

4 For example, see Arend Lijphart, 'The puzzle of Indian democracy: a consociational interpretation', *American Political Science Review*, vol. 90, no. 2, June 1996, pp. 258–68; and Alfred Stepan, 'Federalism, multi-national states, and democracy: a theoretical framework and the Indian experience,' in Shankar Bajpai, ed., *Managing Diversity in*

Democracies: India and the United States (forthcoming); and Eswaran Sridharan, 'Electoral rules, representation and power-sharing in India's democracy,' presented for the Conference on Constitutional Idea and Political Practices: fifty years of the Republic, University of Pennsylvania, Institute for the Advanced Study of India, New Delhi, 23–25 January 2000.

5 See Giovanni Sartori, *Comparative Constitutional Engineering: an inquiry into structures, incentives and outcomes*, London: Macmillan, 1994.

6 This is argued eloquently by Sunil Khilnani, *The Idea of India*, London: Hamish Hamilton, 1997. The following relies largely upon his discussion in Chapter 4.

7 In retrospect, the Assembly was astonishingly unrepresentative. It consisted of approximately three hundred members, who by and large shared certain markers: anglicised elites who were legally trained, urban-living, high caste and upper class. However, they managed to design a polity which unwittingly allowed a transfer of power in many sections of society in ways initially unimagined. See Sunil Khilnani, 'Democracy,' presented for the Conference on Constitutional Idea and Political Practices: fifty years of the Republic, University of Pennsylvania, Institute for the Advanced Study of India, New Delhi, 23–25 January 2000.

8 This informed Nehru's vision of development through a modern economic regime guided by state planning, which was contested on both moral and economic grounds in successive generations. Unfortunately these issues are beyond the scope of this paper.

9 These are drawn to great effect by James Tully, *Strange Multiplicity: constitutionalism in an age of diversity*, Cambridge: Cambridge University Press, 1994.

10 To paraphrase James Tully's notion.

11 These are summarised in Lijphart, 'The puzzle of Indian democracy'.

12 This point is made by Sunil Khilnani, 'Democracy'.

13 The following relies upon Partha Chatterjee, 'Secularism and Toleration,' in his *A Possible India: essays in political criticism*, Delhi: Oxford University Press, 1998.

14 See Chatterjee, 'Secularism and Toleration'.

15 Regional party acronyms are commonly TDP – Telugu Desam Party, DMK – Dravida Munnetra Kazhagam, AGP – Asom *Gana* Parishad, ADMK/AIDMK – All-India Dravida Munnetra Kazhagam, and TMC – Tamil Maanila Congress (not to be confused with the later Trinamool Congress in Bengal). A third group, which I won't address here, was of course the Left bloc, which played a critical role in blocking the BJP.

16 For instance, see Sudipta Kaviraj, 'The general elections in India,' *Government and Opposition*, vol. 32, no. 1, Winter 1997: pp. 3–25.

17 Samata party in Bihar, largely on tactical grounds; and with the *Shiv Sena* in Maharashtra, which owed more to shared (though not equally) ideological affinities; Lakshmi Parvati's TDP (NTR) in Andhra Pradesh; Naveen Patnaik's Biju Janata Dal in Orissa; Ramakrishna Hegde's Lok Shakti in Karnataka; Mamata Banerjee's Trinamul Congress in West Bengal; the Loktantrik Congress and BSP faction in Uttar Pradesh; and Jayalalitha's AIADMK in Tamil Nadu. The latter was, in turn, allied to the Tamizhaga Rajiv Congress (TRC), Janata Party, Marumalarchi Dravida Munnettra Kazhagam (MDMK) and Pattali Makkal Katchi (PMK).

18 The term was coined by Douglas Rae.

19 The Ministry of Law and the Minister of State for Finance with control of the Department of Revenue, Banking and Insurance, an unprecedented division of responsibility since the latter was customarily within the purview of the Minister of Finance, to the AIADMK; and the Speaker's position in the *Lok Sabha* to the TDP.

20 The appraisal of the senior BJP party leader from Uttar Pradesh, quoted in V Ramakrishnan, 'All for survival,' *Frontline*, 15 (8), April 11–24 1998.

21 Sukumar Muralidharan, 'BJP and friends,' *Frontline*, 15(1), January 10–23 1998.

22 This theme partly informs an original study of the ways in which political agents in India skilfully implemented policies of economic liberalisation despite strong expectations against their success. See Rob Jenkins' *Democratic Politics and Economic Reform in India*, Cambridge: Cambridge University Press, 1999.

23 Jenkins, *Democratic Politics and Economic Reforms in India*, pp. 121–2.

24 See Adam Przeworski et al, *Sustainable Democracy*, Cambridge: Cambridge University Press, 1995, p. 25. The following set of options match those explained by Adam Przeworksi in the context of strategies to achieve social democracy. See his *Capitalism and Social Democracy*, Cambridge: Cambridge University Press, 1985, p. 102.

25 This point is stressed by Christophe Jaffrelot, *The Hindu Nationalist Movement and Indian Politics, 1925 to the 1990s: strategies of identity-building, implantation and mobilisation (with special reference to Central India)*, Penguin Books India, 1999, p. 548.

26 Przeworksi, *Capitalism and Social Democracy*, p. 112.

27 For instance, see Achin Vinaik, *India in a Changing World: problems, limits and successes of its foreign policy*, Hyderabad: Orient Longman, 1995, p. 123.

28 See Praful Bidwai, 'India defiled, Indians diminished,' *Frontline*, May 23–June 5 1998.

29 Thus for the first time in decades the conflict in Jammu and Kashmir figured in a joint-communiqué on 4 June 1998 of the five permanent members of the United Nations' Security Council.

30 BP Sinha, KS Lal, BR Grover, former Director of the ICHR, and BB Lal, former Director General of the Archeological Survey of India. See Sukamar Muralidharan, 'The *Hindutva* takeover of ICHR,' *Frontline*, July 4–17 1998.

3. Ideological Integration in Post-colonial (South) India: Aspects of a Political Language

1 I am extremely grateful to N.P. Shankarnaraya Rao of Bangalore for the hours he gave to talking about things of great interest to me. Thanks as well to David Gilmartin for reading and commenting on this piece.

2 Narain and Mathur, 1984.

3 Manor, 1983: 725.

4 Kohli, 1991.

5 Fuller and Harriss, 2000: 7–10.

6 Kaviraj 1984, 1991; Chatterjee 1993, 1998.

7 Madan, 1997.

8 Saberwal 1996.

9 Chhibber 1999.

10 Gilmartin, 1998: 1092.

11 Gilmartin, 1998:1080.

12 Gilmartin, 1998:1080.

13 For example Freitag, 1989.

14 Van der Veer, 1994; Hansen 1999.

15 Price, 1996a.

16 Brass 1974.

17 See, for example, Kothari 1970.

18 For example, Brittlebank 1999; Price 1996b; Appadurai 1981; Dirks 1987.

19 Srinivas 1996; Anantha Murthy 1978, 1996.

20 A recent discussion of Narayan's life and works is Pankaj Mishra, "The Great Narayan", in *The New York Review of Books*, February 22, 2001, pp. 44–47.

21 There is evidence for this assertion in the spring of 1997–8 in Bangalore, Mysore City, Dharwar-Hubli, and Sirsi.

22 I refer in this paper to newspapers published in Karnataka editions, not only the *Deccan Herald*, but *The Hindu* and *The Times of India*.

23 *Hindu*, 25/4/98.

24 *Hindu*, 8/2/98).

25 *Times of India*, 10/3/98.

26 *Times of India*, 8/1/98.

27 *Hindu*, 13/5/98.

28 *Deccan Herald*, 22/1/1998.

29 *Deccan Herald*, 11/4/98.

30 *Hindu*, 14/2/98.

31 *Hindu*, 6/2/98.

32 *Hindu*, 24/3/98.

33 *Deccan Herald*, 11/6/98.

34 Raghavan, 11/5/98. I did not use a tape recorder in interviewing. When I use quotation marks in reporting notes from these interviews, these are direct quotes.

35 Raghavan, 11/5/98.

36 GS Hegde Ajjibal, 26/12/97.

37 N. Jayaram, interview, 11/4/98.

38 N. Jayaram, 11/4/98.

39 Ajjibal, 26/12/97.

40 P.S. Jayaramu, interview, 1/4/98.

41 Panduraga Patil, former mayor of Hubli-Dharwar, 28/4/98.

42 K.H. Srinivas, 11/5/98.

43 I used an interpretor during this interview, which took place at the State Legislators Hostel in Bangalore.

44 Gowda, 18/5/98.

45 Raghavendra Rao, 27 April 1998.

46 Srinivas 1996, 172, 176.

47 Srinivas 1996, 173.

48 Zydenbos, 1996: 166–167.

49 Anantha Murthy, trans. Srinivasa Rao, 1996.

50 Nagaraj, 1996: vii–viii.

51 Nagaraj, 1996: x.

52 Anantha Murthy, 1978: 20, 22.

53 Ramanujan, 1978, 141, 142, 143.

54 Fuller, 1992.

55 Shankarnaraya Rao, 4 June 1998.

56 Shankarnaraya Rao, 23 May 1998.

57 Saberwal, 1996, 160, his emphasis.

58 Saberwal 1996, 78.

59 Holmström, 1988: 6.

60 Holmström, 1969, 90–92.
61 Holmström, 1988: 90.
62 Holmström, 1988: 90.
63 Holmström, 1988: 91.
64 Holmström, 1988: 91.
65 Chopra, 1996: 44.
66 *Hindu*, 21/1/98.

4. The Fight for Turf and the Crisis of Ideology: Broadcasting Reform and Contemporary Media Distribution in India

1 The Goenka family are principal shareholders in the *Indian Express*, whereas the Sahu-Jains and their business associates control Bennett-Coleman and Co., publishers of *The Times of India;* Delhi's *Hindustan Times* is owned by the Birla family, one of the largest industrial houses in India; *The Statesman* is owned by a combine that includes among others, two major industrial houses, Tata Sons Pvt. Ltd, and Mafatlal Gagallbhai and Co Ltd. For estimates on the level of concentration in the print media in the post-Independence period, see 'Competition and Monopolies', Report of Press Commission, Part I, Government of India Press, Delhi, 1954, esp. pp. 280–309; Report of the Second Press Commission, vol. 2, Controller of Publications, Delhi, 1982, esp. pp. 238–42. Both reports suggest that the available information, especially that volunteered by newspaper managements, tends to under-report the level of consolidation. For the structure of ownership in the regional language press, see Jeffrey, *India's Newspaper Revolution* (Oxford University Press: New Delhi, 2000).
2 Ibid.
3 See Report, 'Cash boost for Bollywood' by Sanjeev Srivastava, July 25 2001, BBC News Online, URL: http://www.news.bbc.co.uk/hi/english/entertainment/film/newsid_1700000/1700458htm, accessed December 10 2001.
4 Besides Films Division, the second state intervention in film production was the setting up of Film Finance Corporation in 1960. The FFC and its later *avataar*, the National Film Development Corporation, aimed to finance an alternate cinema with modest budgets through production and export of Indian films, imports of foreign films, the import and distribution of raw stock, construction of cinema theatres and development of technology. For an estimate of these state-supported interventions in film finance, see Mira Reym Binford, 'India's Two Cinemas', in ed., John DH Downing, *Film and Politics in the Third World* (New York; London: Praeger, 1988).
5 Owen Lippert and Michael Walker, *The Underground Economy: Global Evidence of Its Size and Impact* (Fraser Institute,: 1997); Colin Williams, Jan Windebank and J Windeband, *Informal Employment in the Advanced Economies: Implications for Work and Welfare* (Routledge, New York, 1998); Kathleen Staudt, *Free Trade: Informal Economies at the U.S.-Mexican Border,* (Temple University Press: Philadelphia, 1998).
6 See for example Gerald Horne, *Class Struggle in Hollywood 1930–1950: Moguls, Mobsters, Stars, Reds and Trade Unionists* (University of Texas Press, Austin, 2001); for an account of the foothold of the Japanese *yazuka* in film exhibition and entertainment shows, see also Junichi Saga, *The Gambler's Tale: a life in Japan's Underworld*, trans. John Bester (Kodansha International, Tokyo: 1991) pp. 195–7.

7 For an investigative account of the intertwined fortunes of Reagan, the MCA and the mafia, see Dan Moldea, *Dark Victory: Ronald Reagan, MCA and the Mob* (Viking Press, New York: 1986).

8 For an analysis of the colonial-modern public sphere and the political implications of the limited size of reading publics, see Veena Naregal, *Language Politics, Elites and the Public Sphere: Western India under Colonialism* (Permanent Black, Delhi: 2001).

9 Jan Breman, 'The Study of Industrial Labour in Post-Colonial India – The Informal Sector: A Concluding Review', eds., Jonathan Parry, Jan Breman and Karin Kapadia, *The Worlds of Indian Industrial Labour* (Sage, New Delhi: 1999).

10 For a detailed study of the informal sector in agriculture, see Jan Breman, *Footloose labour: Working in India's informal economy* (Cambridge University Press: Cambridge, 1996).

11 See Madhav Prasad, The Economics of Ideology' in *Ideology of the Hindi Film: A Historical Construction* (Oxford University Press, Delhi: 1995), especially pp. 40–1.

12 'Report on the Film Industry', *India Infoline Sector Reports*, URL: *http://www.indiainfoline.com/sect/mefi/ch04.html*, accessed on December 12, 2001.

13 It is estimated that there are 12,548 theatres catering to a population of over 1 billion in India, as against 31,000 theatres in the US, which results in 117 theatres per million people, there are only 12.5 theatres catering to a million people in India. See Report on Film Industry, *Screen*, Online edition, August 31, 2001, URL: *http://www. screenindia.com/20010831/freport.html*, accessed December 12, 2001.

14 Madhav Prasad, cited above; see also Barnouw and Krishnaswamy, *Indian Film*, Ist edition, (Orient Longmans, Delhi :1963) pp. 137–9 and 160–9.

15 See 'Report on the Film Industry', *India Infoline Sector Reports*, URL: *http://www.indiainfoline.com/sect/mefi/ch04.html*, cited above.

16 See interview with film-makers Benegal and Gulzar, 'The threats continue...', *Rediff.com*, November 5, 2001, URL: *http://www.rediff.com/entertai/2001/nov/05mafia.htm*, URL accessed December 10, 2001.

17 See Peter Manuel, 'The Advent of Cassettes: New Alternatives to His Master's Voice', *Cassette Culture: Popular Music and Technology in North India*, Indian edition, (Oxford University Press, Delhi: 2001), pp. 60–88.

18 See report by *Syed Firdaus Ashraf* and *Suparn Verma*, 'Gulshan Kumar shot dead!' on *Rediff.com*, URL: *http://www.rediff.com/news/aug/12super.htm*, URL accessed on December 10, 2001. See also Profile on Gulshan Kumar at *Rediff.com*, URL: *http://www.rediff.com/entertai/aug/12super1.htm*, accessed on December 10, 2001.

19 Gulshan Kumar produced two major hits, including *Aashiqui*, his first film, and *Bewaafa Sanam*. Made with completely unknown faces and mediocre scripts, both films were packed with songs, sung by new entrants, but with tunes calculated to ensure that the film would do well.

20 See Report, 'Role of the Dons', *The Week*, Online edition, December 10, 2000, URL: *http://www.the-week.com/20dec10/enter.htm*, accessed December 9, 2001; *India Infoline Sector Reports*, 'Film Production and Film Promotion, URL: *http://www.indiainfoline.com/sect/mefi/ch04.html*, accessed December 9, 2001.

21 See Report 'Cleaning up Bollywood', *BBC News Online*, April 19, 2001, URL: *http://news.bbc.co.uk/hi/english/audiovideo/programmes/crossing_continents/asia/newsid_1283 000/1283350.stm*, accessed December 9, 2001.

22 'See report, 'The threat from the Underworld continues' November 5, 2001, *Rediff.com*, URL: *http://www.rediff.com/entertai/2001/nov/05mafia.htm*, accessed December 10,

2001; also report by Luke Harding, 'Bollywood spins its own mobster yarn', *Guardian Online*, January 15, 2001, URL: *http://www.guardian.co.uk/elsewhere/journalist/story/ 0,7792,422515,00.html*, accessed December 10, 2001.

23 Ed., Ashis Nandy, 'Introduction', *Secret Politics of Our Desires: Innocence, Culpability and Indian Popular Indian Cinema* (Oxford University Press, Delhi: 1998); Ravi Vasudevan, 'Shifting Codes, Dissolving Identities: The Hindi Social Film of the 1950s as Popular Culture', *Journal of Arts and Ideas*, Delhi, vol. 23, no. 4, 1993, pp. 51–85; Ravi Vasudevan, 'Addressing the Spectator of a 'third world' national cinema : the Bombay 'social' film of the 1940s and 1950s', *Screen*, London, vol. 36, no. 4, pp. 305–24; Rosie Thomas, 'Indian Cinema: Pleasures and Popularity', *Screen*, London, vol. 26, no. 3–4, 1985, pp. 116–31.

24 Madhav Prasad, Cine-Politics: On the Political Significance of Cinema in South India', *Journal of the Moving Image*, Calcutta, Autumn 1999, no. 1, pp. 37–52.

25 SV Srinivas, 'Is there a Public in the Cinema Hall?', *Framework*, Online Edition, Summer 2000.

26 Madhav Prasad, 'Signs of Ideological Re-form in Two Recent Hindi Films: Towards Real Subsumption?', ed., Ravi Vasudevan, *Making Meaning in Indian Cinema*, (OUP, Delhi: 2000) pp. 145–67.

27 See Report, 'Cash Boost for Bollywood', BBC News Online, July 25, 2001, URL: news.bbc.co.uk/hi/english/entertainment/film/newsid_1456000/1456962.stm, accessed December 10, 2001.

28 Mumbai's population is currently estimated to be around 20 million. Being the very epi-centre of India's capitalistic growth, its links with business and industry have generated the particular brand of civility based on a work culture that makes Mumbai's ethos quite unique among Indian cities. Indeed, since the 1970s they have quite visibly bred what has been described as a 'robber-baron culture of speculation, hostile take-overs and windfall profits'. Even by the early 1980s, the city's manufacturing sector had gone into a decline. Increasingly, as a result, the rising numbers of the unemployed have been pushed to either rely on the limited increase in trading and allied services or join the ranks of the self-employed by establishing independent petty businesses. On the one hand, the privatisation of public-sector assets has fuelled periodic speculative booms on the city's stock markets, augmenting the pools of money capital in circulation. Simultaneously at the other end of the socio-economic spectrum, inflationary trends impelled by the growing consumerist ethos, shrinking employment in the formal sector, withdrawal of meagre welfare benefits have pushed poorer sections closer to the brink. In such a socio-economic environment, the interfaces between the underworld and the 'cleaner' capitalistic sectors have only proliferated in recent years, even as this milieu has sustained political parties like the *Shiv Sena*, who survive essentially by managing the new capital-politics-crime nexus through a mixture of populist welfarism and organised extortion.

29 See Appendices A, 'The Broadcasting Bill, 1997', eds., Monroe Price and Stefaan Verhulst, *Broadcasting Reform in India: Media Law from a Global Perspective* (Oxford University Press, Delhi, 1998), pp. 191–222; Appendix B, 'Broadcasting Bill: Issues and Perspectives (1996)' in ibid., pp. 223–33.

30 Appendix J, 'Broadcasting in India', 1997, in ibid., p. 296.

31 Appendix B, 'Broadcasting Bill: Issues and Perspectives (1996)' in ibid., pp. 223.

32 Appendix D, 'Secretary, Ministry of I&B vs. Cricket Association of Bengal', in ibid., pp. 258–62.

33 Rob Jenkins, *Democratic Politics and Economic Reforms in India* (Cambridge University Press: Cambridge, 1999); Narendra Pani, Redefining Consveratism: *An Essay on the Bias*

of India's Economic Reform (Sage: New Delhi, 1994); ed., Terence Byres, *The State, Development and Liberalisation in India* (Oxford University Press, Delhi: 1999).

34 Appendix L, 'Survey of National Broadcasting, Cable and DTH Satllite Laws' in ibid., pp. 329–72.

35 See tabular data on media law in a range of Western and Asian countries, ibid., pp. 331–44.

36 See endnotes 29 and 34.

37 See Appendix B in ibid., pp. 223–6.

38 Ibid., p. 230.

39 See Report, 'Uplinking not to hit Star, Zee, Sony', *Business Standard,* Online edition, June 26, 1998, *URL: http://www.business-standard.com/archives/1998/jun/50260698.034.asp,* accessed December 9, 2001.

40 'Indian Boost for broadcasters', July 26, 2000, BBC News Online, URL: *http://news.bbc.co.uk/hi/english/world/south_asia/newsid_852000/852409.stm,* accessed December 12, 2001.

41 'India approves direct home broadcasts', BBC News Online, 2 November, 2000, URL: *http://news.bbc.co.uk/hi/english/world/south_asia/newsid_1003000/100367.stm,* accessed December 9, 2001.

42 See Rashmi Sehgal, 'Cable Wars', *Sunday Times of India* Review, 26 March, 2000. The article puts the cable penetration in India at 24 million homes. However, another estimate puts the figure in 1999 at almost 30 million, with a further break-down offered as follows: 55 per cent of TV homes in urban India and 27.6 per cent TV homes in rural India have access to cable television. See *Cable Waves,* New Delhi, December 1–15, pp. 1, 15.

43 See 'Siticable dents Hathway biz in Delhi, Ahmadabad', *Screen,* Bombay, 13 August, 1999.

44 Informant No 1/Dahisar, Bombay, interviewed on May 15, 1999.

45 Informant No 2/Dahisar, Bombay, interviewed on May 17, 1999.

46 Informant No 3/Dahisar, Bombay, interviewed June 18, 1999.

47 Informant No 3/Bandra, Bombay, and Informant no. 5, Borivli (West), Bombay, interviewed on June 20, 1999.

48 The first three main companies mentioned here are national players, with Siticable, the distribution entity jointly owned by Subhash Chandra and Murdoch, easily the leading cable service in the country, dominating the North Indian market with a presence in at least 45 cities. IN Cablenet has a presence in nine cities, claiming to service a total of 3 million cable and satellite homes in Mumbai, Delhi, Bangalore, Belgaum, Ahmedabad, Nagpur, Indore and Hyderabad, whereas besides its presence in Mumbai, Hathway has networks in the southern states of Tamil Nadu, Kerala and Karnataka.

49 Interviews with IN Network officials, conducted in IN centre, Andhrei (east), Bombay, May 17 and 24, 1999.

50 For a fuller account of cable operator associations that have emerged in Bombay suburbs, see Veena Naregal, Cable Communications in Mumbai: Integrating Corporate Interests with Local and Media Networks, *Contemporary South Asia,* vol. 9, no. 3, 2000, pp. 289–314.

51 'STAR offers lower rates for larger piece of cable pie', *Economic Times,* Online Edition, December 1, 2001, URL: *http:www/economictimes.indiatimes.com/articleshow.asp?catkey=569038520&art_id=483620539&sType1,* accessed December 9, 2001.

52 'Pay channels: view from a MSO', *Screen,* Bombay 28 May, 1999.

53 See 'Cable Official shot dead', *Express News Service,* September 12, 1998, URL: *http://www.indian-express.com/ie/daily/19980912/25550624.html,* accessed December 8, 2001.

54 See 'Hindujas file FIR against ex-chiefs of IndusInd' *Economic Times*, Bombay, August 13, 1999.
55 See fn. 52.
56 'Courtship of Media Moguls', *Business Standard*, September 15, 1998.
57 'News Corp chief executive Rupert Murdoch agrees to let Zee 'manage' three STAR network channels: nature of amalgamation to be worked out', *Business Standard*, July 30, 1998.
58 Interview with Jindal in Ashok Banker, 'STAR's Final Assault', *Business India*, March 15, 1999. Eventually, the deal did not come through, and Zee paid $296 million to buy out Murdoch's stake in ATL and two other joint ventures. However, Murdoch retains his interest in Siticable.

5. The Political Economy of Urban Planning

1 Though Bombay was renamed 'Mumbai' in 1996, I will persist with the original mode of address as featured in most of the official documents discussed in this essay.
2 cf. Kaviraj 1991, p. 89.
3 Thakurdas 1945.
4 Miliband 1973.
5 Rudolph and Rudolph 1987; Lal 1983, pp. 17–18, 30–1.
6 See Bardhan 1994, 1998.
7 Jenkins 2000, pp. 32ff. For an extended treatment of these categories at and since Independence, see Byres 1974, 1981, 1982.
8 See Byres 1998, especially the essays by Byres and Chatterjee.
9 Hawthorn 1991, pp. 25–7.
10 Poulantzas 1973, p. 50.
11 Chatterjee 1998, pp. 101–2.
12 Byres 1998, p. 53.
13 The city accounts for 10 per cent of India's factory employment and added manufacturing value, generates 25 per cent of national income tax, 20 per cent of excise and 60 per cent of customs revenues, regulates 41 per cent of India's domestic and 50 per cent of its international air traffic, 17 per cent of its port traffic, and accounts for 16 per cent of total deposits and 22 per cent of all credit advanced by the banking sector, and 40 per cent of Maharashtra's domestic product (*Economic Times*, June 17, 1994; Swaminathan 1995, pp. 134; 1999, p. 1). The Bombay Stock Exchange accounts for more than 70 per cent of listed capital and 90 per cent of market capitalisation in India (*Business India*, August 9–22, 1999, p. 64), and the Bombay Metropolitan Region contributes 62 per cent of the total industrial value addition at the national level (Confederation of Indian Industry, Western Region).
14 The earliest comprehensive statistics of the city's linguistic character show Maharashtrians, at 50.2 per cent, constituting a very slender majority. Migrants comprised almost 30 per cent of the total population of 800,000, with 10 per cent of the city's residents deemed to have arrived from outside Bombay province. (Census of India, 1881).
15 Chandavarkar 1994, 1998; Ramswamy 1988; Sherlock 1996a.
16 Cushman and Wakefield Global Marketbeat, Summer 1999.
17 For an overview of available poverty estimates for Greater Bombay, see Swaminathan 1999.

18 Breman 1980.
19 Farooqui 1996; Mahadevia 1991.
20 Dossal 1995.
21 Harvey 1973, p. 310.
22 Mahadevia 1998.
23 Centre for Monitoring the Indian Economy, Bombay.
24 Joshis 1976, pp. 60–2.
25 Bhagwati 1993, p. 3.
26 The reference is to the seventeenth-century warrior prince who successfully resisted Mughal rule.
27 Deshpande 1979.
28 Chandavarkar 1994.
29 Chandavarkar, 1994, pp. 219–38.
30 The body of empirical literature on the Bombay labour market confirms widespread segmentation, while disagreeing on the relative impact of human (gender, caste, religious background, education and skills) and non-human (job characteristics, formal and informal components, scale of enterprise) capital variables as determinants of incomes (Deshpande 1996; Khandker 1992; Mazumdar 1979; Swaminathan 1996).
31 Fourth Five-Year Plan Document. Planning Commission, Government of India, pp. 399–400.
32 Shaw 1996.
33 Offe 1984.
34 'Status groups' are founded upon relations of consumption and take the form of 'styles of life' that separate groups from one another.
35 Chatterjee 1993.
36 Shaw 1995; Banerjee-Guha 1995, pp. 108ff.
37 Estimates vary between 3,000 and 10,000 acres.
38 In doing so it ignored recommendations to the contrary by two special committees set up between 1922 and 1930 and 1958 and 1970, and the stipulations of the BMRDA regional plan, which had restricted commercial use to 20 per cent of the land area. The Maharashtra Chamber of Housing Industry is believed to have been instrumental in influencing the choice. (Narayanan 1997, p. 12).
39 Banerjee-Guha 1995, p. 106.
40 The Industrial Location Policy, however, made a special provision for textile mills, which continued to function in the industrial zone within city limits. This was an overt government intervention to protect jobs in the sector, which accounted for over a quarter of the city's employment.
41 Bawa 1987, p. 106, table 32; Deshpandes 1991, p. 136. As for the small-scale sector, between 1974 and 1988, it had a growth rate of 7 per cent in Greater Bombay, as compared to 12 per cent in the rest of the state (Deshpandes 1991, p. 136).
42 Chandavarkar 1994.
43 Banaji and Hensman 1990.
44 Gupta 1982, pp. 81–4.
45 Cited in *The Week*. February 19–25, 1984, p. 18.
46 Mahadevia 1998.
47 Narayanan 1997. This is made explicit in the ULCRA's 'Statement of Objects and Reasons: '...there has been a demand for imposing a ceiling on urban property also,

especially after the imposition of a ceiling on agricultural lands by the state governments.' (1992 edition, p. 1).

48 Interview with former Maharashtra chief secretary, JB D'Souza, dated January 3, 2000.

49 Przeworksi 1991, p. 82.

50 Sundaram 1989, pp. 82–3.

51 Phatak 1996.

52 Sundaram 1989, p. 85.

53 Interview with an official in the department of urban development, Government of Maharashtra. January 14, 2000.

54 *Times of India*, July 24, 1981.

55 EPW 1982.

56 Lamarche 1975.

57 Mahadevia 1998, tables 10, 11.

58 Sen 1981.

59 Swaminathan 1999.

60 D'Souza 1996, p. 390, table 7.

61 SPARC 1994.

62 BMRDA 1995, p. 299.

63 Of the public housing available in Bombay between 1985 and 1991, 57 per cent catered to the 'high-income' category Phatak 1996, p. 187.

64 Lele 1995.

65 *Blitz*, April 8, 1989.

66 The prescribed density, in this case, was 200 units per 10,000 square metres, making housing at the prevalent market rates unaffordable to low-income communities.

67 The observations by the incumbent urban development secretary in this regard are instructive: 'What are the legal provisions for reserving a particular plot of land? Strange though it may seem, there are no provisions! Nor are there any government guidelines about what kinds of land or plots can be placed under a particular category of reservation. Does that mean that a sub-engineer of the Bombay Municipal Corporation decides which plot should be reserved for a garden or a parking lot without any guidelines? The answer is "yes".' (Joseph, D.T., 'Land reservation norms arbitrary', *Times of India*, October 12, 1990).

68 D'Souza 1991.

69 *Daily*, February 23, 90; *Times of India*, May 10, 1990.

70 'Pawar's plots', *Sunday*, July 30–August 5, 1989, pp. 12–18.

71 See Devidayal, Namita. 'Planned Chaos', *Times of India*, September 26–29, 1999.

72 D'Souza 1991.

73 'Planned chaos', *Times of India*, September 28, 1999.

74 Lipton 1977.

75 Chakravorty 1996, table 2.

76 BMRDA 1995.

77 Sainath 1994, p. 195.

78 BMRDA 1995.

79 Subsequently, the state government struck down the area's 'green belt' status, releasing 10,921 hectares for urban use (Banerjee-Guha 1995, p. 117–8).

80 Phatak 1996, p. 187.

81 Mahadevia 1998, p. 19, table 5.

82 *Times of India*, April 21, 1987.

83 Masselos 1995, pp. 201–2.

84 Padgaonkar 1993, p. 25.

85 *Economic Times*, March 4, 1994.

86 BMRDA 1995, p. 12.

87 A report by the Joint Select Committee of the Maharashtra legislature estimated the total *pugree* transactions at Rs.750 billion (around £10 billion).

88 Nijman 2000.

89 Narayanan 1997, pp. 7–8. The ULCRA, which was repealed by the central government in 1999, continues to be in place in Maharashtra, while insignificant changes have been made to the rent control laws.

90 'Emerging market indicators', *The Economist*, February 24, 1996, p. 112.

91 According to the report of the Eleventh Finance Commission (2000, p. 177), in 1989–90, the combined fiscal deficit of the centre and the states stood at 8.21 per cent, while the revenue deficit was 2.58 per cent.

92 Kurien 1992, p. 114.

93 Eighth Plan Document, vol. 1, p. 15.

94 Chakraborty 1996, pp. 256–7.

95 Kundu 1999.

96 cf. Bhagwati 1993, p. 3.

97 Jenkins 2000.

98 D'Monte 1998; LHS 1996.

99 Jenkins 2000, p. 196.

100 *The Indian Express* (September 24, 1996) refers to 'the dichotomy in the chief minister's (Manohar Joshi) stance as he pays lip service to workers and pacifies mill lords.'

101 See Swami, Praveen. 'Preying on Mumbai mill lands', *Frontline*, December 25– January 7, 2000.

102 Kohli 1989.

103 GoM 1997, p. 2.

104 Singh and Das 1995.

105 On March 11, 2000, the Maharashtra government announced the withdrawal of the SRD scheme, which had yielded a mere 3,486 houses over a four-year period.

106 Slums on public land may be 'recognised', 'notified', 'declared' or 'authorised', and the nature of entitlements under each of these categories is determined by the public body that owns the land. Slums on private land and pavement dwellers have no legal entitlements.

107 Sengupta 1999: Table 15.

108 Chatterjee 1998:91.

6. Understanding Local Politics, Democracy and Civil Society: Environmental Governance in Urban India

1 The opinions expressed in this paper are the author's, and do not necessarily reflect those of the World Bank.

2 Mehta, pp. 419–20.

3 In 2001, India's urban population was 285.3 million compared to the total population of United States which was 284.7 million (see U.S. Census Bureau, 2003).

4 See United Nations (2003).

5 Taken as (i) manufacturing, construction, electricity, gas and water supply; (ii) trade, transport, storage and communication; and (iii) financing, insurance, real estate and business services (see Government of India 2003:S-5).

6 Civil society is most commonly understood as the realm of private voluntary associations, from neighbourhood committees to interest groups to philanthropic enterprises of all sorts, between the family and the state but excludes firms. See Hyden (1997) for broader discussion on civil society.

7 See Mehta 1999.

8 E.g. Mathur 1994, 1996a, 1996b, 1999; Mehta 1999; Sengupta 1999.

9 E.g. Dahiya 1999; Sivaramakrishnan 1994, 2000.

10 Such as Beteille 1999; Chatterjee 1997, 1998; Kohli 1988; Mahajan 1999a, 1999b.

11 Beteille 1999; Mahajan 1999a, 1999b.

12 Chatterjee 1997, 1998.

13 Mehta 1999:167.

14 This is evident from the fact that many national magazines and newspapers in India have started city pages and/or metro-supplements. This has been followed by the insertion of city pages in the internet versions of some Indian magazines and newspapers.

15 During the fieldwork, a Chennai Municipal Corporation official declined to provide information to the author because he thought that researchers could release the information to newspapers.

16 Gazette of India 1993.

17 Government of India 1997.

18 (quoted in D'Souza 1999:2984).

19 Ibid.

20 D'Souza 1999, p. 2984.

21 Ibid.

22 (emphasis original, p. 2985).

23 D'Souza 1999.

24 Basu and Das 2000.

25 *Dahiya and Pugh, 2000:176.*

26 Basu 1994.

27 Basu 1994.

28 Kundu 1992, p. 132.

29 Kundu 1992.

30 On this point, also see Mohan (1996) and Sivaramakrishnan (2000).

31 See Hyden 1997.

32 E.g. Chatterjee 1999; D'Souza 1999.

33 (Chatterjee 1999).

34 World Commission on Environment and Development 1987.

35 (United Nations 1993).

36 See Agarwal *et al* 1999; Centre for Science and Environment 1982.

37 See Nirmal 1996; Praja Foundation 2003.

38 See Malik 2001.

39 See Paul 1995.

40 Public Eye, 1996:11.

41 McCarney et al 1995:95.

42 UNDP-World Bank 1999.

43 Sharada Trust was launched by Arvind Mills in 1995 to facilitate the slum improvement experiment in Ahmedabad.

44 SAATH is an Ahmedabad-based NGO that concentrates on youth development and social awareness. It has been active since 1989 with experience in several slums.

45 Established in 1994 in response to the demand from the community of poor, self-employed women in Ahmedabad, MHT is an Ahmedabad-based organisation for specialised housing-related activities.

46 SEWA Bank is an urban bank of and for self-employed women. It acted as a financial intermediary in Sanjayanagar by initiating and collecting the community contribution for *Parivartan* and depositing it in individual bank accounts.

47 Communication with M.B. Nirmal, Founder and President of Exnora International, Chennai (1999).

48 Communication with G. Ananthakrishnan, City Editor, *The Hindu*, Chennai (1999).

7. Political Institutions, Strategies of Governance and Forms of Resistance in Rural Market Towns of Contemporary Bengal: A Study of Bolpur Municipality

1 The most important literature on the subject is Atul Kohli, *Democracy and discontent: India's growing crisis of governability*, Cambridge: Cambridge University Press, 1990. Written at the end of the Rajiv Gandhi era against the background of political realignment from the Congress-dominated system to the coalitional structure of government, Kohli has presented a picture of serious political dislocation. He argues that dominant social groups face growing demands from newly organised social groups that often culminate in intense violence. Institutional mechanisms for the resolution of conflict have broken down, the civil and police services have become highly politicised, and the state bureaucracy appears incapable of implementing an effective plan for economic development. While this essay agrees with Kohli's findings, it points out how institutional structures have failed to meet demands from redistribution asserted by working classes in small market towns, it addresses an area which Kohli misses, the rural market towns of Bengal.

2 This trend is reflected in many important works on the subject For example, RP Misra and Kamlesh Misra, *Million cities of India: growth dynamics, internal structure, quality of life, and planning perspectives*, New Delhi: Vikas, 1978. Andrea Menefee Singh, Alfred de Souza. *The urban poor: slum and pavement dwellers in the major cities of India*, New Delhi: Manohar, 1980. Donald B Rosenthal, *The limited elite: politics and government in two Indian cities*, Chicago, University of Chicago Press, 1970. Indeed, an interesting exception and a model for this study is Richard G Fox, *From zamindar to ballot box; community change in a north Indian market town*, Ithaca, NY, Cornell University Press, 1969.

3 It will be simplistic to lump together towns of these diverse sizes in the same parenthesis. Geographers have identified four different patterns of urban growth in India: urban agglomerations meaning smaller satellite towns surrounding large cities such as Calcutta, Bangalore and Madras; urban clusters or towns comprising more than 100,000 people located in close proximity forming clusters rather than urban agglomeration; urban shadow – the antithesis of urban cluster – where a city does not have another town within a 75-mile radius; and urban dispersals implying the existence of small and medium size agricultural market towns supported by villages. See R Ramchandran *Urbanisation and Urban Systems in India*, Delhi: Oxford University Press, 1991, pp. 146–50.

4 For a detailed description of the region in the nineteenth century see WW Hunter, *Annals of Rural Bengal*, 7th ed., London, Smith, Elder, 1897, New York, Johnson Reprint Corp., 1970.

5 Suchibrata Sen 'Itihas' in Sauro Kumar Basu, ed., *Mahakuma Parichay Bolpur*, Calcutta, Basumati Corporation, 1995, p. 10.

6 Ibid., p. 11.
7 See for details LSS O'Mally, *Birbhum District Gazetteer*, Calcutta, Government of India Press, 1910.
8 Suchibrata Sen, 'Itihas' in Sauro Kumar Basu, ed., *Mahakuma Parichay Bolpur*, Calcutta, Basumati Corporation, 1995, p. 11.
9 Siddheswar Mukhopadhayay 'Samkhipto Parichiti' in Sauro Kumar Basu, ed., *Mahakuma Parichay Bolpur*, pp. 154–5.
10 GK Lieten, *Continuity and Change in Rural West Bengal*, New Delhi, Sage, 1992.
11 Anandamoy Sen, 'Krishi O Sech Sikhsa' in Saura Kumar Basu, ed., *Bolpur Mahakuma Parichay*, pp. 39–56.
12 Ibid., p. 48.
13 Ibid., p. 48.
14 Ibid., p. 48.
15 Arijit Ray, 'Paribahan O Jogajog', in Saura Basu, ed., *Bolpur Mahakuma Parichay*, pp. 71, 74–5, 77.
16 For a study of the impact of the expansion of irrigational facilities on agriculture see Harriss, J, 'What is happening in Rural West Bengal? Agrarian Reform, Growth and Distribution', *Economic and Political Weekly*, June 12, 1993, pp. 1237–47.
17 For Details see Siddheswar Mukhopadhayay, 'Bolpur Smakhipto Parichiti' in Sauro Kumar Basu, ed., *Bolpur Mahakuma Parichay*, pp. 154–7.
18 Sauro Kumar Basu, 'Nibedan' in Sauro Kumar Basu, ed., *Bolpur Mahakuma Parichay*, p. x.
19 'Bolpur Mahakumai abosthito banker talika', Sauro Kumar Basu, ed., *Bolpur Mahakuma Parichay*, p. 167.
20 Anandamoy Sen, 'Sikhsa' in Sauro Kumar Basu, ed., *Bolpur Mahakuma Parichay*, pp. 82–4.
21 Dr. Sitaram Bandopadhayay, 'Swashthya o Paribar kalyan', Sauro Kumar Basu, ed., *Bolpur Mahakuma Parichay*, pp. 92, 93–4.
22 'Adivasi' is the literal Bengali translation of the term 'Aboriginals'. It is used now to connote 'tribal' groups in India. The word dalit means oppressed. The term dalit is used here to indicate the former untouchable social groups.
23 Ashim Adhilari, 'Janabinyas' in Sauro Kumar Basu, ed., *Bolpur Mahakuma Parichay*, pp. 14–15.
24 Ibid.
25 Ibid.
26 Interview with Manik, a rickshaw driver from Nichupatti, 22 December, 2000.
27 Interview with Ganesh Murmu, a Santhal rickshaw puller and inhabitant of Balipara near Santiniketan, 20 December, 2000.
28 Informal discussions with Biren Ghosh and Salien Mishra, two prominent local political activists working on the left of the CPI(M).
29 Interview with Rabi-ul Haque, Head Mason from Santiniketan area, 7 January, 2001.
30 Interview with Sauro Kumar Basu, 9 July, 2001.
31 Recent analyses of official data shows that after nearly two decades of stagnation, agricultural production – particularly the output of foodgrains – accelerated from the mid 1980s onwards. Between 1969–70 and 1979–80, the growth of foodgrains production in West Bengal was much lower than the rest of India (1.7 per cent per annum in comparison to 2.5 per cent for India as a whole), lagging far behind the rate of increase of population. From 1978 to 1991, however, West Bengal's foodgrains output grew at an average rate of 4.6 per cent, compared with 2.8 per cent for the country as a whole.

For an examination of the debates regarding West Bengal's performance in agricultural production in the 1980s and early 1990s see Saha, A and M Swaminathan, 1994, 'Agricultural Growth in West Bengal in the 1980s', *EPW*, March 26, pp. A-2–A-11; Datta Ray, S, 1994, 'Agricultural Growth in West Bengal', *EPW*, July 16, p. 1883–4; Rogaly, B et al., 1995, '*Sonar Bangla?* Agricultural Growth and Agrarian Change in West Bengal and Bangladesh', *EPW*, July 22, pp. 1862–8.

32 Mukherji, B and S Mukhopadhyay, 1995, 'Impact of Institutional Change on Productivity in a Small-farm Economy: Case of Rural West Bengal', *EPW*, August 26, pp. 2134–7.

33 Harriss, J, 1993, 'What is Happening in Rural West Bengal? Agrarian Reform, Growth and Distribution', *EPW*, June 12, pp. 1237–47.

34 A similar view has been advanced by Bates in one of his classic works on Africa. For details see Bates, RH, 1981, *Markets and States in Tropical Africa: The Political Basis of Agricultural Policies*, Berkeley, University of California Press.

35 Discussion with Biren Ghosh and Sailen Mishra, two prominent local CPI(ML) activists.

8. Action, Autonomy and Political Rights: Towards a Theory of 'Political Literacy'

1 I am grateful to Dr Sudipta Kaviraj for comments and discussions on the paper. I would also like to thank Drs. Maya Unnithan, Sanjay Seth, Francesca Orsini, Radhika Chopra and Shireen Rai for detailed written comments.

2 Subordination is not treated here as a relative experience of disadvantage but refers to those constraints, both moral and social, which affect our abilities to put into effect our chosen desires.

3 To point to the different self-expressions is only to earmark the differences that exist in the language used to describe the self. It is not to claim that these self-understandings exist in isolation of the other.

4 Capacities associated with moral autonomy are higher-order capacities for self-criticism, evaluation and the ability to 'revise one's ends in terms of arguments and evidence to which one rationally assents; we assess the basic demands of such personal autonomy for the goods through which we express basic respect for its development, exercise and realisation, and we universalise such demands to other persons who by definition, share these capacities'. See David AJ Richards, 'Rights and Autonomy', in Christman, ed, *The Inner Citadel: Essays on Individual Autonomy*, Oxford University Press, 1989.

5 The *sathins* are the primary workers within the Women's Development Program (WDP) sponsored by the State Government of Rajasthan (Northwestern India), in keeping with the principles enunciated within the sixth five-year plan. Their first point of contact with these ideas (according to most of the *sathins*, they had heard of nothing resembling the idea of individual rights within living memory) was through the resource persons (consisting mainly of academics and women's activists) who organised a series of workshops, or training camps as they are known, in order to prepare them for their developmental tasks.

It must be clarified at this point, that although the *sathins* admitted to never having any prior contact with the discourse of rights, this essay does not in any way assume them to have been non-autonomous before their contact with the idea of rights.

6 Dworkin 1988.

7 (Dworkin 1988; Benn 1976). According to SI Benn, 'to be autonomous one must have reasons for acting, and be capable of second thoughts in the light of new reasons; it is not to have a capacity for conjuring criteria out of nowhere'. Benn, SI, 'Freedom, autonomy and the concept of a person', *Proceedings of the Aristotelian society*, vol. lxxvi, 1976, pp. 109–30.

8 Gary Watson (1975) makes a distinction between *valuing* and *desiring* as being crucial to the understanding of free action. According to him, 'it is possible that what one desires is not *to any degree* valued, held to be worthwhile…and second, although one may indeed value what is desired, the strength of one's desire may not properly reflect the degree to which one values the object: that is, although the object of a desire is valuable in the situation and yet one's desire for it may be stronger than the want for what is most valued'. See his 'Free Agency', *Journal of Philosophy*, volume lxxii, no. 8 (1975).

9 Meyers 1998.

10 According to Lorraine Code, 'theorists [and here she is referring to Whitbeck and Baier] who take communality and interdependence as their starting point seem better able to accommodate the requirements of autonomy than theorists who take autonomous existence as the "original position" are able to accommodate the requirements of the community'. See Code, 'Second Persons', in Hanen Marsha and Nielson Kai, eds, 'Science, morality and feminist Theory, Calgary: University of Calgary Press, 1987.

11 According to Schneewind, these are separate questions. See Martin Sosna, Thomas C Heller and David E Wellbery, eds, *Reconstructing Individualism*, Stanford University Press: California, 1986.

12 It must be pointed out here that the philosophical possibility of disconnecting our action from the thinking processes that precede it is not entirely new. There have been two kinds of references to such a distinction in some of the writings of the autonomists such as that by Gerald Dworkin (1988). The first distinction is that between autonomy of judgement and autonomy of action and privileging the former over the latter, and the second is the one between 'being autonomous' and exercising autonomy (Lindley 1983). Gerald Dworkin proposes that autonomists must make a distinction between autonomy of judgement and autonomy of action. According to him, the 'arguments in favour of allowing people to determine for themselves what is right are more compelling than those that favour of allowing people to act in accordance with their beliefs'. This distinction is also important because not only do we not always express what we truly desire in our actions but also we do not always value what we desire. Therefore our actions cannot always be explained in terms of reference to our beliefs. It must be pointed out that while these distinctions are important, their philosophical premise is impoverished. It is based on the presumption that persons are autonomous regardless of the social and moral circumstances of their lives.

13 I am here using sociological individualism to mean what Raymond Boudon calls individualism in 'its sociological sense'. According to him, individualism in its 'sociological sense, a society is taken as individualist when the autonomy conferred upon individuals by law, custom, and social constraints is very wide'. See Raymond Boudon, 'Individualism in the social sciences' in J. Leca and P. Birnbaum, eds, *Individualism: Theories and Methods*, 1990.

14 Sachs, David, 'How to Distinguish self respect from self esteem', *Philosophy and Public Affairs*, vol. 10, issue 4 (Autumn 1981), 346–60.

15 Leca, Jean, 'Individualism and Citizenship', in Leca and Birnbaum, eds, *Individualism: Theories and Methods*, Oxford: Clarendon Press, 1990.

16 The *Jati* or caste *panchayat* is one of the four kinds of traditional *panchayats*, which continue to exist despite the introduction of 'modern' *panchayat* institutions functioning on the principles of inclusion and universal adult franchise. The other traditional *panchayats* are the general meeting type of *panchayat*, the Kisan Lagdar *panchayats* in its limited form and the situational *panchayat*. The *Jati*, consisting of caste elders, performs judicial functions, settles cases of violations of caste norms and rules, and dispenses punishments. For instance, the punishment for intercaste marriage is outcasting; for most offences, the punishments range from fines to organising feasts. See Mario and Zamora, *The Panchayat Tradition: a North Indian Village in Transition, 1947–62*, Reliance Publishing House: New Delhi, 1990. As recent as the year 2000, it has been estimated that nearly 21,450 *Jati Panchayats* existed in Rajasthan. Rajasthan has an unenviable record of *Jati Panchayat* activities. On the 6 June, 1992, 17 Harijans were massacred by persons belonging to higher castes who had been ordered by their *Jati Panchayat* to do so. The castes which have strong *Jati Panchayats* are mostly *Kumawat, Meena, Gujjar, Meghwal, Jats, Meos* etc. (see Tomar, KS, 'Jatiya Panchayats: still Prevalent in Rajasthan', *Hindustan Times*, November 21, 2000.

17 I borrow this term 'recognition respect' from Stephen Darwall. While Darwall regards recognition respect as laying the moral guidelines for treatment of other persons, by referring to 'recognition respect' in this essay I am drawing attention to the desire of persons to be treated as persons. According to Darwall, there are two kinds of respect: recognition and appraisal. These two distinctions also correspond to what have been referred to elsewhere as objectivist and subjectivist conceptions of self-respect. Darwall defines recognition respect for persons as giving 'appropriate weight to the fact that he or she is a person, by being willing to constrain one's behaviour in ways required by that fact'. As opposed to recognition respect, the objects of appraisal respect are 'persons or features which are held to manifest their excellence as persons engaged in some specific pursuit'. See Stephen Darwall, 'Two Kinds of Respect', *Ethics*, vol. 88, issue 1 (Oct 1977).

18 Dillon 1992; Massey 1983; Darwall 1981; Spelman 1979.

19 Massey 1983, p. 249.

20 Dillon 1992, p. 56.

21 Dillon 1992; Spelman 1978.

22 Feminist encounters with theory are clearly marked by a number of stages. I am not referring here to the phases of feminism characterised by the liberal, socialist and the radical, but rather drawing attention to the various experiences of different women, which draw upon alternative resources of feminist epistemological practice in order to articulate their concerns. Perhaps, the critiques of moral theory as androcentric, while in many ways correct, do not appreciate many other aspects – such as rights – that can provide a language within which many struggles for self respect may be articulated.

23 See Mary Lyndon Shanley and Uma Narayan, eds, *Reconstructing Political Theory: Feminist Perspectives*, Polity Press, 1997. See in particular Elizabeth Kiss, 'Alchemy or Fools Gold? Assessing Feminist Doubts about Rights' in the same volume. According to her, cultural feminist and feminist communitarians critique the abstract, ahistorical and asocial principles that inform liberal ideas of the 'good'. Feminist legal scholars highlight the hidden male agendas behind the universalist language of law. Feminist post structuralists 'charge that rights language is bound up with socio-linguistic hierarchies of gender and with outdated patriarchal fictions of a unitary self'.

24 I owe the distinction between conceptual and natural language to Dr Sudipta Kaviraj.

25 There were two (indirect) exceptions to the state being the first point of contact with the idea of rights. One of them was a daughter of a former military man and the second *sathin* is married to a 'malaria Inspector'. It is important to note that both these men were and are employees of the state.

26 The interchange between *adhikar* as rights and *adhikar* as power especially by elected local government representatives was brought to my notice by Shail Mayaram, Personal Communication.

27 The word *Haq* is a derivative of *hkk*, whose use is now obscure. Its meaning is 'recovered by reference to the corresponding word in Hebrew' where it means to 'to cut in', to inscribe' and thereby refers to a permanent law or statute which necessarily does not have a particular normative content. It is an Arabic word, which is also available in Hebrew, Persian, and in some of the older Semitic languages such as Aramic, Phenician, and Mendian. Its earliest use in Arabic can be traced to pre-Islamic poetry where it means ' something right, true, just, and real'. In the Koran, its fundamental meaning is 'established fact', and therefore 'reality', and the meaning 'what corresponds to facts' and therefore 'truth' is secondary. In Arabic and Persian dictionaries the following meaning are prescribed for *Haq*: to be just, right, obligatory, make, or decide to be just. (Persian) truth, correctness, rightness, rightful possession, property, one's due, duty, proper manner, true, authentic, real, right, fair, good and reasonable, correct, sound, valid (Cowan Milton, ed., *A Dictionary of Modern Written Arabic*, London: George Allen and Unwin, 1971). In the earliest dictionaries of the Hindustani language *Haq* is defined as a right (see John Gilchrist, *A dictionary, English and Hindoostanee...* London, 1790) and as equity, due, reason, doom (John Fergusson, *A Dictionary of the Hindostan Language*, London, T Cadell, 1773). Giving an example of the use of the word, the author says: *Burra Faheb Fubb Quoy hukk infaaf kurrta*, which he proceeds to translate as 'the governor does justice and equity to everybody), In a later dictionary, compiled by Joseph Taylor, (1808) *Haq* appears as 'just, right, true, the deity, justice, rectitude, lot, portion, equity'. The plural of *Haq* is *Hoqooq*, which refers to rights, duties, laws, just, claims. In *A Dictionary of Urdu, Classical Hindi and English* by John T Platts (Oxford University Press, 1884), *Haq* is said to have the following meanings: just, proper, right, true, correct, rectitude, justice, equity, right title, privilege claim, due, lot, portion, the truth, and true god.

28 Some of the other meanings of *Haq* (or to have a right) are *insaf* (justice), *nyao, adalat* and *dad*. See Forbes Duncan, *A Dictionary of the Hindustani and English* 2nd edition, London, WMH Allen & Co, 1858. Some of the meanings of the term *Haqq*, according to the Urdu to English dictionary, are: just, right, true, right, portion justice, duty, claim, truth, and God.

29 Interview with *Sathin* Prem of Teetariya village, 'If there happens a child marriage and if the news gets around then our life becomes terrible. The villagers gather around us and think that we must have been the ones to inform the police or other officials. Especially on *akha Teej*, the villagers really trouble the *sathins*. However, the village women do support us'.

30 Tara Rathore, the *Pracheta* of Jamwa Ramgargh cluster of *sathins*. (*Pracheta* literally means a 'person of learning and commitment'. In the WDP she is the principal animator and is in charge of supervising the selection as well as activities of the *sathins*.)

31 Chandrakanta, ex-*sathin* of Chandlai (interviewed 8 March, 1999):

    I left the WDP because my husband and mother in law did not like it. This program involves speaking to men. I had to speak to the *Sarpanch* and the other eleven members of the *panchayat samiti*. He forbade me to speak to men. Then people started saying things to my husband that I was talking to the *Sarpanch* all the time and that I was having illicit relations with him. They started spreading rumors about other men and me. They spread rumours about women who come out of the house.

32 According to Kiran Dubey, property rights are considered to be contentious and are not encouraged much by the WDP office, though the right of women to be registered as co-owners of property is encouraged.

33 *Nata* is a practice alternative to marriage, which is recognised under customary law and is prevalent among the lower castes in Rajasthan. It takes place when either of the partners in a marriage is deceased or is abandoned as a result of a marital dispute. Usually a sum of money is agreed to by the man to either the woman's father or husband or the members of her marital family. The relationship thus entered into never enjoys the sanctity accorded to marriage; in fact the woman is often treated as inauspicious and never invited to participate in religious or other ceremonies within the family. See Shobhita Rajan, 'Violence Against Women' in *Situational Analysis of women and Children in Rajasthan*, Jaipur: IDS, 1990.

34 The need for support mechanisms was brought up a number of times by Manphooli Devi, the lady *Sarpanch* of *Lakhariyawas*, who spoke of her fears of resorting to independent action. She spoke of the need to have someone that she could turn to and who in turn could offer her support, as the women in her village were not brave enough to come out in support of her.

35 The villages that comprise *Dosara Panchayat* are: *Dosara, Mandaliya, Loonpura, Prempura, Mooratpura, Surastipura, and Saitlitya*. Mohan Kanwar belongs to *Mandaliya*.

36 The visibility of women within political institutions at the local government level was one of the objectives of the 73rd amendment to the constitution, which was adopted by the Parliament in 1992. The amendment act reserved one-third of the seats in the local governing bodies for women. Rajasthan, along with several other states, already had a *panchayat* system in place, albeit a relatively dormant one plagued by infrequent elections, and a hierarchical and an unrepresentative character. The new system of local governance is a three tier structure consisting of the village level (the *panchayat*), the block level (*Panchayat Samiti*) and the district level (*Zilla Parishad*) In addition to these three tiers, the New *Panchayati* Raj Act 1994 (Rajasthan) granted constitutional status to the *Gram Sabha* (village council) which is composed of all the eligible voters in the village. The *Gram Sabhas* are required to congregate at least four times a year in order to discuss local development and the budget. In a recent addition to the 1994 Act, the government of Rajasthan has enacted the Rajasthan *Panchayati Raj* (Amendment) Ordinance of 6 January which makes it mandatory for the Quorum of the *Gram Sabha* to proportionally represent women, Scheduled castes and tribes and other *backward* castes. The Quorum must be formed of at least one tenth of the *panchayat's* eligible voters.

The village *panchayats*, presided over by a *Sarpanch*, have the following local development functions: education, water, sanitation, health, maintenance of census records, agriculture, family welfare, cottage industries, co-operative societies etc. They have the power to raise taxes over vehicles and buildings etc. The *panchayat Samiti*, presided over by a *Pradhan* and an *Up Pradhan* or a deputy *Pradhan*, form the second tier of local government. They are involved in the planning and implementation of state plans, including those on community development, animal husbandry, education, rural housing etc. It also can levy taxes.

The *Zilla Parishad* rests at the top of the tiered structure and is a district-level institution. The Members of Parliament and of Legislative assemblies of the district, the *Pradhans* of the *Panchayat Samitis*, the Block development Officer and the President of the Co-operative Bank are the *ex officio* members of this body. It exercises coordinating and monitoring functions of the other two tiers and distributes grants to the *Panchayat Samitis*.

As a direct consequence of the implementation of the 73rd amendment act there are 10 women *Zilla Pramukhs*, 80 women *Pradhans* and 3064 women *Sarpanchs* within the *panchayat* bodies in Rajasthan.

See *Government of Rajasthan Instruction of Statutory Social Audit of Rural Development Works*, Jaipur 2000 and also *Development of Women and Children: A Brief on Efforts Made in Rajasthan*, Department of Women and Child Development Government of Rajasthan.

37 A *Sarpanch* is the chairperson of the *panchayat*, which is a village-level local body.

38 Mackenzie and Stoljar, eds, *Relational Autonomy: Feminist Perspectives on Autonomy, Agency and the Social Self*, New York: Oxford University Press, 2000. The authors 'analyse the implications of the intersubjective and social dimensions of selfhood and identity for conceptions of individual autonomy and moral and political agency'. See especially Mackenzie, 'Imagining oneself Otherwise', in the same volume, in which she explains how a 'restrictive or oppressive cultural imaginary may limit an agent's capacities for self definition, self transformation and autonomy' (p. 143).

39 Mackenzie and Stoljar 2000, p. 4.

40 Interview with Kalyani, Mokumpura: 'what *Purdah* is this, it's just a little *Purdah*, we are speaking, it's only that our eyes are not being seen'.

41 A ward *panch* is a member of the village *Gram Panchayat*.

42 It must be emphasised here that this is an unbroken narrative.

43 Bourdieu describes the properties and movements of the body to be determined by one's social position as well as role. According to him 'Bodily hexis is political mythology realised, em-bodied, turned into a permanent disposition, a durable way of standing, speaking, walking, and thereby of feeling and thinking. The opposition between the male and the female is realised in posture, in the gestures and the movements of the body' see 'Belief and the Body' in Bourdieu, Pierre, *The Logic Of Practice*, Polity Press, 1990.

44 For example, on average an election for *Sarpanch* would be, at a minimum cost, between 15 to 20 thousand rupees. Costs incurred in the hiring of jeeps and tractors for campaigning purposes comprise the majority of the expenses. Related to this financial inability are other problems, such as being unable to muster funds to provide for free-flowing liquor in the quarters where it matters the most. However, many of the women interviewed also expressed their discomfort with the idea of purchasing votes with liquor.

45 Rajasthan tops the country as far as incidence of crime is concerned, according to the recently released national crime bureau report. Crimes against women are the second most common, , at approximately 21.5 per cent of all crimes of IPC. The percentage assumes alarming proportions, particularly keeping in mind that a sizeable portion of these crimes go unreported due to the social stigma attached to them.

46 Interview with *Sathin* Bhanwari Devi of Village Bhateri. 'I don't want to stand for *Sarpanch*. If I want to stand then five men will threaten me. I am scared because the men do all the work themselves and keep all the development schemes for themselves and for those who are aligned with them. Only if the women control the money can women can do some work in the *panchayat*. As it stands women *Sarpanchs* do not control money. Secretaries who are all men often control it.'

47 By 'second hand' moral principles I am not implying that somehow some of us are in possession of moral principles which are 'original' or have been discovered by us but am using the term to highlight the very new acquisition of formal principles of rights in the *Sathin*'s moral repertoire.

48 While this may be acceptable (and there seems to be evidence to prove this) in several cases, this cannot be the whole story. For this assumes that those who have not had any schooling are necessarily incapable of making particular kinds of choices, and conversely, that those who have been through schooling are more adept at making these decisions.

49 A good example is the study of women's status that has been undertaken in anthropology. According to Mukhopadhyay and Higgins 1988, the subject matter of the studies on women's status revolved around the following variables: women's economic roles, mainly within the subsistence sector – including contributions in hunting, gathering and agriculture – although women's contributions within distribution and exchange activities are increasing in profile. Other dimensions of women's lives, include studies on diversity of reproductive activities, on sexuality, women's rituals, religious practices, on the 'culturally constructed ' and 'symbolic nature of gender', motherhood, notions of body, prestige systems, women's culture, women's visual arts, oral literature, poetry and private discourse. According to the authors, there is emerging scholarship on the political activities of women, although much work 'needs to be done conceptually and ethnographically'. See Mukhopadhyay and Higgins, 'Anthropological Studies of Women's Status revisited 1977–86,' *Annual Review of Anthropology*, 1988, 17, pp. 461–95.

50 The aspect of autonomy that falls within the scope of education is referred to as 'intellectual autonomy' (Telfer, Benson). Intellectual autonomy is concerned with the development of one's own judgement and of critical reflection; intellectually autonomous persons do not accept anything without a reason. Intellectually autonomous persons are distinguished from educated persons. While many theorists have drawn extensive lists of virtues associated with the autonomous person (John Benson, Feinberg, Telfer, Dworkin), some (RS Peters) maintain that these virtues can be attained through a particular form of education. RF Dearden sketches one such list, which according to him is a product of education. Dearden includes:

> 1) Wondering and asking, with a sense of a right to ask; 2) refusing agreement or compliance with what others put to him when this seems critically unacceptable; 3) defining what he really wants, or what is really in his interests, as distinct from what may be conventionally so regarded; 4) conceiving of goals, policies and plans of his own, and forming purposes and intentions of his own independently of any pressure to do so from others; 5) choosing among alternatives in ways which could exhibit that choice as the deliberate outcome of his own ideas or purposes; 6) forming his own opinion on various topics that interest him; 7) governing his actions and attitudes in the light of the previous sort of activity. In short the autonomous man has a mind of his own and will typically be no purely natural product, but the outcome of one sort of education.

51 See for instance, David Bridges, ed., *Education, Autonomy and Democratic Citizenship*, Routledge, 1997. Education is purported to relate to at least four of the prerequisites for the functioning of democratic states. These four are: participation and contribution to the affairs of the state; the capacity of citizens to 'sustain their own existence and those

of the state'; ensuring that the social goods extend to all; and that citizens are free to make use of these goods in the interests of their good life. A high quality of empowering education is required to fulfil these prerequisites.

52 'Salma, a ward *panch* in the village of Gegal in Ajmer district'.

9. The Development of Panchayati Raj in India

1 My thanks for their comments on an earlier version of this paper and suggestions to Subho Basu, Patricia Jeffery, Roger Jeffery, Nandini Sundar and Tony Good.

2 F. Perlin, 'Of White Whale and Countrymen' (1978).; R Thapar, *From Lineage to State* (1984); B Stein, *Peasant, State & Society* (1980).

3 See CJ Dewey, 'Images of the Village Community' (1972).

4 LI and SH Rudolph, *The Modernity of Tradition* (1967), pp. 264–8.

5 John Matthai (1915) has an enthusiastic introduction by the British Socialist MP Sidney Webb. The coeval ideological development of ideas of local self-government in India and the United Kingdom is a subject that merits considerable further research. On the orientalist imagining of India see Inden (1990) and Dirks (2001).

6 William Wedderburn, *The Indian Raiyat as a member of the village community: a lecture delivered before the London Institution...on the 10th December, 1883* (London, 1883).

7 M Galanter, *Law and Society in Modern India* (1989), p. 58.

8 See *Report of the Village Panchayat Committee* (Nagpur: Government Press, 1926).

9 M Galanter, *Law, State and Society*, pp. 58–9. Also H Tinker, *Foundation of Local Self Government in India, Pakistan and Burma* (1954).

10 MK Gandhi, *Collected Writings*, vol. 1, p. 93.

11 MK Gandhi, *Collected Writings*, vol. 1, pp. 256–72.

12 Thus, concerning the CWC's decision, against his wishes, that Gandhi should attend Round Table talks if invited, even if the Communal question remained unresolved, provided the 'conditions' were favourable, he wrote: 'though I myself am often described as an autocrat, I consider myself a man who accepts the supremacy of the people's voice, it is in my nature to give in to a *Panch*. *Panch* means the voice of the people. I therefore accepted the resolution passed by the majority.' [from Gujarati]: *Navajivan*, 21/6/1931, in *Collected Writings*, vol. 47, pp. 423–6.

13 MK Gandhi, in *Navajivan*, 23/08/1925, from *Collected Writings*, vol. 28, p. 99.

14 MK Gandhi, *Young India*, 27/08/1931, from *Collected Writings*, vol. 47, p. 363.

15 S. Sarkar, *The Swadeshi Movement in Bengal* (1973): see section on constructive *Swadeshi*.

16 See R. Ray, *Social conflict and political unrest in Bengal* (1984).

17 AM Zaidi, ed., *Speeches of the Congress Presidents* (1985–9). In his speech, entitled '*Swaraj for 90 per cent*', CR Das stated his belief that through Panchayati raj, class struggle and divisions in the nationalist movement could be averted, but without it there would be an explosion in rural areas.

18 D Dalton, *Mahatma Gandhi: nonviolent power in action* (1993), p. 61.

19 Edited from R Mukherjee, ed., *The Penguin Gandhi Reader* (1993), p. 80.

20 AJ Parel, ed., *Gandhi: Hind Swaraj* (1997), p. 189.

21 J Nehru, *The Discovery of India* (1945/1989).

22 Institute of Social Sciences, *Status of Panchayati Raj...1994* (1995).

23 A report published in the mid 1960s, *Co-operative Credit in Raipur District (Factors contributing to Heavy Overdues)*, by C Muthiah of the Agro-Economic Research Centre for Madhya Pradesh (Gwalior 1966), was the final nail in the coffin of the cooperative movement in MP. So damning were its conclusions that for a considerable time it was suppressed.

24 Quoted in RG Fox (1989), p. 183.

25 Institute of Social Sciences, *Status of Panchayati Raj*...ibid.

26 MK Gandhi, 1947, quoted in R Mukherjee, ed., *The Penguin Gandhi Reader*, p. 253.

27 See, for example, *The Madhya Pradesh Panchayats Act, 1962, no. 7 of 1962*, Govt. of Madhya Pradesh Law Dept. (Bhopal, 1962).

28 This problem persists up until the present day, see A Mishra, S Vasavada and C Bates (1998).

29 RG Fox (1989), p. 184.

30 *Report of the Committee on Panchayati Raj Institutions*, (New Delhi: 1978), pp. 5–7. Similar conclusions were drawn by contemporary anthropologists and sociologists, see e.g. Srinivas (1962) and Berrerman (1963).

31 *Report of the Committee on Panchayati Raj Institutions*, p. 173.

32 G Mathew, *Panchayati Raj: from legislation to movement* (1994), p. 85.

33 Ford Foundation report (1992), Gokhale (1988) and Maithani & Rizwana (1992), cited in J Dreze and A Sen, eds., *Indian Development* (1996 and 1998), p. 96.

34 For criticism of West Bengal's rural development programme see Jayoti Gupta (1997). The study is based on 308 case histories from the village of Pashang in Midnapur and highlights the way in which the Bengal agrarian reform programme (Operation *Barga*), which emphasises 'land to the tiller', has tended to exclude women from proprietary rights, as the tillers are customarily men. This is despite the high level involvement of women in elections and in the panchayats.

35 S Nagendra Amdekar, *New Panchayati Raj at Work* (2000). The Rajasthan Panchayati Raj Act of April 1994 established a three tier system of Gram Panchayats at the village level, *panchayat* samities at the Block level and a *Zilla Parishad* at the district level. The chairman at the village level is called the *Sarpanch* and is directly elected. One-third of the seats are reserved for women and reservations for SC, STs and OBC's is in proportion to their population (15–18 per cent). A study of the gram panchayats in Bikaner after elections in 1995 revealed that whilst land-owning upper castes of Rajput and Jats dominated amongst the members, 48 per cent had no education beyond primary level. The overwhelming majority of *panchayat* leaders had an income of less than Rs 50,000 and 68 per cent were entirely new to panchayati institutions.

36 Atul Kohli highlighted political commitment as a key explanatory variable when contrasting the performance of Congress and non-Congress states in *The State and Poverty in India* (Cambridge: CUP, 1987). By contrast, Moitree Bhattacharya, *Panchayati Raj in West Bengal: democratic decentralisation or democratic centralism* (Manak, 2002) suggests that enthusiasm for panchayats has subsided in Bengal since the late 1970s due to excessive political control. She also questions the involvement of women. Much of her data though derives from the early 1990s. The more recent research of Prabhat Datta published in *Panchayats, Rural Development, and Local Autonomy; the West Bengal experience* (Calcutta: Dasgupta & Co., 2001) gives some grounds for greater optimism, pointing to 97 per cent of *panchayat* elections being held on time in November 1997 and a mere 30 per cent complaining of 'moderate' government influence. In the 2002 *panchayat* elections there are further grounds for optimism, three Gram Sansad committees (the level above the Gram Panchaat, coterminus with electoral constituencies) being formed with all-female representation.

37 A recent study of *panchayat* institutions in Dobhi block of eastern UP (HN Singh, 1993, cited in Dreze and Sen, 1996) found that two-thirds of the headmen in 82 surveyed villages were Thakurs, the traditional landowning upper caste. The authors concludes

that these privileged groups are still exercising a tight control on local government institutions, using them 'to their private advantage at the expense of public needs'.

38 G Mathew, *Panchayati Raj: from legislation to movement* (New Delhi: Concept, 1994), ch. 9
'Karnataka puts the clock back'.

39 Amdekar, *New Panchayati Raj*, p. 143.

40 Comments to this effect were made by Kapil Sibal, leading counsel and *Rajya Sabha*
member, at a meeting of the Congress Parliamentary Party on July 14th, quoted in
India Today, July 1998, p. 15. The women's Reservation Bill would have reserved 33 per
cent of Parliamentary seats for women. It failed despite the support of Sonia Gandhi,
Prime Minister AB Vajpayee and leading Congressmen such as Sharad Pawar, owing
to opposition from within the ranks of the major parties, allegedly orchestrated by
(mostly male) representatives of the OBCs, fearful of an erosion of their influence.

41 See Mahi Pal, 'Panchayats in Fifth Scheduled Areas', *EPW*, May 2000.

10. Political Representation and Women's Empowerment: Women in the Institutions of Local Self-Government in Orissa

1 This essay is partly based upon my *A Million Indiras Now? Political Presence and Women's
Empowerment in Rural Local Government in India* (Delhi: Manohar 2004).

2 ISS 1997, p. 7. At this time Jammu & Kashmir and Bihar had not held elections.

3 Article 40 (4) reads: 'The state shall take steps to organise village panchayats and
endow them with such powers and authority as may be necessary to enable them to
function as units of self-government'. Constitution of India, as amended. For a brief
description of the evolution of the Panchayati Raj from pre-independence till today
see Mathew, George, 'Introduction' (Mathew 1995, 1–14).

4 GoI 1957, vol. 1, p. 47.

5 GoI 1957, vol. 1, p. 127.

6 For the role of women, see GoI 1978, pp. 140–2; a list of recommendations follows
later, concerning the issues above see recommendations 111 and 112 (ibid., p. 199).

7 Ibid., pp. 179–80.

8 Ibid., pp. 180–1.

9 Ibid., p. 178.

10 For this and the following see Everett 1979, pp. 101–40.

11 Everett 1979, p. 136.

12 For a quick reference see ICSSR 1988.

13 GoI 1974, p. 303, Paragraph 7.109 b.

14 See Paragraphs 7.112 and 7.113 (GoI 1974, p. 303). For the specific reasons see 7.113
a–g. For dissenting voices see ibid., pp. 355–7.

15 Mazumdar 1997, p. 15.

16 GoI, 1974, p. 304, Paragraphs 7.115–116.

17 ICSSR 1988, pp. 114–15. For the longer version see GoI 1974, pp. 304–5, Paragraph
7.117.

18 GoI 1974, p. 305, Paragraph 7.117–2.

19 GoI 1988, p. 153.

20 For detailed information of State Initiatives to enhance the position of women see GoI
1995.

21 Mazumdar 1997, p. 15.

22 GoI 1988, pp. 153–70.

23 Ibid., p. 156.

24 However, I could not find any information on a 30 per cent reservation in Andhra Pradesh; the last Act before the 73rd Amendment was the Andhra Pradesh Mandala Praja Parishads, Zilla Praja Parishads and Zilla Pranalika Abhivrudhi Sameeksha Mandals Act, 1986, which reserved 9 per cent of seats for women in the Mandala Praja Parishad, and 2 out of 22 chairpersons of the Zilla Praja Parishad (see Mathew 1995, pp. 24–5); at the level of Gram Panchayats a number of seats were reserved for women in the Andhra Pradesh Gram Panchayats Act, 1964, before it was amended in the 1980s, which amounts to between 22 per cent and 25 per cent reservation (Manikyamba 1989); in Karnataka a reservation of 25 per cent for women in the *Zilla Parishad* and the Mandal Parishad (Karnataka had a two-tier-system) was enshrined in the Act of 1983, with elections taking place in 1987 (Mathew 1995, pp. 98–9).

25 Ibid., pp. 164–5. There was one additional recommendation to declare a certain percentage of constituencies as exclusively for women and all executive positions in a certain number of territorial jurisdictions as reserved for women.

26 One problem was that the non-Congress State Governments felt that the Bill vested too many powers in the Governor and the National Government (Chandrashekhar 1989, pp. 1433–5).

27 For a concise theoretical and normative debate arguing for women's political representation through a quota see the seminal work by Phillips 1995.

28 For the Indian case see e.g. Lelithabai 1998; Meenakshisundaram 1995; Pal 1999; Vidya 1997.

29 Batliwala 1993: p. 8.

30 Rowlands 1998, p. 12.

31 Ibid., p. 14.

32 Rowlands also adds 'power with', and 'power from within', which I will not discuss in this essay.

33 Bystydzienski 1992, p. 5.

34 The existing studies are also mainly case studies conducted in a single Indian state. However, cultural background or societal norms are often taken as granted and are hardly mentioned. Another problem is that normally the elected women are the sole source of information, which can lead to misrepresentations. For studies on women in Panchayati Raj after the 73rd Amendment, see for example Athreya/Rajeswari, s.d [study was conducted in 1998]; Kaushik 1997; MARG 1998; Santha 1999; for studies on women in the PRI prior to the 73rd Amendment see D' Lima 1983; Manikyamba 1989; Rajput 1993; Vidya 1997.

35 Orissa was ranked as the poorest state in India in terms of per capita income (Rs 3,028 per annum) and persons below the poverty line (55 per cent) in 1996 (*Haq* 1997, p. 32). For 'backwardness' in social terms see Mohanty 1990 and Pathy 1988.

36 An administrative unit situated between district and village. Most blocks were created in the 1952 under the Community Development Program, as the fulcrum of development administration.

37 In Balipatna 100 per cent of the female Sarpanches and the one *Samiti* Chairperson, and 75 per cent of the ward members were interviewed; in Gania 100 per cent of the elected women in both lower tiers, that is the Gram Panchayats and *Panchayat Samiti*, were interviewed.

38 There is, however, some bias in the male sample. First, comparatively more Sarpanches have been interviewed, as they were seen as important sources of information. Additionally an unintended bias is due to the procedure of reservation. In the event that, for example, two seats are reserved for Scheduled Castes, one has to be reserved for a Scheduled Castes woman. Thus, the percentage of Scheduled Castes in the female sample is much higher than in the male sample.

39 For socio-economic data of other samples see Kaushik 1997, pp. 11ff; Manikyamba 1989, pp. 58ff; MARG 1998, pp. 38ff; Rajput 1993, pp. 34ff; Santha 1999, pp. 40ff; Vidya 1997, pp. 102ff.

40 Not all women could give their age precisely. In these cases either present relatives were asked, or when the answer was, e.g. 'between 35 and 40', it went into the calculation as 37.

41 Kaushik, 1997, p. 11.

42 One *Sarpanch* has primary education only, three Sarpanches and one Samiti Member went to class VI–IX, two Sarpanches, one *Samiti* Member and one *Samiti* Chairperson studied up to class 10, one *Sarpanch* is a Graduate, and one *Samiti* Chairperson is a Post-Graduate.

43 The literacy rates for Balipatna are (excluding the age group 0–6) 80.64 per cent for males and 51.55 per cent for females, making a total of 66.26 per cent (GoO a), s.d., p. 14), and for Gania 71.54 per cent for male and 37.17 per cent for females, amounting to a total of 54.94 per cent (GoO b), s.d., p. 11).

44 At this time 1 US$ was equivalent to Rs 42.

45 That was the figure for the 1992 survey (Government of Orissa, s.d., p. 71).

46 The medium income of the Sarpanches was between 20,000 and 50,000, of the *Samiti*-Chairpersons between 50,000–100,000, whereas ward members had 10,000 to 20,000.

47 cf. Rerrich 1996.

48 In Haryana the Chief Minister even set out a price for villages where candidates came uncontested.

49 This also became obvious during the election to the Vidhan Sabha in February 2000. Many people reported that the voting decision is cast by the whole village (i.e. men of the village), and everybody votes accordingly. However, sometimes these villagers expect and get some amenities from the candidate in question for delivering so many votes.

50 There is an interesting Oriya dictum indicating why people do not want to 'invest' in their daughters' education: 'Jhia, ghia para patarare dia' which translates as 'Daughter and Ghee [you have in order to] put on other people's plates.' I am grateful to Subrata K Mitra for mentioning this proverb to me.

51 Out of the women interviewed during the second field-visit, there were 7 *gaanjhias* (2 unmarried, one divorced, 4 married) and 7 *bahus* (3 young ones without much help in the household and small children, and 4 old ones, either with daughters-in-law or adult children). Thus half of the women interviewed were *gaanjhias* (which was not a conscious selection but was only found out while conducting the interviews); however only 4 of them married. This seems to be a quite a high proportion.

52 For information on this NGO and its work see Harper 1998, pp. 124–31.

BIBLIOGRAPHY

1. Stages in the Success and Failure of Economic Reform in India: a Review of the Literature

Ahluwalia, Montek S, 1999, 'India's economic reforms: an appraisal', in Jeffrey D Sachs, Ashutosh Varshney and Nirupam Bajpai, eds, *India in the Era of Economic Reforms*, New Delhi: Oxford University Press, pp. 26–80.

Bardhan, Pranab, 1984, *The Political Economy of Development in India*, New Delhi: Oxford University Press.

——, 1998, *The Political Economy of Development in India*, New Delhi: Oxford University Press.

Bhaduri, Amit and Deepak Nayyar, 1996, *The Intelligent Person's Guide to Liberalization*, New Delhi: Penguin Books.

Chhibber, Pradeep, 1995, 'Political parties, electoral competition, government expenditures and economic reform in India', *Journal of Development Studies*, vol. 32, no. 1, pp. 74–96.

Currie, Bob, 1996, 'Governance, democracy and economic adjustment in India: conceptual and empirical problems', *Third World Quarterly*, vol. 17, no. 4, pp. 787–807.

Denoon, David BH, 1998, 'Cycles in Indian economic liberalization, 1966–1996', *Comparative Politics*, vol. 31, no. 1, pp. 43–60.

Guhan, S, 1995, 'Centre and States in the reform process', in Robert Cassen and Vijay Joshi, eds, *India: the Future of Economic Reforms*, New Delhi: Oxford University Press, pp. 73–111.

Harriss, John, 1987, 'The state in retreat: why has India experienced such half-hearted liberalisation in the 1980s?', *IDS Bulletin*, vol. 18, no. 4, pp. 31–8.

Jenkins, Robert S, 1995a, 'Liberal democracy and the political management of Structural Adjustment in India: conceptual tensions in the good government agenda', *IDS Bulletin*, vol. 26, no. 2, pp. 37–48.

——, 1995b, 'Theorising the politics of economic adjustment: lessons from the Indian case', *Journal of Commonwealth and Comparative Politics*, vol. 33, no. 1, pp. 1–24.

Jenkins, Rob, 1999, *Democratic Politics and Economic Reform in India*, Cambridge: Cambridge University Press.

Joshi, Vijay and IMD Little, 1997, *India's Economic Reforms 1991–2001*, Delhi: Oxford University Press.

Kohli, Atul, 1989, 'Politics of economic liberalization in India', *World Development*, vol. 17, no. 3, pp. 305–28.

Manor, James, 1987, 'Tried, then abandoned: economic liberalisation in India', *IDS Bulletin*, vol. 18, no. 4, pp. 39–44.

Manor, James, 1995, 'The political sustainability of economic liberalisation in India', in Robert Cassen and Vijay Joshi, eds, *India: the Future of Economic Reforms*. New Delhi: Oxford University Press, pp. 341–61.

Milner, Murray Jr. and Sukirti Sahay, 1997, 'Victory without the spoils? The irony of *backward* caste politics in a liberalizing economy', Paper presented at a Conference of the American Sociological Association, Toronto, Canada, 9–13 August 1997.

Pani, Narendar, 1994, *Redefining Conservatism: An Essay on the Bias of India's Economic Reform*, New Delhi, Sage Publications.

Panini, MN, 1995, 'The social logic of liberalization', *Sociological Bulletin*, vol. 44, no. 1, pp. 33–62.

Paranjape, HK, 1985, 'New lamps for old – A critique on the "New Economic Policy"', *Economic and Political Weekly*, vol. 20, no. 36, pp. 1513–22.

——, 1988, 'Indian liberalisation: Perestroika or Salaami tactics?', *Economic and Political Weekly*, vol. 23, no. 45–7, pp. 2343–58.

Patnaik, Prabhat, 1986, 'New turn in economic policy: context and prospects', *Economic and Political Weekly*, vol. 21. no. 23, pp. 1014–19.

——, 2000, 'Economic policy and its political management in the current conjuncture', in Francine Frankel, Zoya Hasan, Rajeev Bhargava and Balveer Arora, eds, *Transforming India: Social and Political Dynamics of Democracy*, New Delhi: Oxford University Press, pp. 231–53.

Patnaik, Prabhat and CP Chandrashekar, 1995, 'The Indian economy under structural adjustment', *Economic and Political Weekly*, vol. 30, no. 47, pp. 3001–13.

Rubin, Barnett R, 1985, 'Economic liberalisation and the Indian state', *Third World Quaterly*, vol. 7, no. 4, pp. 942–57.

Sachs, Jeffrey D, Ashutosh Varshney and Nirupam Bajpai, 1999, 'Introduction', in Jeffrey D Sachs, Ashutosh Varshney and Nirupam Bajpai, eds, *India in the Era of Economic Reforms*, New Delhi: Oxford University Press, pp. 1–25.

Shastri, Vanita, 1997, 'The politics of economic liberalization in India', *Contemporary South Asia*, vol. 6, no. 1, pp. 27–56.

Sridharan, E, 1993, 'Economic liberalisation and India's political economy: towards a paradigm synthesis', *Journal of Commonwealth and Comparative Politics*, vol. 31, no. 3, pp. 1–31.

Varshney, Ashutosh, 1999, 'Mass politics or elite politics. India's economic reforms in comparative perspective', in Jeffrey D Sachs, Ashutosh Varshney and Nirupam Bajpai, eds, *India in the Era of Economic Reforms*. New Delhi: Oxford University Press, pp. 222–60.

Weiner, Myron, 1999, 'The regionalization of Indian politics and its implications for economic reform', in Jeffrey D Sachs, Ashutosh Varshney and Nirupam Bajpai, eds, *India in the Era of Economic Reforms*. New Delhi: Oxford University Press, pp. 261–95.

2. The Temptations of Presidentialism: An Explanation of the Evolving Political Strategy of the BJP

Bajpai, Shankar ed., *Managing Diversity in Democracies: India and the United States* (forthcoming).

Brass, Paul, *The Politics of India since Independence*, CUP, Cambridge, 2nd edn., 1994.

Chatterjee, Partha, *A Possible India: essays in political criticism*, OUP, Delhi, 1998.

Jaffrelot, Christophe, *The Hindu Nationalist Movement and Indian Politics*, Penguin Books India, 1999.

Jenkins, Rob, *Democratic Politics and Economic Reform in India*, CUP, Cambridge, 1999.

Kaviraj, Sudipta, 'The general elections in India' *Government and Opposition*, Vol. 32, No. 1, Winter 1997, pp. 3–25.

Khilnani, Sunil, *The Idea of India*, Hamish Hamilton, London, 1997.

Lijphart, Arend, 'The puzzle of Indian democracy: a consociational interpretation' *American Political Science Review*, Vol. 90, No. 2, June 1996.

Mitra, Sumit *et al*, 'Review rift' *India Today*, 14 Febuary 2000.

Przeworski, Adam *et al*, *Sustainable Democracy*, CUP, Cambridge, 1985.

Sartori, Giovanni, *Comparative Constitutional Engineering: an inquiry into structures, incentives and outcomes*, Macmillan, London, 1994.

Tully, James, *Strange Multiplicity: constitutionalism in an age of diversity*, CUP, Cambridge, 1994.

Vinaik, Achin, *India in a Changing World: problems, limits and successes of its foreign policy*, Orient Longman, Hyderabad, 1995.

3. Ideological Integration in Post-colonial (South) India: Aspects of a Political Language

Anantha Murthy, U.R., *Samskara: A Rite for a Dead Man*, trans. A.K. Ramnujan (Delhi:Oxford University Press, 1978).

Anantha Murthy, U.R., *Bharathipura*, trans. P. Sreenivasa Rao (Madras: Macmillan India Ltd., 1996).

Appadurai, Arjun, *Worship and Conflict under Colonial Rule: A South Indian Case* (New York: Cambridge University Press, 1981).

Brass, Paul R., *Language, Religion and Politics in North India* (London: Cambridge University Press, 1974).

Brittlebank, Kate, *Tipu Sultan's Search for Legitimacy: Islam and Kingship in a Hindu Domain* (Delhi: Oxford University Press, 1997).

Chatterjee, Partha, 'Community in the East', in *Economic and Political Weekly*. No. 33, 1998, pp. 277–82.

Chatterjee, Partha, *The Nation and Its Fragments: Colonial and Post-Colonial Histories* (Princeton: Princeton University Press, 1993).

Chhibber, Pradeep K., *Democracy Without Associations: Transformation of the Party System and Social Cleavages in India* (Ann Arbor: The University of Michigan Press, 1999).

Chopra, Vir, *Marginal Players in Marginal Assemblies: The Indian MLA* (New Delhi: Orient Longman, 1996).

Dirks, Nicholas, *The Hollow Crown: Ethnohistory of an Indian Kingdom* (Cambridge: Cambridge University Press, 1987).

Freitag, Sandria, *Collective Action and Community: Public Arenas and the Emergence of Communalism in North India* (Berkeley: University of California Press, 1989).

Fuller, C.J., *The Camphor Flame: Popular Hinduism and Society in India* (Princeton: Princeton University Press, 1992).

Fuller, C. J. and John Harriss, 'For an Anthropology of the Modern Indian State', in C.J. Fuller and Véronique Bénéï, eds., *The Everyday State and Society in Modern India* (New Delhi: Social Science Press, 2000), pp. 1–30.

Gilmartin, David, 'Partition, Pakistan and South Asian History: In Search of a Narrative', in *The Journal of Asian Studies*, Vol. 57, No. 4, 1998, pp. 1068–1095.

Hansen, Thomas Blom. *The Saffron Wave: Democracy and Hindu Nationalism in Modern India* (Princeton: Princeton University Press, 1999).

Holmström, Mark, 'Action-sets and Ideology: A Municipal Election in South India', in *Contributions to Indian Sociology: New Series*, No. 3, 1969, pp. 76–93.

Holmström, Mark, 'Action-sets in a Big City: A Social Anthropologist's View of the 1971 General Election', paper presented at the 10th European Conference on Modern South Asian Studies, Venice, 1988.

Kaviraj, Sudipta, 'On the Crisis of Political Institutions in India.' in *Contributions to Indian Sociology, N.S.*, Vol. 18, No. 2, 1984, pp. 223–243.

Kaviraj, Sudipta, 'On State, Society and Discourse in India', in J. Manor, ed., *Rethinking Third World Politics* (London: Longman, 1991), pp. 72–99.

Kohli, Atul, *Democracy and Discontent: India's Growing Crisis of Governability*. (Cambridge: Cambridge University Press, 1990).

Kothari, Rajni, ed., *Caste in Indian Politics* (New Dehli: Orient Longman, 1970).

Madan, T.N., *Modern Myths, locked Minds: Secularism and Fundamentalism in India* (Delhi: Oxford University Press, 1997), cited in Fuller and Harriss.

Manor, James, 'Anomie in Indian Politics: Origins and Potential Wider Impact', in *Economic and Political Weekly*, Vol. 18, No. 19, 20, 21, 1983, pp. 725–735.

Mayer, Adrian, 'The Significance of Quasi-groups in the Study of Complex Societies', in M. Banton, ed., *The Social Anthropology of Complex Societies* (London: Tavistock, 1966) pp. 97–122.

Mishra, Pankaj, 'A New, Nuclear India', in *The New York Review of Books*, Vol. 45, No. 11, 1998, pp. 55–64.

Nagaran, D. R., 'Introduction,' in U. R. Anantha Murthy, *Bharathipura*, trans. P. Sreenivasa Rao, pp. vii–xvi.

Narain, Iqbal and P.C. Mathur, 'Ideology and the Indian Party System: An Essay in Conceptual Cognition', in Kenneth Ballhatchet and David Taylor, eds., *Changing South Asia: Politics and Government*(London: Asian Research Service, 1984) pp. 161–77.

Narasimha Rao, P. V., *The Insider* (New Delhi: Viking, 1998).

Prasad Singh, Mahendra , 'The Dilemma of the New Indian Party System: To Govern or Not to Govern?', in *Asian Survey*, Vol. 32, No. 4, 1992, pp. 303–317.

Price, Pamela, *Kingship and Political Practice in Colonial India*. (Cambridge: Cambridge University Press, 1996b)

Price, Pamela, 'Revolution and Rank in Tamil Nationalism', in *The Journal of Asian Studies*. Vol. 55, No. 2. 1996a, pp. 359–383.

Ramanujan, A. K., 'Afterword', in U.R. Anantha Murthy, *Samskara: A Rite for a Dead Man*, trans. A.K. Ramanujan, pp. 139–47.

Saberwal, Satish, *Roots of Crisis: Interpreting Contemporary Indian Society* (New Delhi: Sage Publications, 1996).

Srinivas, M.N., 'The Quality of Social Relations', in his *Indian Society Through Personal Writing* (Dehli: Oxford University Press, 1996), pp. 163–91.

Van der Veer, Peter, *Religious Nationalism: Hindus and Muslims in India* (Berkeley: University of California Press, 1994).

Zydenbos, Robert J., *The Calf Became an Orphan: A Study in Contemporary Kannada Fiction* (Pondichéry: Institut Francais, 1996).

4. The Fight for Turf and the Crisis of Ideology: Broadcasting Reform and Contemporary Media Distribution in India

Breman, Jan, *Footloose labour: Working in India's informal economy*, CUP, Cambridge, 1996.

Byres, Terence ed., *The State, Development and Liberalization in India*, OUP, Delhi, 1999.

Downing, John D.H., *Film and Politics in the Third World*, Praeger, New York; London, 1988 and Greenwood Press, 1994.

Horne, Gerald, *Class Struggle in Hollywood 1930–1950*, Texas UP, Austin, 2001

Jeffrey, *India's Newspaper Revolution*, OUP, New Delhi, 2000.

Jenkins, Rob, *Democratic Politics and Economic Reform in India*, CUP, Cambridge, 1999.

Lippert, Owen & Walker, M. *The Underground Economy: Global Evidence of its Size and Impact*, Fraser Institute, 1997.

Manuel, Peter, *Cassette Culture: Popular Music and Technology in North India*, OUP, Delhi, 2001.

Moldea, Dan, *Dark Victory: Ronald Reagan, MCA and the Mob*, Viking Press, NY, 1986.

Nandy, Ashis, *Secret Politics of our Desires: Innocence, Culpability and Indian Popular Cinema*, OUP, Delhi, 1998.

Naregal, Veena, 'Cable Communications in Mumbai', *Contemporary South Asia*, Vol. 9, No. 3, 2000.

Naregal, Veena, *Language Politics, Elites and the Public Sphere: Western India under Colonialism*, Permanent Black, Delhi, 2001; Anthem Press, London, 2002.

Pani, Narendra *Redefining Conservatism: An Essay on the Bias of India's Economic Reform*, Sage, New Delhi, 1994.

Parry, Jonathan *et al*, *The Worlds of Indian Industrial Labour*, Sage, New Delhi, 1999.

Prasad, Madhav, *Ideology of the Hindi Film: A Historical Construction*, OUP, Delhi, 1995.

Price, Monroe and Verhulst, S. *Broadcasting Reform in India: Media Law from a Global Perspective*, OUP, Delhi, 1998.

Saga, Junichi, *The Gambler's Tale: A life in Japan's Underworld*, Kodansha, Tokyo, 1991.

Staudt, K., *Free Trade: Informal Economies at the US-Mexican Border*, Temple UP, Philadelphia, 1998.

Vasudevan, Ravi, 'Shifting Codes, Dissolving Identities: The Hindi Social Film of the 1950s as Popular Culture', *Journal of Arts and Ideas*, Delhi, Vol. 23, No. 4, 1993.

Vasudevan, Ravi, *Making Meaning in Indian Cinema*, OUP, Delhi, 2000.

Williams, Colin *et al*, *Informal Employment in the Advanced Economies: Implications for Work and Welfare*, Routledge, NY, 1998.

5. The Political Economy of Urban Planning
The Case Study of Bombay

Banaji Jarius and Rohini Hensman, 'Outline of an IR theory of industrial conflict,' *Economic and Political Weekly* August 25, 1990.

Bardhan, Pranab, *The political economy of development in India*, (Oxford: Basil Blackwell, 1984).

Bardhan, Pranab, 'Dominant proprietory classes and India's democracy,' in *India's democracy: an analysis of changing state-society relations*, ed. Atul Kohli. (Hyderabad: Orient Longman, 1988).

Bawa, V K., *Indian metropolis: urbanisation, planning and management*, (New Delhi: Inter-India, 1987).

Bhagwati, Jagdish, *India in transition: freeing the economy*, (Delhi: Oxford University Press, 1993).

BMRDA (Bombay Metropolitan Regional Development Authority), '*Draft regional plan for Bombay Metropolitan Region 1996-2011*', (Bombay: BMRDA, 1995).

Breman, Jan, 'The informal sector' in *Research: theory and practice*, (Rotterdam: Comparative Asian Studies Programme, 1980).

Byres, Terence J., 'Land reform, industrialisation and the market surplus in India: an essay on the power of rural bias' in *Agrarian Reform and Agrarian Reformism*, ed. David Lehmann, (London: Faber, 1974).

Byres, Terence J. 'The new technology, class formation and class action in the Indian countryside.' *Journal of Peasant Studies* 8. 1981.

Byres, Terence J. 'India: capitalist industrialisation or structural stasis?' in The struggle for development: national strategies in an international context, ed. Manfred Bienefield and Martin Godfrey. (Chichester, New York: Wiley, 1982).

Byres, Terence J., 'State class and planning' in *The state, development planning and liberalisation in India*, ed. Terence J. Byres, (New Delhi: Oxford University Press, 1998).

Chakravorty, Sanjoy, 'Too little in the wrong places: mega city programme and efficiency and equity in Indian urbanisation', *Economic and Political Weekly*, September. Special Number. 1996.

Chandavarkar, Rajnarayan *The origins of industrial capitalism in India: business strategies and the working classes in Bombay, 1900-1940*, (Cambridge: Cambridge University Press, 1994).

Chatterjee, Partha, *The nation and its fragments: colonial and post-colonial histories*, (Princeton: Princeton University Press, 1993).

Chatterjee, Partha, 'Development planning and the Indian state' in *The state, development planning and liberalisation in India*, ed. Terence J. Byres, (New Delhi: Oxford University Press, 1998).

Deshpande, Lalit K., *The Bombay labour market* (Bombay: Department of Economics, University of Bombay, 1979).

Deshpande, Lalit K., 'The Bombay labour market', in *Urban explosion of Mumbai*, ed. M D David. (Bombay: Himalaya, 1996).

Deshpande, Sudha and L K., *Problems of urbanisation and growth of large cities in developing countries – a case study of Bombay*, (Geneva: International Labour Organisation, 1991).

D'Monte, Darryl, 'Redevelopment of Mumbai's cotton textile land: opportunity lost,' *Economic and Political Weekly*. February 7, 1998.

Dossal, Mariam, 'Signatures is space: land use in colonial Bombay' in *Bombay: metaphor for modern India*, ed. Sujata Patel and Alice Thorner, (New Delhi: Oxford University Press, 1995).

D'Souza, J B., 'Will Bombay have a plan? Irrelevance of planners and their plans' *Economic and Political Weekly*. May 18, 1991.

D'Souza, Victor, 'Bombay: a city on the horns of a dilemma' in *Urban explosion of Mumbai*, ed. M D David. (Bombay: Himalaya, 1996).

EPW (Economic and Political Weekly), 'Expensive housing cheap people', Editorial. *Economic and Political Weekly* 17. 1982.

Farooqui, Amar, 'Urban development in a colonial situation: early nineteenth century Bombay', *Economic and Political Weekly*. October 5, 1996.

Flyvbjerg, Bent, *Rationality and power: democracy in practice*, (Chicago, London: University of Chicago Press, 1998).

GoM (Government of Maharashtra), *Guidelines for implementation of slum rehabilitation schemes– in Greater Mumbai*, (Bombay: Slum Rehabilitation Authority, Housing and Special Assistance Department, 1997).

Gupta, Dipankar, *Nativism in a metropolis: the Shiv Sena in Bombay*, (New Delhi: Manohar, 1982).

Harvey, David, *Social justice and the city*, (London: Edward Arnold, 1973).

Hawthorn, Geoffrey, 'Waiting for a text?' in *Rethinking Third World Politics*, ed. James Manor, (London, New York: Longman, 1991).

Jenkins, Robert., *Democratic politics and economic reform in India*, (Cambridge: Cambridge University Press, 2000).

Joshi, Heather and Vijay, *Surplus labour and the city: a study of Bombay*, (New Delhi: Oxford University Press, 1976).

Kaviraj, Sudipta, 'On state, society and discourse in India' in *Rethinking Third World Politics*, ed. James Manor. (London, New York: Longman, 1991).

Khandker, S R., *Earnings, occupational choice and mobility in segmented labour markets of India*, (Washington D.C.: World Bank, 1992).

Kohli, Atul, 'Politics of economic liberalisation in India' *World Development*. 17, 1989.

Kundu, Amitabh, 'Urban poverty in India: issues and perspectives in development.' in *Social Dimensions of Urban Poverty in India*, (New Delhi: National Institute of Urban Affairs, 1999).

Kurien, C T., *Growth and justice: aspects of India's development experience*, (Madras: Oxford University Press, 1992).

Lal, Deepak, *The poverty of 'development economics'*, (Hobart: Institute of Economic Affairs, 1983).

Lamarche, Francois, 'Property development and the economic foundations of the urban question,' in *Urban sociology: critical essays*, ed. C G Pickvance. (London: Tavistock Publications, 1975).

Lele, Jayant, 'Saffronisation of the *Shiv Sena*: the political economy of city, state and nation' *Economic and Political Weekly*. June 24, 1995.

LHS (Lokshahi Hakka Sanghatana), *Murder of the mills: an enquiry into Bombay's cotton textile industry and its workers*, (Bombay: LHS, 1996).

Lipton, Michael, *Why poor people stay poor: a study of urban bias in world development*, (Cambridge, Mass.: Harvard University Press, 1977).

Mahadevia, Darshini, 'Emerging process of residential segregation in metropolitan cities - case studies of Bombay and Madras', Ph.D. thesis. (New Delhi: Centre for the Study of Regional Development, Jawaharlal Nehru University, 1991).

Mahadevia, Darshini, 'State supported segmentation of Mumbai: policy options in the global economy', *Review of Development and Change*. 3. 1998.

Masselos, Jim, 'Postmodern Bombay', in *Postmodern cities and spaces*, ed. Sophie Watson and Katharine Gibson. (Oxford; Cambridge, Mass.: Basil Blackwell, 1995).

Mazumdar, Dipak, *Paradigms in the study of urban labour markets in LDCs: a reassessment in the light of am empirical survey in Bombay city*, (Washington D.C.: World Bank, 1979).

Miliband, Ralph, 'Poulantzas and the capitalist state', *New Left Review*, 1973.

Narayanan, Harini, 'The plot thickens: rhetoric and reality in the context of the Urban Land (Ceiling and Regulation) Act 1976 and its application in Mumbai', Paper presented at Seminar on Work and Workers in Mumbai, November 27–29. (Bombay: Vikas Adhyayan Kendra, 1997).

Nijman, Jan, 'Mumbai's real estate market in the 1990s: deregulation, global money and casino capitalism', *Economic and Political Weekly*. February 12, 2000.

Offe, Claus, *Contradictions of the welfare state*, (London: Hutchinson, 1984).

Padgaonkar, Dileep (ed.), *When Bombay burned*, (New Delhi: UBS, 1993).

Phatak, Vidyadhar, 'Shelter strategy for Bombay' in *Urban explosion of Mumbai*, ed. M D David. (Bombay: Himalaya, 1996).

Poulantzas, Nicos, *Political power and social classes*, (London: New Left Books, 1973).

Przeworski, Adam, *Democracy and the market: political and economic reforms in Eastern Europe and Latin America* (Cambridge: Cambridge University Press, 1991).

Rudolph, Susan Hoeber and Lloyd, *In pursuit of Lakshmi: the political economy of the Indian state*, (Bombay: Orient Longman, 1987).

Sainath, P., 'Bombay riots of December 1992: a report' in *Communalism in India: challenge and response*, ed. Mehdi Arsalan and Janaki Rajan (New Delhi: Manohar, 1994).

Sen, Amartya, *Poverty and famines: an essay on entitlement and deprivation* (Oxford, New York: Oxford University Press, 1981).

Sengupta, Chandan, *Urban poverty and vulnerability in India: nature, dynamics and trends*. (New Delhi: Oxfam [India] Trust, 1999).

Shaw, Annapurna, 'Satellite town development in Asia: the case of New Bombay, India', *Urban Geography*. 16, 1995.

Shaw, Annapurn,. 'Urban policy in post-Independent India', *Economic and Political Weekly*. January 27, 1996.

Singh, P K Das and Gurbir Singh, 'Building castles in the air: housing schemes for Bombay's slum-dwellers', *Economic and Political Weekly*. October 7, 1995.

SPARC (Society for Promotion of Area Resource Centres), 'Waiting for water: the experience of poor communities in Mumbai' (Bombay: SPARC, 1994).

Sundaram, P S A., *Bombay: can it house its millions? A new approach to solving the housing problems of Third World cities* (New Delhi: Clarion Books, 1989).

Swaminathan, Madhura, 'Aspects of urban poverty in Bombay', *Environment and Urbanization*.7. 1995.

Swaminathan, Madhura, *The determinants of earnings among low-income workers in Bombay: an analysis of panel data* (Bombay: Indira Gandhi Institute of Development Research, 1996).

Swaminathan, Madhura, *Aspects of poverty and living standards in Mumbai* (Bombay: Indira Gandhi Institute of Development Research, 1999).

Thakurdas, Purshotamdas *et al.*, *Memorandum outlining a plan of economic development for India*, (Middlesex, 1945).

6. Understanding Local Politics, Democracy and Civil Society: Environmental Governance in Urban India

Agarwal, Anil, Sunita Narain and Srabani Sen (1999) *State of India's Environment 5: The Citizens' Fifth Report*, Centre for Science and Environment, New Delhi.

Basu, Subho (1994) *Workers' Politics in Bengal 1890–1930: Strikes, Riots and Nationalist Agitations*, Unpublished Ph.D. Thesis, University of Cambridge, Cambridge.

Basu, Subho and Suranjan Das (eds.) (2000) *Electoral Politics in South Asia*, K.P. Bagchi Publications, Calcutta.

Beteille, Andre (1999) Citizenship, State and Civil Society, *Economic and Political Weekly*, Vol. 34, No. 36, pp. 2588–2591.

Centre for Science and Environment (1982) *State of India's Environment 1: The First Citizens' Report*, Centre for Science and Environment, New Delhi.

Chatterjee, Ashoke (1999) 'NGOs: An Alternative Democracy', In Hiranmay Karlekar (ed.) *Independent India: The First Fifty Years*, Indian Council for Cultural Relations and Oxford University Press, New Delhi, pp. 280–292.

Chatterjee, Partha (1997) *A Possible India: Essays in Political Criticism*, Oxford University Press, New Delhi.

Chatterjee, Partha (1998) 'Introduction – The Wages of Freedom: Fifty Years of the Indian Nation-State', In Partha Chatterjee (ed.) *Wages of Freedom: Fifty Years of the Indian Nation-State*, Oxford University Press, New Delhi, pp. 1–20.

CMC (1999) *Privatisation of Conservancy Operations: Details*, Chennai Municipal Corporation, Chennai.

Dahiya, Bharat (1999) The Impact of Decentralisation Policies in India, *Habitat Debate*, Vol. 5, No. 4, p. 25.

Dahiya, Bharat and Cedric Pugh (2000) 'The Localisation of Agenda 21 and the Sustainable Cities Programme', In Cedric Pugh (ed.) *Sustainability in Cities in Developing Countries: Theory and Practice at the Millennium*, Earthscan, London, pp.152–185.

D'Souza, J. B. (1999) Local Self-Government and Citizens, *Economic and Political Weekly*, Vol. 34, No. 42–43, pp. 2984–2986.

Gazette of India (1993) *The Constitution (Seventy Fourth) Amendment Act, 1992*, April 20.

Government of India (1997) *The Ninth Five Year Plan*, Publication Division, New Delhi.

Government of India (2003) *Economic Survey 2002–2003*, Government of India Press, New Delhi.

Hyden, Goran (1997) Civil Society, Social Capital, and Development: Dissection of a Complex Discourse, *Studies in Comparative International Development*, Vol. 32, No. 1, pp. 3–30.

Kohli, Atul (1988) 'State-Society Relations in India's Changing Democracy', In Atul Kohli (ed.) *India's Democracy: An Analysis of Changing State-Society Relations*, Princeton University Press, Princeton, pp. 305–318.

Kundu, Amitabh (1992) *Urban Development and Urban Research in India*, Khama Publishers, New Delhi.

Mahajan, Gurpreet (1999a) Civil Society and Its Avatars: What Happened to Freedom and Democracy?, *Economic and Political Weekly*, Vol. 32, No. 20, pp. 1188–1196.

Mahajan, Gurpreet (1999b) Civil Society, State and Democracy, *Economic and Political Weekly*, Vol. 34, No. 49, pp. 3471–3472.

Malik, Iqbal (2001) Managing Garbage, Simply, *Terra Green*, Issue 2, available at <http://www.teri.res.in/teriin/terragreen/issue2/essay.htm>, accessed 11 August 2003.

Mathur, Om Prakash (1994) 'Responding to the Urban Challenge: A Research Agenda for India and Nepal', In Richard Stren (ed.) *Urban Research in Developing World: Vol. 1, Asia*, University of Toronto, Toronto, pp.47–100.

Mathur, Om Prakash (1996a) 'Governing Cities in India, Nepal and Sri Lanka: The Challenge of Poverty and Globalization', In Patricia McCarney (ed.) *Cities and Governance: New Directions in Latin America, Asia and Africa*, University of Toronto, Toronto, pp. 109–124.

Mathur, Om Prakash (1996b) 'New forms of governance', In Nigel Harris and Ida Fabricius (eds.) (1996) *Cities & Structural Adjustment*, UCL Press, pp. 65–71.

Mathur, Om Prakash (1999) 'Governing Cities: Facing up to the Challenges of Poverty and Globalization', In Om Prakash Mathur (ed.) (1999) *India: The Challenge of Urban Governance*, National Institute of Public Finance & Policy, New Delhi, pp. 3–52.

McCarney, Patricia, Mohamed Halfani and Alferdo Rodriguez (1995) 'Towards an Understanding of Governance: The Emergence of an Idea and its Implications for Urban Research in Developing Countries', In Richard Stren with Judith Kjellberg Bell (eds.) *Urban Research in the Developing World, Vol. 4: Perspectives on the City*, University of Toronto, Toronto, pp. 91–141.

Mehta, Asoka (1962) The Future of Indian Cities: National Issues and Goals, In Roy Turner (ed.) *India's Urban Future*, University of California Press, Berkeley, pp. 413–421.

Mehta, Meera (1999) 'Participation and Urban Governance', In Om Prakash Mathur (ed.) *India: The Challenge of Urban Governance*, National Institute of Public Finance and Policy, New Delhi, pp. 163–211.

Mohan, Rakesh (1996) Urbanization in India: Patterns and Emerging Policy Issues, In Josef Gugler (ed.) *The Urban Transformation of the Developing World*, Oxford University Press, Oxford, pp. 93–131.

Nirmal, M. B. (1996) *People's Participation in Environmental Management: Civic Exnora Guidelines*, Classic Prints, Madras.

Paul, Samuel (1995) *A Report Card on Public Services in Indian Cities: A View From Below*, Public Affairs Centre, Bangalore.

Praja Foundation (2003) *Praja Foundation website*, available at <http://210.210.20.30:8080/prajasql/citizen>, accessed 11 August 2003.

Public Eye (1996) Announcement, *Public Eye*, Vol. 1, No. 4, p. 11.

Sengupta, Arjun (1999) Delivering the Right to Development: ESCR [Economic, Social and Cultural Rights] and NGOs, *Economic and Political Weekly*, Vol. 34, No. 41, pp. 2920–2922.

Sivaramakrishnan, K.C. (1994) Is Urban Politics Unique?, *Urban Age*, Vol. 2, No. 2, pp. 10–11.

Sivaramakrishnan, K.C. (2000) *Power to the People? The Politics and Progress of Decentralisation*, CPR–Konark, New Delhi.

United Nations (1993) *Report of the United Nations Conference of Environment and Development*, United Nations, New York.

United Nations (2003) *World Population Prospects: The 2002 Revision* and *World Urbanization Prospects: The 2001 Revision*, Population Division of the Department of Economic and Social Affairs of the United Nations Secretariat, available at <http://esa.un.org/unpp>, accessed 11 August 2003.

U. S. Census Bureau (2003) *State and Country QuickFacts*, available at <http://www.census.gov>, accessed 11 August 2003.

UNDP-World Bank (1999) *Ahmedabad Parivartan*, UNDP-World Bank Water and Sanitation Program-South Asia, New Delhi.

World Commission on Environment and Development (1987) *Our Common Future*, Oxford University Press, Oxford.

7. Political Institutions, Strategies of Governance and Forms of Resistance in Rural Market Towns of Contemporary Bengal: A Study of Bolpur Municipality

Basu, Sauro K. ed., *Bolpur Mahakuma Parichay*, Basumati, Calcutta, 1995.

Bates, R.H., *Markets and States in Tropical Africa: The Political Basis of Agricultural Policies*, California UP, Berkeley, 1981.

Fox, Richard G., *From zamindar to ballot box; community change in a north Indian market town*, Cornell UP, NY, 1969.

Harris, J., 'What is happening in Rural West Bengal? Agrarian Reform, Growth and Distribution', *EPW*, 12 June 1993.

Hunter, W.W., *Annals of Rural Bengal*, Smith, Elder, London, 1897 7th edn.

Kohli, Atul *Democracy and discontent: India's growing crisis of governability*, CUP, Cambridge, 1990.

Misra, R.P., Misra, K., *Million cities of India: growth dynamics, internal structure, quality of life and planning perspectives*, Vikas, New Delhi, 1978.

Mukherji, B., Mukhopadhyay, S., 'Impact of Institutional Change on Productivity in a small-farm Economy, *EPW*, 26 August 1995.

Ramchandran, R., *Urbanization and Urban Systems in India*, OUP, Delhi, 1991.

Ray, S., Agricultural Growth in West Bengal, *EPW*, 16 July 1994.

Rogaly, B., *et al* 'Sonar Bangla', *EPW*, 22 July 1995.

Rosenthal, Donald B., *The limited elite: politics and government in two Indian cities*, University of Chicago Press, Chicago, 1970.

Saha, A., Swaminathan, M., 'Agricultural Growth in West Bengal in the 1980s' *EPW*, 26 March 1994.

Singh, Andrea M., and de Souza, A., *The urban poor: slum and pavement dwellers in the major cities of India*, Manohar, New Delhi, 1980.

8. Action, Autonomy and Political Rights: Towards a Theory of 'Political Literacy'

Baier, Annette, 'Cartesian Persons', in *Postures of the Mind: Essays on Mind and Morals*, Minneapolis: University of Minnesota Press, 1985.

Dillon, Robin, 'Towards a Feminist Conception of Self Respect', *Hypatia*, volume 7, no.1 (winter 1992).

Dworkin, Gerald, *The Theory and Practice of Autonomy*, Cambridge, Cambridge University Press, 1988.

Fergusson, John, *A Dictionary, English and Hindoostanee...*, London, T Cadell, 1773.

Gilchrist, John, *A Dictionary English and Hindoostanee...*, London, 1790.

Government of India, *Crime in India*: National Crime Bureau Report, 1996.

Lindley, Richard, *Autonomy*, Basingstoke: Macmillan, 1986.

Massey, Stephen J., 'Is self respect a moral or a psychological concept?' *Ethics*, 93, 1983.

Meyer, John W., 'Myths of Socialization and of Personality' in *Reconstructing Individualism: autonomy, individually, and the self in Western thought*, edited by Thomas C. Heller, Morton Sosna, and David E. Wellbery (Stanford, Calif.: Stanford University Press, 1986).

Meyers, Diana, 'Agency' in Jagger, Alison M. and Young, Iris Marion eds, *A Companion to Feminist Philosophy*, Oxford Blackwell, 1998.

Spelman, Elizabeth, 'On Treating Persons as Persons', *Ethics*, 88, 1978.

Sosna, Morton, Heller, C Thomas, and Wellbery, David, eds, Stanford: Stanford University Press, 1986.

Whitbeck, Carolyn, 'A different Reality: feminist Ontology in '*Beyond Domination: New Perspectives on Women and Philosophy*', ed. Carol C Gould, Totowa, NJ; Rowman and Allenheld, 1984.

9. The Development of Panchayati Raj in India

Amdekar, Nagendra S., *New Panchayati Raj at Work*, ABD Publishers, Jaipur 2000.

Berreman, Gerald D, *Hindus of the Himalayas*, University of California Press, Berkeley, 1963.

Dalton, Dennis, *Mahatma Gandhi: nonviolent power in action*, University of Columbia Press, New York, 1993.

Dewey, Clive, 'Images of the Village Community: a study in Anglo-Indian ideology', *Modern Asian Studies*, Vol. 6, No. 3 , pp 291–328.

Dirks, Nicholas *Castes of Mind*, Princeton UP, Princeton, N.J., 2001.

Dreze, J., Sen, A. eds., *Indian Development: selected regional perspectives*, OUP, New Delhi, 1996 & 1998.

Fox, R. J., *Gandhian Utopia: experiments with culture*, Beacon Press, Boston 1989.

Galanter, M., *Law and Society in Modern India*, OUP, Delhi,1989.

Gandhi, M.K., *Collected writings of Mahatma Gandhi*, 86 Vols. New Delhi: 1958 –

Ghosh, Jayati 'Voices break the silence: women define their rights and demands within the changing land relations in West Bengal', *The Journal of Women's Studies*, 1, 2 October–March 1997, pp. 59–89.

Government of India *Report of the Committee on Panchayati Raj Institutions* New Delhi: GOI, Ministry of Agriculture and Irrigation, Dept. of Rural Development, August 1978.

Government of the Central Provinces and Berar *Report of the Village Panchayat Committee*, Government Press, Nagpur, 1926.

Inden, Ronald *Imagining India*, Blackwell, Oxford, 1990.

Institute of Social Sciences *Status of Panchayati Raj in the States of India*, Institute of Social Sciences, Delhi, 1995.

Jain L.C., *et al*, *Grass without roots : rural development under government auspices*, Sage, London, 1985.

Maithani, B.R., *Environmental planning for sustainable development of hill areas: a case study approach*, Mittal, New Delhi 1992.

Maithani, B.R., *Case studies on rural poverty alleviation in the Commonwealth*, India Food Production and Rural Development Division, Commonwealth Secretariat, London, 1992.

Mathew, George, *Panchayati Raj: from legislation to movement*, Concept, New Delhi, 1994.

Matthai, John, *Village Government in British India* 1st edn. London 1915, repr. Delhi: Low Price Publications, 1993.

Mishra, A., Vasavada, S. and Bates C., 'How many committees do I belong to?' in N. Sundar, and R. Jeffery (eds.), *Organising Sustainability: NGOs and joint forest management in India* Sage, London,1998.

Mukherjee, Rudrangshu, *The Penguin Gandhi Reader* Penguin, London 1993.

Muthiah, C. *Co-operative Credit in Raipur District (Factors contributing to Heavy Overdues)*, Agro-Economic Research Centre for Madhya Pradesh, Gwalior, 1966.

Nehru, Jawaharlal, *The Discovery of India*, Centenary edn., OUP, New Delhi: 1989; first pub. Calcutta: Signet Press, 1945).

Pal, Mahi, 'Panchayats in Scheduled Areas', *Economic & Political Weekly*, 35, 9 May 6 2000, pp. 1602–1606.

Parel, Anthony J., *Gandhi: Hind Swaraj and other writings*, Cambridge University Press, Cambridge, 1997.

Perlin, Frank, 'Of White Whale and Countrymen in the Eighteenth Century Maratha Deccan', *Journal of Peasant Studies*, V, 2 1978.

Ray Rajat K., *Social conflict and political unrest in Bengal: 1875–1927*, OUP, Oxford, 1984.

Rudolph, S.H & L.I. *The Modernity of Tradition: political development in India*, University of Chicago, Chicago, 1967.

Sarkar, Sumit, *The Swadeshi Movement in Bengal, 1903–08*, OUP, New Delhi, 1973.

Srinivas, M.N., *Caste in modern India and other essays*, Asia Publishing House, London, 1962.

Stein, B., *Peasant, State & Society in Medieval South India*, OUP, Oxford,1980.

Thapar, R., *From Lineage to State: social formations in the mid-first millennium B.C. in the Ganga valley*, OUP, Bombay 1984.

Tinker, Hugh, *Foundation of Local Self Government in India, Pakistan and Burma*, London, 1954.

Wedderburn, William, Sir, The Indian Raiyat as a member of the village community: a lecture delivered before the London Institution … on the 10th December, 1883, Harrison, London, 1883.

Zaidi, A.M. ed., *Congress presidential addresses*, Vols. 3 & 4, Publication Dept., Indian Institute of Applied Political Research, New Delhi, 5 vols., c1985–1989.

10. Political Representation and Women's Empowerment: Women in the Institutions of Local Self-Government in Orissa

Athreya, V.B., Rajeswari, K.S., *Women's Participation in Panchayati Raj: A Case Study from Tamil Nadu*, M.S. Swaminathan Research Foundation, Chennai, s.d [study was conducted in 1998].

Batliwala, Srilatha, *Empowerment of Women in South Asia: Concepts and Practices*, APBAE-FAO, New Delhi, 1993.

Bystydziensky, J. ed., *Women Transforming Politics: Worldwide Strategies for Empowerment*, Indiana University Press, Bloomington, 1992.

Chandrashekhar, B.K., 'Panchayati Raj Bill: The Real Flaw', *Economic and Political Weekly*, July 1, 1989, pp. 1433–35.

D' Lima, H., *Women in local government: a study of Maharashtra*, Concept Publishing Company, New Delhi, 1983.

Everett, J.M., *Women and Social Change in India*, Heritage, New Delhi, 1979.

Government of India, Committee on Plan Projects, *Report of the Team for the Study of Community Projects and National Extension Service*, November 1957, Vol. 1–3.

Government of India, *Towards Equality: Report of the Committee on the Status of Women in India*, New Delhi, 1974.

Government of India, Ministry of Agriculture and Irrigation, Department of Rural Development, *Report of the Committee on Panchayati Raj Institutions* New Delhi, August 1978.

Government of India, *National Perspective Plan for Women, 1988–2000 A.D.*, Delhi,1988.

Government of India, *Towards Empowering Women*, New Delhi, 1995.

Government of Orissa a), District Statistical Handbook 1993: Khurda, Bhubaneswar, s. d).

Government of Orissa b), District Statistical Handbook 1993: Nayagarh, (Bhubaneswar, s.d.).

Haq, Mahbub ul, *Human Development in South Asia*, (Oxford University Press, Karachi, 1997.

Harper, Malcolm, *Profit for the Poor: Cases in Micro-Finance*, Oxford & IBH Publishing Co. PVT.LTD, New Delhi & Calcutta, 1998.

Hust, Evelin, 'Political "Empowerment" of Women through Legislation? Case study Orissa', in Pinto, A. and Reifeld, H. (eds.), *Women in PRI*, New Delhi, ISI, 2001, pp. 166–194.

Hust, Evelin, *A Million Indiras Now? Political Presence and Women's Empowerment in Rural Local Government in India*, Manohar, New Delhi, 2004.

ICSSR, *Status of Women in India: A Synopsis of the Report of the National Committee*, New Delhi, 1975.

Institute of Social Science, *Panchayati Raj Update*, New Delhi, ISS, 1997.

Kaushik, Susheela, *Women Panches in Position: A Study of Panchayati Raj in Haryana*, Centre for Development Studies and Action, New Delhi, 1997.

Lelithabai, K.N., 'Empowering Women Through Panchayati Raj', *Kurukshetra*, August 1998, pp. 9–12.

Manikyamba, P., *Women in Panchayati Raj Structures*, Gian Publishing House, Delhi 1989.

MARG, *They call me Member Saab: Women in Haryana Panchayati Raj*, Multiple Action Research Group, New Delhi, 1998.

Mathew, George, *Status of Panchayati Raj in the States of India*, Concept Publishing Company, Delhi, 1995.

Mazumdar, Vina, 'Historical Soundings', *Seminar 457*, Delhi, September 1997, pp. 14–19.

Meenakshisundaram, S.S., 'Empowerment of Women through the Panchayati Raj', *The Administrator*, July-September 1995, pp. 161–165.

Mohanty, M., 'Class, Caste and Dominance in a *Backward* State: Orissa', in Frankel, F. and Rao, M.S.A. eds. *Dominance and State Power in Modern India: Decline of a Social Order*, Vol. 2, Oxford University Press, Delhi 1990 pp. 321–367.

Pal, M., 'Empowerment of Women Through Panchayats: An Assessment of the Tasks', *Women's Link*, 5 (2), April–June 1999, pp. 20–29.

Pathy, J., *Under Development and Destitution: Essays on Orissan Society*, Inter-India Publications, Delhi 1988.

Phillips, Anne: *The Politics of Presence*, Clarendon Press, Oxford, 1995.

Rajput, Pam: 'Women Leadership at the grassroot level in Punjab', in: Kaushik and Susheela eds. *Women's Participation in Politics*, Vikas Publishing House, Delhi 1993, pp. 31–34.

Rerrich, M.S., 'Modernizing the patriarchal family in West Germany: some findings on the redistribution of family work between women', *The European Journal of Women's Studies*, 3 (1) 1996, pp. 27–39.

Rowlands, Jo, 'A word of the times, but what does it mean? Empowerment in the discourse and practice of development', in Afshar, Haleh ed. *Women and Empowerment: Illustrations for the Third World*, Houndmills, MacMillan, 1998, pp. 11–34.

Santha, E.K., *Political Participation of Women in Panchayati Raj: Haryana, Kerala, and Tamil Nadu*, ISS, New Delhi 1999.

Vidya, K.C.: *Political Empowerment of Women at the Grassroots*, Kanishka Publishers, New Delhi 1997.

GLOSSARY OF NON-ENGLISH TERMS

Adab	courtesy
Adivasi	tribal
Aman	crop
Bahu	daughter-in-law
Biradari	fraternity, kinsfolk, extended family
Bhai log	underworld gang members
Bhaiband	brotherhood, grouping of heads of families of the same lineage in a locality
Boro	cultivation (Bengal)
Brahmadeya	village gifted to a Brahmin group
Caste, Scheduled	former 'untouchable' castes given special concessions in recognition of their disadvantaged status
Backward	former untouchables who converted to other religions, nomadic castes, and low status *sudra* (peasant) castes benefiting from special concessions
Chawl	tenement
Chuda	puffed rice
Crore	ten millions
Dacoity	banditry
Dada	underworld boss
Dalit	oppressed (former untouchable, also usually *'scheduled caste'*)
Desi	indigenous
Gaanjhia	woman married in village of origin
Gana/Jana	clan
Garib manus	poor people

Gaurava	respect
Ghazal	lyric poem
Ghungat	veil
Haq/adhikaar	power
Hat	agricultural market
Hindutva	Hindu cultural nationalism
Holi	Hindu spring festival
Jaggeri	unrefined sugar
Janapada	ancient Indian clan territory
Jati	caste cluster, subcaste
Jatra	folk theatre
Kama	desire
Kamadhenu	cash cow (colloquially); mother of all cows (Hindu mythology)
Khanwal	eating house
Lakh	a hundred thousand
Mahalwari	landlord-based system of revenue settlement
Mahal	landed estate (consisting of several villages)
Mahila mandal	women's group
Maika	maternal home
Majur classer lok	working class people (Bengal)
Mana/mariyade	honour (Karnataka)
Mandir	temple
Manishta/maryadasta	man with a keen sense of self-respect (Karnataka)
Mariyatai	respect (Karnataka)
Masjid	mosque
Math/matha	monastery
Mitra mandal	friendship forum
Moka	face
Moksha	salvation
Nadu	ancient south Indian territorial community
Naxalite	CPI (M-L); militant left group in favour of armed insurrection

Nata	payment similar to bride-price in non-marital relationship (Rajasthan)
Nimna madhayabitta	lower middle classes (Bengal)
Padhi likhi	literate
Palegar/pallegar	chieftain
Panchayat, Panch	traditional village council, group of councillors (trad. 5 in number)
Nagar panchayat	town council or council for a group of villages
Gram panchayat	village council
Jati panchayat	caste council
Parisad	pertaining to an assembly; person present at an assembly
Parivartan	transformation
Patidar/s	joint village landlord, community of joint village landlords (Gujarat)
Periyanadu	supra-village territorial unit in ancient South India
Peta	Mysore turban
Pugree	capitalised rent/head tax
Puja	worship
Purdah	separation or hiding of women from the gaze of men
Sabha,	
Lok Sabha	lower house of Indian parliament
Rajya Sabha	upper house of Indian parliament
Gram Sabha	village assembly
Sach/satya	truth
Sahi	village or hamlet
Sainaks	disciples (commonly followers of *Shiv Sena*)
Samaj seva	social service
Samiti	committee
Samskara	transmigration (title of 1965 Kannada novel by Anantha Murthy)
Sarpanch	head of panchayat

Sathin

female grass-roots or community worker; female associate

Scheduled tribe

adivasis or tribals given special concessions in recognition of their disadvantaged status

Shakha

branch [of political party]

Shiv sena

Shivaji's army

Stannamana/manam

status acquired through political appointment/ status acquired through honourable conduct (Karnataka)

Supari

underworld

Swabimana

self-respect (Karnataka)

Swadeshi

of one's own country/political campaign for home rule (1905)

Swaraj

self-rule

Thana/thanedar

police station/officer

Upanishad

theological and argumentative parts of the *Vedas*

Vedas

ancient Indian religious texts

Zamindari

Landed estate, landed property; land or estate held by a zamindar; the office or tenure of a zamindar; landlord-based system of revenue collection

Zilla Parishad

district council

Zopadpatti

slum

INDEX

Jinnah, Muhammad Ali   41
Joshi, Murli Manohar   31, 35–36, 97

Kargil, war in   xi, 34
Karnataka   xvi, xxiv, 41–62, 183, 189,
   239 n24
Kashmir [and Jammu]   xi, xxv, 27–28,
   34, 216 n29, 238 n2
Kaviraj, Sudipta   29, 40, 215–216, 222
   n2, 229 n1, 231 n24, 243–244, 247
Kerala   181, 183
Kesri, Sitaram   43
Kishore, Acharya Giriraj   38
Kohli, Atul   xii–xiii, 4, 39, 211 n10,
   212, 225 n102, 227 n1, 241, 244,
   247, 249–250
Kolkata   35, 108, 114

Left Front [government, West Bengal]
   xxiv, 126, 129, 132, 136, 143–148
Lok Sabha   xv, xxi, 2, 27, 30, 45,
   182–183, 257
London   86
Lok Shakti Party   xvi, 61

Madan, T.N.   40, 244
Madhok, Sumi   viii, xix–xx, 151–167,
   229–235, 251
Madhya Pradesh   38, 55, 182–184
Manor, James   5–6, 8–10, 39, 212 n22,
   213, n32, 241–242, 244
Metcalfe, Charles   xx, 176, 179
Minorities Commission, the   35
Montagu-Chelmsford Committee   187
   Report   172
Mooji, Jos   viii, xiv–xv, 1–19, 212–214,
   241–242
Multinational corporations   15–17
Mumbai   xvii, xxv, 64, 71–82, 172,
   222 n1
   Communal violence in   101
   Municipal elections in   112–113
   NGOs in   116–117
   Population of   107, 220

protests in   37
riots in   36
urban planning in   83–106, 118
Murdoch, Rupert   68, 81
Myrdal, Gunnar   xi
Mysore   42, 61, 217 n21, 257

Nagaland   180
Naidu, Chandrababu   45
Narayan, J.P.   179
Narayan, R.K.   43
Narayanan, K.R.   22
Naregal, Veena   vii–ix, xvi, 63–82,
   218–222, 244–245
National Democratic Alliance
   [NDA]   21
Nehru, Jawaharlal   3, 10, 23–24, 26,
   84, 90, 177, 215 n8, 236 n21, 252
Nepal   xxiv
New Delhi   xi, 116–117
   Agitations in   37–38

Orissa   xxi–xxiii, 182, 184, 185–210,
   239 n35
   Attacks against Christians in   38

Padiyath, Bhavana   ix, 83–106,
   222–225, 245–248
Panchayat   xxiv, 125, 166–167, 239 n36,
   257
   Gram p.   155, 193, 196, 237 n35,
      239 n24
   Jati p.   155, 230–1 n16
   Mandal p.   180
   Nagar p.   110
Panchayati raj   xx, 144–5, 169–184,
   185
   Raj Institutions [PRI]   xxi,
      186–210
   reform   xx
Panini, M.N.   6, 8, 10, 213, 242
Pakistan, artists in   37
   creation of   24, 40–41, 62
   conflict with India   34